POWER AND COMPLACENCY

All rights reserved. Potomac Books is an imprint of the
University of Nebraska Press.
Manufactured in the United States of America.

Library of Congress Cataloging-in-Publication Data
Names: Lohaus, Phillip T., author.
Title: Power and complacency: American survival in an
age of international competition / Phillip T. Lohaus.
Description: Lincoln, Nebraska: Potomac Books, an
imprint of the University of Nebraska Press, [2021] |
Includes bibliographical references and index. |
Summary: "Power and Complacency: American
Survival in an Age of International Competition"
highlights the disconnect between America's approach
to international competition and the realities of how its
adversaries conceive of war.—Provided by publisher.
Identifiers: LCCN 2020041061
ISBN 9781640122260 (Hardback: acid-free paper)
ISBN 9781640124707 (ePub)
ISBN 9781640124714 (mobi)
ISBN 9781640124721 (PDF)
Subjects: LCSH: Strategic culture—United States—Case
studies. | National security—United States—Decision
making—Case studies. | Balance of power. | Strategy. |
United State—Foreign relations—1989—Case studies.
Classification: LCC JZ1480 .L65 2021
DDC 355/.033073—dc23
LC record available at https://lccn.loc.gov/2020041061

Set in Minion Pro by Laura Buis.

POWER &
COMPLACENCY

AMERICAN
SURVIVAL
IN AN AGE OF
INTERNATIONAL
COMPETITION

PHILLIP T. LOHAUS

Potomac Books

AN IMPRINT OF THE UNIVERSITY OF NEBRASKA PRESS

CONTENTS

PREFACE

In 1945 President Harry S. Truman famously ordered that the eagle on the presidential seal permanently face to the left, toward the olive branches that represented peace. After two long wars, this explanation provided a pleasant rationale for adapting a symbol that had itself undergone many changes over the years. Peace, interpreted narrowly, would indeed become the prevailing norm in the United States—Congress has not formally declared war since the end of the Second World War. In this sense, Truman's decision to reverse the stance of the eagle on the presidential seal was prescient.

Yet few would argue that the United States has enjoyed peace since the 1946 Paris Peace Conference that formally ended the Second World War. Not even five years after Truman's proclamation, the United States found itself embroiled in conflict on the Korean Peninsula. America has remained engaged in near continuous military conflict ever since. Conflict, in fact, has proven to be more of a norm than peace; the historical reluctance of Congress to declare war has not impeded its willingness to repeatedly authorize or fund military engagements since the country's founding. Notwithstanding the poetry of the olive branch and arrows on the presidential seal, peace and war became intertwined.

Debate has ensued in recent years to determine the most useful way to characterize the space of international competition that exists between war and peace. New terms, such as *the gray zone* and *hybrid warfare*, have emerged to describe what are in fact age-old phenomena. To some, these terms are little more than tools used to justify the ever-expanding role of the military in America's foreign policy.[1] To others, the terms are of little benefit whatsoever, as international conflict has always involved many different aspects of national power. There is truth to both these interpretations.

These terms each point to a wider phenomenon: the ability of states and organizations to achieve warlike gains without resorting to war. Since the end of the Cold War, the unquestioned power of the United States has failed to deter the advances of Iran and Islamic extremist groups in the Middle East, of China in the Pacific and elsewhere, and of Russia, not only in Eurasia but also within the United States. None of these actors could directly challenge the American military, yet they continually challenge America across a variety of geographic and political realms. Whether in "gray," "hybrid" or other conflicts, the proficiency of the U.S. military has not translated into lasting, beneficial political outcomes, nor has the primacy of its conventional power effectively deterred adversarial behavior.

Conventional measures of military power have become less useful for understanding the international balance of power. Despite, or perhaps because of, its unrivaled military power, America has failed to develop an effective way of harnessing all tools of national power toward a common end goal. Since the end of the Cold War, no threat has proven existential enough to motivate America to do so. Because of its power, America has grown complacent.

This book explores the causes of the efficacy deficit that has characterized American foreign policy since the end of the

Cold War. Drawing from the literature in international relations and strategic studies, it tests two dependent variables: relative power and strategic predispositions. It finds that relative power has little bearing upon the ability of a country to achieve its foreign-policy objectives but rather explains whether a state will pursue its interests directly or indirectly. Strategic predispositions, informed by immutable realities of geography and, iteratively, by historical experiences of decision-making elites, orient states toward either attrition or maneuver-based strategies. The book employs several case studies to demonstrate its findings.

A nation's ability to achieve its foreign-policy objectives lies in the calibration and interaction of these two dependent variables. As the case studies in this book show, weak powers tend to challenge their more powerful foes indirectly by identifying and exploiting gaps in their adversary's capabilities and strategic priorities. By maneuvering around their more powerful enemy, such actors redefine power imbalances in a manner more suited to their strengths. Although the more powerful actor enjoys superior capabilities, it is hindered by an interest in merely maintaining its power rather than expanding it. In other words, whereas a defensive approach offers the path of least resistance to the more powerful actor, an offensive approach by the weaker actor compensates for its relative paucity of capability.

America's place atop the international power hierarchy and its enduring approach to strategy and warfare have prevented it from effectively adapting to the changing strategies employed by its adversaries. Since the end of the Cold War, America has sought to maintain the status quo through the employment of a series of technological and doctrinal advancements. Air-Land Battle, Shock and Awe, and the first, second, and now third offsets are examples of theories that seek to adapt conflict to suit America's current or projected future strengths. The reader may observe that doctrinal innovations drive change and generally derive from analysis of current challenges in global affairs. Although this is true, few doctrines provide a mechanism for responding to adversarial actions in dynamic operational environments.[2] Rather, most approach their solutions to prevailing strategic challenges with an air of conclusiveness. When circumstances change, new theories attempt to once again reformulate the terms of conflict, and the cycle repeats. Meanwhile, adversaries find ways to undermine each new doctrine or to innovate in their own right. They often find new ways to pursue their national objectives outside of the paradigm that the hegemon—in this case, America—so carefully devised.

America is not the first great power to fall into this trap. History is replete with examples of powerful nations underestimating the nature of the challenges posed by their weaker adversaries. The Romans found the raids of the Germanic tribes annoying but hardly viewed them as a threat to the republic until it was too late. The British found the Boers to be pests but never imagined that their army would be mired in fighting a protracted "small war" against them in South Africa. By the time a nation understands how and why it must adapt, its relative decline is often already a fait accompli. The realization of decline belatedly occurs when, complacent and blinded by prior successes, policies toward adversaries becomes less efficacious.

Over the past twenty years the effectiveness of American foreign policy has declined. In the Middle East, for example, America's outsized power has not resulted in decisive military wins but rather in the need for an extended commitment to maintain fragile and fractious regimes. In East Asia, the assumption that admitting China into the international economic order would result in that country's acquiescence to global trade and security norms has proven incorrect. And in Europe, Russia has faced few meaningful consequences for its revanchist and expansionist behavior, despite that country's comparative poverty. Put simply, the tools designed to maintain American hegemony are no longer working. Whether characterized as the gray zone, the space between peace and war, or international competition, actions taken in this space accumulate to provide revisionist actors with strategic advantages that obviate the need to compete on the "new" terms that America continually attempts to establish. Complacency, bred by power, has led America to falsely believe that it alone is in the position to define the rules of competition with its weaker adversaries.

This book provides two lenses to view this mismatch between means and ends. First, I argue that America's emphasis on the direct application of military force has hindered its ability to address threats indirectly, whether through the military or other tools of national power. The reader may point out that the United States maintains many tools to counter indirect threats; the Department of State, the Department of Treasury, various intelligence agencies, and, within the Department of Defense, special-operations forces each support American interests below the threshold of direct combat. Yet even within these organizations, shaping activities, which are difficult to measure and may take years if not decades to bear fruit, are often shelved or deprioritized in the interest of addressing time-sensitive crises. Within the U.S. military the forces responsible for Civil Affairs, area studies, and Psychological Operations (now known as Military Information Support Operations) have repeatedly seen their budgets slashed in favor of surgical strikes, drone warfare, and procurement programs aimed at maintaining the military's edge at the high end of the escalatory spectrum. An emphasis on direct approaches also encourages escalation, as the United States seeks to compete on a field more suited to its capabilities.

Leaving budgetary and structural considerations aside, a more fundamental question remains: what should these organizations shape toward? Budgetary and structural choices reveal decision-maker priorities, but an analysis of means only partially explains America's failure to counter foreign shaping activities. Ideally, budget decisions flow from strategy, yet most National Security Strategies have given short shrift to shaping activities. Documents that should guide the employment of the government's vast national-security apparatus have become anodyne expressions of intentions and platitudes, far cries from the alignment and vision provided by documents such as National Security Council Memorandum 68. Even the most recent National Defense and National Security Strategies, which were widely lauded by foreign policy experts, do little to define how America should implement a policy of "strategic predictability and operational unpredictability." Effective strategies must account for the ways that resources are employed and relate them to a clear-eyed understanding of the current threat environment.

One of the challenges of developing a coherent approach to shaping activities is that they defy tidy ontologies. Nevertheless, to solve any problem, one must begin by defining it and then mapping it to relevant operational arts. To this end, the first chapter reviews relevant literature to show how relative power and strategic predispositions contribute to an actor's approach to achieving its objectives. In the chapters that follow, the case studies demonstrate how these factors shape the strategic approaches of Russia, China, Iran, and, finally, the United States. The case studies treat each actor's activities empirically, set within a larger framework to explain why some actors are more predisposed to succeeding outside of war than others.

That brings me to the second lens provided in this book: strategic predispositions. These ways of viewing competition, developed additively over time, influence the inclination or disinclination of states to employ shaping activities in the pursuit of strategic ends. A comparison between the opposing strategic approaches of attrition and maneuver demonstrates these dynamics: Attrition-based strategies are of most use to relatively stronger powers, as they bring their power to bear and chip away at the resolve of their weaker enemies. Maneuver-based strategies are generally pursued out of necessity—comparative weakness demands that less powerful actors adapt and maneuver around their adversary's strengths.

Russia, China, and Iran were chosen as foreign case studies because each actor has developed the ability to project power through the conventional military and across diplomatic, informational, and economic realms, either regionally or globally. Each has demonstrated revisionist ambitions, in that they are actively challenging the global order established after the Second World War. Each retains the ability to project power through strategies of either maneuver or attrition, but their distinct histories and predispositions result in markedly different ways of competition. The challenges posed to the United States by Russia, Iran, and China are also unlikely to end anytime soon—if anything, they are poised to expand. Although case studies of Islamic extremist groups or North Korea would prove interesting in this context, they were ultimately not selected for deeper inquiry, as the aforementioned common denominators do not, in my opinion, fully apply.

As the selected case studies in this book demonstrate, adversaries that would seek to upend the status quo approach America primarily with maneuver-based strategies. That, however, is only the beginning of the argument. The book also finds that these actors all possess a predisposition to success with maneuver-based strategies. The geographic position and historical development of Russia, China, and Iran have resulted in a more expansive conception of warfare than typically understood in America, or, indeed, in the West more generally. America's ascent to sole-superpower status has exacerbated these differences, to the detriment of the United States and its allies and to the benefit of revisionist actors.

Before embarking on this exploration, a few acknowledgments are in order. As is always the case with a work of this length, the list of those that have contributed ideas and support to this project could fill a chapter of its own. Nevertheless, a few individuals and institutions bear special mention. First and foremost, I would like to thank my wife, without whose support and encouragement this work would not exist. In a similar vein I'd like to thank my in-laws, for providing a space in beautiful Sonoma County, California, for me to write, and my parents, for their ongoing encouragement. Thanks are in order to Nadia Schadlow and Christopher Griffin at the Smith Richardson Foundation, whose generosity and confidence in my research made possible the fieldwork that supported this book. The scholars and staff of the American Enterprise Institute in general deserve thanks for their support, but specific thanks are due to Gary Schmitt, Rebecca Burgess, Dan Blumenthal, Michael Rubin, and Leon Aron for their comments and thoughts on various chapters; to J. Matthew McInnis for cohosting a workshop on Iranian shaping operations; to Danielle Pletka and Giselle Donnelly for mentorship and guidance; and to my research assistants over the years—Justin Lang, Gregory Graff, John Sakellariadis, and Taylor Clausen—whose fantastic support to my research activities and writing were essential for the success of this project. I was fortunate to benefit from collaboration and interviews with institutions and individuals around the globe, which included the Army Capabilities Integration Center, the U.S. Army War College, the Air Force Warfighting Integration Capability, and the Strategic Landpower Task Force; the Foundation for Defense of Democracies, the Sasakawa Peace Foundation, and the Korea Foundation in Washington, DC; Taiwan Think Tank and Taiwan Brain Trust in Taiwan; the Nippon Foundation and the Ministry of Defense in Tokyo; the Asan Institute for Policy Studies and the Ministry of Foreign Affairs in Seoul; Derasat and the Ministry of Interior and Ministry of Defence in Bahrain; senior foreign relations officials in Abu Dhabi; staff from IDC Herzliya in Herzliya, Israel; Pasi Eronen, Saara Jantunen, Aapo Cederberg, and the staff of the Finnish Institute of International Affairs in Helsinki; Tomas Jermalavičius and the International Centre for Defence and Security in Tallinn; and a certain Russian diplomat, now persona non grata, who unwittingly validated many of my findings about Russia's approach to strategy. Eliot Cohen deserves thanks for encouraging my love of strategic studies research, as do the librarians and research staff at Johns Hopkins School of Advanced International Studies and Stanford University, whose patience with my inquisitiveness greatly assisted in my ability to find optimal secondary-source material. Lastly, I'd like to thank my editor, Tom Swanson, and the University of Nebraska Press for their enthusiasm for and assistance with bringing this project to completion. Each of these individuals and institutions, along with many others, deserve credit for the insights and inspiration they provided, but it bears mentioning that any omissions or errors in this work are my responsibility alone.

POWER AND COMPLACENCY

Introduction

Since the end of the Cold War, the power of the United States has eclipsed any single potential challenger. Yet throughout this period, America has become involved in a number of costly and unsuccessful military ventures. In diplomatic and economic endeavors, success has not correlated positively with America's ability to impose its will, if it so choses, on any other actor. This decline in efficacy is a function of America's power relative to other nations and its approach to competition as manifested in its strategic predisposition to confront its enemies directly with the threat or use of force.

This chapter will serve as a theoretical prelude to the book's case studies, which demonstrate that not all strategic predispositions detract from short-of-war competitive strategies. Though each of the states examined in this work would be at a disadvantage in directly confronting the United States, the ways that they conceive of international competition provide opportunities to exploit the blind spots created by America's outsized power.

This book defines *international competition* as the use of any or all tools of national power to eventuate advantageous strategic outcomes. Although this work primarily focuses on efforts besides combat that shape the strategic environment, it does not view such efforts as a substitute for capable, ready, and effective military forces. Rather, it views military forces as just one tool of national power—one that must be used as part of any effective strategy but should not be viewed as a substitute for diplomatic, informational, and economic tools of statecraft. At an empirical level, the book compares how different orientations and historical experiences have shaped the approach to international relations of several nations and how they seek to achieve efficacy in the realm of strategy.

The Question of Efficacy

How does one measure strategic efficacy? To answer this question, many will first look to the ends of a particular strategy and then compare current circumstances to that idealized result. A prognostic phase may follow, in which ways and means are analyzed to determine how and why the strategy produced or failed to result in the desired ends. Though the ideas of the originating (or current) strategists may have been theoretically compelling, complications of ways and means—or the ill-conceived nature of the strategic ends themselves—sometimes cause strategies to fall short of their potential.

This gap between theory and practice has long been the subject of inquiry—or deliberate avoidance—for Western thinkers. As François Jullien points out in his *A Treatise on Efficacy*, the philosophers of ancient Greece and Rome struggled to find the connective tissue between the two.[1] Machiavelli avoided the question entirely by implying that practice created theory, rather than the other way around.[2] Carl von Clausewitz found interest in the gap between theory and practice when attempting to create a methodical way of thinking about warfare, an act that is inherently unpredictable and chaotic. Antoine-Henri Jomini, Clausewitz's Enlightenment-influenced contemporary, found that a scientific approach to warfare could substantially narrow this gap but could not himself devise a perfect-enough theory to overcome it. Although these strategists came to different conclusions about the relationship between theory and practice, human decisions served as the insurmountable X factor standing in the way of a perfect marriage between theory and practice.

To the Greeks, the essence of decision was the subject of fascination, the least explainable yet perhaps most consequential variable that connected theory to practice and that differentiated success from failure. Despite the evolution from Plato's argument that Forms or Ideas were the most precise representations of reality available to humans to Aristotle's emphasis on empiricism, the latter still recognized the importance of ideas in understanding the world.[3] From here on, a coupling of theory and practice came to define classical understandings of efficacy.[4] The development of the archetypical hero provided a means to explain the transcending of the gap between theory and practice. The hero's ability to employ indefinable prowess at pivotal moments became a marker of true greatness and is evident throughout Greek philosophy, literature, and epic poems.[5] From Odysseus to Homer, Greek heroes overcame enormous obstacles to lead their forces to victory. The Greeks began this tradition in Western thought, though they were hardly the last to employ it. Throughout the Middle Ages, bravery and valor were communicated through heroic archetypes and legends.[6] Implicit in the use of archetypes is the centrality of human agency, in its most exceptional and brilliant form, to achieve strategic efficacy.

In *The Prince*, Machiavelli states that, in peace, one must dedicate oneself to the practice of war in two ways: by action and by study. The former should be adhered to by keeping armies well drilled and organized, essentially a Renaissance version of the concept of readiness, so that armies are prepared to respond in a time of need or surprise.[7] In the latter, Machiavelli proposes an analytic immersion in the geography of the expected battlefield. Both recommendations reduce strategic surprise, but his second recommendation suggests an understanding that practice should inform theory, not vice versa. He suggests that a future prince should mimic or adopt the approaches of successful military practitioners before him, specifically mentioning Alexander the Great, Achilles, Caesar, Scipio, and Cyrus. To Machiavelli, theory was practice, with victory being the sole deciding factor for what is to be followed in a time of war. Once again, human agency—this time in the form of mimicry and validated by victory—connected the hypothetical and the actual.

Von Clausewitz accounted for the sinews connecting theory and practice with his conception of genius in warfare.[8] Intelligence, cunning, and will could combine to overcome theoretical obstacles; inversely, the absence of these factors could discount the explanatory power of even the most ironclad theories. Von Clausewitz further observed the limited utility of theories during crises, the most acute form of chaos. In times of crisis, theory is sidestepped in favor of instinct, which manifests in military genius or results in failure. Because time and current circumstances bind opportunities to achieve the optimal outcome in a crisis, empirical observations necessarily replace abstract theories to become the driver of decisions. Whether the failure of theory was due to the inability of all but the genius to truly understand it or the exceptional ability of the genius to transcend the rules in a moment of crisis, von Clausewitz, like the Greeks and Machiavelli, conceived of strategic efficacy in humanistic terms.[9]

Following the Enlightenment, the opposite view came into prominence through thinkers like Antoine-Henri Jomini, the less quoted though similarly influential contemporary of von Clausewitz.[10] Rather than attributing efficacy to a heroic or intellectually gifted archetype, success or failure in war was the result of a logical system of inputs and outputs, of *military statistics* rather than intelligence, all orchestrated within a *system of operations*.[11] In this view, the inability of the theory to describe reality simply meant that that theory needed pruning or refinement. For Jomini and the generations of strategists that have followed, not always consciously, in his footsteps, theory has provided a framework for analyzing and understanding, for bringing order to disorder. Despite his drive toward a systematic understanding of efficacy, however, Jomini still placed a human ability—rationality—at the center of his explanation of strategic efficacy.

This faith in human agency, bolstered by the Enlightenment, would continue to shape strategic thinking in the West in the centuries that would follow. The employment of scientific and administrative principles in the construction of Napoleonic France's Grand Armée, the use of economic statecraft to bolster military power in the centuries that followed, and ongoing debates about whether efficacy is a function of technocratic mastery or that of the genius outsider (or hero), provide just a few relevant examples.[12] More than a century later, in his sweeping history of Western strategy, B. H. Liddell Hart observed that human reactions, made in response to desperate situations, were the fountainhead of effective solutions.[13] Viewed this way, theory has far less utility to producing effective outcomes than the ability to make the right decisions in a time of crisis.

If we are to accept that strategic efficacy is rooted in human agency, then it follows logically that the absence of the latter should explain a failure of the former. To those who turn to heroic archetypes, the absence of a hero would explain failure. To von Clausewitz, ineffectiveness might be explained by the absence of genius, whether in its most exceptional and individual form or in the form of institutional mastery. To Jomini, the insufficiency of a system of war explained a lack of efficacy. Again, we find that, through the Western lens, human agency is at the center of questions of effectiveness. The glue that binds theory to practice is human agency.

Because of its foundational relationship to efficacy, it is worth exploring the meaning of *agency*. Agency comprises a latent and an active component in the form of capability and will. In the context of war and conflict, capabilities represent the spectrum of means with which an opponent must contend. They act as a deterrent and, when employed, as an instrument to defeat an adversary. Soldiers, strategists, statesmen, and nations all possess innate capabilities, but without acting upon them, or convincingly communicating their intention to act, their talents will have no positive impact on strategic efficacy.[14] The nature of each capability bears upon the decision to employ it; the decision to employ a small team of special operators, for instance, is separate from the decision to use nuclear weapons. The nature of a particular capability, however, is insufficient to understand whether it will be used or whether the adversary perceives that it will be used. Human agency—and strategic efficacy—must thus be thought of as a function of capabilities and a will to act, whether actual or perceived.

Will is a complicated topic, one that philosophers have debated for millennia. At an aggregate or societal level, it manifests differently in various forms of government and is also highly dependent on context. In the Western, liberal democratic mold, societal will acts as a constraint on or amplifier of the will of the leader. In the United States, for example, societal will is expressed through foreign policy vis-à-vis the president, both directly through the vote and public-opinion polls, and indirectly through Congress.[15] The effect of societal will on leaders in authoritarian systems may at first seem de minimis, but in fact it may simply take on a different form. Rather than manifesting through elections, societal will bubbles forth in fits and spurts before being squelched if it is deemed a threat or amplified and institutionalized if deemed an asset. During the Arab Spring, for instance, demands for reform emanating from societies throughout the Muslim world resulted in a wide variety of outcomes, from regime change to the consolidation and expansion of existing power structures.[16] Indeed, the components of societal will may be a combination of unique factors in individual societies, making generalizations at the internal level difficult.

In regard to the question of efficacy and the ability of the United States to assert its will in the international arena since the end of the Cold War, one cannot avoid the question of political will. Factors such as geography, history, economics, and political systems must be examined to understand how and why a state developed a particular suite of capabilities. Furthermore, one must examine these strategic elements to understand the willingness of a society and a leader to act in the interest of the state. Though one may define international competition as the totality of actions taken by each state to maximize its chances of survival in an anarchic system, the manner by which each state pursues its interests is another matter entirely.

Much ink has been spilled discussing the optimal types and amounts of equipment necessary for America to achieve its aims. Such inquiries often echo Jomini and assert that a systematic employment of available technologies will prove sufficient to solve the military challenge of the day. Whether AirLand Battle, AirSea Battle, Network Centric Warfare, or Anti-Access/ Area Denial, American operational constructs have primarily been a prescriptive rather than descriptive affair. Because they assume the existence of the political will to act in accordance with theory, their utility in deciphering the drivers of decreased strategic efficacy is limited. Far fewer studies have ventured to explain the more pertinent question: how human agency, that linkage between theory and practice, has impacted the manner by which America seeks to employ its capabilities.

The remainder of this introduction will outline the dependent variables examined throughout this study that, taken together, contribute to a new way of understanding the achievement of strategic objectives in the international arena. These variables provide lenses for considering how external stimuli and internal developments influence human agency and thus strategic efficacy. The externally focused lens, grounded in international relations theory, illuminates motivations and inclinations to employ certain capabilities, depending on the power of a particular state relative to its adversary. The internally focused lens draws from literature on strategic culture to build a more additive and adaptive concept—strategic predispositions—to the analyst's toolkit. The remainder of the book demonstrates how the strategic predispositions of other states have enabled them to compete with the United States outside the realm of war to overcome their relative lack of hard power.

The Interplay of Powers

What is power? The concept of power has existed since ancient times, and the concept of the balance of power has been in use in European halls of state for centuries. Simply put, the ancient and early modern uses of these terms are of limited relevance in this study. As this book seeks to understand the mechanisms underlying the decline in efficacy of American foreign policy, it is useful to use definitions generated in the wake of the Second World War, when dramatically changed circumstances portended both a new place for America in the world order and a reexamination and reconceptualization of these terms.

In 1957 Robert A. Dahl formalized the concept of power in political and behavioral science by expressing it as "the ability of A to get B to do something that he would otherwise not do."[17] In this simple axiom, we find that power is a function of two variables. In other words, it is not innate, but relative. Dahl demonstrated this through an analysis of the relationship between the president and Congress, but the concept is equally extendable to the field of international relations. It is from here that the concept of *relative power* discussed in this work originates.

If we are to take Dahl's definition literally, the term *balance of power* almost seems redundant: what is power if there is not an object upon which to assert one's will? The term encompasses more than simply the relations between two states (though it includes that also). In use metaphorically since Machiavelli, the concept was cemented by the Congress of Vienna in 1814–15 as a way of understanding how to produce an equilibrium between powers, and, thereby, to reduce the likelihood of interstate conflict.[18] Just as the Congress of Vienna convened to determine a new postwar order, conversations about how to achieve a sustainable peace after the Second World War required discussions about how to balance the competing interests of nation-states. The context, however, was different in just about every other respect, necessitating a reconceptualization of the term. In 1953, Ernst B. Haas attempted to relate the term *balance of power* to postwar circumstances.[19] He delineated four distinct interpretations of the term: the descriptive, the prescriptive, the propagandistic (or rhetorical), and the analytical. This work will primarily use the analytical meaning of the term, that is, as a way of describing the mechanics of power assertion in the international system.

Within the balance-of-power framework exist many levers through which states attempt to maximize their power in an anarchic world system.[20] The availability and usefulness of these levers change, depending on the relative power balance between an actor and its adversary. In 1971 Charles Doran investigated the manner by which the availability and utility of these tools change as declining powers reintegrated into the international system.[21] He later expanded upon this model by expressing relative power as a function of relative capabilities and time. Though elegant in execution, Doran's model suggests a predetermined, parabolic trajectory for relative power and also neglects to account for the multidimensional complexity of relative power dynamics.[22] Similarly, Doran did not address the question of efficacy, except to imply the inevitability of its decrease over time. The mechanistic understanding of relative power as initially expressed by Doran is thus insufficient to understanding mismatches between power and efficacy.

The qualitative work of other scholars from this period is more useful for understanding the balance and interplay of powers in the international system. Some of these works, particularly those from the realist and neorealist schools of international relations theory, build upon the balance-of-power concept by describing the world in terms of power centers around which weaker states orbit.[23] Kenneth Waltz's idea of *bipolarity* helped describe a world centered on the balance of power between two hegemonic states, which at the time of its writing helped explain why the United States and the Soviet Union avoided direct conflict with one another.[24] In retrospect, it is difficult to argue that the United States and the Soviet Union existed in a perfectly static equilibrium. If each actor's perceptions are taken into account, however, there is room in Waltz's theory to explain the balancing process of the two hegemons.

Waltz further argued that weaker states balance both externally and internally against the hegemon—externally through the pursuit of alliances and international cooperation, and internally by mimicry of the hegemon's institutions, technology, and practices.[25] He also provided a third option: the decision not to balance at all. Realist and neorealist theorists tend to view the likelihood of balancing against, versus seeking protection from, the hegemon (*bandwagoning*) as a function of geography and capabilities.[26] We can thus conclude that the smaller the relative power differential between two states, the higher the incentives to engage in balancing activity.

Viewed this way, the Cold War represented a vicious internal balancing cycle between the United States and the Soviet Union, which resulted in the space race, proxy wars, and, above all, the increase in quality and quantity of each state's nuclear-weapons arsenal. The United States and the Soviet Union engaged in a two-part, repetitive game in which each capital made decisions based on its perception of relative power.

Each new advance in the security realm was quickly mimicked by the other superpower, and competing international structures were established to increase the costs of direct conflict to the aggressor. The theory holds.

Viewed differently, however, three limitations emerge. The first problem is one of correlation and causation: it is impossible to know whether the conscious act of balancing or the very advent of the annihilative power of nuclear weapons did more to discourage direct conflict between the two "poles." Second, as T. V. Paul discusses, superpower balancing does not explain conflicts initiated by lesser powers against more powerful ones, as was the case when China entered the Korean War against the United States in 1950, Egypt challenged Israel by invading the Sinai in 1973, and Argentina confronted the United Kingdom when it invaded the Falklands in 1982.[27] Third, conflict initiation for domestic reasons, such as an upwelling of societal will to act against an external threat, does not map easily onto a model that treats conflict as a function of power dynamics only between rather than also within states.

With these limitations in mind, bipolarity was only a stabilizing force in the Cold War if we limit our view of conflict to direct, armed confrontation between the two superpowers. Because nuclear weapons reduced, if not precluded, the efficacy of direct conflict between the two most powerful actors, the pursuit of strategic objectives simply shifted to an indirect plane. The United States and the Soviet Union expanded their power through alliances and mimicry cycles expressed through arms races and proxy conflicts. In periods when both felt secure in their power relative to their rival, arms controls and other forms of what Thomas Schelling calls the "dialogue of competitive armament" ensued.[28] Between such periods, the balancing activities of the two hegemons were a function of their perceptions and fears of comparative weakness.

This repetitive cycle eventually produced nuclear weapons arsenals that threatened to destroy the world many times over. The advent of mutually assured destruction incentivized the development of ways to think about competition that leveraged military power either without using it or by applying it selectively, beneath the threshold that would risk escalation to nuclear war. Although these dynamics informed, and served as the impetus for, their works, Thomas Schelling's *Arms and Influence* and Alexander George and William Simons's *The Limits of Coercive Diplomacy* contain lessons that are also instructive for thinking about how relative power shifts, in a modern context, find their expression in competition outside of armed conflict.

Schelling begins with the simple observation that the "power to hurt . . . is a kind of bargaining power."[29] Not coincidentally, much of his work focuses on limited wars, that is, ones whose aims are less than the total destruction of another society. Such wars, in his estimation, were the products of ongoing bargaining processes between the belligerents, in which the scope and outcome of limited engagements were continually in tension.[30] The concept of compellence, or compelling an adversary to submit to one's will, undergirds much of Schelling's analysis. Many tools outside of total war exist to compel an adversary to behave in a desired manner, and most of them only rely upon the credible threat of violence rather than the actual act of combat. Violence is generally thought of as similar to the threat of annihilation, but it could also be thought of as an act that will hurt target societies in other ways, whether through damage to critical infrastructure, undermining of political will, or demotion of one's status in international affairs. These acts narrow the strategic options available to an adversary, even if they do not include physical violence. Put differently, the most violent act of all may be the neutralization of an adversary's ability to achieve its goals.

Alexander George and William Simons's work takes a more defensive approach to the interaction of powers. To them, compellence is akin to blackmail, fundamentally offensive, and only used to prevent an adversary from undertaking a particular action. Coercive diplomacy, on the other hand, seeks to halt ongoing actions, to "deal with the efforts of an adversary to change a status quo situation in his own favor," and to "back a demand on an adversary with a threat of punishment for noncompliance that will be credible and potent enough to persuade him that it is in his interest to comply with the demand."[31] Although it is clear that George and Simons view the threat of military action as a tool to enhance the effectiveness of diplomatic negotiations, force positioning and other non-combat military decisions and operations represent a military expression of coercive diplomacy. The positioning of American military assets in Japan, for example, communicates to North Korea and China alike the potential consequences of noncompliance with diplomatic demands. Likewise, the positioning of IRGC (Islamic Revolutionary Guard Corps) Quds Force elements and Russian troops in Syria increases the risk calculation to Israel and the United States of wider involvement in the Syrian conflict. The separation of military and diplomatic strategy envisioned by George and Simons is artificial, in practice if not in theory.[32]

The influence of these two works on American strategic thinking, though strong, was attenuated by the fall of the Soviet Union. Because each was the product of an international system in which mutually assured destruction precluded direct conflict, the ascent of the United States to sole superpower status drew their utility into question.[33] Systems for thinking about the dynamics of a bipolar world seemed less relevant, or at the very least, outdated in the new, unipolar system in which the United States remained the sole superpower.

Perceptions, both internal and external, are essential to understanding how America's efficacy declined during the zenith of its relative power. Internally, America's new unipolar position created the perception that the liberal international order would not only continue but also expand; the unquestioned power of the United States portended American supremacy in perpetuity. Externally, not all were satisfied with this new arrangement, nor did all view U.S. preponderance as beneficial to their interests. This became clear in the aftermath of the attacks of September 11, 2001, but discontent had been brewing for many years prior. As the United States involved itself in a number of military conflicts, weaker powers gained many opportunities to refine their mimicry of the hegemon.

Rather than adapt to the growth in sophistication and power of other actors, the United States, still perceiving itself as the unquestioned singular superpower, repeatedly attempted to shape conflict in terms that suited its military superiority. However, the rapidity and precision with which adversaries identified weaknesses and nullified technical gains through mimicry decreased the effectiveness of these efforts. Had the United States begun thinking of itself as one pole in a system of several (even if the power of some was latent), its behavior may have mirrored the cycles of weakness and strength that characterized the interaction of the superpowers in the Cold War. Instead, weaker powers continued to mimic the United States and developed asymmetric responses to progressively narrow their relative power gap.

As its rivals have found ways to circumvent or obviate American power, the theories discussed in this section suggest that the United States would begin to shift its strategy in reaction to the narrowing of its relative power. To understand why the shift has proven so difficult for the United States, we must examine enduring patterns in its decision-making process that exist independently from its relative position in the world. Here, we find that predispositions inherent in the American way of war militate against the development and implementation of a comprehensive approach to international competition at the operational and tactical levels—the very levels where competition is most keen.

Similar to how human agency connects theory to practice in the Western tradition, the ways bridge resources and the attainment of ends. Also like human agency, the ways represent the intellectual and the rational—the human element of strategic success. Both ways and human agency manifest in many forms, which are a function of the infinitely varied perspectives of human decision-makers. To make sense of these variations, one must accept a certain level of generalization. Examining how different groups perceive of, and act to counter, threats provides insights that a comparison of military balances alone could not reveal.

Such is the basic premise upon which the idea of *strategic culture* was built. The term first came into use in 1977 in a RAND Corporation report written by Jack Snyder, in which the author questioned whether American analyses of the Soviet Union's decision-making process suffered from a mirror-imaging problem.[34] The idea of *national character* dates back much further: nineteenth-century scholars defined it as including morality, government type, religion, and intellectual capacity, and scholars from the mid-twentieth century asserted that it could shape policy decisions.[35] Difficulties in achieving a precise definition of *nation* and *character* led to the decline of this term among sociologists, anthropologists, and historians. In the context of international security, the semantic drawbacks of the concept were outweighed during the Cold War by a pressing need to understand how the adversary understood warfare.

Nevertheless, *strategic culture* has generated its fair share of controversy. Since Snyder's original report comparing the United States and the Soviet Union, scholars have debated the extent to which history, geography, and political culture inform decision-making processes and whether these factors have resulted in substantive or merely stylistic differences in approaches to strategic decision-making.[36] In a seminal

essay, "Thinking about Strategic Culture," Alistair Iain Johnston criticized the "first generation" of literature on the topic
(to which Snyder's work belongs) for its "cultural determinism" and "homogeneity." To Johnston, first-generation literature implicitly suggested that strategic culture, however defined,
was inescapable and immutable and failed to address the possibility of multiple strategic cultures emerging within a group.[37]
After reviewing the second and third generations of literature
on strategic culture, Johnston attempted to develop strategic
culture as a variable that exists outside of behavior.

This essay sparked a strong reaction from another scholar,
Colin Gray, who presented an opposing viewpoint: strategic culture is inseparable from observable behavior, and it
merely paints a picture of the context in which decisions are
made.[38] The inescapable subjectivity of strategic cultural analysis, according to Gray, precluded its isolation as a dependent
variable that could directly explain decision-making processes.
Culture, after all, is dynamic; furthermore, elite or decision-
making culture may not entirely overlap with that of a broader
society. Gray's definition indeed avoids the pitfall of determinism, but its nihilistic flavor arguably creates more problems
than it solves.[39] As for Johnston, Gray's theory was a prime
example of the homogeneity and the cultural determinism
that he criticized in earlier works on the topic.[40] The impasse
between these two authors has prevented the emergence of a
universally accepted definition of strategic culture.

Despite this, the term continues to appeal to strategists if
for no other reason than it provides a way to describe the je
ne sais quoi of an adversary's behavior. The lack of a common
definition, though problematic in one sense, may also be useful in that it forces analysts to consider their own definition
of the term. Ignoring strategic culture is also problematic, as
doing so has the potential to amplify biases and to blind analysts to contrasting adversarial assumptions and methods.[41]
An analysis that failed to consider the conscious and uncon-

scious factors that affect adversarial decision-making would, oddly enough, exhibit the same pitfalls that Johnston identified in Snyder's work. In other words, strategic culture provides a method for analysts to mitigate their own biases, to gain an understanding of how historical developments peculiar to a people result in particular structures and processes, and ultimately to understand the logic—or lack thereof—that drives an adversary's actions.

Though each analyst may weigh them differently, the factors that comprise strategic culture—history, geography, and political dynamics—are universally applicable. Alastair Iain Johnston is best known for his China-studies scholarship, and other thinkers in this field, such as Andrew Scobell, have incorporated the concept into their analyses of Chinese strategic thinking.[42] Although his definition of strategic culture differs from that of Johnston, Colin Gray updated and expanded Snyder's original work on Soviet strategic culture to describe Russia's way of war.[43] Others have subjected Iran, the United States, and Israel to similar analyses.[44] Just as Net Assessment expanded the analysis of military balances beyond a simple enumeration of forces, strategic culture provides a way for understanding why others make decisions that may, at first glance, seem confusing or irrational.

Strategic culture is also useful for understanding how foreign actors conceive of international competition. However, two caveats are in order. First, studies of strategic culture often focus on the military decision-making process, but ways of competition encompass more than just military maneuvers. This study will show that, by illuminating how different actors define war, strategic culture is also a useful concept for analyzing the different toolkits that foreign powers bring to bear in their competitive relations with other states. Second, because neither the ways of war nor the ways of competition are as static as the term *culture* implies, this study will use the term *strategic predisposition* in place of *strategic culture* to emphasize the point drawn out in the previous section: states behave differently depending on their power position relative to their adversaries. This term also allows analysts to avoid the semantic pitfalls inherent in the word *culture*, which has driven the scholarly impasse outlined previously. It is difficult for one person, or a group of persons, to change a culture. Awareness of a predisposition, however, allows the possibility of not only changing it but also avoiding it entirely. This understanding far better reflects the role that human agency plays in determining the efficacy of a particular strategy.

To develop a framework for understanding ways of competition, one must first begin with how individual actors conceive of war. As the case studies in this book highlight, *competition* and *warfare* are analogous to some, with violence merely being one (and often not the most preferable) instrument of persuasion. Perhaps the most literature has been written on China's expansive view of warfare, but Russia and Iran similarly do not limit their perceptions of warfare to combat. All of these countries have, at some point in their long histories, gone through extended periods of defensiveness, real or perceived subjugation, and protracted struggles for influence against adversaries of greater strength. Over time, these historical experiences resulted in strategic predispositions that prized opportunism and agility, and that prioritized the achievement of warlike gains outside of war.[45]

Unlike the other cases in this book, the United States has exhibited a predisposition toward what Russell Weigley defined as a "strategy of annihilation."[46] Rather than organizing its military based on the actions of a militarily superior foe, the United States—especially since its ascent to sole-superpower status—focused on maximizing efficiency and optimizing its military to win against any enemy through attrition.[47] Thus, efforts to shape the strategic environment are often viewed as mere steps on the escalation ladder rather than as ends unto themselves. It makes little sense to go to the effort of shaping an environment when one is confident of victory in any direct confrontation.

Geography—if not a surplus of relative power—has frequently afforded the United States the luxury of assuming that it could set competitive terms vis-à-vis its adversaries. Yet this has, in fact, rarely been the case. The majority of America's military engagements have not involved direct confrontation with near-peer adversaries, yet despite its inferior effectiveness against weaker enemies, the United States has continually pursued strategies of attrition.[48] America's narrow definition of warfare and its predisposition toward attrition-based strategies have resulted in a number of failures or strategic stalemates against nominally weaker foes.

The narrowness of this strategic predisposition, as applied to broader international competition, could be mitigated by a concerted application of nonmilitary tools of national power to a specific strategy. Such capabilities—diplomatic, economic, informational, and others—are essential components of a successful grand strategy. For structural as well as cultural reasons, however, executing a "whole of government"—much less a "whole of society"—approach has proven problematic for the United States. Outside of periods of existential threats or, as discussed in the prior section, times when it perceived itself as in a position of parity or weakness in relation to its adversary, the United States has found difficulty aligning diplomatic, economic, and informational tools of power with its military strategy. A focus on instruments rather than intended effects—on means rather than ways—has created silos of influence that hinder attempts to coordinate and integrate efforts over the long run. Strategies of annihilation are optimal for short-term solutions, but international competition is a long-term, complex affair.

The alternative approach to annihilation, favored out of necessity if not predisposition by relatively weaker powers, is one of maneuver. This strategy is both less costly and more oriented toward long-term strategic thinking. Robbed of the ability to confront their adversary directly, the weaker power will focus on how it might exploit an enemy's weaknesses across a host of domains—military, social, psychological, and political— and will organize its military accordingly. The result is generally a nimble, flexible, and responsive force. Employing this strategy from a position of weakness risks total annihilation as the adversary shrinks the decisive time horizon and applies overwhelming force. Employing this strategy deliberately, however, mitigates these concerns, especially if paired with the development of superior military tools for use in the event that escalation to direct conflict occurs. It is a strategy that requires patience and opportunism. In low-intensity conflicts such as insurgencies, hybrid warfare, and competition outside of war, practitioners of the maneuver approach enjoy a distinct edge.[49]

The challenges posed by low-intensity warfare are neither new nor unique to the American experience. Whether they manifest in the form of substate insurgencies or as part of hybrid warfare strategies, hegemons have long struggled to adapt attrition-based approaches to nominally weaker enemies. Despite the explosion of counterinsurgency literature that followed the U.S. invasion of Iraq, the ideas contained within it were hardly unique. Insurgent tactics defined the success of the Maccabees against the Romans in the second century BCE, of Americans and Boers against the British, and of the Viet Cong against the Americans during the Vietnam War, to name just a few of many examples.[50] Similarly, though Frank Hoffman first posed the idea of modern hybrid warfare in a 2007 essay, other scholars have shown that history is replete with examples of hybrid conflicts.[51] The fact that these topics are repeatedly reexamined shows the intractability of the problem.

The long history of low-intensity warfare and competition outside of combat has led many countries to develop capabilities relevant to both strategic approaches. Russia, China, and Iran do this effectively. The relative power balance between these actors and the United States favors these approaches. America's hesitance or inability to adapt—in short, its complacency—cedes entire realms of competition to its adversaries, even though it already possesses the relevant capabilities. Indeed, as direct confrontation has decreased in recent decades, the use of special-operations forces (SOF) has increased.

Since the establishment of United States Special Operations Command (USSOCOM) in 1987, America has relied mainly on special-operations forces to address military competition short of war. This is in part due to the circumstances of the Command's founding: the failed mission to rescue hostages from the American embassy in Tehran.[52] Noncombat operations required many skill sets that previously had no natural home in the broader military apparatus and that were viewed with skepticism by many senior leaders in the military and elsewhere.[53] Viewed one way, the establishment of USSOCOM marked an awakening of the need to increase the maneuverability of the American military.

Viewed differently, however, the establishment of the command marked an attempt to fold maneuverability within the predominant American predisposition toward strategies of annihilation and attrition. Throughout the 1990s—as was the case during the Second World War and in Vietnam—SOF were consistently used as a supplementary force to larger military operations that still employed annihilative strategies. Operational models continued to emphasize the importance of "dominating" and "destroying" an enemy via the overwhelming application of force.[54] Efforts to shape and adjust the operating environment before or after conflict were minimized. It was not until the counterinsurgency campaigns of the 2000s that the skills endemic to SOF—regional and language expertise, operational agility, and psychological warfare among them—again became prized.

Thus far, the changed operational environment has translated to an increase in utility for SOF rather than a fundamental change to how the U.S. military or the government views international competition. Whereas many of America's adversaries developed capabilities for competition outside of war that encompass all the tools of national power at their disposal, the United States has relegated its efforts in this realm to less than 5 percent of its standing military force.[55] Diplomatic, informational, and economic instruments of national power have been overlooked in favor of SOF. These instruments continue to function but not in the coordinated and integrated manner exhibited by America's adversaries. The problem comes into starker relief when one views facets of national power in terms of effects rather than tools: a tiny subset of the military, no matter how capable, cannot create the same impact in the diplomatic, information, military, and economic realms as could an entire government working in concert.

Promising signs of change have become apparent in recent years. The United States Army, for example, has a center devoted to the study of operational maneuver, and its discussions about "multi-domain conflict" reflect an acceptance of multiple planes of combat. At a military-wide level, the recent Joint Concept for Integrated Campaigning provides a compelling theoretical framework for the military to appreciate the overlapping competitive, cooperative, and conflict dynamics that comprise international relations. At the strategic level, the National Defense Strategy and National Security Strategy issued by the Trump administration framed the international threat environment as one of competition among great powers.

These efforts mark an essential step toward developing an American way of competition. Yet it remains to be seen whether and how the theoretical frameworks and ideals laid out in recent documents will translate into practice. Here again, the question of human agency and the formulation of ways becomes paramount. The United States faces structural, legal, and political limitations on how it combines and coordinates instruments of power that its competitors—including Russia, China, and

Introduction

Iran—do not. The Joint Concept for Integrated Campaigning, for example, leans heavily on coordination with interagency partners, but the extent to which those partners, such as the U.S. Departments of State and Commerce, will be able, willing, or required to go along with the Joint Staff's concepts is unclear. For all that the Trump National Defense Strategy (NDS) and National Security Strategy (NSS) did to align the government around a specific set of objectives, they did not address implementation. Moreover, they risk perpetuating a view of competition that is centered on "great powers," thus framing the threat environment as one of realpolitik rather than one of relative power dynamics and differences in strategic predispositions.

An important difference between the strategic predispositions of the United States and the other cases outlined in this book is the former's view of the diplomatic, informational, military, and economic realms of competition as delegable to distinct organizations and the latter's ability to use each organization under its command to create effects in each competitive space. The sequestration of competitive efforts to specific organizations—diplomacy to the Department of State, economics to the Departments of Commerce and the Treasury, and so on—exacerbates the bureaucratic silo effect that the United States must overcome to build an effective "whole of government approach." Meanwhile, for reasons of strategic predisposition, governance, and necessity, America's adversaries use different organizations under their control to effect change within each realm—the use of "merchant" vessels by China to create military effects, the use of informational tools by Russia to create economic and diplomatic effects, and the use of the Revolutionary Guards by Iran to create informational effects are just a few examples.

In short, America's adversaries have developed a keen understanding of the indirect approach, whereas America continues to approach its goals in each competitive realm directly. This difference may be the most significant hindrance to the formulation of an American way of competition in a multi-polar world.

Pivotal Nature of the Current Moment

Relative power and strategic predispositions help explain the options and decisions of any set of leaders. The details of these two variables are, in the short term, primarily out of the control of any group or nation. However, the relationship between them is a function of human agency. Much like agency ties theory to practice, it also explains whether groups transcend contemporary circumstances and historical experience to succeed or allow these variables to limit outcomes. It is at this connection where societal will and perceptions generate a decisive impact on whether a country thrives in its current circumstances or declines.

The combination of waning unipolarity and a predisposition toward strategies of domination threaten to blind America to the shifting sands of international relations. The United States is hardly the first power to struggle with overcoming old habits as its relative power declines. The Roman Empire was unable to respond effectively to internal and external pressures and changes before eventually being overtaken by determined barbarians.[56] The British Empire declined mostly because of its inability to change; Aaron Friedberg referred to the empire as a "weary titan."[57] The Soviet Union, China, and Persia each underwent periods of decline that stemmed from their failure to correctly interpret and act upon power shifts and upon established patterns of governance and behavior. These empires attained levels of power that seemed insurmountable, but their complacency ultimately blinded them from adapting to maintain their relative position.

To be fair, there are essential differences between the pressures that led empires to decline and those faced by America. The external pressures on Rome came from adjacent territory. Although Britain could have extended its hegemony in the short term, it is hard to argue the long-term viability of the empire's reliance on foreign resources to supplement its indigenous economic, demographic, and geographic constraints.[58] Neither China nor Persia were truly global powers at the time of their decline, and the Soviet Union's contest with the United States prevented it from attaining the global hegemony that the latter went on to enjoy.

In the abstract, however, each of these powers experienced a slow erosion of their primacy followed by a situation that brought their diminishment into stark relief. After centuries of difficulty balancing internal issues with the need to placate and tame the diverse constituencies residing along its border regions, the Western Roman Empire could remain in denial about its problems no longer once the barbarian Odoacer claimed the Roman throne. Even after relinquishing much of its global responsibilities to the United States, Britain could continue to view itself as a global power until its embarrassingly poor performance during the Suez Crisis in 1956.[59] The Ming dynasty in China remained confident in the perpetuity of its power long after changing circumstances should have challenged its assumptions, until a combination of internal and external pressures eventuated its collapse.[60] Although the state of a nation's military is not the only indicator of a nation's decline, a decisive loss is often the coup de grâce that breaks the illusion of perpetual power.

The current historical moment portends a similar situation for the United States. As its relative power has declined markedly, not just from the postwar high of the 1950s but also from the post–Cold War interlude of unipolarity, the strategic outlook is shifting in ways that, if not addressed adroitly, may make this decline permanent. The illusion that its power could not be challenged was drawn most starkly into relief by the attacks of September 11, 2001. However, the terms of international competition had been changing long before that event and continued to evolve afterward. As the inadequacy of America's predisposition to strategies of annihilation came into focus as the country struggled to consolidate political gains in Iraq, state actors saw an opening to further challenge the primacy of the hegemon. From a lower level on the relative power hierarchy, these actors leveraged aspects of their strategic predispositions in a manner that would confuse the United States and draw into question the power of its military. Meanwhile, the United States has remained complacent, thus obscuring the ability of American decision-makers to see the implications of changing power dynamics while also impeding efforts to adapt to maintain the status quo.

To reassert what it views as its rightful position in the world, Russia has built upon the legacy of the tsarist and Soviet eras to expand its influence and sow chaos within societies of its adversaries. Russia has leveraged new tools, such as social media, as well as established institutions, such as the Russian Orthodox Church, to shape and constrain the strategic options available to its adversaries and to increase the perception of its power. Militarily, Russia has responded to America's strategic predispositions by developing methods to exploit its weaknesses—such as hybrid warfare via the so-called Gerasimov doctrine—and by investing in capabilities long neglected by the United States—such as electronic warfare and nuclear weaponry. Although America is not the sole, or in many instances the primary, target of Russian destabilization efforts, the cloud of suspicion surrounding Russia's involvement in the 2016 election demonstrates Russia's understanding of the importance of diminishing the perception of American power.

China has similarly positioned itself to improve its regional and global standing while undermining the rules-based international order that the United States and its regional allies established after the Second World War. By manipulating international legal norms and controlling dissent from the Communist Party of China's official line within its borders (and increasingly beyond them), China has taken steps to regain its place as the regional hegemon of the East Pacific. Its military strategy similarly supports these goals. The People's Liberation Army has publicly stated its intention to become the unchallenged power in the vast Pacific region between China's mainland and Guam and, after carefully studying America's operational approaches, has taken a holistic approach to information and cyber warfare simultaneously rooted in ancient Chinese texts and modern understandings. Like the rising powers before it, China has made incremental changes to the status quo that, over time, truncate the strategic options of the hegemon and reduce the relevance of its outsized power.

In the Middle East, the expansionist and revolutionary regime in Tehran has similarly sought to expand its power and diminish the options available to the United States and its regional allies. Though support to proxies through the Revolutionary Guard Corps receives the most media attention, these activities comprise only one line of effort that Iran has pursued to increase its regional clout. It has also engaged in sophisticated financing schemes and cyber-warfare activities, leveraged like-minded religious communities in other countries, and engaged in a "soft war" that it purports is in response to information warfare waged against it. Militarily, it has become a leader in the development of asymmetric capabilities that circumvent the power of its adversaries and has pioneered corresponding military techniques, such as swarming and the aforementioned support to proxies throughout the region. Iran's activities have the potential to remake the regional order in an image that will significantly reduce America's influence, regardless of the military forces that remain.

This book will not assert esoteric knowledge about these developments; those matters are better left to regional experts. It will, however, based on years of interviews and extensive research, demonstrate how these activities, and America's lack of efficacy in responding to them, have accreted power from the United States and reduced the power differential between it and its adversaries. It will catalogue competitive strategies in the space between war and peace and show how each nation's strategic predisposition either aids or detracts from its effectiveness in this realm. The book will show that competition in international affairs is a constant, not a new development nor an exception to the norm, and will contribute to discussions about how the United States may still use its outsized power to shape dynamics in a manner that maximizes efficacy. Because human agency, on aggregate and at the individual level, will determine whether America can bridge the gap between power dynamics and its strategic predisposition, the book concludes with modest recommendations for America's current leaders to better address these dynamics. America has the capabilities (quantifiable means to accomplish a goal, like number of tanks) and capacity (ability to use those means, which encompasses factors like political will and tactical acumen) to compete outside of war, but a change in perceptions will be required to bridge the gaps between theory and practice and between power and complacency.

1

Russia

Conceptualizing Competition Short of War

The Russian nation has governed an immense landmass bridging Asia and Europe for more than three centuries, but rather than engendering a sense of durability, Russia's size has fostered insecurity among generations of its leaders. Although Russia's vast hinterlands protect its interior from foreign aggressors, most of its population lies within geographic Europe. Aside from brutal winters, little stands between Russia's political heartland and would-be invaders from the West. Hence, geography forces the defense of western Russia to the forefront of the Kremlin's national-security agenda, motivating a pursuit for a strategic buffer zone that, by default, extends into Eastern Europe.[1]

A string of military defeats toward the end of the nineteenth century cemented this strategic imperative in the minds of Russian military planners.[2] But military considerations alone did not prompt Russia's encroachment on Europe's historical borders. The sweeping changes brought about by the Industrial Revolution introduced an additional set of rationales, both economic and political, for the westward expansion of the Russian Empire.[3] Unlike its eighteenth- and nineteenth-century

European neighbors, tsarist Russia thus sought to expand contiguously and in the direction of its European neighbors, just as the rest of Europe looked further afield for colonial gain.[4] Yet even within its borders, Russia harbored many different creeds and ethnicities, a reality that incentivized the gradual Russification of areas under Moscow's control.[5]

Rapid expansion during the tsarist period exacerbated existing governance challenges for the sprawling Russian state. Managing a diverse and swelling population required more than just assimilationist policies directed at internal minority groups. Notwithstanding the varied ethnic and geographic backgrounds of the ruling family, Russian military and political elites developed a messianic outlook during the tsarist period to rationalize national expansion through the Russification of outside groups.[6] Popular adherents of this view cast Russia as the Third Rome: a fount of modern civilization to which non-Russian peoples should submit.[7]

The tsarist era also laid the foundation for predispositions and organizations that would resurface later in Russian history. The utility of deception, for example, was first demonstrated in the tsarist era: the concept of a Potemkin village traces its roots to eighteenth-century Russia, when Prince Grigory Potemkin constructed fake villages to create the impression of prosperity to a transiting Catherine the Great.[8]

The relationship among the state, its security services, and the population in Russia also has pre-Bolshevik antecedents. After its establishment in the nineteenth century, the internal police force known as the Third Department eventually gained enough power to influence "not only every branch of the [Tsar's] administration . . . but also the development of all aspects of national life, political, social, and cultural."[9] This organization eventually morphed into the Russian Imperial Police, or Okhrana, whose integrated domestic and foreign activities were a foundation for future Soviet approaches to espionage and counterespionage.[10]

Although Lenin and the Bolsheviks promised a radical departure from tsarist-era Russia, certain tsarist approaches and organizations transcended questions of ideology. The Okhrana, for example, were among the Bolshevik's top targets, yet Lenin and his compatriots nevertheless appreciated the organization's function. Lenin believed that a strong central government offered the key to establishing and enforcing socialist utopia; the strength of the state would thus rest in equal parts on coercion and inducement.[11] The heavy hand of the state would enforce order, and supreme faith in the Russian nation would sustain and legitimize the state's tactics.[12] Lenin thus shared the tsarist view of the population as an object of control rather than, as in capitalist democracies, one of persuasion or management. The Bolshevik mindset and ideology further created a need for population control: Lenin and his acolytes rejected the peace-war duality common in the West and instead viewed international politics as a "continuing state of conflict and struggle."[13] In function if not in name, Communist Russia found reason to maintain tsarist-era mechanisms of population control to promulgate and enforce its new ideology.[14]

Lenin also found use in other tsarist approaches. The perceived universality of the Communist mission, for example, mirrored the messianic expansionism that characterized the tsarist period. Yet again, Soviet Russia's choice to embark on a system of government with international proselytization at its core set it apart from its neighbors across Europe, many of which turned inward to remedy the societal ills laid bare by the First World War.[15] Moreover, communism's evangelism dovetailed with the long-held Russian goal of creating strategic depth in Eastern Europe, or Russia's strategic culture.[16] This alignment of geopolitical and ideological goals, rooted in enduring strategic imperatives, would sustain an expansionist approach to international affairs for decades to come.[17]

Once they attained power, the Bolsheviks, now organized through the Communist Party, soon developed methods to export their revolution. These tools took the form of formal organizations such as the Third International Committee but also included informal mechanisms that were more pernicious. For example, many of the more than one million Russian émigrés and refugees scattered in Western cities supported communism and joined local Communist Party chapters. By 1920 in Chicago, for example, 75 percent of Communist Party members were émigrés.[18] Soviet agents did not limit their efforts to friendly groups of émigrés. Through a program called the Trust, Soviet agents penetrated immigrant groups hostile to communism and leveraged them to feed misinformation about the Soviet government to Western intelligence agencies.

During the interwar years, the Soviets considered the United States a low intelligence priority, below the United Kingdom, Poland, France, and Germany.[19] The stock market crash of 1929, however, provided the Soviet Union with an opportunity to sow doubts about the wisdom of laissez-faire capitalism, particularly within the American left. The egalitarian promise of communism appealed to many interwar American progressives, and the Communist Party of the United States gained greater prominence in leftist political circles.[20] This environment created opportunities for Soviet operatives to recruit American agents.

Initially, the activities of American agents were limited to economic and industrial espionage. That situation changed in 1933 when President Franklin Delano Roosevelt decided to grant official recognition to the Soviet Union.[21] Official recognition, it was thought, would allow the Soviets to increase their trade with the United States at a time when opportunities for domestic economic growth were limited. Along with increased trade, however, came the establishment of a permanent Soviet embassy in Washington and consulates in New York and San Francisco. Soviet officials quickly moved civilian and military-intelligence elements into these facilities to take advantage of the diplomatic cover, and source recruitment expanded dramatically.[22]

In addition to targeting New Deal Democrats in Washington, intelligence elements from the New York consulate began to foster relationships with the Communist Party of the United States of America (CPUSA).[23] At the time, the U.S. government did not inquire into employees' affiliation with subversive political organizations, which allowed the Soviets to specifically target CPUSA-affiliated federal employees.[24] By the late 1930s, the Soviets had developed a broad network of sources in the U.S. government. Meanwhile, the Soviets pursued industrial targets in the chemical, steel, oil, finance, shipbuilding, automotive, and aircraft production sectors.[25] Due to the economic benefits of trade with Russia, commercial, scientific, and technical intelligence collection was largely tolerated in the United States, enabling the establishment of a large, informal collection network.

Not all were willing to turn a blind eye to Soviet activities on American soil. The Federal Bureau of Investigation attempted to counter industrial espionage, and the U.S. Congress investigated "subversive" Communist activities but was generally unable to reach strong-enough conclusions to warrant retaliatory measures.[26] Quelling communism wasn't the first priority: many in government, as well as the public, were preoccupied with the growing threat of fascism.[27] The announcement of the Molotov-Ribbentrop Pact in August 1939 ushered in anti-Communist sentiments within the executive branch of the U.S. government.[28] By this point, however, the Soviets had already established a sophisticated intelligence-collection network, which they leveraged against the United States and others throughout the Second World War.

Declassified cable traffic between Soviet intelligence agents in the United States and their overseers in Moscow provides a glimpse into the scope of sensitive information acquired by the Soviets. In addition to regular reports from the War

Production Board, the Soviets received descriptions of the state of the U.S. steel, synthetic rubber, ceramics, shipbuilding, and aircraft industries.[29] With respect to military intelligence, Soviet sources sent information about U.S. military intelligence-training processes and ammunition-production figures to Moscow, as well as designs for prototype T-70 tank destroyers and 155 mm guns and details about U.S. plans to develop long-range B-29 bombers.[30] On the political front, a cable from 1943 describes the relationship between FDR and Vice President Henry Wallace and includes a discussion of how "little the Vice President seems to know" about FDR's thoughts about Operation Overlord, the upcoming invasion of France.[31] This information was obtained through both high-level contacts with access to senior officials and low-level contacts who may have had otherwise legitimate relationships with U.S. manufacturers.[32] By 1943 the Soviets had a highly granular picture of the U.S. industrial posture, insight into innovative and sensitive technological development, and access to senior executive-branch leaders.

The Soviets were also adept at leveraging American policy developments to extend the reach of their economic-influence activities and espionage operations. With the extension of Lend-Lease aid to the Soviets in October 1941, the Soviets used their previously gained knowledge of the U.S. industrial base to expand their American ties. Some of the money that Stalin saved as a result of Lend-Lease was redirected to Russian trade representatives in the United States to bolster their relations with manufacturers.[33] Russian trade representatives used the surplus funds to obtain "hundreds of pounds of uranium and heavy water" for use in the Soviet Union, and others exploited FDR adviser Harry Hopkins's desire to help Russia by requesting to visit the construction facility for the B-29 Superfortress, although they were ultimately rebuffed.[34]

Espionage in the years leading up to and including the Second World War was not the exclusive domain of the Soviets, nor was the United States the only or even primary target of its efforts. The degree of access that Moscow obtained in the United States, however, demonstrates the contrasting understandings of warfare held by the United States and the Soviet Union. Whereas the United States remained focused on the most immediate enemy, Germany, the Soviet Union extended mechanisms of influence deep into the societies of its ostensible allies.

The Soviets drew from the Western canon of military literature for its standalone merit and to improve their understanding of foreign contemporaries. Yet their readings of such texts, when viewed through the expansionist lens of communism, reflected a different and more expansive understanding of warfare than that held by their American counterparts. Lenin believed that the military and political aspects of war (along with the organizational and rhetorical aspects) were inseparable and interdependent—a stark contrast to the Western view that war is subordinate to politics.[35] Later military strategists would expand upon Lenin's insights. The writings of the preeminent and widely read Soviet strategist, Aleksandr Svechin, for example, treat the conduct of offensive and defensive political warfare campaigns with a level of seriousness and detail that Americans would typically reserve for kinetic war planning.[36] As the military became more politicized under Stalin, the expansive ideology of communism mixed with the development of strategic and operational doctrines.[37] This infusion of ideology into military art further blurred the line between politics and war. Soviet strategic doctrine thus came to regard politics as inseparable from war; both were struggles that should involve all aspects of national power. Within this paradigm, battlefield combat was only the most violent expression of ongoing political struggle but hardly the only realm of conflict deserving of a coordinated and comprehensive response.

This comprehensive view of the mechanics of war had important implications for how the Soviet Union attempted to gain strategic, operational, and tactical advantages over its adversaries. The authoritarian nature of the Soviet system, moreover, facilitated the development of long-term planning functions and a sustained strategic patience. Whereas American cultural and institutional norms prohibited the use of deception as a legitimate tool of state policy, the consequentialist moral code of communism looked favorably upon deception so long as its aims conformed to the advancement of Communist ideology.[38] Thus, by the early 1940s the Soviets had incorporated deception—or *maskirovka*—into strategic, operational, and tactical plans and had developed deception campaigns for both foreign and domestic audiences.[39] While the United States developed plans for propaganda and political warfare in times of battle, the Soviets developed a web of contacts over time that could then be leveraged if the opportunity arose—whether inside or outside the confines of war, as the term is understood in the West.[40] Rather than focusing on security crises as they arose, the Soviet Union deliberately fostered vectors of influence during times of nominal peace for use during any conditions of international affairs.

Because the Soviets believed that international affairs were perpetually characterized by conflict and struggle, their deception campaigns transcended civil-military boundaries as understood in the West. The contrasting U.S. and Soviet perceptions about the proper role of propaganda illustrate this point. Whereas the United States began to abandon its information agencies at the end of the war, the Soviet Union redoubled its efforts to shape and influence how domestic and foreign audiences perceived communism and capitalism.[41] As early as September 1946, the U.S. embassy in Moscow requested to extend Voice of America broadcasts into the Soviet Union to counter the anti-American propaganda broadcasted by the Soviet state.[42] This proposal, however, was thwarted by a lack of dedicated resources and a desire on the part of Washington to ramp down wartime information campaigns.[43]

By the 1950s, the Soviet Union had developed an extensive international network to conduct influence operations. Though the Red Scare taking hold in the United States focused the public's attention on avowed Communists allegedly, and sometimes actually, in their midst, U.S. government records reveal a more nuanced internal understanding of the sophistication and pervasiveness of Moscow's methods of influence. In 1953, the United States Information Agency (USIA) concluded that the Soviet government dedicated as many as 325,000 staff to the production of agitation propaganda ("agitprop").[44] The report further indicated that the combined foreign broadcasting hours of Voice of America and BBC were only half those of their Soviet counterparts, a gap that widened by a factor of four by 1958. In a report published that year, USIA catalogued the exponential growth of Soviet-funded foreign-language publications, broadcasts, documentaries, art exhibitions, and films, as well as support for a wide range of national and international organizations around the world.[45]

In addition to overt methods of influence, the Soviets built on the espionage network they had established in the United States before the war.[46] Besides the political, military, and economic research organs, Soviet intelligence doctrine provided for injection of misinformation into target societies, acquisition of sensitive industrial secrets from them, and penetration of their intelligence services.[47] Although each of these efforts entailed significant overlap, the United States treated them in a compartmentalized fashion, both in terms of the information flow about them and the responsible organizations for addressing them.[48]

Moreover, for all the knowledge of Soviet activities aimed at the United States, gleaned from USIA reports and intelligence intercepts, the ambiguous nature of Soviet influence operations complicated American attempts to counter them. No intelligence-collection capability available to the United States, the Central Intelligence Agency concluded in a 1957 Special National Intelligence Estimate, "provided invariable proof against deception."[49] As a result, determining how best to think about and articulate Moscow's activities proved extremely difficult. In a 1960 speech, Senator Thomas J. Dodd characterized Soviet active measures as "an integrated offensive on every plane of human activity—the economic, the political, the diplomatic, the psychological, the social, the cultural—a war conducted by stealth and with Pavlovian techniques."[50] The Soviets appeared to be both everywhere and nowhere at the same time.

Meanwhile, America was establishing its own system for projecting influence abroad. Just as the Soviets viewed capitalism as an existential threat, the U.S. government viewed the spread of communist ideology as anathema. Notwithstanding the strategies provided in National Security Council Memorandum 68, Kennan's long telegram, or the deterrence theories developed by the likes of Thomas Schelling, America's approach to competition with the Soviet Union remained comparatively fragmented, especially with respect to Soviet active measures and efforts to counter them.[51] Whereas the Soviet Union drew from the views of its Bolshevik forebearers— which held that tactics, programs, and organizations were in fact inseparable—the relationship between these concepts was far more complex in America.[52]

Senator Dodd was accurate in his characterization of the nature and pervasiveness of the Soviet threat. Because the destructive power of nuclear and thermonuclear weapons largely precluded their use, nonnuclear and nonkinetic means, or *active measures*, remained the primary Soviet tools to counter the spread and influence of capitalism.[53] The use of proxies throughout the world supported the expansionist imperative of communism and reflected a paternalistic impulse on the part of Moscow to "provide guardianship to" like-minded regimes across the globe.[54] With respect to the United States, Richard Shultz and Roy Godson induced from a review of available literature the following objectives of Soviet active measures:

1. To influence American, European, and world public opinion to believe that U.S. military and political policies are the major cause of international conflict and crisis.

2. To demonstrate that the United States is an aggressive, militaristic, and imperialistic power.

3. To isolate the United States from its friends and allies (especially those in NATO) and to discredit those states that cooperate with the United States.

4. To discredit the U.S. and NATO military and intelligence establishments.

5. To demonstrate that the policies and objectives of the United States are incompatible with those of underdeveloped nations.

6. To confuse world opinion concerning Soviet global ambitions, creating a favorable environment for Soviet foreign policy.[55]

The stature of Soviet organizations responsible for the conduct of active measures indicates the high priority placed on them by the Communist Party of the Soviet Union (CPSU). The Politburo reviewed and decided on matters of day-to-day governance and then passed directives along to relevant government ministries for execution. For issues deemed of specific interest to the international Communist movement, however, the CPSU maintained a separate chain of command that avoided ministerial interference and provided direct control to CPSU leadership.[56] For the most part, the conduct of active measures took place through this alternative structure and thus avoided much of the bureaucratic friction that characterized the permanent ministries. Organizations within this structure attracted the most ambitious senior servants, which, over time, further extended and compounded the CPSU's ability to guide the direction of the international Communist movement. The three organizations responsible for active measures—the CPSU Central Committee's International Department, its International Information Department, and the KGB—belonged to this category.[57]

These three organizations maintained distinct functional responsibilities. The International Department of the Central Committee, which expanded upon the legacy of Lenin's Comintern, coordinated relations with international front organizations, communist and revolutionary forces that had not gained controlling power over their home countries (including the Communist Party of the United States), and the Soviet Academy of Sciences' research organizations.[58] Although the reach of the International Department extended into the first world, by the late 1960s the department's focus shifted to conducting political warfare in nonaligned areas.[59] The department managed a web of international front organizations that advocated for Soviet-friendly policies or, more generally, for socialist principles such as the international solidarity of workers. The department's vast research arm oversaw the production and annual distribution of thousands of socialism-themed foreign-language titles and developed links with foreign academics.[60] Operationally, the International Department maintained a low profile in order to "affect . . . the behavior of foreign governments and political movements without revealing Moscow's role as actor."[61] Aiding front groups that supported the Palestinian Liberation Organization in the 1960s, supplying socialist manifestos to build momentum for Salvadoran revolutionaries in 1980, and creating cooperation agreements with "progressive" political movements such as that of South Yemen in the late 1970s are but a few examples of the organization's reach.[62]

The efforts of the International Information Department complemented, informed, and often overlapped those of the International Department, so much so that the International Department finally absorbed it in 1986.[63] The organization's responsibilities included distributing propaganda and molding media narratives through state-run wire services, periodicals, and radio broadcasts. In a certain sense, it was not unlike the United States Information Agency. Yet, as previously discussed, the volume of material generated by the department far eclipsed that of its U.S. counterpart and expanded further over time (from 1960 to 1970, weekly hours of Soviet-backed external broadcasting doubled from 1,047 hours to 2,155 hours).[64] The highest levels of the CPSU coordinated the output of the International Information Department and tailored it for both foreign and domestic audiences.[65] In addition to covering news from a Soviet perspective, these outlets also spread forged documents and disinformation created by the third, covert arm of the Soviet Union's apparatus for the conduct of active measures: the Central Security Bureau, or the KGB.

The KGB, which traces its roots to the establishment of the Extraordinary Commission for Combatting Counter-Revolution and Sabotage (the Cheka) in 1917, maintained responsibility for internal security, overseeing foreigners inside the Soviet Union, counterintelligence, and most clandestine activities abroad, including covert efforts to influence the international information environment. The organization grew adept at creating forged government documents, which served as "proof" of nefarious or duplicitous American plots. As Director of Central Intelligence William J. Casey observed in 1985, the injection of such "half-truths, lies, and rumors" into the international press served to "discredit free world policies [and] individuals" and undermine trust in the consistency and validity of American policy directives.[66] Other intelligence officials attested to the use of dozens of forged documents throughout the Cold War, which included fake plans to overthrow the Greek and Ghanaian governments and a fake plot to assassinate the pope.[67] Blatant forgeries were quickly discredited by the U.S. government but nonetheless provided fodder for anti-American groups and conspiracy theorists around the world.

Disinformation planted directly into the press, an art also mastered by the KGB, proved more difficult to control. The organization became adept at exploiting the open nature of foreign media outlets and at leveraging social anxieties over current affairs. Because news agencies lacked credibility, the KGB planted falsehoods in Western media outlets, hoping that misinformation would spread virally as journalists attempted to provide comprehensive coverage of an issue. For example, to reframe the conversation about Soviet-downed Korean Air Lines Flight 007 in 1983, Moscow found "obscure Western publications" to plant the idea that the passenger airline was in fact on a U.S. spy mission.[68] Western news outlets covered the disinformation as a valid counterargument, even though it had no basis in fact.

Several years later, when the HIV/AIDS crisis emerged, the Soviet Union propagated the idea that the U.S. government created the virus via genetic engineering at the U.S. Army Medical Research Institute.[69] This falsehood reinforced ongoing Soviet claims about U.S. biological warfare activities and undermined allied confidence in the presence of U.S. troops on their soil. The claim was so audacious that it provoked a public response from the U.S. Department of State and a rebuttal from Soviet Premier Mikhail Gorbachev, who, in a manner similar to the current Russian tactic of dismissing unwanted criticism as Russophobic, claimed that the American response was simply the latest example of "nourished hatred" for the Soviet Union.[70]

The KGB also fostered relationships with individuals and organizations abroad to compromise them, intimidate them into passive submission, or leverage them against their home governments. Such efforts were aimed not only at foreign diplomats but also at foreign elites, agents of influence, and paramilitary organizations. These relationships were viewed as essential to the subversion of non-Communist ideologies abroad and to countering the subversive activities of Soviet exiles.[71]

The KGB recruited agents of influence throughout Western and so-called neutral countries. They hailed from a variety of professional backgrounds but shared a unique access or ability to shape perceptions and events in a manner useful to the Soviet Union, and they often sympathized with the

Communist movement. In the United Kingdom, for example, the KGB's predecessor organization famously recruited the so-called Cambridge Five network in the 1930s, and in the 1970s, the KGB attempted to recruit the Bishop of Southwark after he gave a speech lambasting England's social injustices.[72] In France, the KGB worked closely with journalist and publisher Pierre-Charles Pathé on the overarching themes of his writings and established a toehold in the French intelligence establishment.[73] Given its pivotal position in Cold War politics, the KGB maintained relationships with many agents of influence in Finland, and in Denmark it recruited a Britain-bound journalist to pursue Margaret Thatcher.[74] Such activities extended to American soil. That the nature of the KGB's relationship with Harry Dexter White, a prominent economist and high-ranking U.S. Treasury Department official, is still the subject of debate demonstrates the subtlety and sophisticated tradecraft employed by the organization.[75]

KGB active measures extended outside the realm of opinion shapers and policymakers. Although support to foreign militaries was officially the responsibility of the armed forces and the GRU (the Main Intelligence Directorate, the KGB's military counterpart), the KGB provided covert support to a host of paramilitary and resistance movements that were of particular interest to Communist Party leadership. In the 1970s, the Soviet Union provided the Palestinian Liberation Organization with support in the form of money, equipment, and training and later deputized its Eastern European satellite states to provide financial assistance to terrorist groups.[76] Although initially focused in Africa, by the 1980s the KGB supported "national liberation" movements in Central America in coordination with Cuba and may have also supported the Irish Republican Army in Northern Ireland.[77]

The use of active measures shifted with domestic and foreign events throughout the Cold War. After attenuating activity during détente, the Soviets increased the use of active measures in the latter 1970s, particularly with respect to nuclear developments in Europe.[78] The increased interest in active measures during the early 1980s suggests that the Reagan administration's hard line toward Moscow may have further incentivized the use of active measures, although it is also possible that increased attention to Soviet active measures in the United States revealed ongoing activities that had gone unrecognized during the 1970s.

Later in the decade, Mikhail Gorbachev's pursuit of glasnost and perestroika drew into question the expansionist imperative that underpinned Soviet military doctrine and many of the CPSU's active measures.[79] Of course, not only were glasnost and perestroika antithetical to the Soviet Union's security posture; also, their success hinged on a concept unfamiliar to the Russian people—namely, property rights. In Russia, ultimate authority over property—both real estate and intellectual property—had historically resided with the state.[80] Russia's rocky transition to a market-style economy merely confirmed the rigidity of this principle: the old ruling class largely retained its hold over property, while the less fortunate struggled to make ends meet.[81] The perception within Russia of Western impatience, disinterest, and smugness toward their attempts at democratic transition helped curdle the population's sense of hope into bitterness.[82] By the end of the short-lived experience with capitalism, Russians yearned to reestablish its country as a great power. This process entailed not just the pursuit of international prestige but also a reintroduction of Soviet tools of power in a post-Communist context.

Contemporary Competition Short of War

As Russia's short experiment with Western-style democracy gave way to oligarchy and kleptocracy, the Kremlin reconstituted a model of centralized governance. Russia's messianic view of international affairs, and its long-established understanding of strategic competition, once again propelled its foreign policy. Driven by a desire to restore Russia to its former glory, this was apparent in both word and deed, particularly after the ascendency of Vladimir Putin.

In a June 2000 white paper published not long after his election, Putin articulated the core objective of his foreign policy: the "formation of a good neighbor belt along the perimeter of Russia's borders." It was a bold reaffirmation of what Russia and the Soviet Union had historically viewed as its sphere of influence, but the policy was presented in terms that were easily digestible to foreign audiences. To create the belt of "good neighbors," Putin emphasized the "greater role [that] is being played by the economic, political, scientific and technological, ecological, and information factors" of relations between states.[83] The white paper led many to believe that Putin would pursue his objectives in accordance with the norms of the rules-based, post–Cold War international order. This conclusion rested on two key misconceptions: first, what the Kremlin meant by the term *good neighbor* and, second, that an emphasis on nonmilitary means of influence equated with a pacifist foreign policy. The former simply reflects unfamiliarity with Russian history; the latter reflected the West's narrower understanding of war.

Although Putin couched his original foreign policy proclamation in dovish terms, his bellicosity became more evident over time. Since Putin's ascension to the presidency, Moscow has undertaken a series of coercive and hostile actions against its neighbors and the West. In 2008, Putin invaded and annexed Crimea, launched an assault on Ukraine's Donbass region, and intervened to prop up the Bashar al-Assad regime in Syria several years later.[84] More recently, Moscow interfered in the U.S. election via cyber and information warfare and deployed ballistic missiles to the Eastern European enclave of Kaliningrad.[85] But Moscow's hostile actions often take a more ambiguous form. Since Putin came to power, Moscow has leveraged business relationships, energy policy, broadcast media, the Russian

Orthodox Church, local ethnic Russian populations, and legacy networks from the Soviet period to wield "coercive power" toward states along Russia's periphery.[86] In addition, Moscow has increased the frequency of military exercises that simulate a NATO invasion along the country's western flank, allowing it to probe NATO's resolve under the pretense of acting defensively.[87] Because of the deftness with which he has directed Russia's foreign policy, Putin has, to a sufficient degree, escaped charges of aggression and bellicosity within his electorate.

The United States and its allies have taken some actions to deter Russian aggression in Europe. The United States, for its part, launched the European Reassurance Initiative in 2014, which continued during the Trump administration. As its name implies, the program aims to reaffirm America's commitment to European security by increasing combined exercises, training, capacity-building efforts, and coordination, as well as through the rotational presence of American troops along NATO's eastern flank. America's allies in Europe have also taken steps, both collectively and individually, to improve their defenses against ongoing Russian influence activities and to deter future hostilities. At the collective level, NATO and the European Union have established several thematic centers of excellence to provide member states with a coordination and analysis mechanism to address and constrain the wide variety of Russian activities aimed at Europe. Individually, many member states have begun conversations about increasing their defense budgets or conducting other long-overdue defense reforms.

The question still remains, however, as to whether these efforts are enough—enough to deter, enough to coerce, enough to, in the words of Philip Breedlove, "change Russia's calculus."[88] Many of Russia's tactics exploit Western societal norms or borrow from Western approaches to warfare. They also stem from a fundamentally different understanding of conflict boundaries, conditions, and temporality than that held in the West, one that has developed over centuries. Unless the United States and NATO adapt in kind and see their differences with Moscow as Russia does—as an ongoing conflict—Russia will continue to improve its strategic position.

Old Techniques, New World Disorder

Although Putin's government bears little resemblance to the Soviet system, the strategic culture of his security services remains similar. Deception and provocation measures have been reapplied to a more globalized and connected world, but they still serve the same functions: to provide Russia with strategic advantages externally and to rally and distract the domestic population. The string that ties Russia's current use of active measures to that of the Soviet era lies in Putin himself. A low-level officer in the KGB at the time of the revolution, Putin led the KGB's legacy organization—the Federal Security Service (FSB)—during the mid-1990s, a period characterized by rapid expansion of the FSB's responsibilities in the realms of internal security, international monitoring, and telecommunications.[89] Upon his ascent to the Kremlin, many of Putin's former colleagues from the intelligence world were folded into his inner circle of advisers. Furthermore, many of the KGB officers who chose not to transition to the FSB instead went into private security in banks, the media, and large corporations and brought the contacts and mindset that they had gained in the KGB with them. The progressive consolidation of the Kremlin's power among this new elite has centralized the state's apparatus and represents a return to previous governance models. At the time, these changes were underappreciated in the West. So too was Putin's return, despite his rhetoric to the contrary, to a foreign policy approach reminiscent of the expansionist models of his Soviet and tsarist predecessors.

The West's reaction to Russia's invasion of Crimea and the Donbass illustrates this point. Even though Russia's approach to achieving its objectives in both locations borrowed heavily from Soviet and tsarist strategy, some Western observers interpreted the writings on nonlinear warfare of Valery Gerasimov, chief of the General Staff of the Armed Forces of Russia, as indicative of a new doctrine of hybrid warfare.[90] Use of the term, which has come to be understood as the combination of asymmetric and nonkinetic warfare with conventional war, has succeeded in mobilizing and organizing coordinated responses to Russian aggression along NATO's eastern flank. The term, however, is not without its problems. First, and as demonstrated previously, the Kremlin has employed variations on hybrid warfare for centuries. Second, the nomenclature *hybrid warfare* has the potential to confound more than clarify. Gerasimov's hybrid warfare bears little resemblance to that as originally conceived, which refers to the combination of state-organized warfare and insurgency-style tactics, such as that employed by Hezbollah in the 2006 Lebanon War.[91] Most important, hybrid warfare does not offer a complete picture of Russian strategy. Gerasimov's writings fail to capture several elements endemic to Russia's approach to geopolitical competition, thereby conveying—perhaps deliberately—a narrower view of Russian strategy than exists in practice.

Terminology is important insofar as it creates a taxonomy, and from a taxonomy follows doctrine and plans oriented around a particular understanding of the world. As suggested in the aforementioned historical analysis, Russia's perception of warfare does not conform to rigid classifications. Rather than adhering to a phased, escalatory conflict model, the Kremlin views conflict through a continuum, one that emphasizes the importance of preconflict operations and that is adaptable to suit individual conflicts.[92] Vulnerabilities are exploited via a range of tools, regardless of the category into which the vulnerability falls.[93]

So why does Russia use the term *hybrid warfare*? As it turns out, the Kremlin adopted the term from the West, where it first came into vogue. Indeed, borrowing from Western models and concepts is common practice for many militaries, including Russia's. For example, after observing the ascendency of special operations forces in the West, Russia expanded the capabilities of its elite *spetsnaz* units to form a "special operations command."[94] It is has also observed the American use of private military contractors in conflict zones and as a result has begun to relax, in action if not letter, its prohibition on their use.[95] Russia's fundamentally weaker position vis-à-vis the West has left it little choice but to monitor how neighbors and adversaries approach warfare. Given the many NATO and American military engagements since the end of the Cold War, Moscow has had ample opportunity to learn.

Of course, this tendency to mirror Western approaches does not always succeed. Since the reign of Peter the Great, Russia has swung between periods of admiring and then vilifying the West, and the tipping point between these eras often hinges on periods of failed reform. At the time of the Bolshevik revolution, for example, Russia was a largely agrarian society that had not yet developed the large working and middle classes that, in Marx's analysis, were a prerequisite for the transition to communism. Translating Marx's ideas to a Russian context, as both Lenin and Stalin recognized, required rapid economic development and thus an authoritarianism that stood outside the utopian ideals expressed in communist theory. Whether because of a lack of aptitude or will or because of cultural differences, Western modalities do not always translate into Russian modalities in ways that Russian leaders are willing to accept.

Russia's failed experiment with democracy provides a more recent example. According to the Kremlin's narrative, Russia suffered humiliation and rejection after attempting to join the liberal democratic order in the 1990s. Meanwhile, NATO expanded into lands that were previously in Moscow's orbit.[96] A deep cynicism developed toward the West, which would have a profound impact on how Russia viewed its place in the world. "Foundations of the State Cultural Policy," a 2014 document signed by Vladimir Putin, codified this emergent cynicism, calling for a Russia that maintains cultural distinction from Europe through its rejection of liberal, Western social values.[97] This cynicism is not shared by all in Russia, leading to a cold coexistence between admiration and disdain for the West within Russian society. While Russian elites enjoy lives of global mobility and indulge in Western lifestyles, consumer goods, and property, the general population must play by a different set of rules set forth by a Kremlin that is officially hostile to Western norms.[98] Russia's treatment of dissidents, from homosexuals to journalists and to those like the band Pussy Riot, illustrates a renewed emphasis on cultural homogeneity with which the bulk of Russia's population must contend.

Russia's experiment with Western-style democracy provided its leaders with enough knowledge of the system's strengths and weaknesses to subvert it, or at least to project Russia's own failings onto the West in a manner that would stymie Western efforts to counter it. Old tools of Soviet subterfuge proved applicable to the new context. Using the teachings of Lenin as inspiration, ex-Soviet practitioners of disinformation, including ex-KGB agents who had now spread throughout society, began to weave deception and provocation into information campaigns aimed at liberal democracies.[99] Meanwhile, an increasingly unequal distribution of wealth and nostalgia for past greatness bred a public dissatisfaction that was assuaged by overt displays of strength. Those opportunities arose first with respect to Georgia, then Crimea, and then Ukraine.

Simultaneously, many of the institutions and characteristics of Western societies that had defended against such measures in the past had devolved: civic engagement had decreased,[100] several generations of elites had been educated to view the world through a postmodern, relativistic lens,[101] and resources had been turned away from tracking Russia, which was no longer seen as an existential threat.[102] Thus, as the West grew comfortable with the idea that liberal democracy had won the ideological war with communism, the vulnerabilities created by pluralism were no longer mitigated by knowledge and defenses against Russian subversion. Although Putin's expansionist military campaigns forced the world's attention, they were merely the culmination of a multipronged campaign to shape the social, political, and economic dynamics of Russia's periphery to the Kremlin's advantage.

Social, Political, and Economic Influence Operations

Freedoms of speech and individual rights are inherently vulnerable to foreign propaganda attacks, and recent trends have exacerbated their susceptibility to manipulation. Propaganda now passes through the information environment with an exponentially greater speed and reach than ever before possible. An erosion of trust in institutions, the fragmentation and segmentation of the media, and the rising disconnect between many elites and their countrymen have further broken down the defenses that open societies once had in place to counter malicious information. Putin's Russia has exploited these vulnerabilities through the media, cyber operations, and individuals sympathetic to the Russian cause.

Russia targets its information operations at the general public and also at specific audiences, such as political or business communities. Regardless of the target, such efforts aim to tear at the seams in the social fabric, erode trust in institutions, and widen the divide between leaders and the populations they serve. By sowing chaos and encouraging an environment of distrust and discord, these efforts increase Moscow's maneuverability across a number of domains.

Information and Cyber Operations

The collapse of the Soviet Union heralded an era not only of confusion and lawlessness in Russia but also of great opportunity. This was as true for individuals as much as it was for the government. In *The Red Web*, authors Andrei Soldatov and Irina Borogan trace the foundations of what has become the Russian approach to surveillance and information control back to the Soviet era. The authors detail, for example, how the lack of established norms regarding the relationship between private internet providers and the government allowed the latter to establish an unfettered ability to monitor all internet traffic in the country, access that would later allow for content filtering. While control of the domestic information space facilitated the suppression of unflattering and subversive material, the Kremlin soon realized that the internet outside Russia was just as much of a "battleground for information warfare."[103]

The Soviets had long considered information manipulation as a critical aspect of warfare; some considered it even more important than direct confrontation on the battlefield. Over time, the Soviets and their Russian successors developed a body of theories to analyze the deployment of information as a political and military tool. These theories, known together as reflexive control, grew out of long-standing practices of *maskirovka* and treated disinformation and deception as means to elicit a desired and advantageous response rather than as a method to conceal intentions.[104] In application, reflexive control concentrates on exploiting or weakening the filter that a decision-maker—or member of the public—uses to sort true or useful information from false or useless information. In information or other types of war, the side with the most sharply developed reflexes, or ability to "imitate the other side's thoughts or predict" its reactions, will have the "best chance of winning."[105] The internet represented a new environment for information warfare and thus for reflexive control: a medium through which both state and substate actors could use information to provoke specific responses from their adversaries.

If it is true that the Kremlin views the internet as a space controlled by America and designed to promulgate its ideas, reflexive control helps to explain the Kremlin's aggressive use of information warfare and cyberattacks on the internet.[106] Unlike the West, which views information and cyber operations separately, the Kremlin views them as parts of "multidisciplinary campaigns" that should reach social, military, intelligence, communications, education, and cyber vulnerabilities in target societies.[107] Because it is easier to avoid attribution for hostile activities in the cyber realm, the Kremlin employs its cyber arsenal with regularity to both collect information and to intrude into its adversaries' systems.[108] The sheer number and variety of attacks conducted by Russia, along with the creation of units designed to spread misinformation with impunity across the web, indicate the ambition and scale of Russia's activities in the cyber domain.[109] In the recent past, Russia has launched distributed denial-of-service attacks at energy and finance ministries in Georgia, Lithuania, and Estonia and performed network intrusions and phishing scams against government agencies, think tanks, and political communities in the United States.[110] As part of reflexive control, these actions tested filters and shaped perceptions, within target populations, that Russia is a powerful and formidable foe.

The problem of attribution obscures the full scale of Russia's cyberattacks: even when evidence suggests that an attack has originated in Russia, definitively attributing it to the Russian government has proven difficult. Although cyberspace-attribution issues were apparent as early as the 2008 Georgia-Russia conflict, they continue to allow Moscow to deny involvement in cyberspace crises suffered by its adversaries.[111] For example, the Ukrainian government contends that Russia is behind the numerous cyberattacks launched against it since before the seizure of Crimea, including a series of electrical-grid attacks[112] from 2015 to 2016 and the NotPetya attack in 2017.[113] Evidence of direct Russian involvement, however, remains elusive. Similarly, the Ukrainian government underwent a series of cyberattacks during and immediately after the Maidan protests in December 2013. Though the "hacktivist" groups that launched these attacks are ideologically aligned with Russia, the official distinction between the Kremlin and the perpetrators provided Moscow with enough plausible deniability for the attacks.[114] The wave of cyberattacks against Estonia following the 2007 Bronze Night demonstrations show that even when the motives for involvement are clear and when internet protocol addresses and the presence of Russia-linked botnets suggest, at a minimum, state complicity with attacks, linking specific activities to the Russian government has remained difficult.[115] For its part, Moscow seems knowledgeable about and willing to exploit this capability gap. When confronted with suspicions of involvement, to undermine the accusers' claims the Kremlin will often ask for hard "proof" that is impossible or imprudent for a government to provide, blame others for the original creation of cyberattack vectors, or simply deny agency over involved parties.[116]

The activities of the cyber espionage group Fancy Bear (also known as Sofacy or APT28), which private-sector firms have assessed is likely affiliated with Russian intelligence, highlight these dynamics. Although Putin has denied any link to the group, Fancy Bear nonetheless pursues targets that align with Russia's national interest, such as Georgia, Eastern European governments and militaries, international security organizations such as NATO and Organization for Security and Co-operation in Europe (OSCE) and private-sector firms in the aerospace, defense, energy, and media sectors.[117] The group, along with another collective known as Cozy Bear, was also behind the intrusion into the servers of the Democratic National Committee (DNC) in advance of the 2016 U.S. presidential election. In June 2017 Putin acknowledged that "patriotic hackers" may have targeted the DNC but has repeatedly denied any state involvement in the operation. The U.S. intelligence community assessed with high confidence that, on the contrary, Putin had directed a vast influence campaign directed at the United

States, but the protection of sensitive sources and techniques precluded their ability to provide the proof underlying the unclassified version of their assessment.[118] Subsequent cyber-attacks against the U.S.-based Hudson Institute and International Republican Institute, despite evidence from Microsoft, were similarly denied.[119] Although the proof of Russia's involvement with hacker collectives is substantial, the attribution problem that plagues cyber forensics more generally has created a space for such groups to combine state-level resources with the asymmetric advantages more commonly associated with substate actors.

Even if Russia were to admit its involvement with "patriotic" hacking collectives, it is unclear what, if any, consequences would follow such an admission. Russia has actively sought to shift international internet governance norms and conventions in order to maximize its sovereignty over the information space within its borders. The creation of "multistakeholder" and "internationalized" internet governance—long advocated for by Moscow, Beijing, and Brasilia in particular, especially following the Edward Snowden revelations—has unlocked new opportunities for governments to extend their control over how the internet is perceived and processed within their own borders.[120] Such policies are justified in international forums as necessary to protect Russia from technologies used by "the West to topple regimes in countries where the opposition is too weak to mobilize protests" but are also used to restrict domestic internet activities more generally.[121] What were once considered highly technical and apolitical international forums focused on internet governance have thus become intensely political, with Russia, China, and others advocating for the ability to control their own internet in the name of "sovereignty." An internet that resembles the relatively anarchic system of modern international relations provides much more space for maneuver than a system that, previously, was more akin to a book publisher. This space has proven ripe for the activities of state-affiliated groups such as Fancy Bear and for the promulgation of state-sponsored propaganda through the internet.

It is worth reiterating that the internet is only the newest medium through which information operations are conducted. Other tools—such as print media, leaflets, television, and radio broadcasts—remain important avenues to influence specific audiences. The utility of these mediums has changed little since they were used in Soviet times. Yet Russia's relative openness and connections to the rest of the world as compared with the Soviet Union has created opportunities to refine information warfare techniques in ways that were not previously possible. Kremlin-friendly "journalists" have attempted to gain employment in Western news outlets, and Russian outlets hire Western journalists for a number of roles, both off- and on-camera, and for both domestic and foreign consumption.[122] When aimed at Western media consumers, such efforts exploit the credibility of familiar faces and media practices and confuse the audience's ability to filter propaganda from factual, objective information. The content of Kremlin-funded Russia Today (RT) international television network, for example, is a far cry from the grainy agitprop of the Cold War era.[123] The channel has adopted a slick marketing campaign that implores viewers to "question more" and accordingly sows skepticism among its audience about the trustworthiness of national leaders.

Russian information operations take on many guises and, leaving aside state-sponsored networks, rarely display overt connections to the Kremlin. Depending on the target and the purpose at hand, Russian information operations manifest in two forms: "creative" measures, which promulgate new and politicized narratives, and "destructive" measures, which seek to sow doubt and confusion about preexisting narratives. Both approaches employ reflexive control in that they are most effective when aimed at the weak link of a target's information filter.

Creative measures exploit commonly held beliefs, heuristics, and shibboleths in a target society to perpetuate a new and politically desirable way of understanding the past or the present. In a domestic context, the Kremlin combines appeals to the public's sense of patriotism and religiosity to whitewash past or current events and foretell a return to Russia's glorious past.[124] By sidestepping present conditions to focus on initiatives supposedly required to return Russia to its rightful place among world powers, the regime creates a powerful connection between nostalgia and hope and likewise positions Russia as an ascendant yet aggrieved nation. In so doing, actions that may otherwise have been labeled aggressive or revanchist are recast as defensive reactions to hostile aggressors.[125] According to this script, Russia plays the righteous victim, always absolved of wrongdoing.

After the Kremlin settles on a new narrative, organizations and individuals aligned with the Kremlin push it out through new and old forms of media.[126] Such communications campaigns saturate the media environment with a single interpretation of events in order to establish the boundaries of acceptable debate and alienate dissenters. Often, the Kremlin simultaneously deploys destructive measures to neutralize opposing voices. Dismissals of counterpoints as Russophobic and more tawdry and personal character assaults against dissenters help silence those who disagree and sustain a veneer of social cohesion.[127] Manipulating public opinion thereby enforces unanimity across society, providing a valuable, if superficial, fount of democratic support for the regime's foreign policy objectives.

The narrative surrounding Novorossiya provides a clear example of how the Kremlin uses creative measures to build support for specific policies. Putin first mentioned this term in response to a question-and-answer session in 2014, not long after the invasion of Crimea; it refers to a formerly Russian-controlled section of modern Ukraine and has its roots in the tsarist era.[128] By reminding native Russians of these historical ties, the Novorossiya narrative frames an international conflict as a local one and triggers a sense of obligation toward ethnic Russians living in Ukraine.[129] Moreover, by invoking Russia's former greatness and its embarrassment at Ukraine's turn toward the West, the term stokes a defiant but unifying strain of Russian nationalism. The injection of this concept into the domestic public discourse thus reframes naked violations of international law as noble pursuits consistent with Russia's noble past. What the West decries as a violation of international norms, Russia views—or claims to view—as a domestic problem outside the purview of the international community.

By contrast, destructive measures aim to foment chaos by undermining societal trust in the institutions and authority structures that underpin democratic decision-making processes. The Kremlin has employed destructive measures against its adversaries, including the United States, for quite some time, but its efforts are most acute in Eastern Europe. According to a working group convened as part of research for this book and comprised of Eastern European experts, Russia believes that war with the West has already begun and Eastern Europe represents the most proximate front.[130] The participants, who hailed from countries long targeted by Russian information operations, viewed the weaponization of information as a natural measure to advance Russian interests and erode confidence in domestic institutions in target societies. Executed effectively, they warned, destructive measures create a vicious cycle in which declining institutional trust opens more space for alternative voices to corrode traditional authority structures.

Indeed, as the Kremlin's manipulation of the Novorossiya narrative suggests, the Kremlin often interweaves creative and destructive measures in the same information operation. Destructive measures create receptive audiences for policies favorable to the Kremlin by attacking traditional social institutions and eroding the public's faith in them. The Kremlin then injects new narratives into the information environment that, if not always overtly pro-Kremlin, nonetheless undermine the West and benefit Moscow. In addition to state-sponsored internet trolls, the Kremlin deploys individuals affiliated with respected institutions—contemporary instantiations of the Soviet-era "agent of influence"—to discredit contrasting viewpoints and push hostile narratives.[131] Destructive measures also reduce the appeal of liberal democratic governments to native Russians, who otherwise might resent Russia's domestic political structures and admire the freedoms enjoyed in open societies. These measures shape foreign and domestic political environments to be less resilient to, if not directly compliant with, the Kremlin's interests.

In addition to increasing Russia's maneuverability within democratic societies, information operations also reduce the appeal of democratic governments within the domestic Russian population by painting democratic societies as chaotic, divided, and weak. This is the perhaps the most important aim of information operations, as the current regime's power is inversely related to the will and ability of the population to demand reforms. Recall that Putin's fixation with reclaiming the near abroad derives from a revisionist instinct to restore Russia's privileged place in the international sphere, the country's expansionist tendency rooted in Russia's history and national psyche as discussed earlier in this chapter, and an existential fear that the regime could collapse from the outside in. Understood this way, it becomes clear why plurality, diversity of opinion, and an engaged and empowered citizenry represent a threat to the autocratic regime in Moscow—and why jingoistic rhetoric if not actual military campaigns consolidate the regime's authority.[132] After all, if a so-called Color Revolution could succeed in Ukraine, it could in Russia. Evidence that Russia is reclaiming its rightful place in the world provides a potent distraction from the discontent that might otherwise fuel calls for reform.

This work will not treat Russian interference in the 2016 U.S. election in depth, as separating the truth of what occurred from the charged and partisan nature of the current debate is a task best left for future historians. However, the activities of the Internet Research Agency, the well-documented attempts to sow discord within American society via social media campaigns and targeted information leaks, and the Kremlin's subsequent denial of involvement mirror the tactics of information warfare outlined in this section and earlier in this chapter. Support to populist political candidates on both the left and the right—whether official, financial, or through shadowy information campaigns—similarly mirrors the Russian modus operandi in other Western nations, a subject to which we will now turn.

Political, Economic, and Ecclesiastical Influence Operations

Russia's support for nationalism and cultural solidarity dovetails with the populist, nativist, and traditionalist political narratives that have resurged in recent years. This is more than a coincidence. The Kremlin has expanded its financial and intellectual ties with likeminded political organizations across Europe and used its economic position—especially in the energy sector—to prevent the adoption of anti-Russian policies. In addition, it has used its relationship with the Russian Orthodox Church to forge stronger links to segments of Western society that reject secularism and multiculturalism and to foster greater connections with its European diaspora.

Russia weaves together political and economic influence operations in a mutually supportive manner that exploits dissatisfaction with status quo policies and leverages the Kremlin's clout in sectors vital to Europe's economy. The confluence of interests between foreign political parties and the Kremlin, especially vis-à-vis Putin's United Russia party, extends far beyond Eastern Europe into some of the most stalwart defenders of the liberal democratic order in the West, including France, Germany, and the United Kingdom. In each of these countries, nativist resentment toward the prevailing order—expressed variably in hostility toward Muslim immigrants, anti–European Union sympathies, or antiestablishment sentiments—are exploited by political parties with support from the Kremlin. Where anti-Russian sentiment limits opportunities for direct political involvement, Moscow pulls from the information-operations toolkit to undermine the standing government or leverages its economic clout to pressure politicians into adopting pro-Russia or Russia-neutral stances.[133]

Russian involvement in the continent's energy sector is central to understanding the Kremlin's motivation—and ability—to influence European politics. As of 2014, oil and natural gas sales accounted for 68 percent of Russia's total export revenues, making energy the single most important contributor to the Russian economy.[134] Despite taking measures to decrease reliance on Russian fuel (such as the third energy package), as of 2015 Europe still relied on Moscow for more than a quarter of its oil, gas, and solid-fuel imports. Russian-sourced fuel thus remains the largest contributor to Europe's overall energy source portfolio.[135] In an attempt to maintain market shares and reduce resistance to price discrimination policies, Russian energy companies often adopt aggressive business practices that undermine pan-European energy initiatives. For example, after the EU unveiled a plan to provide surge capacity to countries highly dependent on Russian energy supplies, Russian companies responded by advancing plans to extend the scope of their European pipeline network—an effort that, if successful, would undercut the viability of alternative suppliers.[136]

Russia uses similar tactics at the national level and often interweaves them with political-influence campaigns. The country has shown an ability to adapt its approach to suit changing circumstances and personalities in each country's political, economic, and social milieu, which complicates any attempt to create blanket categorizations of Russia's activities in Europe. Nonetheless, many of Russia's efforts are opportunistic and thus theoretically preventable—although the costs of doing so often outweigh the short-term benefits of continued trade with Moscow. The extent and nature of a particular country's relationship with Russia, particularly whether the country is a NATO member and whether it was part of the Communist bloc, provide a rough framework for analyzing vectors of influence.

FORMERLY COMMUNIST NATO MEMBERS

Although many of these countries, including the Baltic States, Poland, and a number of other states in Eastern and Southeastern Europe, joined NATO to reduce Russia's meddling in their internal affairs, vestiges of Russia's historic involvement in and relationships with these countries have been difficult to excise. Across former Soviet-bloc countries, these ties constrain the agendas of mainstream political leaders and empower fringe groups that find common cause with Moscow.

This situation is particularly visible in the Baltic states and the four states of the Visegrád Group: Poland, the Czech Republic, Slovakia, and Hungary. Here, links with Russia, particularly in the energy sector, have long been recognized as a potential threat to national security. The Czech Republic, for example, depends on Moscow for 65 percent of its oil and, physically speaking, all of its natural gas and for the maintenance of much of its military equipment.[137] Although less dependent militarily, Poland and Hungary are similarly—if not more—reliant on Russian energy exports than the Czech Republic.[138] Pipelines linking these countries to Russia and their landlocked position, with the exception of Poland, limit their ability to obtain fuel from other sources. Whereas the Czech Republic has increased its gas imports from Norway, for example, the fuel must still transit through pipelines that terminate in Russia.[139] Diversification into alternative energy sources could, theoretically, ameliorate Visegrád dependence on Russia, but Russia has inserted itself into these sectors as well. In 2015, for example, Russia issued a $10.8 billion loan to the Hungarian government to expand its Paks nuclear power plant.[140]

Energy-sector and other business links in the Visegrád states provide Russia with ample opportunities to assert its agenda, whether through foreign agents, information campaigns, or direct finance or other support to like-minded political groups. In the Czech Republic, for example, Russia has found a friend in President Milos Zeman despite a pro-Western legislature. Russia backs a host of marginal political groups and has waged an aggressive propaganda campaign.[141] Russia maintains close ties with Hungary's far-right Movement for a Better Hungary (Jobbik Party), which has grown into the country's third-largest political party, and has promised increased economic ties to court leaders of the most prominent political party, the Hungarian Civic Alliance.[142] Despite frequent crackdowns on Russian espionage and a public that overwhelmingly holds hostile views toward Moscow,[143] Euroscepticism among the Polish working class has given rise to the populist Zmiana Party, which the Kremlin has been quick to support.[144] Lastly, in Slovakia, Russia has supported a range of groups, from organized crime rings to the Slovak National Party and the neofascist People's Party of Our Slovakia.[145]

The Baltic states, like their Visegrád neighbors to the south, inherited much of their energy infrastructure from the Soviet era. Although this situation caused Estonia, Latvia, and Lithuania to rely on Russian gas imports after independence, in recent years they have made significant strides in diversifying their energy portfolios. Estonia and Latvia, for example, have increased domestic production of shale oil and the use of renewable energy such as biomass.[146] Lithuania, which became heavily reliant on natural gas after the 2010 closure of its sole remaining nuclear power plant, has focused instead on supply risk reduction; opening the Klaipėda floating liquefied natural gas terminal in 2014 gave Vilnius the means to import more gas from Norway than from Russia for the first time in 2016.[147] Moreover, construction is underway on two pipelines, the Gas Interconnection Poland-Lithuania and the Balticconnector between Finland and Estonia. Together, these pipelines will connect the region to the gas-transport infrastructure of the rest of Europe.

Decreased dependency on Russian gas has reduced a key vulnerability in the Baltic states, but other leverage points remain. Russian nationals, which make up more than a quarter of the population in Estonia and Latvia, have chaffed at the Euro-centric outlook of mainstream political parties and remain oriented toward Russian media. Business elites in these countries have been "co-opted through bribes, financial incentives and the 'appeal' of Russian business culture, which is network-rather than market-driven."[148] Because these networks are part of the fabric of everyday life, and because Russia remains one of the largest trading partners of the Baltic states, separating legitimate activities from nefarious ones has proven difficult.[149]

Moscow's degree of agency in advancing the political and economic activities of ethnic Russians is often unclear. Yet because "the creation of an arc of friendly neighbors" is an official Russian foreign policy goal, it would be illogical for the Kremlin to not advance its interests in former Communist-bloc countries where it maintains the greatest means of influence. The vectors provided by Russia's ongoing ties to these countries increase the Kremlin's opportunities to advance its interests without direct involvement or while maintaining plausible deniability. Although the leaders of these countries are often stalwart supporters of NATO, their populations are less homogenous, and the reality of infrastructural, cultural, and economic links with Russia creates powerful incentives for some politicians to look eastward for support.

OTHER NATO COUNTRIES

Russia's use of political and economic levers is not limited to NATO members in its near abroad. The comparative lack of cultural, historical, and economic ties between Russia and other NATO members limits the pervasiveness of Russia's influence campaigns but not their effectiveness, particularly when the end goal is to stoke internecine divisions. For Russia, the benefits of pursuing active measures against legacy NATO members mirror those of similar efforts in former Communist-bloc states: they hamper unity and create conditions that allow the Kremlin to extend its reach and power, test the resolve of NATO member states, and present very low risk to Moscow.

On the political front, alignment with Putin has become synonymous with rebelling against the established European and transatlantic order, providing momentum to groups that might otherwise remain on the fringe. Far from hiding connections with Moscow, nationalist and populist groups often flaunt their connections with, and proximity to, the Kremlin. France's Front National (FN), Germany's Alternative für Deutschland, the United Kingdom's Independence Party, and populist movements in Austria, Belgium, and Greece have coordinated with, received varying degrees of funding from, or offer their outspoken support to Russia.[150] Led by France's Marine Le Pen, these movements have attempted to extend their reach beyond national borders and into the European Parliament through the Europe of Nations and Freedom (ENF) voting bloc, which has consistently attempted to block legislation that would curtail Russian influence operations in Europe.[151] In this environment, Russia thus has every incentive to continue testing the limits of how much meddling NATO members will accept.

While not as deep as that between Russia and former Soviet states, the economic relationship between legacy NATO members and Russia also provides Moscow leverage. Many countries remain dependent on Russia for a large slice of their energy needs: as of 2015, the European Union as a whole relied on Russia for approximately one-third of its gas and oil supplies.[152] Infrastructural limitations and Europe's growing disenchantment with nuclear power—with the exception of France—have stymied efforts to diversify fuel sources and increase energy independence.[153] Energy and trade considerations (Russia is the European Union's third-largest trade partner) have the potential to drive a wedge between EU-wide economic and security considerations; Angela Merkel's balking at the codification of U.S.-led sanctions in 2017 is a case in point.[154]

For the time being, Russia's active measures against current NATO countries are mostly aimed at fomenting discord and undermining support for existing institutions, including the EU and NATO itself. Operations directed at prospective NATO members, particularly recently, have taken on a more direct and dramatic tone. In October 2016, for example, two Russian agents allegedly facilitated a coup attempt in Montenegro.[155] Since the country's accession into NATO in June 2017, Russia has redirected its efforts toward other Balkan states and indirect influence campaigns. In recent years Russia has sought to expand its security ties with Serbia, Macedonia, and Bosnia and has gone on a buying spree of Balkan media properties.[156]

NON-NATO EUROPEAN UNION STATES

Whereas Russia seeks to undermine unity within the alliance with its operations toward NATO states, operations directed at non-NATO states aim to prevent NATO expansion and to further expand and solidify Russia's sphere of "friendly neighbors." These two goals sometimes overlap, depending on the location of the target and the nature of Russia's historical relations with the target country. In the case of the unaligned Nordic countries, Sweden and Finland, years of directed Russian propaganda have inured much of the public to disinformation campaigns.[157] Nonetheless, Russia has adapted to this environment by supporting disaffected groups, deploying disinformation through local surrogates, appealing to business and development interests, and attempting to discredit voices that call attention to these efforts.

In Sweden, where the government has no major pro-Russian political faction to advocate for Moscow's interests, Russia blends information campaigns with public diplomacy efforts and advances its interests with economic and military intimidation.[158] Nevertheless, Russian entities have engaged with groups and individuals on Sweden's right and left political fringes that advocate for a radical departure from the liberal democratic status quo.[159] Although the connections between the Kremlin and Swedish entities remain unclear, fringe voices in Sweden nonetheless advocate for policies that suit Russian interests and help create a more permissive environment for future operations by sowing societal discord.

Economically, Sweden is far less dependent on Russia than many of its neighbors to the south.[160] But Sweden still relies on Russia for more than a quarter of its crude-oil supply, and trade issues have caused tension between the two countries in recent years. For example, the Russian firm Gazprom attempted to rent harbor space in the Swedish island of Gotland for its Nord Stream 2 construction operations but faced rejection after Stockholm questioned the wisdom of allowing a Russian firm access to the strategic location in the Baltic Sea. In early 2017 the Swedish government dropped objections to Gazprom leasing additional space at Karlshamn, perhaps because of the government's superior ability to monitor Russian activities in the mainland port.[161] The Gazprom incident demonstrates the continued intent of Russian firms to entrench themselves in the Swedish market and the balancing act between economic and security interests that Stockholm must consider in its relations with Russia.

The Kremlin's involvement in Finland mirrors its operations against Sweden, but at a much higher volume (if not effectiveness), due to the country's historic relations with, and proximity to, Russia. Although Helsinki views its relations with Moscow as needing constant management and calibration, Finland's experience of war with Russia prompted the development of a sophisticated civil-defense system that—combined with a cultural predisposition against corruption—has minimized opportunities for Russia to influence Finland's political process. Buoyed by a relatively homogenous population and an excellent education system, Finland has been touted as a success story in its ability to mitigate the effects of Russian propaganda.[162] Russia has nevertheless found ways to create leverage within Finnish society. By combining subversive information campaigns, investments in Finnish critical infrastructure, and politicized and militarized activities along its shared border with Finland, Russia consistently prods Finland's physical and psychological defenses.

Although Finnish society may identify overt Kremlin propaganda with ease, Russia has adapted its information campaigns to inflame societal wedge issues, shame prominent critics of Russia into silence, and encourage and support Finnish voices that support Russia's interests. Rather than directly address its dissatisfaction with Finland's tilt westward, for example, Russia has pushed a narrative that Finland is "sidelined within the European Union," which appeals to the small group of Finns that view Finland as having a culture and perspective that it distinct from Europe.[163] Two outspoken Kremlin critics— Jessikka Aro and Saara Jantunen—have received threatening text messages and been the subject of public smear campaigns aimed at discrediting their research on Russia's information warfare techniques.[164] Meanwhile, Russia continues to host Kremlin apologist Johan Bäckman, who used his standing as a docent at the University of Helsinki and an affiliate of the Russian Institute of Strategic Studies to highlight the plight of the supposedly marginalized Russian population in Finland.[165] These efforts pollute the information space and intimidate those who might speak out against Russia's tactics.

The indirect creation of leverage within the information space mirrors Russia's approach to gaining influence in Finland's economic sector. Whereas in much of Europe Russia has used its domination in the oil and gas sectors to force difficult decisions upon politicians, Russia has instead attempted to gain a toehold in Finland's indigenous nuclear-power capabilities. In 2015 Russia attempted to circumvent the laws requiring Finnish or EU-majority ownership in the joint venture Finnish-Russian Fennovoima nuclear power plant through a Croatia-based shell company. Finnish authorities intervened after discovering the true nature of the investment arrangement.[166] The government has also intervened to halt the sale of strategic real estate to Russian nationals, who had been purchasing tracts of land near military outposts and in the sensitive border region of South Karelia.[167] The Russian government dismisses the Finnish government's actions as Russophobic and asserts that Finland is of little strategic interest.[168] Nevertheless, the acquisition of strategic properties would prove useful to Moscow should conflict between Russia and Finland ever again commence.

The cases of Sweden and Finland demonstrate Russia's flexibility in adjusting active measures to suit varied circumstances and interests. Russian-sponsored activities in these countries force leaders to consider the domestic consequences of closer ties with NATO, an organization that is still attempting to define a way forward for countering Russia's destabilizing behavior. In some ways, Russian influence in these two countries mirrors its approach to current NATO members. It differs, however, in that it is less direct, more subversive, and thus more difficult to track and counter.

COMMONWEALTH OF INDEPENDENT STATES

The tactics aimed at countries in Russia's near abroad—which include many current or former affiliates of the Commonwealth of Independent States (CIS)—mirror many of the tactics previously discussed but also include higher levels of political and economic leverage due to the extent of historical ties between Russia and these nations. Here, active measures have also set the stage for military action.[169] Prior to the 2008 invasion of Georgia, for example, Russia employed political and economic measures against Tbilisi that proved advantageous once the military phase of the conflict commenced.[170] On the political front, Russia's long-standing support for the leadership of the breakaway provinces of Abkhazia and South Ossetia, which undermined the central government before the conflict, proved useful once it made the decision to invade. Meanwhile, on the economic front, Moscow levied sanctions against Tbilisi and drew into question the status of thousands of Georgians working in Russia, whose remittances were vital to Georgia's economy.[171] Active measures are a step along a conflict progression, one that may ultimately result in armed conflict.

Because of Ukraine's importance to Russia's conception of its near abroad, the country has been the subject of Russian political and economic influence measures since its inception. The circumstances surrounding the seizure of Crimea and the conflict in the Donbass beg the question of why Russia viewed 2014 as a propitious time to act militarily. The moment was opportunistic for several reasons: the legislature had recently passed a resolution that removed the protected minority status of Russian nationals in Ukraine, the government itself was in transition, and the Maidan protests of 2013 demonstrated the extent to which many in Ukraine had developed an affinity for the West.[172] To the Kremlin, losing Ukraine to the West would have raised a number of unacceptable questions inside Russia about the domestic political situation.[173] The recent Ukrainian experience illustrates the dangers of letting down defenses against Russia's behavior and the risks of threatening the Kremlin's core interests.

Such lessons were not lost on Belarus, historically one of Moscow's closest allies. Despite recent attempts to diversify its trading position, Belarus remains highly reliant on Russia. In exchange for the country's loyalty, Russia has provided Belarus with preferential pricing on oil and natural-gas imports; in 2007, Belarus paid three to five times less for Russian gas than neighboring Poland.[174] Russia is also Belarus's largest trading partner by a large margin, accounting for 57 percent of Belorussian imports from Russia and 45.1 percent of its exports in the first half of 2017.[175] Seeking to make such ties permanent, Putin suggested in 2002 that Belarus should dissolve and join the Russian Federation, causing offense to Belarusian President Alexander Lukashenko and leading him to assert Belarus's independence from the Kremlin's positions.[176] Russia responded by increasing its use of active measures in Belarus—particularly in the information space. Russia's state broadcasters, who dominate the Belarusian market, disparaged Lukashenko's policy decisions, pushed a narrative that economic ties to Russia are preferable to those with Europe, and brought attention to Belarusian political scandals.[177]

From Russia's perspective, Belarus's strategic location on the border of NATO and alongside the Suwalki Gap provides ample reasons for Moscow to maintain close ties with Minsk. Russia has long sought to establish permanent military bases on Belarusian soil—requests that Lukashenko continually rebuffs.[178] Russia has responded by signaling its comparative strength: Russia pursued maneuvers on Belarusian soil during the quadrennial Zapad exercises in 2017, which surprised Belarusian and Western analysts alike.[179]

In addition to direct pressure applied to political and economic elites in former Soviet states, Russia has also benefited from alternative election monitoring efforts that legitimize flawed election practices and undermine faith in democratic processes.[180] These alternative structures provide useful counterpoints to the sometimes-inconvenient findings of internationally recognized election-monitoring groups such as the OSCE. Hostility between Russia and the OSCE began when the Color Revolutions between 2003 and 2006 in Ukraine, Georgia, and Kyrgyzstan ushered in regimes "unfavorable to Moscow."[181] From 2007 to 2008, Russia, Belarus, and Uzbekistan responded by putting barriers in place to prevent OSCE–Office for Democratic Institutions and Human Rights (OSCE-ODIHR) from accessing their respective elections, and Russia attempted to restrict funds to the organization.[182] These regimes had come to see OSCE-ODIHR as a mechanism for Western "interference in internal affairs" and began issuing alternative findings through the CIS Interparliamentary Assembly (IPA-CIS). Frequent contradictions of OSCE findings and the organization's domination by Russian monitors, however, eroded the credibility of IPA-CIS.[183]

Beginning in the early aughts, several nonprofit organizations emerged to provide a more "neutral" alternative to the OSCE-ODIHR. These organizations provide reports that contradict OSCE findings in a manner similar to IPA-CIS, but their "neutral" status—and their incorporation of non-CIS participants[184]—impart a veneer of legitimacy that has proven useful to authoritarian regimes. The most prominent of them, the Commonwealth of Independent States–Election Monitoring Organization (CIS-EMO),[185] serves as a main contractor for much IPA-CIS work and consistently issues views opposed to those of OSCE-ODIHR.[186] During the 2004 Orange Revolution in Ukraine, CIS-EMO officials attempted to legitimize the election of pro-Kremlin candidate Viktor Yanukovych, despite clear evidence of fraud. The following year, the organization opposed OSCE-ODIHR findings in Uzbekistan, Tajikistan, and Kyrgyzstan.[187] The organization has also attempted to delegitimize non-CIS elections, to cast European domestic policies as hypocritical, and to justify Kremlin policies using the language of human rights.[188]

Although the nature of the Kremlin's involvement in the activities of CIS-EMO and its affiliates is unclear, Moscow openly lauds and cites the organization and its subcontractors. The reasons for this affinity are threefold. First, these groups' conclusions muddy the truth about the conduct of elections. By providing an alternative narrative that international election standards have been met even when evidence suggests otherwise, these groups empower authoritarian regimes to maintain the appearance of adhering to international norms without actually having to do so.[189] Second, the increasingly pan-European nature of these organizations metastasizes favorable ideas deep into Europe. One of Russia's ongoing points of contention with OSCE missions is that they do not include a balance of opinions from "east and west" of Vienna;[190] not only do these organizations provide that balance, but they also hold views that align with the Kremlin's interests. Third, these organizations assert that facts about elections are actually opinions. This undermining of trust in authoritative election assessments creates an opening for alternative forms of "democracy," and thus provides additional leeway to Russia for how it mixes elements of democracy with authoritarianism on its own soil.

Political and economic active measures are inexpensive, are easy to spread, and, through the use of proxies, pose little attribution risk. If applied effectively, they yield long-term benefits—strategic and otherwise—for the perpetrator, while avoiding the risk associated with more coercive forms of influence. They are also additive: each action builds on the other and creates additional influence opportunities as the target's understanding of reality shifts. Taken together, they create points of leverage that provide opportunities to compel a target to one's will and reduce its strategic options.[191] Russia's recent activities in Europe demonstrate that political and economic influence operations are often subtle enough that their effectiveness bears fruit before the targets understand that they are under attack.

RUSSIAN ORTHODOX CHURCH AND OTHER ENTITIES

Much like Russia has reconstituted Soviet tactics of influencing political and economic decision makers, it has also turned to the church to amplify cultural and ideological ideas that suit its interests. The reader may find this assertion counterintuitive, given the Soviet Union's general hostility toward religion. Yet the Soviets were quite adept at leveraging the few religious institutions allowed to practice openly within the borders of the USSR, as well as foreign religious institutions, to advance their aims. In exchange for permission to operate, for example, churches—as well as mosques—were expected to promote the interests of the state to foreign audiences.[192] International ecumenical councils, although aware of Moscow's motives, were largely willing to accept the ideological agenda as the price of maintaining a connection with their Soviet cobelievers. Meanwhile, the Communist Party of the Soviet Union oversaw connections with foreign religious front organizations to spread socialist ideas, generally cloaked in the guise of maintaining peace.[193] Although most Western believers saw through this rhetoric, the front groups remained effective at spreading Soviet ideology or sympathy in the third world, where their affiliations were less known. Just as in tsarist times, the Soviet government recognized the utility of the church in advancing its aims and thus maintained a careful suzerainty over religious activities inside its borders and sought to influence the narratives promulgated through religious institutions outside them.[194]

With the collapse of the Soviet Union, the relationship between church and state began to change. One might trace the genesis of this shift back to Gorbachev's loosening of restrictions on church activities before the fall, but the real marker of the church's newfound importance came with the failed coup in August 1991. As tensions rose in the months preceding the event, Alexy II, the head of the Russian Orthodox Church (ROC), led discussions between opposing sides and claimed that the coup had faltered due to "divine intervention" resulting from the faith of parishioners.[195] Russia's parliament chose the Cathedral of the Assumption in Moscow to convene its first post-coup sessions, and Boris Yeltsin himself expressed gratitude to the patriarch. This comingling of church and state interests would have been unthinkable during the Soviet era.

In the years that followed, religious institutions in general and the ROC in particular began to reconstitute their property holdings and expand their reach. By 1995 the ROC had grown strong enough to pursue "concrete policy initiatives" that aligned with the beliefs and motivations of its leaders.[196] But instead of beseeching its government overseers as it might have done in the past, the church's post-Soviet position allowed it to work with the Kremlin on a more equal footing. The Russian constitution paved the way for these new terms, as it held that church and state should remain separate. In calling for a spiritual renewal in its 2000 National Security Concept, however, the state signaled that it would still maintain an active interest in the activities of the church.[197] This interest in spiritual renewal, encouraged by the church, has led the state to pursue policies that consolidate the power of the ROC in the name of creating spiritual unity.[198] For its part, in 2000 the ROC attempted to define its proper role with respect to the state in the *Social Concept*, a publication that crafted guidance for the church on a number of social and political issues. The document advanced the pre-Soviet vision of church-state relations known as *symphonia*, which provides space for the church to enter into a "cooperative relationship with the state, in a joint endeavor to better society."[199]

By the end of the 1990s, the relationship between the church and the state in Russia had thus grown into one of a mutually beneficial association, in contrast to the long-standing previous arrangement that was more akin to the relationship between patron and benefactor. In 2007 Alexy II oversaw the reunification of the church with its foreign contingent, the Russian Orthodox Church Outside Russia, ending an eighty-six-year schism that expanded the numerical and rhetorical influence of the Moscow Patriarchate.[200] Citing the overwhelming majority of Russians that identify as Orthodox, the church soon began to make demands of the state, such as installing Orthodox chaplains in the military and injecting Orthodox teachings into the curriculum of Russia's public schools.[201] These demands were at first ignored, but the state began to acquiesce in 2008 with the election of President Dmitry Medvedev and the ascension of Kirill I to the patriarchy of Moscow.

Since Putin's reelection in 2012, the church and the state have reached new heights in cooperation, an arrangement that benefits both entities.[202] From Putin's standpoint, the church provides a "veneer of historical and cultural legitimacy"; from the church's perspective, cooperation with the Kremlin reinforces its "position as a moral arbiter for society."[203] In addition to receiving access to the military and public-education systems, Patriarch Kirill maintains an influential role in crafting and promoting policies that benefit the church. The church has encouraged restrictions on speech and assembly, for example, as well as harsher punishments for those who speak out against Russian Orthodoxy.[204] In so doing, the church helps propagate a Russian national identity distinct from the secular cosmopolitanism of Western Europe.[205] Reciprocally, state propaganda frames the West's supposed moral vacuity as a product of its secularity and encourages Russians to seek refuge in the Orthodox Church. Under Kirill I, the Moscow Patriarchate has become a unifying force among adherents, one that reinforces the nationalistic tendencies of the Russian state and perpetuates critiques of Western norms.[206]

Kirill's initiatives do not reflect the opinions of everyone in the church, which has many factions that hold differing views about the appropriate level of engagement with social and political issues. As the *Social Concept* and symphonia imply, however, the Russian Orthodox Church views itself as sharing many of the same core interests as the state, particularly on moral issues. If there is a moral dimension to a particular policy (and few policies are devoid of morality), the church, or certain factions within it, take an active interest.

The church's interests do not end at Russia's borders. The priorities of the church and the Kremlin, in fact, often converge on policy toward Orthodox believers outside Russia, especially in countries where Orthodoxy predominates. In Moldova, senior Orthodox priests have worked to block their country's integration with the West.[207] In Romania, over 40 percent of the population lives in rural areas dominated by the Romanian Orthodox Church, which promulgates pro-Russian political opinions.[208] (Pro-Russian views are less common in urban Romania.) In Serbia, the Russian Orthodox Church denigrates actors as varied as NATO, Albania, and the Croats, suggesting that they may in the future destroy Orthodox shrines, while enflaming social tensions linked to the spread of gay marriage and gay pride.[209] In each of these cases, the ROC portrayed Moscow as bastion of Russian Orthodoxy and as the lone protector of religious traditionalism against the corrosive forces of Western secularism.

The Russian government does not wield its influence over the church overtly, as in the past. The church has fewer qualms openly collaborating with the state. Because of its influence on the government and the high percentage of Russians who identify with the Orthodox faith, as the church is a vector through which prevailing societal attitudes on moral—and sociopolitical—issues are transmitted to the Kremlin. If, as has been the case for the past twenty years, the fundamentalists assert their views more effectively than other groups, the church will continue to advocate for their priorities. This phenomenon leads to a feedback loop between the Kremlin and the ROC, which plays out not just in Russian society or among foreign adherents but also in the international political arena. Thus, while Putin and the church may view their arrangement as mutually beneficial, those with opposing viewpoints may view it quite differently.

Military-Shaping Operations

Shaping activities in the social, cultural, political, and economic realms of society eat away at a given area's resilience to Russian meddling and help set the conditions for decisive military victory. The invasion of Georgia, the seizure of the Crimea, the invasion of Eastern Ukraine, and operations in Syria demonstrate the extent of Russian hard power. But other less obvious displays of military power also serve as powerful tools of influence. As with the softer forms of shaping discussed previously, they seek to confuse, confound, and intimidate adversaries. The pace of Russia's military modernization; its aggressive incursions into the airspace, sea space, and ground space of surrounding countries; and the increased frequency and changing nature of its military exercises obscure the Kremlin's strategic intent and create misleading impressions of Russia's military capabilities and capacities.

Military Modernization

Russia's current military modernization dates back to the 2008 invasion of Georgia, which exposed significant vulnerabilities in its military. Known as the New Look package of defense reforms, the Kremlin aimed to reform the structure of the military from the Soviet model, which relied on mass mobilization, to a Western model built around professional soldiers; revamp the military's doctrine to reflect modern challenges; and provide the military with new equipment to replace Soviet-era weaponry.[210] The invasion of Crimea in 2014—vastly more efficient than the earlier Georgia campaign—showcased how much progress Russia had made toward achieving these goals.[211]

Although the success of Russia's recent military forays confirms these investments have already borne fruit, Moscow continues to invest in military modernization. By 2020, the Kremlin aimed to modernize 70 percent of its army's equipment, upgrade its already superior electronic warfare capabilities, and field new "aircraft, nuclear-powered submarines, tanks, [and] air defense systems."[212] Plans beyond 2020, approved through the second State Armament Program in late 2017, include an increased focus on precision weaponry, "intellectual weapons," and nuclear-deterrence systems.[213] International sanctions incurred after the Crimea invasion and declining oil prices raise questions about the Kremlin's ability to sustain these investments, but Putin has thus far proven adept at martialing fears of Western encirclement to justify outsized defense spending.[214] In May 2018, Putin announced that the Russian Air Force would receive 160 new aircraft, 500 new armored vehicles, and 10 newly commissioned warships by year's end, along with a hypersonic vehicle in 2019.

These ambitious modernization plans have significant economic limitations, especially under the current sanctions regime. Russia's investments in its military represent a fraction of U.S. expenditures, and some argue that the Russian Ministry of Defense's plans are overly optimistic.[215] There is also a danger of reading too much into Russia's military successes. One might argue, for example, that Russia could not replicate its success in the Crimean Peninsula in less permissible territory. Given the local population's support for Russian intervention and Moscow's heavy reliance on its elite *spetsnaz* units, its best-resourced outfits, it is difficult to tell how much genuine progress Moscow has made.[216]

Perhaps because of the challenge of modernizing an army on a limited budget, Putin has placed nuclear weaponry at the core of Russia's modernization strategy.[217] Compared with other investments in Russia's armed forces, Putin's efforts at redeveloping Russia's nuclear forces have made significant progress.[218] On the strategic front, each leg of Russia's nuclear triad is undergoing modernization: Russia has, or in the coming years will procure, eight Borei-class ballistic submarines, build four hundred intercontinental ballistic missiles (ICBMs), and reopen the production line for the Tu-160 Blackjack bomber, in addition to updating its existing Tu-160s.[219] Lastly, Russia's newest ICBM, the thermonuclear-armed RS-28 Sarmat, will likely be operational by 2022.[220] Thus, while the United States has reduced its nuclear arsenal, Russia has likely developed nuclear-capable cruise missiles, short-range ballistic missiles, and aircraft.[221]

The Kremlin has already begun to leverage its growing nuclear toolkit. In 2016, Russia deployed nuclear-capable Iskander missiles to the European enclave of Kaliningrad, raising concerns about Putin's willingness to use tactical nuclear weapons.[222] In addition to Putin's tendency to highlight the strength of Russia's strategic forces in official speeches, Russia dropped the Soviet "no first-use" policy with respect to nuclear weapons and instead "reserves the right to use nuclear weapons first if the survival of the state is threatened by conventional means."[223] The lack of clarity regarding the size, location, and composition of the forces in Kaliningrad injects additional ambiguity into an already assertive nuclear posture, and it amplifies Russia's ability to intimidate foes on its Eastern European periphery.

In addition to upgrading Russia's nuclear forces, Putin has made steps toward reforming the structure and doctrine of Russia's special operations forces. While Moscow has long relied on specialized units to intervene in its near abroad,[224] these units were traditionally scattered across the Russian government.[225] (The GRU, for example, was affiliated with the Federal Security Service and the Main Intelligence Directorate.) However, after Russia's poor performance in the 2008 Georgian War, Putin decided to establish a centralized Special Operations Command (SOC), which could address the operational gaps exposed in the wartime deployment of GRU-affiliated *spetsnaz* units. Modeled loosely on those that exist in the West, SOC has an estimated 250 servicemen across five special operations divisions, in addition to 1,250 support staff.[226] After the military reforms that began in 2008 and the creation of SOC in 2011, several *spetsnaz*-GRU were relocated to the newly established Special Operations Command, which was the new tool for limited intervention.

Incorporating many specialized units into a single command could have increased effectiveness of Russia's short-of-war military actions. The use of established units instead of the soc in recent conflicts, however, shows that Russia still has much to learn in leveraging an integrated special operations command. The soc deployed in Crimea, but *spetsnaz-GRU* brigades and the Naval Infantry ultimately intervened to help secure key buildings.[227] When Moscow turned its political objectives toward eastern Ukraine, where the risk of direct conflict was much higher than in Crimea, the Kremlin again chose the *spetsnaz*-GRU over the soc. Whereas the outfit has refrained from direct conflict in eastern Ukraine,[228] approximately one thousand *spetsnaz*-GRU soldiers were operating behind Ukrainian lines in 2015, destroying supply trains, attacking convoys, and conducting reconnaissance.[229] Contrary to its usual role, the outfit also has provided training to partisan forces, both local to Donbass and recruited from Russia. The ultimate utility of Special Operations Command hence remains an open question, as does the distinction between its role and that of the better-established *spetsnaz* units.

Across conventional, nuclear, and special-operations domains, Russia is pushing its military units to operate in new ways and with modernized equipment. Although the success of modernization efforts and operational reforms remains an open question, Russia's forces have found an increasing number of circumstances to test and develop tactics in the field. Recent incursions into foreign territories and a number of military exercises demonstrate that Russia has learned much since the beginning of the New Look.

Incursions and Training Exercises

Incursions into foreign territories serve two purposes: to test the strength, responsiveness, and resolve of a target state and to collect valuable information about or prepare the territory for future conflict. During the Soviet era, the United States and Russia played a careful but well-orchestrated probing game via prescheduled overflights, facility inspections, and close approaches to each other's airspace.[230] Unlike in the past, however, Russia's recent incursions into Western airspace are neither predictable in terms of timing and location, nor agreed to in advance. Nor are such incursions limited to the air: Russia has also violated the sea space and ground space of its near abroad, actions that are often conducted in tandem with shaping efforts in other domains.

The pace of these incursions has increased year over year since 2012. Over the Baltic states, for example, NATO jets scrambled to intercept Russian aircraft 160 times in 2015, a 15 percent increase from the prior year.[231] And in Turkey, even after airspace violations led to Ankara shooting down a Russian jet, Russia again crossed Turkish airspace on its way to Syria, claiming, "There is no such thing as NATO airspace."[232] These incursions, particularly involving bombers, have extended outside Russia's near abroad to countries such as the United Kingdom, the United States, Sweden, and Japan.[233]

The Kremlin plays a similar game at sea, often with submarines. As of February 2016, Russian submarine activities in the North Atlantic had reached Cold War levels, and intrusions near populated coastal areas have also been on the rise.[234] One particularly brazen incursion involved a Russian submarine entering the Stockholm archipelago, which revealed the significant limitations of Sweden's ability to detect foreign submersibles in its territorial waters.[235] In March 2017 Russia deployed a spy ship off the coast of Georgia, not far from the U.S. Navy's ballistic-missile submarine base at Kings Bay, and in September and May 2018, the United States intercepted Russian bombers off the coast of Alaska.[236] Cumulatively, these incursions reveal the response times of target nations, allow for the collection of intelligence via on-board sensors, and, at the strategic level, reveal the extent to which countries are willing to appease Russia in order to avoid conflict.

With respect to ground activities, Russia tends to rely heavily on disinformation campaigns to obscure its direct involvement.

For example, in Donbass in 2014, Russia denied transporting weapons into the region, claiming to have sent "humanitarian convoys" into Ukraine. In truth, Moscow concealed the delivery of heavy artillery to Donbass under the cloak of night.[237] Simultaneously, the Kremlin waged information campaigns and leveraged its political influence inside Ukraine to deflect accusations against it.[238] Lastly, in the final stages before the conflict, Russia deployed *spetsnaz* operatives to the region and recruited new ones from the local population, both of which operated in military uniforms without identifiable insignia (as the infamous "little green men").[239] Each of these actions obscured the nature and extent of Russian involvement, thereby undermining responses to Russian aggression from observers in Ukraine and the West.

Russia's recent involvement in Syria highlights Moscow's growing use of private military contractors, which promises to further obscure the Kremlin's involvement in conflict zones. Private contractors such as the Wagner Group (previously known as Slavonic Corps) operate similarly to American security firms, but the details of their arrangements with Moscow remain shrouded in mystery. Notably, the Kremlin has not officially acknowledged Wagner's involvement in Syria.[240] Meanwhile, Russian-backed private security firms have begun operating in Libya, reflecting Moscow's expanding role in the Middle East, and Russian security officials seem keen to learn from American experiences with private military contractors.[241]

Intimidation and signaling do not always require incursions. Russia's frequent training exercises mold threat perceptions and are used as tools of information warfare. Here too, the element of ambiguity obscures true intentions. Between September 2012 and September 2018, Russia conducted twenty-seven mostly large-scale exercises that simulate various kinds of battles against NATO forces. Those held in Russia's Far East in September 2018 were the largest ever held in both Russian and Soviet history. The exercises prior to that, held in September 2017, simulated Russia's defense of ally Belarus in a conflict with a "hypothetical" enemy invading through the strategic chokepoint known as the Suwalki Gap. The exercise showed the importance Russia continues to place on Belarus and offers a number of clues about the evolution of the Russian military's doctrine and capabilities. In addition to the increased use of unmanned aerial vehicles, the exercise focused on electronic warfare and the related creation of Anti-Access/Area Denial "bubbles" at various echelons of the escalatory and electro-magnetic spectrums.[242] The exercise also featured information *maskirovka*: the level of logistical support employed suggested a much higher number of actual troops deployed than the official number, and despite Russian denials it remains unclear whether its troops remained in Belarus after the conclusion of the exercise. Although NATO conducts a fair number of exercises on its own, they have typically been smaller and not explicitly linked to conflict with Russia.[243]

NATO and Eastern European nations must take these exercises seriously, as they sometimes presage forthcoming military actions. For example, the Kremlin practiced deploying *Iskander* missiles to Kaliningrad in 2015 and then actually deployed the missiles there a year later.[244] Russia also conducted the Caucasus frontier exercise just months before launching its military campaign in South Ossetia in 2008. The regularity of these exercises normalizes aggressive behavior, running the risk that Russia's neighbors will mistake actual military operations for exercises. (This is particularly important because the Kremlin designs its exercises and incursions to project an image of power that may exceed Russia's actual capabilities.) By intimidating smaller countries, Russia has developed a knack for keeping its enemies on high alert, which drains resources and distracts observers from many of Russia's other, less obvious shaping activities.

Conclusions

Since the time of the tsars and following on to the present day, the Russian state has honed techniques to maximize its influence while minimizing the resources expended to do so. Russia's strategic predisposition to competition outside of war stems from its geographic and historical place on the margins of Western civilization, being neither of it nor apart from it. This close acquaintanceship and the transmutation of Western ideas into Russia over the past century has yielded a trove of information about the weaknesses of the West—weaknesses that the Russian state has keenly exploited particularly during times of nominal "peace." As the concepts of pluralism and representative democracy that underpin Western systems of government have come under question in recent years, Russia has stood ready to add fuel to the fire.

Yet despite Russia's many efforts to propagate influence throughout its near abroad and elsewhere, it is worth considering the country's weakness relative to the West, particularly with respect its economy.[245] Although Russia's economy grew at the fastest rate in six years in 2018 (which is still far lower than the growth Russia enjoyed during Putin's first term), it is unlikely that this growth will be sustainable or that it will result in material improvements for the average Russian citizen. With an economy highly dependent on natural-resource extraction, moreover, Russia is vulnerable to shifts in international energy prices.[246] In the short term, such fluctuations may not prevent Putin from funneling money into military-modernization efforts. In the medium to long term, however, single-sector dependency, slow growth rates, and demographic declines will begin to squeeze Moscow's ability to compete with the West in combat or in scenarios short of war. Whether this situation increases the willingness of the Kremlin to lash out at its neighbors will depend on whether sufficient cost-imposing measures are in place to deter it.

Russia is comparatively weak with respect to a direct confrontation with the collective power of NATO. Although it currently holds advantages in specific contingencies, such as a surprise invasion of the Baltics, NATO and the United States could mitigate these through a more assertive force posture and selective military modernization and acquisitions, through deeper cooperation with regional partner nations. The success of such efforts will hinge, however, on more than military deterrence. Countering the perception of Russian power, particularly during times of peace, will mitigate the most valuable and pernicious effect of the Kremlin's shaping activities: the reduction of targeted societies' will or ability to resist.

To create the impression that Russia has returned to its former superpower status, Vladimir Putin has undermined faith in democratic processes, manipulated foreign political outcomes, used economic realities as leverage, sown chaos through social media and cyberattacks, and modernized the means and ways of the armed forces under his command. Outside Russia, these activities feed a narrative of ascendency and power, which in turn draws more attention to the Kremlin's activities and amplifies their effectiveness. Inside Russia, such achievements are either denied and dismissed as Russophobia or uplifted as examples of the strength of the Russian state. Yet these perceptions belie a country whose demographic and economic decline is inevitable and already apparent. This is perhaps the greatest quandary facing the West: highlighting Russian activities increases the Kremlin's power to influence, whereas ignoring or downplaying them creates additional avenues for active measures.

From an internal standpoint, the United States and the West should use the legislative and legal tools at their disposal to decrease the influence of Russian information campaigns, economic leverage, and political meddling. In the United States, where free speech protections limit government intervention into public debates, the government should continue to cooperate with the private entities that act as content gatekeepers to reduce the prominence of material emanating from Russian sources. Although the Trump administration has increased sanctions against Kremlin affiliates, potential for reform remains with respect to anonymous shell corporations and the access that Russian expatriates enjoy in the American property market. On the political front, foreign financial contributions to American candidates are already forbidden, but travel to Russia has received far less scrutiny. In the wake of the 2016 election, the risks of cooperating with or even meeting with Russians have increased in the United States, but this has not been as true on the domestic political scene for many of America's allies. More than anything, as will be discussed further in the concluding chapter, the United States and its allies need to adopt a more holistic understanding of how Russia competes outside of combat and adjust their institutions and public diplomacy efforts accordingly.

With respect to external efforts, Western national-security agencies and militaries should selectively apply and coordinate countermeasures to mitigate Russian influence while remaining careful to not ascribe undue influence to the Kremlin. In Russia's near abroad, where Russian influence is strongest, partners and allies should be supported in their efforts to counter the Kremlin's attempts at meddling in their internal affairs. When democratic institutions are under attack, this chapter has shown that Russia frequently denies involvement or resorts to moral equivocating. In order to be effective, responses to, say, an attack against a partner nation's energy grid or a seizure of sovereign land must be met with swift condemnations and the provision of resources to assist the targeted nations withstand or resist the Kremlin's intrusions. Simply stated, flourishing and strong democracies, particularly within Russia's near abroad, pose the greatest threat to the legitimacy of the current power establishment in Moscow.

Such efforts naturally run the risk of "provoking the bear," but such risks are mitigable through the creation of effective deterrence and cost-imposition strategies throughout the escalatory spectrum. In addition to the subjects discussed, low-end deterrence may also take the form of selectively demonstrating American capabilities in offensive cyber operations, of developing world-leading capabilities in the realm of artificial intelligence, and of supporting dissident groups within Russia. A recent report of the RAND Corporation details a host of cost-imposition strategies that would further constrain Russian behavior and change the Kremlin's calculus when considering the value of launching military operations, hybrid or otherwise.[247] Some of the solutions discussed include expanding U.S. energy production, increasing the scope of sanctions, providing lethal aid to Ukraine, and increasing research and development into long-range strike aircraft and missiles.

To neutralize the threat posed by Russia, the West should thus apply a combination of resolve, military deterrence, and cost-imposition strategies. It should also be prepared to support the Russian people before and especially if the current regime begins to falter. At the end of the Cold War and for the decade that followed, the United States overlooked the importance of this last consideration and missed an important opportunity to fold Russia into the international system. The populist appeal of a leader like Vladimir Putin, who promised to restore self-respect if not greatness to his countrymen, grew from an environment in which average Russians saw little fruit from the pains of the transition to democracy. The West's recent experience with populism has demonstrated the value of supporting the spread of democracy and liberalism and laid bare the dangers of allowing narratives of grandeur to cloak inconvenient realities.

2

Iran

Conceptualizing Competition Short of War

The crucible of time forged a distinct Iranian identity from a wide variety of geographic, climatic, linguistic, religious, and ethnic features. This identity—rooted in pre-Islamic notions; tied to geography, language, and Persian ethnicity; and augmented by the adoption of Shiite Islam—echoes through the ages and influences Iran's relations with its neighbors to this day.[1] Its location at the crossroads of East and West further enriched and shaped Iranian culture. Geography unified Iran by securing it against many attempts at foreign domination, but its mountains and deserts also divided it. At times it was little else than an absolute monarch or common enemy that bound the strands of this tapestry.

Beginning with Cyrus the Great, the rulers of the nation we now call Iran sought to further secure their holdings through expansionist conquests. Strategic depth not only protected Persia but also provided it with goods unavailable in the dry, mountainous lands of the Persian homeland. These conquests also spread Persian sensibilities. For most of its history, Persian society was more advanced than its proximate neighbors, and the empire's expansionism intertwined with a desire to civilize other peoples.[2] At its height, the Persian Empire stretched from India to the shores of the Mediterranean Sea.

This penchant for cultural proselytization also manifested when Persia eventually came under foreign domination. When the Arabs invaded Iran in the fifth century AD, for example, their achievements in literature, the sciences, and public administration lagged behind those of the Persians. Despite contemporary tensions between Iran and its Arab neighbors, the contributions of the former to Islamic civilization are many.[3] Particularly under the Abbasid caliphs in the sixth and seventh centuries, Persian influences in the Arab world became "stronger and stronger, Persian models were followed in the court and the government, and Persians . . . [played] an increasingly important part in both political and cultural life."[4] Thus even while under foreign control, Iran exported its cultural capital. Similar patterns of maintaining influence and a distinct yet expanding identity are evident during the occupations of the Mongols, British, and Russians.[5]

During times of occupation, the survival of Iranian civilization depended on a mixture of Iranians assimilating into foreign civilizations and the occupier assimilating into Iranian ways. The noted contributions to Islam did not happen through osmosis; they occurred because of the willingness of the local Zoroastrian priestly caste to convert to Islam and then help shape its development.[6] The arrival of Shi'ism under the Safavids yielded a vehicle through which Persian leaders could both absorb and exert influence.[7]

Shi'ism underpins many core elements of Iranian national strategy. It bolstered the sense of otherness in Iran's perception of itself vis-à-vis its neighbors, supplied a unifying narrative, and provided a ready tool for extending Iranian power. In particular, because Shi'ism developed as a minority and persecuted strain of Islam, the sect's historical experience with *taqiyya*, a Quranic device allowing for a "concealing of true intentions," is more expansive than that of Sunni Muslims.[8] Particularly during times of occupation, this device preserved Shi'a communities faced with the onslaught of their more numerous Sunni counterparts.

Just as important, the rise of Shi'ism had specific geopolitical consequences by tying Iran to Shi'a holy cities in Mesopotamia, such as Najaf and Karbala, which not only bound the Iranian Shi'ites and their Arab brethren but also led to formalized systems of clerical exchange that cemented the two holy cities (in modern-day Iraq) as objects of Persian interest if not always influence.[9] Over time, Iran developed facilities for clerical training of its own, most notably in Qom, and exported its particular interpretation of Shi'ism to faithful communities throughout the Muslim world.

The Safavid era (1501–1722), marked the fusion of Shi'ism with a system for governance. In addition to popularizing Shi'ism, Safavid-era religious leader Muhammad Baqir Majlisi advanced the idea that rulers possessed a supernatural ability to interact with the "hidden imam," or "twelfth imam"—a central figure in Shi'a Islam.[10] By "using the religious authority of *ahadith*[11] to convince common folk to disengage from intellectual, social, and political inquiries," Sultan Hossein, influenced by Majlisi's ideas, began the process of reorienting authority from the state to religious figures and created the foundation for the ultimate authority of clerics now evident in the Islamic Republic.[12]

Through the prism of Shi'ism, one might better understand the senses of otherness, superiority, and righteousness that undergird Tehran's approach to its neighbors and world affairs more generally. But because Shi'ism was not adopted as the dominant confessional practice until the reign of the Safavids, nearly nine hundred years after Islam arrived in the lands of Persia, Iran's influence is not attributable to Shi'ism alone.[13] As would occur when the Safavids introduced Shi'ism to Iran, strategy and ruling principles from the pre-Islamic era underwent a "process of Islamisation" and were thus bequeathed to later rulers.[14]

To preserve its rich history, Iran has sought to fold past traditions into contemporary contexts and simultaneously impart its own perceptions and knowledge onto its neighbors. The Safavids established religion as a primary vector for the transmission of ideas into and out of Iran, but the process of importing, co-opting, and then exporting ideas to increase influence is evident throughout Persian history. This cycle of reinvigoration provides the means of adaptation for many societies, but the centuries of the cycle repeating itself in Iran has refined the country's ability to weaponize it. Rather than allowing this cycle to dilute its identity, Iran reconstitutes and fortifies its sense of identity and cultural prowess by injecting its perceptions and knowledge into the cultural, scientific, and economic milieu of neighboring lands. The religious, economic, and military vectors through which this cultural transfusion occur also provide pathways to influence and co-opt competing regimes.

Whereas this process was once limited by geographic constraints, the relevance of Iran's reinvigoration cycle has expanded along with the number of powers wielding regional influence in the modern Middle East. In the opening years of twentieth century, Iran found itself in the crosshairs of stronger countries, namely the United Kingdom and Russia. Iran's interactions with Western powers began genially, but the public soon came to blame foreign meddling for the decline of Iran's power and prestige.[15] The Japanese defeat of the Russians in the Russo-Japanese War and the Constitutional Revolution in Russia provided a confidence boost to anti-imperialist voices around the world, including those in Iran. The Iranian public soon began to demand a greater voice in their government's conduct in domestic and foreign affairs.[16] Clerics and mullahs joined with merchants and revolutionaries to demand reforms, leading to the establishment of a representative assembly, the *majles,* for the first time. The advent of the Majles is a prime example of how Iran internalized a foreign model and adapted it for domestic use.

One finds similar dynamics at play in the lead-up to the Islamic Revolution in the 1970s. Mohammad Reza Shah was increasingly viewed as beholden to Western influence, and the modernization push he oversaw clashed with the important place of religion in the lives and identities of many Iranians.[17] The bitter memory of the 1953 coup backed by the U.S. Central Intelligence Agency and a concurrent rekindling of Iranian society's connections with its past bolstered calls for Iran to return to its roots.[18] Thus, the populist musings of Ayatollah Ruhollah Khomeini began to find resonance even within the intellectual class and the enlisted military.

Populist animus toward Western influence only partially explains the prerevolutionary military's interest in Khomeini. Despite declaring the start of a "new Persian empire" and overseeing a sizable military buildup, Mohammad Reza never built a strong bond with the conventional army, also known as the Artesh, and undermined his own authority through his proposed Westernization reforms.[19] In contrast, Khomeini had clear ideas for the Iranian military, and in the years leading up to the revolution he forged relationships with guerrilla groups such as the Mujahedin-e Khalq. The military's royalist officer class remained Khomeini's main obstacle to authority within the military; in the early days of the revolution, he created the Islamic Revolutionary Guard Corps (IRGC) as "a counterweight to the regular military, and to protect the revolution against a possible coup."[20]

Even at that time, a central feature of the revolution was its exportability.[21] The purported universality of the revolutionary message tied in well with the evangelistic orientation honed over centuries of Iran's history, as well as a sense of religious kinship and obligation to Shi'a communities throughout the Middle East. After all, anti-Americanism was not an Iranian invention, nor was the Islamic fundamentalist phenomenon unique to Shi'ism. Yet with the success of the revolution, the clerics were able to craft a narrative that folded irredentism, the promise of a restoration of greatness, and a return to lost traditions into one attractive package. The result was the formation of a new sort of nationalism for a country that had never adopted the Western sense of the term.[22] In combination with the revolutionary, evangelical zeal of the clerics, Iranian nationalism began to take on a more outward-looking stance. The stage was set for the reinvigoration cycle to begin once again.

Contemporary Competition Short of War

The Islamic Republic's leaders are fond of arguing that Iran has not initiated a war against its neighbors in three hundred years—a claim that is truer in letter than in spirit.[23] The Artesh, which is tasked with defending the homeland and maintaining internal order, has acted in a manner consistent with Iran's professed restraint from waging war against its neighbors. But the Artesh's activities are but a fraction of Iran's military activities, particularly since the foundation of the Islamic Republic. Iran's constitution provides a separate and parallel military status to the IRGC and tasks it with protecting the Islamic nature of Iran's government. The Revolutionary Guard's mandate has expanded significantly since the 1970s, and the group now represents a separate security organization that answers directly to Tehran's clerical leadership.[24]

Given the central role of religion in Iran's system of government, the Revolutionary Guard's growing role in Iran's national-security affairs should come as little surprise. While the Artesh is ultimately subordinate to the Supreme Leader, who is commander in chief, the professional military is not as highly trusted, not as powerful, and not as well connected in government, the economy, or society writ large. Thus, although the Artesh represents Iran's conventional military capabilities and provides a baseline of security in Iranian society, short-of-war capabilities largely fall within the purview of the Revolutionary Guard.

The dichotomy between the Revolutionary Guard and the Artesh makes more sense in the context of how Iran views its strategic landscape. Iran sees conventional forces as limited to protecting the nation from existential threats, which are few and far between due to its strength in relation to its neighbors.[25] Protecting the ideological position of the regime and projecting power throughout the region are central to Tehran's strategy, and an unconventional approach is better suited to these goals than a conventional one. Tehran has nimbly equipped the IRGC and especially the Quds Force, its paramilitary component, to carry out subtle operations that are far more likely to promulgate Tehran's ideology and to extend its influence than would conventional operations waged through the Artesh.[26]

The increase of the IRGC's utility vis-à-vis the Artesh has eventuated the IRGC's substantial growth over the past several decades.[27] Although initially a small group of hardline supporters, the Revolutionary Guard adopted a formal military structure during the Iran-Iraq War and grew over time in size and scope. The IRGC currently has around 150,000 soldiers and oversees the domestic Basij Resistance Force, which may consist of up to one million full time members and up to four to seven million if part-timers are also counted.[28] Formalizing the IRGC's structure and adding the Basij, an auxiliary force that serves as a tool for social control and the policing of morality, enhanced the former's utility and reach, which now includes its own air force, navy, and ground elements, along with substantial links to the Iranian economy and civil society.[29]

Similar to how the clerics relied on insurgent groups to rise to power, they tasked the Revolutionary Guard with fomenting instability in countries throughout the Middle East. Beginning with the Iran-Iraq War in the 1980s, Iran began engaging with Shi'a groups outside of Iran to export the revolution, first through the Office of Liberation Movements and then through the IRGC-Quds Force.[30] This was done not only through support to Artesh efforts in Iraq during the Iran-Iraq War but also through assistance to the nascent Hezbollah organization, which would go on to support Shi'a populations throughout the Middle East. While religion was a primary driver of the revolution's success in Iran, Iran's fundamental opposition—or resistance—to status quo powers helped it find sympathetic partners across the region.[31]

Proxy forces are particularly useful for Iran's approach to international competition. In an updated volume on Iran's strategic culture, Michael Eisenstadt described several factors intrinsic to how Iran sees strategy that illuminate the utility of proxies and other behaviors distinct to the Iranian way of war.[32] First, he identified indirection, ambiguity, and strategic patience as hallmarks of Iranian strategic culture and noted Tehran's emphasis on reciprocity and proportionality. He further demonstrated the primacy of moral, spiritual, and psychological components of competition in Iranian strategic thought—elements that are only faintly present in how the United States sees international competition.[33]

By positioning themselves as the international defenders not only of Shi'a but also of oppressed populations worldwide, Iran leverages spiritual, moral, and psychological dimensions to flexibly advance its ideological position. Regarding the spiritual and moral dimensions, *taqiyya* allows for flexibility with the truth unburdened by the stigma associated with lying in the West, while specific and repeated Quranic mentions of the moral dimension of warfare still lend legitimacy to the regime, its supporters, and those whom they support.[34] From a psychological perspective, the regime frames the world as separated into two camps: those who dominate (the forces of global arrogance or *mustakbirin*) and those who resist (the downtrodden or *mustazifin*).[35] In addition to initiating social renewal and mobilization, the reinvigoration cycle returns one to the position of dominance from a current state of resistance. Viewed this way, there would be no contradiction between resisting the current dominant powers, whether British, American, or Arab, and simultaneously sowing discord in Iran's near abroad.

Iran's distinct approach to international competition also manifests in the hard-power realm. Indeed, each of these features helps explain Iran's strategy for developing a nuclear weapon. Since it began pursuing a nuclear-weapons capability in the 1950s, it has shrouded its progress, placing research facilities deep inside inaccessible mountain ranges and denying the very existence of the program despite copious evidence to the contrary.[36] When international inspectors took interest in one facility, Iran shifted operations to other facilities. The Joint Comprehensive Plan of Action (JCPOA), known colloquially as the Iran deal, would have allowed Iran to create an industrial-scale nuclear infrastructure after about fifteen years, which plausibly could have then served as a cover for a nuclear-weapons program.[37] When one considers Iran's emphasis on patience, its moral flexibility, and the experiences of loss and glory embedded within the collective memory of its people, however, the JCPOA was less of a foreign policy triumph than a stopgap delaying the inevitable.

Old Techniques, New World Disorder

The end of the Cold War altered the strategic landscape in the Middle East and created opportunities for Iran to reassert itself as both the vanguard of Shi'ism and the predominant regional hegemon. To maximize its potential strategic gains, Tehran waited for the right moment to engage. American-Iraqi tensions throughout the 1990s kept Iran's two principal adversaries distracted from the Iranian position, and by playing both sides during these conflicts Iran was able to avoid retribution from either party. At the same time, American campaigning in Iraq presented Iran with the opportunity to observe the strengths and vulnerabilities of America's approach to warfare.[38] Iran's subsequent actions suggest that it recognized the weaknesses in America's approach to campaigning, which underappreciated the scope and scale of the challenges presented by unconventional and insurgent combat.[39]

Thus, by the time that the United States returned to Iraq in 2003, Iran was well positioned and highly incentivized to take advantage of the collapse of Saddam Hussein's regime and the secularist Ba'ath Party. Tehran had previously established extensive contacts with local Shi'a groups, deep networks in the southern half of Iraq, and a variety of indirect levers of influence through the Shi'a clerisy. Meanwhile, America's Shock and Awe approach to the invasion, conducted without a clear stabilization plan, released resentments among the various ethnic and confessional groups that Saddam's authoritarian rule had long suppressed.[40] When the United States reorganized the nascent Iraqi government and established a path to empowerment for the Shi'a majority, it presented Iran with a clear avenue to exert influence on its neighbor at the highest levels of government.

Iran claimed that the purpose of its involvement in Iraq was to promote stability, but it had the opposite effect. Using diplomatic, informational, military, and economic aspects of national power, Iran complicated America's attempts to stabilize the country and extended its own influence in terms of both hard and soft power.[41] Iran's operational gains were apparent from the initial days of the conflict—some reports indicated that Iran had quietly encouraged the White House to oust Saddam and that Iran's involvement with proxies in Iraq began not long after the U.S. invasion.[42] The adaptability and subtlety of Iran's presence in Iraq, however, stymied the Multi-National Force from meeting the Iranian challenge.

As the years dragged on, Iran began to consolidate enduring strategic gains. For example, during and after the war, organizations such as the Supreme Council for the Islamic Revolution in Iraq and Muqtada al-Sadr's Jaysh al-Mahdi maintained ties with Iran, even as they criticized it. Iran continues to enjoy influence with some members of the mainstream Shi'a Dawa Party.[43] Iran's involvement in Iraq, however, was only Iran's initial step toward gaining a stronger foothold throughout the Middle East. Saddam's ouster created a pathway to establish an arc of influence from Iraq to the Mediterranean Sea, made all the more possible by Iran's continued support of Lebanese Hezbollah.[44] As America's regional presence has declined, Iran has filled the power vacuum by employing the IRGC to strengthen ties with groups throughout the crescent.[45]

Despite these strategic gains, Iran's leaders recognize that military influence is only one component of power. From the very founding of the Islamic Republic, Iran's leaders recognized the threat posed by Western cultural prowess.[46] In 2009 Ayatollah Ali Khamenei solidified this concept with his description of a "soft war" or *jang-e narm* waged by the West against Iran. This "war," which weakened the population's resolve via "cultural tools [and] through infiltration of society," had accelerated via modern communications tools such as the internet.[47] The Islamic Republic's Armed Forces General Staff soon established a "soft war headquarters" to better counter creeping Westernization in Iran. Yet for all of the power that Khamenei ascribed to the West, the decrease of the latter's willingness to exert hard power to back up its soft war had created a golden opportunity for Iran to shift from a defensive position in the social, political, and economic competition to an offensive one.

In some cases Iran simply adapted old models to suit contemporary circumstances. In others it learned from peers how best to take advantage of a weakening regional order. In yet others it used diplomacy to reestablish vectors of influence in the context of the information age. In all cases, Iran had laid the foundations of its influence long before the opportunity to increase it became apparent. Thus, at the appropriate moment Tehran was able to advance its cycle of reinvigoration and renew its sense of place and purpose in the world once again. With its immediate environs significantly destabilized, Iran was poised to expand its regional influence in a manner not seen since before the Islamic Revolution.

Social, Political, and Economic Influence Operations

The implosion of Iraq and Syria and American reluctance to remain engaged in the Middle East created new opportunities for Iran to foment discord, instrumentalize proxy groups, and leverage its economic clout to reinvigorate itself and advance the nation's strategic interests. The JCPOA, which dismantled the international sanctions regime in place for many years prior, strengthened and emboldened Iran. And although sanctions levied by the Trump administration curtailed Iran's economic position, America's anticipated withdrawal created an opening for Iran to strengthen its position through proxy groups and influence operations. Despite increasing unrest at home and the death of Qasem Soleimani, Iran remains well equipped to take advantage of the chaotic security environment of its surroundings.

The Middle East of 2021 presents a fertile ground for the exercise of influence operations, particularly as various states continue to grapple with the demands for democracy and representation unleashed by the Arab Spring. Ironically, these demands have provided Iran with a new rhetorical vector through which to justify its behavior. To undermine Gulf monarchies, for example, Iran has appropriated the democratic spirit of the Arab Spring to excuse its subversive support for sympathetic populations and causes in neighboring countries.[48] This rhetorical approach exploits the ideological fault lines of the West's alliances with the Gulf States and also perpetuates the narrative of the West waging a soft war against the wider Muslim *umma*. Viewed through this lens, the Arab Spring was not a movement about democracy but rather an Islamic awakening in which the wider Muslim world has realized the importance of uniting against the pernicious soft influences of the West.[49] Coupling narratives of victimhood with expansionary ambitions mirrors Iran's past, but technological developments are allowing Iran to weaponize these narratives in new and unexpected ways. Tehran leverages state-run media platforms and cultural institutions to promulgate these views.

Information and Cyber Operations

Iran's approach to warfare differs from that of the United States in two key ways: its mechanisms and its emphases. Iran intertwines information and psychological operations into every interaction with the enemy and considers armed conflict as less effective than, and subordinate to, nonmilitary modes of competition.[50] Although it is still up for debate whether Iran would behave this way if it were more powerful than its adversaries, Iran has a long strategic tradition of using diplomacy and information warfare to preserve and expand its sphere of influence.

As with other realms of influence, Iran has built upon past traditions to wage an information war suited for contemporary circumstances. The Islamic Republic twists the Shi'a theological concept of *taqiyya*, which allows for "pious dissimulation" of religious beliefs to protect oneself from persecution, into a rhetorical tool for a state under siege.[51] When applied in the modern information environment, in which untruths spread like viruses and attain the status of facts within loyal subgroups, *taqiyya* provides a justification for the dissemination of misinformation while still allowing Iran to present itself as a moral and just actor. Because Iran is a self-styled theocratic state, one must also examine its foundational text, the

Quran, to understand how it perceives warfare. Although an analysis of Islamic jurisprudence and the extent of its influence on Iran's way of war is outside the scope of this work, the emphasis on spiritual and moral dimensions of warfare found in certain Quranic passages cannot be excluded from a comprehensive understanding of the Islamic Republic's approach to competition.[52] A theocratic state operating under such principles communicates with fervor and focus but not necessarily with an emphasis on objective truth.

The narrative underpinning Iran's strategic messaging is straightforward; the constellation of outlets through which it spreads information, less so. In terms of messaging, Iran's strategy for external mass media involves emphasizing Iranian power and influence, maintaining opposition to the United States and Israel, and presenting itself as pan-Islamic while highlighting offenses against Shi'a populations.[53] In line with its historical ethos, the messages are often delivered via rhetorical tools such as pointing out examples of Western hypocrisy and casting the world in terms of "good" (Iran and the oppressed populations of the world) and "evil" (Western oppressors). In terms of mechanics, Tehran promulgates its ideas through a variety of state-owned media outlets, state-owned cultural institutions, and government-backed covert operations.

Tehran does not hold an exclusive grip on the information available to its citizenry. Although the possession of satellite dishes is illegal in Iran, the Islamic Republic of Iran Broadcasting organization (IRIB) found in 2013 that 42 percent of Iranians illegally watched satellite TV broadcasts and that 70 percent of families possessed satellite dishes.[54] Ownership rates of satellite dishes differs across the country, with ownership rates reportedly higher in Tehran than in more conservative Qom.[55] Nevertheless, viewership of foreign television broadcasts in Iran appears to be on the rise. Though the Islamic Republic does not release official viewership statistics, BBC

Persia found that its audience in Iran nearly doubled between 2012 and 2013, from approximately 6 million to 11.4 million.[56]

Audience reach does not always equate with increased influence. Though diaspora journalists recognize the importance of satellite broadcasts for providing alternative viewpoints to the Iranian public, a 2012 BBC-Gallup poll indicated that 86 percent of Iranians still consider the IRIB as their "most important source" of information.[57] In a country where 96 percent of the population considers television their "most important source of news," IRIB's domestic position remains unchallenged—which may partially explain why officials have turned a blind eye to satellite-dish possession.[58]

IRIB's mission extends beyond shaping the perceptions of Iranians and into the soft war of the global media market. The organization's mission is to "strengthen the country's cultural solidarity" in the "battlefield" of world media in which there is an "intensifying . . . war."[59] The IRIB runs multiple domestic and international TV channels and radio stations and is the sole producer of media within Iran. In recent years, IRIB has expanded to include channels in English, Arabic, and Spanish, adding to its collection of foreign-language broadcasts that already included Bosnian, Azerbaijani, Mandarin, Malay, and Albanian.[60]

IRIB also oversees the operations of international Arabic-language channels Al-Alam, Al-Kawthar TV, Sahar TV, iFilm, and PressTV. Each of these networks serves a different market segment. For example, Al-Alam is the primary outlet for the Iranian regime's perspective on current events. Al-Alam's purpose, according to one of its spokespersons, is to "improve cooperation between people in the region" by exposing regional Muslims to "the Iranian view of Islam and how Iran has translated that view into a government free from American influence and into a stable, multi-ethnic society."[61] Al-Alam may be Tehran's answer to Qatar-owned Al Jazeera and Saudi-backed Al Arabiya.[62]

Al-Kawthar, Sahar TV, and iFilm are cultural-export vehicles that offer religious content, travel and leisure material, and Iranian movies, respectively. Although limited in their reach compared with many Western media outlets, these stations broadcast Iran's perspective beyond its borders and likewise foster a sense of solidarity within the international Shi'a *umma*. Al-Kawthar, for example, promulgates Shi'a interpretations of Islamic ideas as well as the sermons and opinions of the Twelver Shi'a clerics. Although not primarily political in orientation, Al-Kawthar and other culturally focused media outlets still provide Tehran with an important soft-power tool to perpetuate the common destiny of Muslims in general and Shi'ites in particular.[63]

Although Al Jazeera's viewership dwarfs that of Iran's state-backed media ventures, Al-Alam and Al-Manar, another news outlet, have enjoyed particular popularity among Gulf Shi'ites. According to a May 2011 Bahraini government survey, 90 percent of Bahraini Shi'ite respondents watched Al-Alam for news.[64] Thus, even though the ruling family of Bahrain are Sunni Muslims, the majority of its population, who are Shi'a, have their perceptions of current events shaped by Iranian media.

Iran's information campaigns are not limited to targeting majority Shi'a or other proximate Gulf States. As suggested by the number of languages in which IRIB broadcasts, its target audiences extend beyond the Shi'a and Muslim communities and into the West. Likewise, its tactics are not limited to state and cultural information campaigns; Iranian media outlets also take active steps to undermine the legitimacy of Western and Sunni Muslim regimes. PressTV, for example, presents itself as a resource to build bridges between Iran and the English-speaking West, yet CEO Mohammad Sarafraz reportedly tasked employees with "exposing the plots of propaganda networks of the enemy" on the occasion of the channel's founding.[65] This has led to negative reactions abroad, such as in the United Kingdom, where the government revoked PressTv's broadcast license for its coverage of an imprisoned journalist's "confession" to espionage, and in India, where Jammu and Kashmir banned PressTv after the channel showed an incendiary program alleging that Muslims were burning the Quran.[66]

Iran's information campaigns extend beyond broadcasting. Tehran's network of affiliated cultural institutions and the activities of Iranian intelligence agencies provide an additional avenue to inject Iran's perspective into foreign discourses. The Islamic Development Organization, for example, which has the largest budget of any Iranian cultural organization and is overseen by an appointee of the Supreme Leader, promulgates Tehran's viewpoints through Iranian universities, the English-language daily newspaper *Tehran Times*, a cinema franchise, and a publishing house.[67] In 2010 the organization published a statement noting the role of "subversion, internet war, creation of radio-television networks" in "Soft War";[68] a senior IRGC official subsequently described soft war as a way to "force the system to disintegrate from within," with the system being the international media.[69]

Iran recognizes soft war as the means to solidify its preferred interpretation of Islam. The Ahl al-Bayt News Agency (ABNA), founded in 2005, provides an interpretation of world events that conforms to the Islamic Republic's religious and political worldview. Owned by the ecumenical Ahl al-Bayt World Assembly, the agency increases Iran's influence—and exposure to its interpretation of events—within the wider Muslim *umma*.[70] Though the network is primarily focused on current events, it also provides religious content, and its extensive coverage of the "mistreatment" of Shi'a populations led both Saudi Arabia and Bahrain, according to an Iran-based outlet, to ban the network in 2005.[71]

Cultural centers and university partnerships established by Qom's Al Mustafa University and the Department of Disinformation of the Iranian Ministry of Intelligence and Security (MOIS) provide additional means to disseminate information. Al Mustafa University has established relationships and cultural-exchange programs throughout the Muslim world, Europe, the Americas, and Africa. While many of these programs have educational value, the curriculum has inspired some graduates to lead militant Shi'a movements in their home countries.[72] In Syria, Iraq, and Afghanistan, Al Mustafa University–trained clerics have returned from Qom to run or serve in local Shi'a militias, showing that the historical separation between religion and politics espoused by Iran's seminary schools has frayed.[73]

The Department of Disinformation, one of the largest divisions of MOIS, is charged with "creating and waging psychological warfare against the enemies of the Islamic Republic" and has a hand in controlling domestic access to the internet and shaping online narratives.[74] The Iranian government began restricting access to telecommunications shortly after the Islamic Revolution in 1979, but censorship on foreign media outlets and social media sites ticked up after the 2009 Green Revolution.[75] Despite such measures, Tehran recognizes that it could do more through the internet to counter Western narratives and to promote its own. Whereas Iran has demonstrated sophistication in adapting its message to address international developments throu MOIS and other institutions, it has not yet devised the ability to wage a concerted cyber information campaign in the way that Russia and China have.[76] However, the disruptive effects and audaciousness of Iran's cyber warfare and cyber-spying capabilities, if not their breadth and depth, are on par with those of Russia and China.

The 2010 Stuxnet virus attack on the Iranian uranium enrichment facility prompted Tehran to invest heavily in cyber-defense and cyber-warfare capabilities.[77] In 2012 Iran established the Supreme Council of Cyberspace, which includes representatives from the IRGC, militias, intelligence agencies, and the media who answer directly to the Supreme Leader.[78] The body, which has been charged with overseeing all of the government's cyber activities, also has the ability to enact laws. The group oversees the IRGC's Cyber Army, which allegedly includes thousands of hackers and bloggers, and the cyber activities of the Passive Defense Organization, whose mandate of overseeing "measures taken . . . to reduce the probability of and minimize the effects of damage caused by hostile action" has long been central to waging soft war.[79] These represent only the most well-known of Iran's cyber organizations; efforts to enlist the population in defense of the homeland have the potential to create a much larger web of Iranian cyber capacities in the future.

Iran did not wait to fully establish its bureaucratic capacities to begin ramping up its activities in the cyber domain. Also in 2012, Iranian hackers showed their budding prowess by attacking Saudi Aramco's information-technology infrastructure.[80] Iran also allegedly undermined critical infrastructure security in the United States through a series of intrusions and attacks, including a 2013 series of intrusions into computers at the New York Stock Exchange, Bank of America, and AT&T and an attack against the technical infrastructure of a dam in the suburbs of New York City.[81] More recently, the U.S. Department of Justice announced in March 2018 that IRGC-backed hackers had attacked over one hundred American universities. This aggressive approach contrasts with the more deliberate and long-term methods pursued by other leading cyber-warfare powers.[82]

In the lead-up to JCPOA negotiations, Iran increased its cyber activities and resourcing for cyber capabilities. Faced with temporarily foregoing the pursuit of a nuclear deterrent, Iran quietly shifted investment toward developing its cyber-warfare tools.[83] Investments made in IRGC-backed hacker groups, such as Rocket Kitten and Tarh Andishan, allowed Iran to expand the scope of its industrial-espionage efforts to target the critical infrastructure of U.S. allies, such as South Korea and Canada.[84] Iranian hackers also launched spear-phishing attacks against outspoken Iran critics and individuals in the U.S. defense industry. In these and other efforts, they have expanded their knowledge of, and access to, a wide variety of America's critical infrastructure, from power grids to refineries.[85]

Although attacks against critical infrastructure have generated the most press in the West, Iran's capability and willingness to hack into messaging systems and intervene in domestic internet traffic also deserve mention. Following the Green Revolution, in which social media and messaging services fueled widespread protests, Iran worked with Western companies to bolster its domestic information-control capabilities.[86] These capabilities continued to expand as the years went by: by 2016, for example, Rocket Kitten breached secured messaging applications such as Telegram.[87] In addition to stifling domestic discourse, these capabilities also provided Iran with a means to shape political discourse beyond its borders; the use of regime-backed trolls and bot-nets on social media sites to intimidate, refute, and shame dissidents is on the rise. Iran has demonstrated a willingness to block access to social media, as it did in the winter of 2017–2018 amid widespread domestic protests.[88] Far from existing as isolated lines of effort, information and cyber operations are often used in coordination with tools in the political, religious, and economic influence realms.

Political, Religious, and Economic Influence Operations

Iran's longstanding ties with Shi'a communities throughout the Middle East have established a variety of unconventional levers of influence. By fostering relationships with foreign community leaders sympathetic to Iran, leveraging its religious authority to create local allies among foreign populations, and by wielding its economic clout, Iran has proven adept at advancing its strategic interests without recourse to conventional military power. All three soft-power influence campaigns provide additional avenues of leverage for Tehran to achieve its goals without resorting to war.

The political and religious levers available to Tehran are numerous. Iran's political influence has grown since Iraq's Shi'a population returned to prominence, and the repressive treatment of Shi'a populations in some nearby Sunni-led states has produced numerous opportunities for Iran to support its religious brethren. Iran has exploited these ideological and religious commonalities to undermine the authority of neighboring regimes and to lay the groundwork for expanded influence in the region.

Nowhere has Iran's soft influence increased more than in Iraq. The withdrawal of American troops in 2011 exacerbated this trend, but Iranian meddling in Iraq's affairs ticked up years earlier. Shortly after the launch of Operation Iraqi Freedom, Iran increased its support to Shi'a political and insurgent groups in order to support the establishment of a compliant Iraqi government.[89] In Iraq, Iran has deftly adjusted its support in level and kind based on its strategic intent and the needs of the local population. For example, Tehran offered training and financial support to Shi'a militias, offered refuge in Iran to Muqtada al-Sadr, and, in the religious sphere, co-opted friendly clerics and pitted them against the quasi-independent clerical establishment in Najaf.[90] On the political front, Iran leveraged its previously established ties to Dawa, Iraq's predominantly Shi'a political party, to push policies favorable to Tehran.[91]

Much like the Shi'ites in Iraq, Shi'a communities throughout the region often accept Iranian resources because of a lack of alternatives more than because of enduring affinity.[92] In Bahrain, for example, the crackdown on Shi'ites by the ruling Khalifa family following the Arab Spring led many in the Shi'a community, particularly the youth, to warm to the idea of cooperating with Iran.[93] Efforts to better integrate Shi'a into the fabric of society could disincentivize the cooperation of these groups with Iran, but such efforts must be more than symbolic. [94] In Saudi Arabia, for example, representatives of the Shi'a population hold seats in the country's Consultative Assembly, but the body has little power. Despite the gains made from providing Shi'a voices with a political outlet, the arrest of popular Shi'a political figure Nimr al-Nimr in 2012 (and eventual execution in 2016) became a rallying call for Shi'a protesters and militants in Iran and the Gulf.[95] Saudi Arabia's marginalization of Shi'a populations, often done out of fear of the consequences of their own domestic political empowerment, has thus created a pretext for Iran to expand its influence by "saving" the Shi'a population from its "oppressors."

Iran's theocratic system of governance amplifies its use of religious mechanisms of influence. Although Shi'a communities throughout the Gulf generally seek to maintain distance from Tehran, the theological schools at Qom have long attracted Shi'a clerics to study in Iran and learn Farsi, especially during Saddam Hussein's rule in Iraq. Tehran uses the appeal of its religious institutions to its advantage, instilling its worldview in the clerics it trains. When trainees return home, some retain their views and gain loyal followings. Nimr al-Nimr spent fifteen years in exile in Iran.[96] Sheikh Isa Qassim, spiritual leader of Bahrain's now-banned Al-Wefaq Party, studied and taught in Qom from 1994 to 2001 under religious figures close to Khomeini.[97] Aspirant Shi'a clerics may also study in Najaf, Iraq, but doing so does not necessarily free aspiring Shi'a clerics of Iranian influence, as Iranian intelligence operatives reportedly target pilgrims to religious sites in Iraq for recruitment.[98] The training of clerics allows Iran to spread its ideology, sow dissatisfaction within minority Shi'a populations, and therefore foment the very discord that it later points out as a reason for its continued leadership.

While the Iranian state promulgates a specific view of Islam, the question of how to divide revolutionary energy between Shi'a and Sunni populations remains the subject of debate within elite Iranian clerical circles. This has manifested in contrasting approaches toward organized evangelism. In 1990, Iran sponsored the formulation of the Ahl al-Bayt World Assembly (ABWA) as a counterweight to the Tehran Ecumenical Society, which had at the time "developed tendencies towards encroachment on the Sunni world."[99] The new organization, sought to "gain control over the political, social and religious affairs of Shii communities throughout the world" and to consolidate the Islamic Republic's leadership over these groups.[100] Today, ABWA oversees its own media outlet (the Ahl al-Bayt News Agency discussed previously), publishes political and religious manifestos, and convenes annual conferences in Tehran.[101] The conferences infuse the messages and approaches taken by the many outlets in Iran's media constellation with state- and theologically sanctioned guidance. At ABWA's 2015 conference, for example, seven hundred guests from 130 countries joined Iranian attendees to hear a speech from Ayatollah Khamenei which touched upon religious, political, and revolutionary themes.[102]

Iran's ability to use religion—and clerics—as a tool of influence also extends into the financial realm. Shi'ites often provide support, sometimes unwittingly, to Iran and Iranian-backed proxy groups through the payment of *khums* (tithes) to Iran-based clerics. These donations, which may amount to hundreds of millions of dollars, have been funneled to support Shi'a militias across the Middle East.[103] Lebanese Hezbollah, for example, receives financial aid from Iran.[104] Although Hezbollah claims to use these tithes exclusively for charity, at the very least they free up other resources for use in military activities.[105]

Lastly, Iran uses religion as a cynical pretext to retain footholds in countries where it holds strategic interests. Through organizations such as the Imam Khomeini Relief Committee, Iran provides humanitarian aid and infrastructure support throughout the Middle East and beyond.[106] In addition to creating goodwill and boosting Iran's international standing, these charities serve as conduits for the IRGC to recruit among, and establish connections with, the local population.[107] These connections are then leveraged to advance Iran's national interests, further the spread of the state's specific version of Shi'a Islam, or both.

In some cases, Iran does not even bother to conceal the intentions behind its charitable work, particularly in poor countries. In Afghanistan, for example, the IRGC's Basij set up a headquarters in Herat in 2016 to recruit fighters for the Syrian Civil War, often providing "charity" handouts of legal documents, wedding gifts, and cash to achieve their goals.[108] And in Iraq, Iranian charities have begun recruiting women to travel to Iran and learn about the strategic commonalities between the two countries in exchange for practical training in hairdressing, knitting, and computer skills.[109] Such activities blend religious and economic incentives to endear a local population to Iran's aims. Charities, however, represent just a small fraction of Iran's use of economic levers to further its strategic interests; its other efforts deserve separate treatment.

ECONOMIC INFLUENCE

At first glance, it may be tempting to dismiss Iran's economic activities as irrelevant to its strategic priorities. For years, Iran endured crippling economic sanctions and, despite a well-educated population, trailed many of its neighbors in economic development. Its status as an international pariah, however, Iran has incentivized Iran to develop sophisticated tools to influence the economic decisions of strategically significant individuals and entities.

These economic approaches differ depending on their target. Domestically, the ruling regime and its subordinates positioned themselves to maximize the benefits of the sanctions relief provided by the Joint Comprehensive Plan of Action—particularly with respect to oil revenues—and set about establishing a "resistance economy" to help Iran weather future attempts to coerce it through economic pressure. Internationally, the prosperous Revolutionary Guard and other Tehran-linked entities have provided direct financing to proxy groups and pursued profitable ventures that expand Iran's strategic leverage in the Gulf and beyond.

The IRGC has positioned itself as the most important single player in the domestic economy. Its unquestioned loyalty to the ruling regime in Tehran has allowed the group to slowly extend its resource base to include many sources outside of official government control. This began in the early 1990s, when the government's decision to cut military expenditures threatened the economic position that IRGC members had gained during the Iran-Iraq War. What began as side projects in engineering and contracting morphed over time into effective "control of much of Iran's construction sector, oil industry, automobile manufacturing, and electronics," amounting to nearly a quarter of Iran's economy, perhaps more.[110] In addition to fostering support for the IRGC within the Iranian population and providing the IRGC with reliable sources of extra-governmental income, these enterprises provide critical resources for the IRGC's military activities.[111]

The IRGC's domestic economic clout complicates the investment environment in Iran and further inhibits foreign attempts at isolating Iran's civilian economy from the shadow economy of the ruling regime. Like many developing countries, Iran established free-trade zones to experiment with trade and capitalism in a controlled environment. The Supreme Council of Iran's Free Trade, Industrial, and Special Economic Zones contends that it created free and special zones to help

Iran make its mark in a globalized economy.[112] These zones, however, have also become centers for the illicit transfer of funds and goods by the IRGC and other groups. By allowing visa-free entry and exit and creating an environment free of restrictions on the transfer of foreign and Iranian currency, they allow for sanctions circumvention and ease weapons transfers, such as in 2010 when a company based in Kish Island provided material support and weapons to Hezbollah on behalf of the IRGC.[113]

Having learned from its experience enduring crippling sanctions, the Iranian government reacted to the withdrawal of the United States from the JCPOA by falling back on its "economy of resistance" policies, which promote domestic self-sufficiency. In his statement announcing the program during the last sanctions regime, Ayatollah Khamenei highlighted the program's aim to reduce unemployment, manage inflation, and increase Iran's economic dynamism to "stand up against the enemy's threats."[114] After years of sanctions that engendered a mindset of "economic jihad," the resistance economy would encourage a host of economic actors, inside and outside Iran.[115] Further, the plan would increase the autonomy of the Iranian economy and promote the development of a domestic human capital—all of which would reduce Iran's reliance on foreigners.[116]

Meanwhile, the IRGC has retained its central position in Iran's economy and has expanded its economic interests beyond Iran's borders. In recent years, the IRGC has continued to use untracked financial exchanges, known as *hawala* systems, to illicitly transfer money, extend the reach of its international automobile-manufacturing enterprise, and exploit Emirati free-trade zones to engage with the wider world.[117] The presence of IRGC-backed entities in UAE free-trade zones provides additional opportunities for Iran to monitor the development of UAE relations with the United States and other countries.

During the years of increased flexibility that followed the signing of the the JCPOA, the IRGC extended its influence in countries throughout the Middle East by providing funds, equipment, and training to armed groups.[118] Although the economic benefits of these activities are difficult to quantify, sums ran into the billions of dollars per country or organization.[119] Such sums, whether cloaked in a veil of charity or transactional, gave Iran significant leverage with target populations.

Although the JCPOA boosted Iran's economy, sanctions alone are not a panacea to the problem of Iranian soft power. Rather than halt its economic activities, sanctions have the inconvenient side effect of pushing Iran's economic influence activities into the shadows. Moreover, Iran has found ways to either circumvent the sanctions or to exploit differences between the sanction regimes imposed by different countries.[120] Through a web of shell companies linked to Iranian financial institutions, Iran has invested in real estate, acquired sensitive military equipment, and created clearinghouses to launder "charity" money for other purposes.[121] While sanctions introduce friction into Iran's economic activities, they are insufficient to counter its clandestine transactions.

Much like Iran's leaders have used religion as a pretext to develop relationships that may later serve a strategic purpose, so too have they understood the utility of economic relationhips. Yet because the United States has overlooked the role of these relationships in the long-term foreign policy goals of other countries, it has not allocated adequate resources to trace them.[122] As Paul Kennedy observed in *The Rise and Fall of the Great Powers*, ambitious economic reforms—especially when coupled with attempts to create autarky—eventually create opportunities for military revitalization and subsequently for challenges to the status quo.[123] Any future sanctions relief would provide Iran's leaders with the opportunity to expand its economy and also its unconventional and conventional military capabilities. It is hard to argue how such relief would inhibit the Iranian regime from pursuing its regional and international security goals and harder still to argue how these goals might align with those of the United States.

Military Shaping Operations

The softer levers of power chronicled in the previous section complement and enhance the effectiveness of military power, but they do not replace it. Effective shaping combines soft mechanisms of influence with the capability and capacity to use force.[124] In kind, the evolution of the strategic landscape shapes priorities and how capabilities are then employed. The strategic choices that Iran made in developing its military means and those that it supports by proxy hint at its security ends: protection of the homeland, undermining U.S. influence in the Middle East, elimination of Israel, and expansion of Iran's maneuverability throughout the region. To gain a more complete picture of Iran's security ends, however, one must also examine how Iran employs the means currently at its disposal.

Iran's inferior military balance as compared to the United States and its allies in the Gulf belies its regional ambitions.[125] Whether due to a calculation of its comparative advantages or to a predisposition toward low-intensity conflict, Iran has invested in systems that yield advantages in asymmetric combat, has supplemented with investments in missiles and, has opportunistically made copycat versions of Western technologies.[126]

Yet even if sanctions had not limited Iran's ability to modernize its conventional forces, regional developments over the past twenty years make investments in asymmetric capabilities a logical choice. America's toppling of Iraq, Iran's bitter enemy, reduced Tehran's need for a conventional deterrent and provided opportunities for Iran to test its asymmetric capabilities through support to Shi'a militia groups. Meanwhile, America's tendency to deploy large vessels to the Persian Gulf and Iran's inability to compete at that level of capability have led Iran to emphasize nimble, high-speed systems that create asymmetric advantage through operational ambiguity and flexibility.[127]

Iran has found similar advantages, as well as a modicum of deniability, through its support of terrorist and Shi'a militia groups throughout the Middle East. Internally, the IRGC's expanded presence in Iran's economy has provided the organization with the funds necessary to improve its capabilities and capacities. Externally, this has resulted in increased IRGC involvement with numerous organizations throughout the Middle East that share Iran's interests. Involvement with Shi'ite militias in Iraq and with Lebanese Hezbollah are the best known cases, but the IRGC also provides aid to Hamas, supports Shi'ite groups in Syria, aids the Houthis in Yemen, provides arms to Bahraini resistance elements, and recruits fighters in Afghanistan and Pakistan.[128] In addition to providing support in combat zones, IRGC trains favored militants in Iran and at satellite training facilities in Sudan and Lebanon.[129] As policy analyst Matthew Levitt has detailed at length, the organization has established transit points even further afield, from Latin America to Southeast Asia to Europe and, with Hezbollah, has attempted to establish sleeper cells to target American and Israeli interests abroad.[130] Although the effectiveness of Iran's efforts to gain a foothold in Latin America is debatable, mitigating its efforts requires a redirection of resources and cooperation that could serve other purposes.

Countering this extensive international network requires Iran's adversaries to expend resources to track, mitigate, and defend against present IRGC activities and to attempt to anticipate future ones. IRGC activities have become weaponized in their own right, even without the backing of an able conventional force. It's little surprise, then, that for much of the past twenty years Iran's conventional army, the Artesh, has faced neglect.

Iran's approach to naval forces mirrors the emphasis it places on asymmetric capabilities for its ground forces. During the Iran-Iraq War, in what has been called "the most sustained assault on merchant shipping since the Second World War," Iran attacked hundreds of merchant vessels to create economic and security impacts that extended beyond the conflict with Iraq.[131] In line with this approach, Iran has continued to focus on the development of asymmetric capabilities over conventional ones at sea. Rather than developing blue-water power-projection capabilities, such as with carriers or advanced destroyers, it has thus far poured its resources into developing midget submarines and speedboats.[132] Limitations on technology and equipment imports due to sanctions partially explain this decision. Yet as is the case with the IRGC's activities, an asymmetric strategy on the sea also projects power, although in unconventional ways.

The Iranian navy cannot match the firepower of the U.S. navy, but Iran's smaller vessels can outmaneuver American carriers and destroyers, which are better suited for high-end, conventional conflict. Leveraging a nimble fleet at quantity allows Iran to move in to and out of the range of American ships and test the boundaries of American resolve. Thus, the United States frequently finds itself needing to make high-stakes operational decisions that, if not executed carefully, could provide Iran with a public-relations win.[133] A U.S. miscalculation would lead at the very least to embarrassment: the 2012 incident in which the United States attacked an Emirati pleasure craft after mistaking it for an Iranian vessel, resulting in the death of two Indian men, and the 2016 capture of ten U.S. sailors who had allegedly entered Iranian waters are cases in point.[134] Instances such as these aid Tehran's attempt to frame itself as a victim of an overreaching America and undermine the American public's confidence in the efficacy of the U.S. security posture.

Iran's use of the military to shape perceptions is not limited to the naval domain. In February 2017, Iran launched a series of military exercises on the heels of President Donald Trump's warnings of a new round of sanctions.[135] Tehran framed the events as a show of defiance against the United States, which had recently put Iran "on notice" for testing a nuclear-capable ballistic missile. Yet when confronted by the United States and others for its behavior, Iran is quick to point out that it is merely seeking to defend itself from a system that has been set up to restrict the freedom of developing countries.[136]

Thus far, Iran has increased its influence while using asymmetric capabilities to deter and distract its adversaries. But while Iran will likely continue to develop its asymmetric capabilities, it will also need to develop conventional capabilities to fulfill its stated goal of becoming a regional power. Indeed, there are signs that this shift has already begun. In September 2016, Ayatollah Khamenei mentioned the need to invest in Iran's defensive and offensive military capabilities to better protect the Iranian homeland.[137] Subsequently, Mohammad Hossein Baqeri, chief of staff of the Iranian armed forces, echoed this more assertive posture, stating that Iran intends to establish naval bases in Yemen and Syria.[138] The mentions of offensive capabilities are noteworthy because Iran has long framed its international activities as defensive.[139]

In addition to a precision-guided-missile force, long-range air power, and close-support capabilities, Iran has also suggested that it would like to develop a blue-water navy. Whereas Iran has long used foreign systems to fill in knowledge gaps in its indigenous defense industry, the temporary lifting of sanctions under the JCPOA expanded foreign procurement options. It did not take long after the lifting of sanctions for Iran to showcase a domestic version of an S-300 surface-to-air missile system that it acquired from Russia, and its newest armored vehicle "fuses U.S. and Chinese tank designs."[140] The sophistication of Iran's indigenous defense industries is questionable, for now, but an influx of money and outside influences could change this.

In the future, a modernized Iranian military, combined with already formidable asymmetric capabilities and deep relationships with regional nonstate partners, could level the playing field between Iran and its regional adversaries. Adding nuclear capabilities to Iran's arsenal—hardly a foregone possibility in the medium to long term—would exacerbate Iran's tensions with the Gulf Cooperation Council (to say nothing of tensions with Israel) and raise the stakes of direct military confrontations. But given Iran's considerable investments in military and nonmilitary shaping activities, Iran may be on the path to achieving regional preeminence even without the acquisition of nuclear weapons. At least until Iran views itself as the dominant player in the Middle East, its self-perception as leader of the resistance will necessitate the continued use of asymmetric tools of influence.[141] The cyclical nature of Iran's reinvigoration and renewal, however, suggests that it will wage soft war in the future regardless of its relative level of power. The tools of soft war may simply be intrinsic to Iran's conception of international competition.

Conclusions

Iran is a case study in the importance of weighing nonmilitary factors when determining regional power balances. Despite two decades of sanctions, the country has used unorthodox and relatively inexpensive tools, from mass-media campaigns to clerical indoctrination and from strategic economic investments to relationships with proxy groups, to extend its reach. Yet the predisposition of Iranian civilization to extend its strategic reach using nonkinetic means is neither a product of the sanctions regime nor of the Islamic Republic. As described early in this chapter, Iran's political, economic, and cultural expansionism is a defining feature of its place in the world. Through successive cycles of reinvigoration, Iran has renewed both its regional status and the vitality of its civilization. That this process happens at the expense of Iran's adversaries is part of its genius and part of what makes it as applicable today as it ever was.

If Iran's power were to increase, its efforts to influence and mold the strategic environment to its advantage would likely become more pronounced. Moreover, if Iran's hard-power capabilities were to increase, its soft shaping activities would also become more difficult to counteract. Hard power lends credibility to soft-power efforts, and future economic gains would create more opportunities for Iran to expand its influence throughout the region. In modern times, Iran's aggressive pursuit of shaping operations has occurred from a position of weakness, yet the ambitions of the leaders of the Islamic Revolution suggest that future strategies may feature a more even mix of shaping and hard-power tools.

Time horizons represent the most important difference between how Iran and the United States approach international competition. As a millennia-old civilization, Iran's leaders realize that five, ten, even one hundred years may pass before the realization of its core strategic goals. Within this paradigm, it makes sense to invest in relationships and techniques that have little measurable payoff in the short term; to study, integrate, and then apply an adversary's most effective strategies; and to grow hard military power patiently so as to avoid direct conflict while the power balance is tipped against one's favor. Each of these steps would yield dividends if the requirement for direct military confrontation were to arise.

Throughout its existence, Iran has gone through several cycles of empire, defeat, and reinvigoration, but it has always endeavored to maintain its position as a key regional influencer and power broker. The presence of outside guarantors of security, first the United Kingdom and then the United States, has thus far limited Iran's regional ambitions. The recent uptick in the Gulf States' ability and willingness to defend themselves could mitigate the lack of an outside guarantor.

But the current situation in Iraq reveals that any premature withdrawal or reliance on partners before they are ready could have a dire impact on regional security. Presence is important, but so are the intellectual and material capabilities brought to bear. Understanding that shaping activities are endemic to Iran's conception of warfare and not simply a function of its current, relatively weak position is an important step in understanding what kind of adversary Iran has been and will continue to be.

3

China

Of all the case studies examined in this book, Chinese thinking on strategy and warfare dates back the furthest. Although the precise dates of the works that make up the canon of ancient Chinese strategic thought are unknown, *Six Secret Teachings* and Sun Tzu's *Art of War* date back to at least the fourth century BCE, possibly earlier.[1] Prior to the existence of many other civilizations, the Chinese were already codifying an advanced way of thinking about warfare.

Throughout its history, China has grappled with internal rebellion, civil war, and aggression from weaker and more powerful actors in its periphery. Rather than incorporating responses to each of these challenges into a comprehensive way of war, however, Chinese leaders have recognized the need to address different security threats with a variety of tools—not all of which involve violence. China's approach to strategic challenges, as Alastair Johnston observed, is "highly contingent," such that "the effect of an a priori ranking of strategic preferences is mediated by a powerful notion of absolute flexibility."[2]

Given the Chinese emphasis on strategic flexibility, is it possible to define a Chinese way of war? Several common threads run through Chinese military thought. Despite the continued emphasis on flexibility and adaptation, ancient Chinese military thinkers recognized the deep and mutually reinforcing linkages among domestic governance, military victory, espionage, deception, and diplomacy.[3] Sun Tzu's oft-quoted aphorism "the highest excellence is to subdue the enemy's army without fighting at all" implies that the Chinese prefer not to fight.[4] Yet Sun Tzu goes on to say that "the side that knows *when* to fight and *when not* to will take victory" [emphasis added].[5] An accurate reading of Sun Tzu thus reveals a different picture: certain victory is the only occasion that warrants engaging in combat.

The tumultuous early centuries of Chinese history demonstrated the value of strategic timeliness and its necessary precondition: preparation of the preconflict battle space. China did not coalesce under a single ruler until the Qin dynasty in 221 BCE.[6] Frequent internal clashes among warring feudal factions characterized the Shang and Zhou dynasties—the periods from which several ancient Chinese military texts derive. The tumult of these early years imparted an enduring prioritization on unity and order in Chinese society and established a rigid system of civil-military relations in which military thought was both idolized and made unavailable for public consumption.[7]

The ancient military canon contained another important lesson for practitioners: Advantages in size and quality of an army do not guarantee success in war. Rather, a multiplicity of factors that extend beyond the conventional battlefield—such as social cohesion, the ardor of one's soldiers, and success at outmaneuvering the enemy—determine the outcome of a campaign.[8] Molding the strategic environment to one's advantage and initiating the decisive battle at the opportune time were understood as the keys to success in warfare.

The concept that an object's potential emanated from its placement and interrelationship with other objects shaped ancient China's understanding of the world. This concept, known as *shih*, had applications to Chinese politics, art, architecture, and war.[9] In a military context, producing optimal shih required patience and planning to ensure that "disharmonies" within the state or the military's structure or morale did not prevent success.[10] The "strategic configuration of power," as shih has often been translated, could allow for victory against a superior foe or, conversely, defeat against a weaker enemy.[11] Ensuring victory thus required not only tactical acumen or clear linkages of ends, ways, and means but also the establishment of strategic advantage long before the outbreak of war.

The concept of shih arises throughout ancient Chinese military texts. Sun Tzu analogizes shih to "the onrush of pent-up water tumbling stones along" and likens efforts to analyze one's own shih to observing the "rolling [of] round boulders down a steep ravine thousands of feet high."[12] Modern descriptions range from those of Michael Pillsbury, who sees shih as a duality comprised of deceiving others to do one's own bidding and "waiting for the maximum opportunity to strike,"[13] to those of Chinese author Lin Yutang, who describes it as an aesthetic and philosophical notion of what a situation will become, as in "the way the wind, rain, flood or battle looks for the future, whether increasing or decreasing in force, stopping soon or continuing indefinitely, gaining or losing, in what direction and with what force."[14]

Taoist principles of balance and continuity and an understanding of the world as cyclical rather than linear underpin the concept of shih.[15] It manifests in a recognition of the interrelationships among people, places, things, and intentions; "the weather, terrain, diplomacy"; and "spies and double agents, supplies, logistics . . . intangibles of surprise and morale."[16] This lens renders outcomes dependent on incremental adjustments to one or more fundamental elements. Identifying the fundamental elements, understanding the relationships among them and their relative positions, and weighing their relative importance all contribute to the momentum that leads to a particular outcome.

Shih should not be thought of as a conceptual framework but rather as a philosophical understanding that informs Chinese culture, which includes the manner by which its military thinkers approach strategy. To the ancient Chinese military thinkers, attaining the optimal strategic configuration of things extended beyond force allocation. It involved the management and regulation of people—domestic and foreign, soldier and civilian—at the earliest possible instance. In Huang Shin-kung's *Three Strategies*, for example, the author tackles the dicey question of how to approach an equally matched opponent. To do so, he recommends winning over "the minds of the valiant" and "shar[ing] likes and dislikes with the common people," a clear recognition of the importance of public opinion in warfare.[17] *Questions and Replies between T'an Tai-tsung and Li Wei-kung* echoes this concept. In it, the discussants conclude that "attacking does not stop with just attacking . . . cities or . . . formations. One must have techniques for attacking minds."[18] In *Six Secret Teachings*, the discussants list twelve "civil offenses" that when "employed together" constitute a "military weapon."[19] These measures include diplomatic tactics, classic espionage techniques, and psychological manipulation measures designed to bend an enemy leader to one's will without engaging in combat. Thus, from a very early stage, Chinese thinkers understood the importance of social will in waging effective warfare, as well as the many tools available to leaders that circumvent the need for battle or increase the likelihood of success once combat becomes inevitable. All of these tools reflect the ubiquity and centrality of shih in warfare as understood by the ancient Chinese.

Some scholars have developed a literal interpretation of shih, in which it indicates a lack of willingness to engage in combat at all.[20] However, such interpretations overlook the psychological essence of shih, as evidenced by calls for mass readiness in the classic texts. By creating a deterrent and a means to achieve victory, these ancient mobilization initiatives affected the perceptions and will of the population under Beijing's control and on enemy forces alike. For example, in the *Ssu-ma Fa*—a fourth-century BCE guide to governance that focuses on "the problems of motivating men, manipulating spirit, and fostering courage"—the author argues that "authority comes from warfare, not from harmony among men." In a manner that would echo in the later teachings of Mao, he goes on to outline steps to succeed in warfare: first "solidify the people," then "analyze the advantages [of terrain]; impose order on the turbulent . . . nourish a sense of shame; constrain the laws; and investigate punishments." Sun Tzu, who maintained that the "best military policy is to attack strategies; the next to attack alliances; the next to attack soldiers; and the worst is to assault walled cities," provided concise guidance for the relative place of combat in competition with adversaries.[21]

To the ancient Chinese, military policy encompassed a wide range of tools, of which combat was only one. In ancient times as now, however, attacking strategies and alliances alone would not always result in desired policy ends. Neither combat nor violence is entirely separable from strategy. At the operational level, some argue that the Chinese tended to resort to violence more often than Sun Tzu's aphorisms would suggest.[22] This makes more sense when one considers the paramount emphasis placed by classical Chinese military thinkers on flexibility and adaptability. To them, there was no one-size-fits-all approach to warfare. The ancient texts imply that the level of effort placed on attacking strategies and alliances is adjustable to different types of enemies.[23] Whereas a high level of effort would be placed in these stages against a more powerful or equal foe, China's historical behavior indicates that violence occurs much more quickly against weaker enemies.

The geographic and strategic milieu of ancient China provides context for the thinking of the ancient military strategists. At the dawn of Chinese civilization, the Han Chinese occupied the fertile plains among the tributaries of the Yellow and Yangtze Rivers. Natural barriers surround this area: ocean to the east, mountains to the west, jungles to the south, and deserts to the north. However, these areas also harbored other groups of people, many of whom were hostile to the Han. Moreover, the sedentary and agrarian characteristics of Chinese civilization stood in contrast to those of the nomadic and tribal groups that surrounded it, leading to constant insurgent attacks against the Han's pastoral homeland. The relationship with other settled groups, including those across the Yellow Sea such as the Japanese, did not gain strategic significance until much later.[24] For most of its existence, China remained the most powerful entity in the region; the civilizations of the Near East and the West posed little threat to this order.

To mitigate the threat that these groups posed to China's heartland, the Han would ultimately incorporate the western deserts of Xinjiang, the southern jungles bordering Burma and Thailand, the semi-tundra of Manchuria, and areas to the north beyond the Great Wall in their country. Each of these acquisitions created strategic depth or prevented the procurement of resources by other powers.[25] Outright acquisition of these lands did not occur until the nineteenth century or later, but China long exercised influence in these regions by means of force and diplomacy.

The Song dynasty (960–1127) marked the beginning of a golden age in Chinese technological development: gunpowder, the compass, and printed books were invented during this period.[26] Yet because the influence of Confucianism also reached its zenith at this time, intellect began to supplant militarism as the preferred tool for solving China's conflicts with its neighbors. The advent of the bureaucratic examination system created a powerful class of civil servants, and consequently, the military began to decline in influence.

Some twentieth-century Western historians interpreted the rising influence of Confucian thought among the Chinese elite during the Song dynasty as creating a pacifistic approach to international relations that explains modern Chinese behavior.[27] Later scholarship, however, has refuted this interpretation, claiming that the primary source material used in earlier arguments painted China's approach to its neighbors in overly rosy terms.[28] As Yuan-kang Wang describes in his deconstruction of these theories, the Song dynasty appeared pacifistic because it needed to shore up its power base in advance of the inevitable conflict with its more powerful northern neighbor.[29] Confucianism, he demonstrates, did not manifest a pacifistic nature. Rather, it served as a means to solidify morale, achieve victory through economy of force, limit the use of force, and develop strategies that reestablish the natural balance of world affairs. Similarly, grand fortifications were not built primarily for reasons of frontier defense but rather as a means to manage the contrasting nomadic and sedentary ways of life present along the outer limits of Chinese civilization.[30] As Wang later states when reviewing Chinese security posture under the Ming dynasty (1368–1644), "defense became the chosen strategy only after China had lost the capability to launch offensive campaigns."[31]

Viewed differently, China had simply developed a system for minimizing threats and dividing potential challengers to its power. Beginning in the Han dynasty (206 BCE–220 AD) and on through the nineteenth century, China used the *tributary system* as a principle tool to manage its affairs with lesser powers.[32] This structure placed China at the center of the known world and relegated lesser powers to a vassal position. The system entailed the provision of gifts to the Imperial Court in exchange for access to trade and, in some cases, the promise of protection.[33] Read by some as evidence of China's preference for soft power over hard power, the tributary system created a framework for China to influence the internal affairs of other countries and also for the Sinicization of nearby territories.[34] Further, it helped China minimize threats to its hegemony and territorial periphery.[35]

Much debate surrounds the purpose and nature of the tributary system, which provided numerous benefits to vassal states.[36] By definition, however, vassal states acceded to China's position as the region's dominant power and thus relinquished the option to challenge that order. For China, the vassal arrangement unlocked a mechanics of influence that helped to perpetuate its position. The vassal system ensured a reliable flow of trade that benefited both parties, but China could also use the system to "mollify foreign states" and thereby eliminate "external pressures by adopting a conciliatory position" instead of mounting a military campaign.[37] The tributary system allowed China to undermine or co-opt coalitions of potential opponents, thereby weakening their ability to rebel—a logical approach for a nation that had long contended with asymmetric threats to its power.[38] Chinese regional dominance precluded vassals from viable alternatives to this structure.

Ming China's position as the region's unquestioned hegemon understandably bestowed great benefits on it. It helped China "maintain foreign relations, preserve a dominant position in East Asia, and maintain peaceful borders."[39] It also positioned China as a central destination and source for the trade of international goods, via transcontinental roads and also via sea. Although China had long traded with proximate neighbors such as Japan via sea routes, this era saw the voyages of Zheng He, a military commander who expanded China's interests beyond East Asia, into the Indian Ocean, and as far away as eastern Africa.[40]

China

The goal of preserving Beijing's unquestioned authority sustained the tributary system and the trade network on which it was based. Sometimes, as the military confrontations in which Zheng He and land forces engaged during the period show, demonstrating that authority required the use of force.[41] Although China ultimately prevailed against Japan during the latter's invasion of the "model tributary" state of Korea in the late sixteenth century, its tepid victory was a sign of China's overextension and a harbinger of the times to come. Without a credible deterrent, tributary states would have fewer incentives to provide Beijing with favorable trade terms, much less allow expansive influence in their own foreign affairs.

Overextended and overly confident in the perpetuity of its power, China failed to adapt to changing international and domestic dynamics. Its power relative to other civilizations, including the increasingly persistent Europeans, thus declined. Its inferior grasp of technology and its sclerotic governance system hindered the flexible responses advocated by the ancient military thinkers. In addition, domestic troubles began to chip away at China's internal stability. An interlinking confluence of events—including famine, runaway inflation, internal rebellion, and an influx of European goods on Chinese markets—led to the end of the Ming dynasty in 1644.

Violence and chaos throughout China marked the collapse of the Ming dynasty, which resulted in the rise of the highly militaristic Qing dynasty. In addition to numerous conquests, this period saw the deliberate militarization of Chinese culture, which would lay the groundwork for the advent of Chinese nationalism that would follow the dynasty's collapse.[42] Echoing earlier aphorisms about the importance of fortifying domestic support for military conquests, Qing rulers endeavored to create the "appropriate cultural environment" to support imperial power. Taken at face value, the period of expansion and consolidation that followed serve as an important counterpoint to modern arguments that all of China's wars have been defensive in nature. Even if one accepts that the conquests of the Qing period were a form of preemptive defense, they demonstrate China's past willingness to resort to violence when alternative methods of control and influence failed to produce the desired results. Yet it is also noteworthy that, particularly in the later years, many of these conquests resulted in failure. Internal unrest further distracted Beijing from realizing its ambitions, and the arrival of European powers further complicated regional dynamics. The Qing dynasty is thus rightly remembered as the beginning of China's period of humiliation and subjugation to outside powers.

The years that followed the collapse of the Qing dynasty would see the rise of European modes of thinking transposed into a Chinese context. Early Chinese adopters of nationalism, capitalism, and communism interpreted each ideology through the lens of the ancient thinkers. As Chinese leaders in each school of thought emerged, they also drew from the teachings of the ancient military classics, as evidenced in the teachings of Mao Zedong in particular. Based on these lessons, China would slowly rebuild its once-formidable security apparatus and reclaim its position as a significant military and economic power.

Contemporary Competition Short of War

In 1911, the Qing dynasty fell, ending two thousand years of Chinese imperial rule. The empire had grown weak, and when it fell at the hands of philosopher Sun Yat-sen and his revolutionaries, it was only a shell of its former glory.[43] The Chinese imperial system had survived many periods of relative weakness in the past, but there were other factors at play this time. In particular, the permeation of Western ideas among the Chinese people generally and in coastal areas especially produced rapid changes to China's economic and political outlook, dynamics to which the Qing rulers failed to adapt.[44] These factors aided in the rising influence of competing gov-

China

ernance paradigms that appealed more to the emperor's subjects, elites in particular, than did the imperial system.

Although Sun Yat-sen's revolutionaries were instrumental in ending the monarchy, they ultimately lacked the military strength to consolidate power over the entire country.[45] As a result, after the ouster of the last emperor in 1912, China descended into a period of martial rule, dominated by fragmented warlord states. In this chaotic milieu, Western ideas began to permeate more deeply into Chinese society, as evidenced by the May Fourth Movement in 1919 and the subsequent establishment of the Chinese Communist Party (CCP) in 1921.[46] These competing governance paradigms would lead to intense internal strife in the decades to come.

The resulting clashes between the Kuomintang (KMT) and the CCP again thrust China into a period of turmoil. Sun Yat-Sen's successor, Chiang Kai-shek, launched the Northern Expedition in 1926 with the aim of reunifying all of China under KMT rule. This sparked a civil war between the nationalists and the communists that would not conclude until 1949. The Japanese invasion during the Second World War led to alliances of convenience at various times between the KMT and the CCP (as well as with the Soviet Union), but the surrender of the Japan in 1945 forced the reemergence of differences between the two parties. The KMT retained much of the military power and control of many of the urban centers at the end of the Second World War, but war against the Japanese had exhausted its forces. Having garnered the support and tutelage of the Soviets, the CCP managed to push KMT leadership to retreat to Taiwan by 1949. The CCP then founded the People's Republic of China (PRC) in Beijing, and the KMT continued to lead the Republic of China from its base in Taiwan.

The KMT's exhaustion was not the only reason for its loss of the mainland. Although both the nationalist ideology of the KMT and the Marxist ideology of the CCP had roots in

Western thinking, the CCP proved more adept at translating its ideology into a movement of mass appeal.[47] Sun Yat-sen's three guiding principles of nationalism, democracy, and "people's livelihood" marked a reconceptualization of, and evolution from, the Confucian principles underpinning China's dynasties.[48] Sun, educated in the West, presented his principles as a mixture of Chinese traditional thinking and Western ideas. But the principles nonetheless remained ill-defined enough for both Chiang Kai-Shek and Mao Zedong to claim fidelity to them.

Chiang's and Mao's different interpretations of the three principles manifest in their approaches to economic development, the lack of which, both leaders agreed, prevented China from achieving independence from foreign powers. Both Sun Yat-sen and the KMT saw the road to development through cities. The KMT also saw foreign investment as a necessary, if temporary, tool to promote concentrated industrial development.[49] Mao, on the other hand, concentrated on appealing to the masses of Chinese agrarian peasants, particularly those in the countryside. Unlike the KMT, he eschewed foreign investment altogether.[50] Further, Mao argued that the rural peasantry (instead of the industrial proletariat, which dominated Western iterations of communism) would serve as the movement's vanguard.[51] Both parties promoted variations on socialism, but Mao's emphasis on the rural population gave him a distinct numerical edge.

Faith in the inevitable arc of history drove Mao's approach to warfare, governance, and economic development. He consistently ordered his priorities sequentially: at a grand strategic level, for example, he advocated focusing first on military morale, then on social morale, and only then on expelling the enemy.[52] His reading of Carl von Clausewitz's observation that "war is a continuation of politics . . . by other means," unlike readings in the West, appears to emphasize the *separation* of politics and war. In this view, war becomes the outcome of

China

failed political processes, rather than an option to attain political objectives at any point of a leader's choosing.[53] Sequencing is also evident in his writings on battlefield strategies: first, gain the support of the population through propaganda; next, focus on gaining control of the countryside; only then concentrate on nodes of power, such as cities.[54]

Mao's populist emphasis is also evident at the operational level of his theorizing. In navigating the complexities of fighting a civil war and a foreign power simultaneously, for example, Mao placed particular importance on guerrilla warfare.[55] The people, unified through propaganda and militarized though a "popularization of military knowledge," would provide the backbone of forces for "the people's war," supported by a guerrilla military that simultaneously progressed into a regular army.[56] After first securing the countryside, he advocated for the encirclement of the enemy's power bases. Then, having made necessary preparations to ensure victory, his army would deal the enemy "a crushing blow," replenishing his army's resources with looted material.[57] Mao saw Chinese way of war as distinct from those pursued by other nations—informed by uniquely Chinese heuristics and at once population-centric, deliberate, and only reluctantly pursued.

Echoing the concept of shih developed by his ancient Chinese forebears, Mao saw conventional kinetic conflict as only the final and most violent phase of a competition whose outcome was decided long before war began.[58] In a speech that has contemporary antecedents in Chinese behavior, he likened international competition to the act of eating a fine meal: one should focus not on the entirety of the meal but rather on each bite, "it is impossible to swallow an entire banquet in one gulp."[59] To Mao, the inevitable progress of history occurred sequentially and deliberately, requiring patience and calculation on the part of the vanguard. It could occur only after the realization and weaponization of the military and the realization of popular support, whether in the preparatory phase of war or in battle after political processes have failed.[60]

Mao struggled to bring reality in line with the clear strategic vision he had set for China. Despite Beijing's early attempts to forge a closer relationship with the United States, the North Korean invasion of South Korea resulted in the Truman administration's renewal of support to the Taiwan-based KMT, eventually leading to the first Taiwan Strait crisis in 1954.[61] As the situation in the Korean peninsula continued to deteriorate, Mao faced the prospect of war with the much more powerful United States. Though reluctant to become involved in Korea, Mao continued to monitor the conflict, all the while preparing the Chinese army for the worst contingency.[62]

As the prospect of an American presence along its northern frontier represented an unacceptable level of strategic encirclement, China intervened in the Korean conflict in October 1950.[63] In line with the thinking of ancient Chinese strategists, Mao's generals constructed operational plans that centered on deception, surprise, and numerical superiority that exploited the overextended position of the American military.[64] The ensuing offensive succeeded in pushing UN and American forces south of the 38th parallel, but the relative backwardness of the Chinese military prevented Mao from achieving a decisive victory.[65] His decision to stand up to the "imperialist" United States established China as a power in its own right that, though lagging behind the West technologically, could nonetheless mobilize its population and employ shrewd strategic thinking to protect its interests not only within its territory but also along its periphery.[66]

During the remaining two decades of his chairmanship, Mao focused on economic and cultural developments in the Chinese mainland and further sought to cement China's independence. As China scholar John Fairbank notes, Mao's rebuilding process echoed Chinese historical patterns of collapse, new beginnings, and rebirth, and also reinvigorated the traditional

Chinese conception of "a single authority coterminous with civilization," a state-based economy, and an orthodox doctrine for governing all human activity.[67] A lack of national resources and the devastation brought about by internal initiatives, such as the Great Leap Forward of the late 1950s and the Cultural Revolution of the 1960s and 1970s, stymied the evolution of China's strategic approach.[68]

As the People's Republic of China found its economic and international footing under Mao's successor, Deng Xiaoping, its strategy began to evolve beyond the people's-war doctrine advocated for by Mao.[69] Continued tensions with the Soviet Union prompted the People's Liberation Army (PLA) to reassess longstanding doctrine and devise plans to modernize its aging equipment. Though many viewed these initiatives as limited to nuclear warfare, Beijing reconfigured its deterrence posture at every level of the escalatory spectrum.[70] By the early 1980s, China had either moved away from the concept of people's war or prepared its military to fight a people's war in "modern conditions."[71] Either way, economic and technological constraints prevented the full realization of Beijing's modernization plans.

With the disillusion of the Soviet Union in the early 1990s, the Chinese military found itself at a strategic crossroads.[72] On one hand, threats to China's strategic interests stood at a modern-era nadir. Still, the economic reforms implemented by Deng Xiaoping finally provided enough wealth to support significant investments in military modernization. Although senior Chinese military leaders refrained from discussing their thoughts publicly, Western analysts began to notice an evolution in Chinese military doctrine, such as the refinement of a "flexible response" approach to nuclear deterrence and, though aspirational at the time, a noticeable orientation toward technical aspects of power, such as "air and naval power projection . . . electronic countermeasures, information warfare, antisatellite weapons," and "laser and precision-guided weapons."[73]

As China grew more powerful, its skepticism of the Western-led world order grew.[74] In the PLA and Chinese society writ large, an increasing sense of nationalism tested the CCP's commitment to pursuing a conciliatory path in the international sphere.[75] Nationalist angst manifested in antipathy toward Japan, which was still detested because of its invasion of the Chinese mainland five decades prior, and the United States, which faced increasing criticism following the accidental bombing of the Chinese embassy in Belgrade in 1999.[76] Despite these developments, China joined the World Trade Organization in 2001, a decision heralded as evidence of the "near universal acceptance of [the] rules-based" international system. As time would show, this landmark decision did not equate to a principled commitment to the post–World War II world order.[77] Rather, China understood that its position of relative weakness necessitated temporary accommodations to the prevailing international system.

Old Techniques, New World Disorder

As China's political and economic outlook evolved in the 1990s, Chinese leaders undertook reforms of the nation's military doctrine and its conception of international competition. As keen observers of the U.S. military, the PLA noted the evolutionary technology employed at the time by the American military, particularly during Operation Desert Storm.[78] In the United States, Operation Desert Storm heralded a revolution in military affairs (RMA), a new era of weaponry and capabilities, of precision-guided missiles, of Shock and Awe, in which technological advancements had obviated the need for high casualty counts in warfare.[79] American analysts saw this revolution as an unassailable assertion of ingenuity and strength. The conclusions drawn by Chinese observers differed.

For one, the PLA observed that the central premise of war no longer consisted of forcing an enemy to submit to one's will through the threat and use of violence. The American RMA signaled a shift to a more limited—in terms of violence—but also more comprehensive—in terms of employable means—method of "forc[ing] the enemy to serve one's own interests."[80]

It was not so much the advanced systems used by the United States in Iraq that impressed the Chinese but rather the coordination of a wide variety of weaponry. Rather than approaching battle through traditional lines of attack, the new technologies allowed for a selective engagement with targets unlike any before seen in the history of warfare. This allowed for casualty minimization, which the United States saw as more humane though China perceived as a weakness.[81] Whereas Chinese military leaders would place their troops in unwinnable circumstances simply to bring out their bravery, America's conception of war now sought to spare its soldiers from encountering direct combat at all.[82]

In other words, the Chinese recognized that the decisive factors of war were shifting from the realm of the physical battlefield to the virtual, from the realm of the strategic to the informational, and from the realm of soldiers to the populations of a globalized world.[83] Warfare would become less lethal but also more pervasive, less restricted by geography but also more precisely targeted. In this new warfare, intangible resources such as political will, psychology, international law, and financial mechanisms would become weapons as important as the most expensive and advanced military equipment.[84] In this conception of unrestricted warfare, in which war occurs across an unlimited number of domains, order derives from limited objectives rather than the limits of a battle space. Violence does not become unnecessary but rather shifts from the focal point to a detail, a coda to a much larger and comprehensive system of international competition.

Although the United States ushered in this new form of warfare, America did not, from the Chinese perspective, comprehend the implications of the shift. This disconnect created opportunities that played to China's advantage: its comparative military weakness could be overcome through the subtle manipulation of circumstances across an increasing number of domains. To the Chinese, the United States obsessed over technology for technology's sake or, perhaps, to minimize casualties. Either way, Chinese military leaders were puzzled by America's tendency to acquire new systems without first defining how they would satisfy specific strategic and tactical requirements.[85] They echoed their ancient predecessors in observing that, although the means of victory may have shifted from the killing of soldiers to achieving information superiority, the fundamental nature of war would not change: wars are won through incisive strategy and tactics, not through technology alone. China would now endeavor to attain victory by employing all available means to achieve limited and well-defined interests.[86]

In studying the United States and its military, Chinese strategists realized that the United States still had vulnerabilities that stemmed from its power. Because it encountered enemies from a position of strength, the United States grew to assume that it would be able to set the terms of its encounters with its enemies. However, as the terrorist attacks of September 11, 2001, revealed, this had led to weaknesses in defense and, more intractably, a lack of response mechanisms to address asymmetric threats. China recognized the outsized psychological impact that terrorist attacks caused as compared with the relatively minimal amount of effort employed to conduct them.[87] Such attacks were both modern embodiments of ancient strategies and emblematic of how wars would be fought in the future.[88]

Lessons and observations from prior decades influenced Chinese observations of America and its revolution in military affairs, particularly within the PLA. As Andrew Scobell detailed in his analysis of Chinese strategic culture, the Chinese perceived the United States as possessing an expansionist and amoral approach to warfare, which contrasted to China's "defensive" and principled approach.[89]

The historical record, however, bears out a certain amount of flexibility with the term *defensive* on the part of the Chinese. Since the time of Mao through the rest of the twentieth century, China framed and rationalized its military actions in terms of *active defense*, a concept flexible enough to apply to nearly any scenario.[90] Though China, according to Scobell, viewed the United States as an expansionist and hegemonic power, capability gaps rather than pacifism limited its ability to constrain the proximate activities of America and its allies.

As the aughts turned into the twenty-teens, China, emboldened by a decade of explosive economic growth, finally had the means to restructure its military and security apparatus to match the thinking of PLA generals. Chinese strategic culture, with its traditional emphasis on unconventional tools of warfare, was ideally suited for a brand of international competition less dependent on killing. In the years to come, China began developing equipment, such as precision-strike capabilities and unmanned aerial systems, that would bolster its ability to compete in casualty-averse modes of warfare.[91] Meanwhile, *net-centric warfare* further distributed war fighting into the realm of the internet, another bloodless—yet increasingly central—realm of competition. The Chinese could draw on the strategic frameworks set forth by their ancient forebears to integrate revolutionary technologies and new tools into a twenty-first-century approach to warfare.

The "Three Warfares"

The rapid military modernization and improvements in human and economic capital in China during the past twenty years have dramatically expanded the possible power configurations available to Beijing. Western analyses of China's economic and military rise have largely focused on indexes of growth and future technological capabilities. Yet, to Beijing, these developments are not as important in isolation as they are in relation to one another: the propensity, or shih, inherent in its new position provides the greatest opportunity. Recognizing this, and consistent with the concept of active defense, the PLA devised a plan to achieve dominance in each realm and escalatory phase of international competition. In 2003 the PLA released a new concept document that provided guidance to precondition "key areas of competition" to China's favor.[92] The document outlines three separate lines of effort, or warfares, that, when pursued in tandem, amount to the application of ancient theories in a modern, connected, and integrated context. If there were any doubt about the PLA's level of seriousness with respect to these approaches, a more recent PLA document, the 2013 *Science of Military Strategy*, equates the importance of noncombat uses of military power with kinetic warfighting.[93]

The three warfares include psychological warfare, media warfare, and legal warfare. Psychological warfare demoralizes a population and conditions it to accept specific changes to the status quo, whether in security arrangements, social norms, or economic circumstances.[94] Through media (or public-opinion) warfare, public-diplomacy efforts create favorable opinions within the elite and broader segments of target populations. Legal warfare manipulates international and domestic law in a manner that advances national interests.

Before delving into each of the warfares, several points are worth emphasizing. First, this work will treat each line of effort separately, but the success of the three warfares lies at the intersections among them—each is an interdependent element of a paradigm that maximizes opportunities to gain strategic advantages short of armed conflict. Second, the three warfares are not a substitute for military modernization but rather amplify the effectiveness of noncombat modes of competition. Third, the PLA has clearly stated the targets of its three warfares as

China's domestic audience, the global public, South China Sea claimants, and the United States, which dispels the narrative that Beijing seeks to find its place in the preexisting international system rather than pursue policies to disrupt it.[95]

Fourth, China has a formidable and experienced bureaucracy to implement the three warfares concept. The People's Liberation Army has overseen a component responsible for the waging of political warfare, or "liaison work," since the 1930s, and the General Political Department (GPD) of the PLA, in concert with counterparts in the Ministry of State Security, has expanded its aims to include implementation of the three warfares across the four target populations.[96] The three warfares are thus supported by the full complement of powers within established military and party organs, not just a specific unit or specialty within them.

Lastly, the three warfares do not reflect new ideas so much as indicate a revival of the ideas of ancient Chinese thinkers applied to contemporary circumstances. The approach reflects the timeless Chinese tendency to leverage a position to maximize future advantages across a number of conditions and operational levels. In the words of Sun Tzu, "in battle, there are no more than 'surprise' and 'straightforward' operations, yet in combination, they produce inexhaustible possibilities," an aphorism that remains as useful and relevant today as when those words were written in the fifth century BCE.[97]

Examining the application of the three warfares illustrates these points. Although the three warfares have global applicability, each of the four main audiences targeted through the concept have populations, military deployments, or territorial claims in the seas off the coast of China. Examining how China operates toward countries that have a significant interest in the future balance of power in the East and South China Seas—including Taiwan, Japan, Korea, Southeast Asian states, and the United States—provides a window into the multifaceted approach that China takes toward applying this concept.

In keeping with the Chinese emphasis on shaping the battlefield long before the outbreak of overt conflict, psychological
operations influence enemy perceptions of the international
balance of power. The most pervasive of the three warfares,
psychological warfare blends wisdom from ancient thinkers
with the tools and deterministic outlook of Marxism as understood by Mao.[98] Whereas China views the West as employing psychological operations as a means of "promoting . . .
hegemonic strategy, which is designed to create turmoil and
divisions within other countries," China views its psychological operations as a means of "spreading truth and justice . . .
and of exposing the enemy's plot to confuse, corrupt or pen-
etrate China's mental space."[99] Chinese psychological operations have both offensive and defensive mechanisms, chosen
depending on the relative strength of the target. These mechanisms include presenting one's own side as just, emphasizing one's own advantages, undermining the opposition's will
to resist, encouraging dissension in the enemy's ranks, and
neutralizing the psychological operations of other actors.[100]
In practice, these activities are all designed to create leverage
points within target populations.

Although it is tempting to think about Chinese psychological warfare as a distinct discipline, it is more useful to recognize it as a dimension to Chinese behavior across a range of
mediums, from military-force positioning to economic policy. Revealing its own antisatellite capabilities, positioning
forces on contested islands, threatening the restriction of visa
applications, and defending state sovereignty in international
forums all have psychological impacts on foreign perceptions
of China. By crafting the perception that its ambitions are foregone conclusions, Beijing can shape opinions—in both public and policymaker circles—before they develop into policies
that would harm China's interests.

As the original target of Beijing's political warfare, Taiwan is arguably on the receiving end of China's most fervent psychological warfare campaign.[101] A 2016 conference in Taipei on the subject, held under the Chatham House Rule, revealed many contemporary examples of Chinese psychological warfare aimed at Taiwan's government, military, businesses, and population intended to reinforce the "1992 consensus" on the existence of one China with separate governments. Although this consensus has increased predictability and stability in relations between the Chinese mainland and Taiwan, it has also had pernicious effects. By expanding and formalizing political and economic ties across the Taiwan Straits, Beijing has increased the mechanisms through which it can wage psychological warfare against Taipei.

The Taiwanese have long feared the leverage that Beijing would gain if Taipei become economically dependent on the mainland. Yet in the run-up to the 2008 election, Ma Ying-jeou made a convincing case about the merits of closer ties between Taipei and Beijing that helped him win that year's election. Soon after his victory, President Ma began the unprecedented reestablishment of the Three Links, consisting of economic, transport, and postal connections between Taiwan and the mainland. Beijing and Taipei negotiated an increase in the number of approved tourist visas, moving the number of annual mainlanders in Taiwan from 250,000 in 2008 to more than four million by 2015.[102] Later agreements established formal trade links, which opened eighty Chinese sectors and sixty-four Taiwanese sectors for cross-strait competition by 2013.[103]

The economic boost foretold by Ma did come to pass, mainly from tourism and, to a lesser extent, from increased trade.[104] But the economic boon also created openings for mainlanders to infiltrate Taiwan under the guise of tourism or business activities, contributing to what had become a "total permeation" of the PRC into Taiwan's intelligence and technical infrastructure.[105] The opportunities for political and psychological leverage created by increased economic ties were more than fortuitous; they were deliberately planned by the CCP.[106]

The effects of Taiwan's attempts to bolster ties with the mainland created avenues for Beijing to influence Taiwanese morale and resolve that outlived the Ma administration.[107] The additional pressure points established through the Three Links became apparent soon after the 2016 election of Tsai Ing-wen, whose Democratic Progressive Party has advocated Taiwanese independence in the past. In addition to harassing Tsai in the lead-up to the election via aggressive social-media trolling, Beijing also restricted the number of Chinese tourists allowed to visit Taiwan, amounting to a 16 percent reduction in mainland visitors from 2015 to 2016.[108] During a trip to the PRC, mainland handlers fed Taiwanese scholars misinformation that Beijing had given up on peaceful unification and was planning to launch a cross-strait invasion in the coming year. This information was then broadcast upon the scholars' return to Taipei, amplifying what was otherwise a minority opinion on the mainland.[109] Because the impact of these activities is a function of threat perceptions, the combination of a growth in influence opportunities through the Three Links and increased military capabilities has greatly influenced the potency of psychological warfare activities against Taiwan.

Taiwan is not the only country to contend with the balancing act between security and economic interests vis-à-vis China. The demise of the Trans-Pacific Partnership has removed a powerful counterbalance to the voluminous share of trade between China and other nations in East Asia and has reinforced Chinese rhetoric regarding its increasingly pivotal role in international trade. Beijing's increased regional economic leverage has left Japan, South Korea, and other Southeast Asian nations carefully weighing their responses to Chinese security provocations, to the point where, during field research interviews conducted by the author from 2015 to 2016, many would only discuss Chinese activities on the condition of anonymity. Although these interviews revealed anxiousness toward China's increasingly assertive behavior, many also indicated a growing acquiescence or ambivalence about China's activities among regional populations. Many raised questions about the reliability of the America's presence in the region and expressed a growing awareness of the need to develop strategies for countering China that were independent of American involvement.

In Japan, for example, multiple officials described a reluctance to perform freedom-of-navigation exercises in international waters claimed by the Chinese, saying that doing so would risk an unacceptable level of conflict escalation. For its part, China's repeated incursions into Japanese waters have reflected its "borderless" mentality while conditioning the Japanese population to accept its activities as a new normal.[110] In other words, China's naval activities have created an *expectation* of Chinese incursions, regardless of how illegal they might be. In a similar vein, China's unilateral declaration of an air defense identification zone (ADIZ) in the East China Sea in 2013 challenged Japan's claims to the disputed Senkaku Islands while also "amplify[ing] the fears and anxieties" of the Japanese people and "destabiliz[ing] the legal reasoning of Japan and other international powers with respect to China's claims in the East China Sea and elsewhere."[111] Although historic animosity between Japan and China may limit the power of Chinese psychological warfare against the Japanese population—China's disapproval rating with the Japanese public reached 86 percent in 2016, according to Pew—mixed messages from America regarding its willingness to curtail Chinese behavior may exacerbate Beijing's psychological warfare efforts, as would any increased economic linkages between Japan and China.[112]

South Korea faces a similar, if not more urgent, predicament as Japan due to North Korean provocations and China's relationship with the Pyongyang. Reliant on the United States for security, South Korea has nonetheless entertained building stronger relationships with Beijing for the better part of the past ten years.[113] Although working with China on strategic matters "makes little sense" while the Democratic People's Republic of Korea (DPRK) remains a security threat to South Korea, China's ability to increase or reduce pressure on Pyongyang through its trade and foreign direct-investment policies reaches far beyond the borders of the Hermit Kingdom.[114] South Korea cannot discount this factor when deciding whether to pursue policies that might anger China.

Whereas China must prod and test defenses and incrementally change perceptions of the status quo with its northern neighbors, power imbalances to the south enable China to unilaterally mold the security environment to suit its interests. China's island-building activities in the South China Sea provide a case in point: none of the competing claimants could challenge China's behavior on their own, and American inaction reinforced regional perceptions about Beijing's hegemonic claims over the region.[115]

Beijing's overtures to Vietnam and the Philippines demonstrate the opportunities created by America's abdication of leadership in the region. Although relations between Beijing and Hanoi and between Beijing and Manila remain rocky owing to repeated territorial and resource disputes in the South China Sea, the Chinese-led Regional Comprehensive Economic Partnership may prove tempting to Hanoi, Manila, and other Southeast Asian states.[116] The demise of the Trans-Pacific Partnership has countries throughout the region considering alternative trading partnerships, and China has proven willing to fill the gap. The Belt and Road Initiative, though overhyped in terms of the financial gains it provides Beijing,[117] nonetheless creates the impression of China's rising prowess. Participation in any of these trade arrangements will create economic linkages that, however temporary, would prove hard to replace if they disappeared.[118]

While people in the United States tend to view psychological operations as the purview of a small cadre of military officials, psychological factors loom large in China's grand strategy. Attention to psychological conditions permeates China's economic, military, and diplomatic actions on the international stage. Although the specific tools are flexible, a single string ties these disparate activities together: the manipulation of shih for the strategic benefit of Beijing.

Media, Public Opinion, and Information Warfare

Media and public-opinion warfare compliment and add to the effectiveness of psychological warfare. Contemporary PLA thinkers have furthered Mao's recognition of propaganda's utility through the use media platforms for peacetime messaging to create Confucian harmony in an increasingly unequal society.[119] It is little coincidence that the four main goals of Chinese propaganda—to "tell China's story," to counter hostile foreign propaganda, to counter Taiwanese independence proclivities, and to promote awareness of China's foreign policy—align with the goals of the three warfares more generally.[120]

The narratives tied to these overlapping themes differ depending on context. Domestically, the state produces and supplies major broadcast-network content, allowing for significant leeway in manipulating and censoring the information environment in ways that benefit the CCP.[121] Outside its borders, Beijing tailors information warfare to suit its strategic ends with respect to specific scenarios. Whereas in Southeast Asia the Chinese military might use state-run outlets to threaten military action against smaller nations, China employs a subtler strategy toward more powerful nations, often combining military and civilian strategic information campaigns to supplement the targeting of political elites behind closed doors.[122] As the following cases demonstrate, China's information-warfare efforts shape public and elite opinion in ways that allow Beijing maximum maneuverability and flexibility on the global stage.

MEDIA, PUBLIC-OPINION WARFARE IN PRACTICE

Examining China's ability to influence the information environment within its borders provides insight into how Beijing might approach media and public-opinion warfare under ideal conditions. China's domestic media market is the largest in the world, as is the size of its population with internet access.[123] Yet as China's interaction with the outside world has increased, the CCP has also sought to balance censorship and economic growth or, as one author put it, to "maximize the benefits and minimize the risks" of the "growing interaction between Chinese and global discourses."[124] The domestic-propaganda line thus complements the line intended for foreigners: at home, Beijing promotes CCP values and suppresses criticism of government policies; abroad, it seeks to extend the influence of Chinese culture, businesses, and security interests.[125] Both narratives encourage harmony and pride in China's domestic audience, allowing Beijing to direct additional resources toward its foreign-policy and security goals.

The Chinese government has a vast communications infrastructure available to communicate its messages, and it closely monitors the public's interaction with these platforms. The CCP primarily distributes its viewpoints to the public via Xinhua, its official news agency, and its products are then broadcast through the "big three" mouthpieces: China Central Television (CCTV), China National Radio, and China Radio International. The CCP also possesses a number of bureaucracies that spread favorable information through cultural institutions, to the party rank-and-file, and within the military.[126] It controls many newspapers, such as the influential *People's Daily*; newsletters; the state educational system; indoctrination squads, charged with delivering messages to specific populations; and a system of loudspeakers that reach every sizable village and neighborhood within China's borders.[127]

The Chinese internet, although tightly controlled with respect to content from outside China, provides a platform for state-sanctioned search engines, microblogging platforms, and social-media outlets. The Chinese population also has access to more than one thousand individual television channels, to professional publications, to city newspapers, and to entertainment tabloids—many of which have no direct connection to the CCP.[128] In this sense, the Chinese government has allowed the market to determine the supply of content, but only for materials that bear no threat to the established status quo, such as some entertainment media and popular-level publications about science and military matters.[129]

For more sensitive matters, the government employs both active and passive measures to control and manipulate content generated by its own population. Active measures include censoring and the various message-delivery vehicles previously mentioned, and passive measures include internet content filters and local reporting programs. In addition to a wide variety of technical tools, the CCP employs an army of "internet opinion analysts" to police content: as early as 2013, it employed two million citizens in this role.[130] Although unprecedented in scale, these capabilities are similar in character and pervasiveness to those used by past authoritarian regimes, from which the CCP gleaned and adapted many of its methods.[131]

The CCP's thinking about how, and to what end, to use this power has evolved from distributing Marxist leaflets to facilitating the transmission and creation of a flexible narrative that enlists the public as a central participant rather than just a target.[132] Embracing social media has been key to this shift in the CCP's thinking. Superficially, social media is a natural tool for a quasi-Communist organization. The premise of social media, which provides individuals with opportunities to deepen links with like-minded individuals online, aligns well with Mao-ist goals of empowering the population to achieve its collective destiny. Yet social media is also useful for other reasons: with the resurrection of the "mass party line," the CCP also uses social-media platforms to distract its population from a governance style that bears increasingly little resemblance to Maoism.[133] In addition to enlisting the population to perpetuate the ideas that, whether practiced or not, form the backbone of the CCP's rhetorical claim to authority, social media and robust public conversation provide the CCP with a means to monitor ordinary citizens.[134]

Despite copious investments in communications infrastructure and technology, the CCP has had less success influencing media directed at foreign audiences. Much of these difficulties center on the Chinese press's lack of credibility among foreign audiences.[135] A Chinese journalist stated in 2011 that "if the Chinese people no longer trust the *People's Daily*, the New China News Agency [Xinhua], and CCTV, why should people elsewhere be expected to trust them?"[136] A British study of Chinese media penetration in England found that English university students receiving a degree in China studies did not use CCTV for news coverage and used it in only limited quantity for Chinese history or culture, suggesting a high degree of skepticism about the quality of Chinese-funded news media.[137] Yet because the main target audiences of China's foreign propaganda are Taiwan, Hong Kong, and Chinese-speaking populations abroad, the credibility of Chinese-run media outlets among a wider population may be beside the point: Chinese speakers will know that the organizations reflect policy priorities that will impact their communities, whether the message is credible when compared with other sources or not.[138]

China's covert attempts to influence narratives among elites and target populations abroad, especially in its near abroad, have enjoyed more success.[139] To affect public audiences, Beijing uses techniques similar to those used by Russia to pollute the information environment.[140] Disinformation campaigns allow Beijing to circumvent the lingering credibility problems of its state-run institutions while also avoiding attribution and extending a message's reach. Toward elites, Beijing has used economic incentives and its image as a protector of sovereign rights to persuade countries to accede to Beijing's priorities. Coordination of these activities through China's comparatively streamlined command-and-control apparatus allows Beijing to conduct political warfare, or "the logical application of Clausewitz' doctrine in a time of peace," against its adversaries.[141] Depending on the nature of the information challenge, Beijing may combine propaganda, subversion, perception management, influence operations, extensive investigations, disintegration work, "friendly contacts," and psychological operations into a cocktail of capabilities that are infinite in their deployable permutations and rapidly adaptable to changing circumstances.[142]

As an acknowledged target of Beijing throughout the world, Taiwan provides a useful window into China's techniques. With respect to disinformation, Beijing has long taken advantage of the cultural and linguistic ties that it shares with Taiwan to undermine local faith in democratic institutions, "exacerbate divisions between political parties" and within civil society, and "raise suspicions of treasonous intent" toward former military officials in order to wound national morale.[143] Such campaigns feature broadcast-news segments and print stories sympathetic to Beijing's outlook through state-backed and independent media outlets.[144] They also extend beyond the media into civil society, such as through economic pressure placed on individuals and businesses with interests on the mainland, a group that has grown in size significantly since President Ma's Three Links.[145]

Elsewhere in East Asia, China issues threatening statements and leverages its economic clout to communicate the risks of going against Beijing's wishes. When South Korea decided in July 2016 to allow the deployment of American THAAD launchers on its soil, for example, Beijing responded with a number of punitive measures, including the delay of exports, pressure on Korean businesses, and the abrupt cancellation of a planned celebration for the twenty-fifth anniversary of China–South Korea diplomatic relations.[146] Although such actions may seem superficial to outside observers, they activate and enflame the large segment of the population that views cooperation with China favorably and create pressure on leaders to acquiesce to Beijing's wishes.[147]

Closer cooperation among East Asian states, when outside a China-centric framework, has also resulted in punitive actions by Beijing. Although the United States has long sought closer bilateral cooperation between Japan and South Korea, especially with regard to North Korea, China has typically viewed such arrangements with suspicion. When Seoul and Tokyo passed the long-delayed General Security of Military Information Agreement (GSOMIA), for example, China assessed that it would only "aggravate antagonism and confrontation on the peninsula."[148]

Through a Western lens, many of the actions in this section would not fall into the category of "media and public-opinion warfare." The integrated, overlapping, and mutually reinforcing nature of each of the three warfares, however, demands a systems-analysis approach that considers how actions taken by Chinese leadership affects perceptions and decisions of target populations across a host of issues. One may not consider the construction of islands in the South China Sea an act of media warfare at first glance, for example. Yet the very act of flouting international law for security gains sends a message to regional publics and populations that typical constraints may not deter China from expanding its influence. It would be fair to expect that capitals across the region and in the wider international community would note Chinese behavior and take it into account in their decision-making processes. Although in many ways another form of information warfare, China's behavior in international legal regimes deserves separate treatment.

For international law to carry weight, a sovereign nation-state must calculate that the benefits of abdicating some authority to international bodies outweighs the costs of diminished control over international disputes.[149] This view of legal authority, itself an extension of the concept of the social contract, has no direct analogue in Chinese views on jurisprudence. Thus, despite China having signed many treaties recognizing supranational influence over the conduct of some aspects of its foreign-affairs agenda, Chinese views on the purpose of law are in perpetual tension with the relinquishment of sovereignty implied by the existence of international law. Although the precise manner by which China defines sovereignty is a subject of considerable debate, the most important question may be whether Beijing believes that sovereignty should extend to other countries, particularly ones it perceives to be within its orbit, at all.[150]

The development of Chinese legal thought over the centuries suggests a broader understanding of *sovereignty*, at both a societal and international level, than exists in the West. Confucianism and Legalism, two schools of thought developed during the Warring States Period (475–221 BCE), serve as the foundation of Chinese legal thinking. Both frameworks predate the social contract and certainly the development of international legal regimes. Confucian thought held that "long-term order could only exist under a single ruler," precluding the possibility of interstate relations between coequals, as conceived by Western thinkers.[151] Confucianism thus recognizes, even idealizes, the authority and sovereignty of the state, but—in zero-sum fashion—treats the existence of external authorities as a perpetual threat. In contrast, Legalism focused on the attainment and "consolidation of absolute power."[152] Although considerable debate existed between the two schools, both held that sovereignty could not truly exist in the presence of coequal powers that could challenge one another's authority. Both schools of thought also emphasize the instrumentality of law, that is, its use as a tool of social control, in contrast to the modern Western view of the *rule* of law.[153]

Maoist thinking expanded on these themes, extending the instrumental view of law to the realm of ideology.[154] Because a view of law as a constraint on authority never developed in China, legal tools became a logical way to promulgate ideology within the state and eventually beyond it. In 1996 Jiang Zemin recognized the legitimacy of using international law as a "weapon to defend the interests of [the Chinese] state," and PLA officers were instructed to not view international law as a constraint on their actions.[155]

The West has also used law in an instrumental fashion, a fact that was not lost on Chinese observers.[156] PLA officers observed that being "the first to set up regulations" allowed America in particular to raise the practice of legal warfare to a "fine art."[157] They further observed the manner in which the United States used its prominent position in the United Nations to build international support for military actions that were, from Beijing's standpoint, merely an expression of American interests.[158] Thus, by the early 2000s China viewed itself lagging behind the West in the use of law as a source of authority in international affairs.

As China's capabilities and resources expanded, it has become more assertive in implementing Jiang's recommendations. Even before its entry into the World Trade Organization, China exhibited disregard for internationally recognized intellectual-property laws, which weighed down Sino-U.S. relations.[159] By 2009, using a pre-Communist document as a pretext, China submitted the "nine-dash line" map, which essentially claimed the entirety of the South China Sea as sovereign Chinese territory.[160] As the recent development of military facilities on islands in the South China Sea indicates, China's participation in international legal regimes creates opportunities to advance its interests in concert with the two other warfares while creating the false impression that it intends to recognize the authority of, or abide by, international law.

LEGAL WARFARE IN PRACTICE

The official adoption of the three-warfares construct in 2003 marked an expansion of Chinese efforts in the international legal realm, in both ambition and capacity. Whereas many countries would view legal warfare as the purview of diplomats, the primary responsibility for legal warfare in China resides with the military.[161] Many, if not all, of the PLA's lawyers work in the General Political Department's legal bureau, enabling close coordination with sections of the GPD responsible for psychological and information warfare.[162] This arrangement has facilitated the incorporation of legal considerations into every decision relevant to preparation of the battlespace, from interactions with international institutions and the legal regimes they oversee to decisions about force disposition, commerce, and bilateral diplomacy. Regardless of the realm of international law in question—whether maritime, aviation, space, or cyber—the aim of this coordinated approach to legal warfare is the same: to provide legal justification for actions that advance sovereignty rights and that "mitigate possible political repercussions of China's military actions."[163]

In maritime disputes, China has used questionable interpretations of international law to advance its interests in the East and South China Seas. Many of its arguments hinge on its historic use of specified areas, first-use principles, and geology, rather than on prevailing definitions of territorial suzerainty provided in legal regimes such as the UN Convention on the Law of the Sea (UNCLOS). Using historical maps and pretexts from domestic legislation, China builds a narrative that its claims, particularly in the South China Sea, predate and supersede the jurisdiction of international maritime law.[164] China also seeks to undermine UNCLOS jurisdiction over its claims on philosophical grounds, calling for an interpretation of the law that reflects "non-hegemonic, non-American forms of global governance"—ostensibly to better incorporate China's own views of sovereignty on the high seas.[165]

Thus, despite being party to the treaty, China repeatedly questions whether UNCLOS jurisdiction applies to its claims. In the lead-up to the recent South China Sea tribunal decision, for example, China preemptively dismissed the ruling as "null and void," as "having no binding effect on China" and claimed that the tribunal's decision "eroded the integrity and authority of UNCLOS."[166] China took this position despite having agreed to the specific UNCLOS provision that places the ultimate decision in the hands of the arbiters, not the parties involved.[167] The legal validity of the argument, however, turned out to be less important than the Chinese government's persistence in communicating it. A global diplomatic and media campaign resulted in forty countries—many of which maintain deep and vital economic links with Beijing—expressing their support for China's position.[168]

In a statement before the U.S.-China Economic and Security Review Commission, a U.S. Navy attorney characterized China's position as hinging on two questions: whether China will claim sovereignty over land features in the South China Sea and whether it will exercise "jurisdictional rights" related to its claim, which would afford it additional control over the seas near the islands.[169] This analysis illuminates the multistep process in which legal mechanisms build on each other, possibly leading to a transformation in the perception and reality of regional security dynamics. China might first seek small wins based on jurisdictional technicalities, and then build on them to expand its authority over targeted territory, such as

China

through expanded exclusive economic zones or increased control over proximate sea lanes of communication.[170]

Because China's actions are frequently designed to build support for Beijing's preferred narrative rather than to win any argument in international tribunals, other countries often have little choice but to acquiesce to Beijing's demands, particularly when Beijing refuses to accept a court's findings.[171] Thus in the most recent spat over South China Sea claims, China's refusal to accept the court's ruling left the Philippines with the choice of directly confronting China militarily, attempting to exert pressure through its then-tenuous relationship with the United States, or accepting a new status quo.[172]

As the South China Sea case demonstrates, China employs legal warfare to lay a foundation for actions in other realms of international competition. Legal steps provide a mechanism to test international and adversarial responses, at which point other mechanisms may be used to further strategic ends. In the South China Sea, for example, after questioning the jurisdiction of UNCLOS, China began building atolls in the Paracel Islands to cement its position vis-à-vis Vietnam, which also holds claims in the area.[173] Originally claiming that the islands were for civilian use, China ultimately outfitted the larger of the islands with harbors, helipads, airstrips, and surface-to-air missile batteries.[174] Thus, after assessing the willingness, or lack thereof, of the international community to challenge its actions, Beijing extended its military capabilities into a contested area, thereby raising the stakes for any state or international court that may wish to challenge its claims in the future.

The arena of international aviation provides another example of legal warfare's utility for gauging international reactions to transgressions of the status quo. In November 2013 China unilaterally claimed an ADIZ over a wide swath of the East China Sea, including over the disputed Senkaku Islands.[175] In establishing the zone, Beijing cited security concerns and pointed to the use of ADIZs by other nations around the world, including the United States. In addition to requiring that aircraft passing through the zone identify their affiliation and purpose—ostensibly to provide a buffer for Beijing to identify and prepare for unspecified airborne security threats—the zone provided an additional legal mechanism for China to bolster its claims to the disputed Senkaku Islands.[176] Neighboring countries and the United States have largely ignored the zone. As the Chinese have begun to refer to the area as sovereign airspace, however, the zone could be used to justify retaliatory measures against foreign aircraft.[177] In other words, the ADIZ gauged international reaction to an audacious Chinese claim, bolstered preexisting claims to exclusive use of the area in the air and on the water, and provided the basis for future military actions.

Legal warfare has also been used to achieve strategic gains in emerging security realms such as space and cyberspace. The question of whether and to what extent international laws covering terrestrial conflict should apply to cyberspace has remained inconclusive since the inception of the internet. For outer space, the applicability of these laws has remained inconclusive for decades. In the meantime, world powers have developed contrasting approaches to the militarization of each domain. The ongoing legal limbo on conflict in cyberspace and outer space provides ample opportunity for legal maneuvering and holds potential consequences for the utility of international law in regulating international conflict.

For instance, UN principles of the right to self-defense are at least extendable to the keystone text for the international legal regime governing activities in space, the UN Outer Space Treaty.[178] Some argue that activities in space are also subject to international humanitarian law and other regimes that codify internationally agreed-on conduct of states in warfare.[179] Presumably, this would include the International Law of Armed Conflict, which limits when nation-states may engage in war with each other. Legal regimes such as these have driven many decisions on the potential militarization of space, even though space as a field of war was the stuff of science fiction at the time of their adoption.[180]

One main point of departure in international conceptions of the militarization of outer space revolves around the nature of systems that fall outside the jurisdiction of preexisting treaties, namely conventional, or nonnuclear, weaponry. The United States characterizes the activities of its military in space as exclusively nonaggressive, whereas China initially adhered to a more narrow interpretation of international law that limits activities in space to peaceful purposes.[181] During the 1990s, China noted America's increased reliance on space-based systems for communications and, increasingly, for the delivery of precision munitions.[182] Unlike the United States, Beijing saw little difference between aggressive action taken *in* space and aggressive action taken *via* space. Given this interpretation of events, ramping up the development of space-based technologies made strategic sense for Beijing, a pursuit made possible by its increased capabilities.

Although Chinese rhetoric on space in the 1990s implies a dovish outlook about the subject, concurrent and subsequent conversations in the Chinese military paint a different picture. The legal points of departure between China and the United States sparked debate in Chinese military leadership about how to advance Chinese interests in what they characterize as the "fourth territory" of conquest (in addition to air, land, and water).[183] The rough consensus that appears to have won out is that space should be considered as part of warfare in an informationized environment, meaning that it should be thought of as an additional realm of competition among states and one that China should seek to dominate.[184] Chinese behavior in space thus facilitates and intensifies the effectiveness of multiple lines of efforts, including the three warfares generally and legal warfare specifically.

The human and economic interactions in cyberspace are far more varied and voluminous than in outer space, but the legal regime for cyberspace is at a much earlier stage than space law.[185] The lack of mutually accepted terminology, norms, priorities, and relationships among national governments has created an environment that encourages countries to pursue independent policies that conform to their own interpretations and interests. Some countries have argued that national sovereignty should extend into cyberspace, as evidenced by a proposal submitted by China and other members of the Shanghai Cooperation Organization that would "extend . . . notions of sovereignty and territorial integrity to the digital space."[186] This approach contrasts with that of many Western nations, including the United States, which consider the cyber domain as outside the realm of national sovereignty and as a vehicle for the open exchange of ideas and commerce.[187] Additional areas of divergence include the applicability of international law to the cyber realm, including the Law of Armed Conflict, and the perceived attainability and desirability of international standards for the governance of cyberspace.[188]

In each of these cases, China has argued for policies that allow for increased levels of state sovereignty, which has had important implications for both domestic and international cybersecurity policy. On the domestic front, in 2017 China passed a revised cybersecurity law that outlines a host of restrictive requirements applicable to any and all persons and businesses operating in China.[189] In addition to limiting the transfer of "sensitive" knowledge—broadly defined and including information belonging to private firms—outside China, the law also calls for the protection of "critical information infrastructure" undergirding a wide variety of fields from energy to finance, public services, and e-governance.[190] Because the law is applicable to foreign firms as well as to Chinese nationals, it supports China's international claims to state sovereignty in cyberspace and isolates information that, in much of the rest of the world, would be part of the public domain.

When one considers the fact that China views warfare as increasingly in the realm of information, the leverage gained by Beijing's domestic internet policies has serious implications for future conflicts in cyberspace and beyond. Underscoring the centrality of cyberspace to China's conceptions of future warfare, the deputy chief of the General Staff of the Chinese military stated in 2013 that "in the information era, seizing and maintaining superiority in cyberspace is more important that seizing command of the sea and command of the air were in World War II."[191] Because China does not recognize the applicability of the Law of Armed Conflict in cyberspace, its view of proportional responses are opaque, as is its understanding of the delineation between military and civilian targets.[192] Although the norms and legal regimes governing international cybersecurity are still evolving, China has already begun to consider how to position itself to succeed in future cyber conflicts.

In practice, legal warfare has become a central means for China to achieve strategic ends. Whereas the United States has yet to incorporate legal mechanisms into a comprehensive approach to national-security challenges, its capacity to do so far exceeds that of China.[193] The sheer number of lawyers in the United States as compared with China and the level of specialization in the profession represent a formidable and underused resource for waging legal warfare in both commercial and diplomatic matters. Further, as China has noted, the fact that the United States helped to establish current international legal norms gives it a distinct advantage in using legal mechanisms to counter Chinese behaviors. Yet the United States and its allies have not yet devised a way to build from this position in a manner that would protect its position in the international order or that would at least constrain China's revisionist behavior.

America's failure to take the three warfares fully into account in its strategy toward China has created numerous opportunities for China to gain strategic advantage without resorting to overt conflict. Despite closely monitoring military and capabilities modernization in China, the United States' has failed to account for the additional ways that these tools may be used in a highly informationized environment. Quite simply, the United States is overlooking a fundamental shift in the relative decisiveness of the factors of warfare, one that was largely of its own making.

Military-Shaping Operations and Modernization

The evolving application of power discussed in the prior section is all the more concerning given the rapid development of modernized systems, capabilities, and doctrine in the Chinese military. Components of the PLA and its naval and air force have recently undergone a massive reorganization designed to make Chinese forces more adaptive to naval and air threats.[194] An expanding "gray fleet" of coastal patrol vessels and fishing boats augments modernizing naval forces, enabling China to project power further from its mainland. Meanwhile, China has reformed its approach to cyber warfare, including the creation of the new Strategic Support Force within the PLA.[195] In addition to utilizing internet-based tools of information warfare, the new organization centralizes cyber engagement to align tools with the larger needs, requirements, and goals of the Communist Party. China's military-modernization efforts, especially when considered jointly with knowledge gleaned from cyber espionage, are beginning to close the technological gap that has long separated China's capabilities from those of the United States.

Cyberwarfare and "Information Supremacy"

China's recognition of the central importance of information dominance to international competition has led to increased investments in tools and organizations for waging cyber warfare and espionage. Although an important component, the output-based psychological and information warfare described earlier in this chapter represents only a fraction of the much larger effort to attain informational dominance in cyberspace. In addition to using surveillance and information-control strategies domestically, China is developing new technologies and organizational models to obtain information from, and wield power over, the networks of adversaries both near and far.

The emergence of cyberspace and outer space as focus areas for the Chinese military has important strategic implications, especially for deterrence. Rather than being treated as separate disciplines, as is the case in the West, cyberspace and outer space are thought of as components of what the PLA has referred to as *integrated strategic deterrence*.[196] This concept recognizes the increasingly contested nature of cyberspace and outer space and folds nuclear and conventional forces into a wide-reaching defense system designed to deter adversaries in each realm of international competition.[197] Yet the PLA also recognizes that the "diversity of understanding" of deterrence concepts in cyberspace and outer space limit the extent that China should rely on deterrence alone in these realms.[198] Instead, China exploits the lack of mutual international agreement on what constitutes an act of aggression in cyberspace to experiment with hostile and provocative acts.[199]

Meanwhile, China has taken advantage of the fact that its norms of behavior in cyberspace differ from those espoused by the West. The Chinese government, quasi-independent cyber militias, and China-based independent hackers have pursued an aggressive stance in cyberspace; these actors frequently avoid blowback because of the difficulty of tying specific actions back to the Chinese government.[200] Actions originating from China range from the relatively benign phishing, malware, and denial-of-service attacks to more sophisticated operations such as GhostNet, an intelligence-gathering network discovered in 2009 that infected upward of 1,300 computers worldwide.[201] Following several years when the number of cyberattacks and espionage operations originating in China decreased, cyberattacks originating from China had ramped up once again by 2018 as competition over telecommunications infrastructure increased.[202]

As Beijing's primary target, Taiwan shows the potential of Chinese cyber-operations pervasiveness. Chinese cyberattacks have provided Beijing with near total informational awareness of some of the most sensitive inner workings of the Taiwanese government and political parties.[203] Such infiltration allows for the application of information-warfare techniques in otherwise trusted circles, undermining the credibility and effectiveness of governing institutions. Techniques to achieve control include sophisticated phishing campaigns, or "cyber missiles," that arrive as malware-laced messages written in idiomatic, full-character Mandarin.[204] Even if officials do not respond to such campaigns or if defenses prevent unwanted intrusions, the mainland's attempts to test the strengths and weaknesses of Taiwan's networks are relentless: a former Taiwanese government official with a background in information technology reported that the mainland launches "hundreds of thousands, perhaps more" new computer viruses at Taiwan every day.[205] In addition to testing defenses, these efforts convey that resistance is ultimately futile, degrading morale and increasing the chances of acquiescence to Beijing's aims. Thus, the attacks have psychological impacts as well, undermining the perception of, and commitment to, independence from the mainland within Taiwan's population. Other institutions in Taiwan also suffer from persistent Chinese intrusion attacks.

As another named target of China's three warfares, America has also been extensively targeted by Chinese cyber operations, particularly with respect to sensitive technological and personnel information. Prior to the public cyber rapprochement between Xi Jinping and then-President Obama, well-documented Chinese cyber intrusions generated a stream of stolen intellectual property.[206] Some of the most audacious incidents include the formation of hacking rings aimed at stealing information from American national labs, attacks against the U.S. Department of State, the breach of sensitive U.S. Office of Personnel Management personnel records and U.S. Navy data, and the pilfering of blueprints for the F-35, America's flagship fifth-generation fighter jet.[207] Such activities had an estimated multibillion-dollar impact on the U.S. economy and an immeasurable impact on U.S. national security.[208]

The cybersecurity agreement between China and the United States during the Obama administration likely resulted in a short-term attenuation of Chinese cyberattacks against the United States, but the short-term gains that the United States may have made from entering into the agreement contrasted with the long-term benefits that China received. As the platform underlying what China has reimagined as "informationized warfare," cyberspace does not represent to China its own discipline so much as a new realm for applying time-tested strategies.[209] In a 2000 paper published on the application of information operations in the internet age, Chinese analysts listed ten different stratagems that would lead to information supremacy. The stratagems, which rely heavily on deception and the establishment of latent capabilities, include concepts such as thought-directing, intimidation, "all-encompassing deception," and information contamination. The overall goal of applying these stratagems, according to the authors, is to dissuade an enemy from launching information attacks "in order to achieve objectives without direct fighting."[210]

The stratagems not only echo the thinking of ancient Chinese strategists but also are applicable outside the information realm. Although this volume treats efforts in cyberspace separately from the modernization initiatives taking place elsewhere in the Chinese military, China treats them as part of a single package of deterrence and deception. The question of whether China has decreased active intrusions into American systems is thus less relevant than how it is integrating the ability to do so into its longer-term military strategy.

Modernization of Chinese Armed Forces

Although Chinese strategists across time have emphasized the superiority of achieving strategic ends without fighting, they also recognized the importance of a formidable fighting force. China lagged Western and regional powers in capabilities and reach for much of the nineteenth and twentieth centuries. China's economic growth in the twenty-first century has allowed it to rapidly modernize its armed forces and narrow or close previous capability gaps. Modernization initiatives have changed the regional balance of power by shifting military-capability balances vis-à-vis China's adversaries and amplifying the impact of the three warfares. Considering both of these dynamics together is essential to understanding how China has come to challenge aspects of the international order.

Over the past twenty years, China has pursued modernization initiatives across a broad spectrum of military capabilities and has pursued "sweeping organizational reforms" designed to enable flexible and rapid responses to a wide variety of threats.[211] Military-equipment upgrades and capability enhancements have augmented structural reforms to enhance China's position in the informationized conflict environment. Capability enhancements have extended Beijing's ability to defend its territory, enforce the one-China status quo, and project power both near and far. China's rapid military modernization thus changed the extent to which its adversaries— real and potential—are willing to challenge, reject, or accede to Beijing's demands.

STRUCTURAL AND STRATEGIC REFORMS

For all the observations of the U.S. military and subsequent discussions of how to transform the armed forces to better compete in an informationized environment, the structure of the Chinese military has changed little since the 1990s. In November 2015, however, Chinese President Xi Jinping outlined concrete steps that will allow the armed forces to respond with increased agility across a number of domains.[212] These changes take the Chinese military from a mainland-defense posture to one with the potential to conduct "active defensive" missions along the country's periphery with increased swiftness.[213]

The ongoing structural reforms, codified in a 2015 white paper and largely implemented by 2020, seek to improve command and control in the armed forces. Currently organized into regions, the reforms realign the PLA command structure into theaters or joint commands,[214] which enhance cross-service coordination and address the lack of uniformity in systems, doctrine, and approaches that existed prior to the country's dramatic economic transformation. The integration of ground forces throughout each of the services in China previously obviated the need for joint commands; however, the recent reforms also call for establishing a separate PLA Army to oversee ground operations. To better coordinate command and control among all services, the reforms establish clear lines of authority in the Central Military Commission, thereby enhancing the CCP's ability to ensure doctrinal uniformity across the theaters.[215]

The reforms extend beyond the military realm to directly address civil-military relations, which in China have long been characterized by a "bifurcation between civilian and military elites."[216] Dubbed *civil-military integration*, these reforms call for "uniformity in standards" between military and civilian infrastructure, technology, and industries. They also increase cross-fertilization between military and civilian educational institutions in part to "boost awareness" and create a common understanding of the national defense among general and elite populations.[217] Lastly, they call for increased connections between civilian and military efforts in the space, sea, and air domains and for "shared use" of mapping, navigation, and other national resources. These efforts, which build on Xi Jinping's successful anticorruption campaign, further consolidate power in the CCP while weaving nominally civilian efforts into national-security endeavors.[218] This dissolution of civil-military boundaries would also enhance efforts to compete in the informationized space, which overlaps considerably with work performed in the civilian domain.

In terms of strategic thinking, much of the white paper remains unchanged from prior versions. Along with the National Security Law passed around the same time as the revised white paper, however, the text indicates that Beijing intends to prioritize capability development in the maritime, space, and cyber realms.[219] Indeed, China has continued to develop its capabilities in these three realms and has made advances in applying three-warfares techniques to achieve strategic gains outside overt conflict. If implemented, the structural changes will enhance China's credibility by augmenting these efforts with new hard-power capacities.

Meanwhile, China has demonstrated that it will continue to seize strategic advantage in its "new" focus areas.[220] After the publication of its prior military strategy in 2012, China pursued an aggressive stance in the South China Sea, launched countless cyberattacks, and continued to modernize its weaponry. Rather than exceptions to a period of restraint, these developments fit a pattern of incremental expansion that dates back at least to the 2003 PLA document detailing China's "key areas of focus."[221] Rather than heralding a new era in Chinese strategic approach, modernization and structural changes will enhance the effectiveness of lines of effort that are already well underway.

SERVICE-SPECIFIC MODERNIZATION AND REFORMS

For the first time in more than a decade, the 2015 military strategy reiterated China's "no first use" nuclear-weapons policy.[222] Although seemingly innocuous, the timing of the inclusion suggests an attempt to assuage international concerns about China's nuclear-force modernization efforts. For the past ten years, China has progressively diversified its ground-based nuclear weapons holdings, a "trend that has continued" since the release of the 2015 military strategy.[223] In addition to developing an updated version of its nuclear medium-range mobile ballistic missile, China also developed a dual-capable intermediate-range mobile ballistic missile, tested a new version of its intercontinental ballistic missile, modernized various airframes, and upgraded the Second Artillery Corps, which oversees ballistic missiles, from an independent branch to the full-service PLA Rocket Force.[224] China still appears to store nuclear warheads and missiles separately, although some in the military have called for China to change this policy and take a more aggressive stance.[225] The increased flexibility and survivability of China's ballistic-missile force complicates escalation dynamics with its adversaries and, particularly with Taiwan, will require additional investments in defensive measures to counter.

Ground forces are undergoing a similar transformation from a relatively static force to one prepared for "transtheater" mobility.[226] In addition to structural changes that facilitate greater interaction among PLA Army divisions, the PLA has outfitted its ground forces with advanced equipment to enhance command, control, and communication in combat and has continued to bolster its rotary-wing component and precision-guided munitions capabilities.[227] The largest in the world by personnel count, China's military has long been criticized for its focus on quantity over quality. Yet ground-force exercises held over the past several years indicate recognition that internalizing change, whether technological or structural, takes practice. To erode the static emplacement of specific capabilities that has long prevented agile threat responses in the PLA ground forces, recent exercises have focused on cross-theater mobilization. Other exercises have focused on live fire for artillery and air-defense brigades to test real-time communications and targeting software.[228] The technology and doctrinal reforms demonstrated by these capabilities will add to Beijing's ability to respond to ground crises in a manner consistent with their informationized conception of modern warfare. The successes of these measures will improve not only Beijing's ability to counter agile adversaries, such as the insurgent groups near China's eastern frontier, but also its ability to counter more sophisticated adversaries.

Historically, China has emphasized ground-forces power more than maritime power. This has changed in recent years. The most recent defense white paper calls for abandoning the "traditional mentality that land outweighs sea" in strategic importance, including calls for the PLA Navy (PLAN) to expand its attempts to boost power-projection capabilities and to consolidate its ability to influence littoral environments near and far.[229] Although China's slow development of aircraft carriers has received much attention—Beijing has commissioned two, both with capabilities inferior to Western carriers—the PLAN's concurrent modernization of other maritime power-projection capabilities warrants greater concern.[230] In addition to developing "surveillance and precision-strike capabilities [that] put at serious risk Western surface ships, large military aircraft, and arguably any land system," China has bolstered its expeditionary capabilities through humanitarian missions and projected power off the coast of Africa using destroyers.[231] When considered alongside China's rapidly modernizing submarine fleet and the establishment of remote naval bases, such as one formed in Djibouti in 2017, the PLAN has devised means of projecting influence in nontraditional yet potentially highly effective ways.[232] Ultimately, these capabilities may obviate the need to develop sophisticated carriers for high-seas power projection, particularly to counter the United States.[233]

China has developed ways of countering its adversaries in the East and South China Seas that challenge prevailing ways of thinking about the naval balance of power. Like those of its neighbors, China's Coast Guard is an integral part of the nation's active defense. It takes on roles in disputed territories that blur the line between military actions and those of a nominally civil defense force.[234] The Chinese Coast Guard penetrated the territorial seas of the Senkakus, for example, an average of seven to ten times per month between 2012 and 2015, but in such an irregular pattern as to confuse any retaliatory response.[235] The establishment of Chinese military outposts on artificial islands in the South China Sea and elsewhere add additional complexity to the line between civil and active defense.

Vessels of the "maritime militia" have proved even more difficult to counter, as they frequently serve a primary role as civilian fishing vessels and are staffed with civilian volunteers who have received training and direction from the Chinese government.[236] These vessels are particularly useful for clandestine surveillance but could also be outfitted with military-grade weaponry. The use of fishing and coastal-defense forces for military purposes has a storied past in the history of warfare.[237] But in an environment of informationized warfare, a bout with a nominally civilian vessel could have dire consequences for the attacker, and the sheer size of the Chinese fishing fleet could overwhelm a challenger's ability to counter their malign activities, whether in intelligence collection or asymmetric warfare.[238]

The maritime militia offers just one example of how China uses hard-power tools in unconventional ways to gain advantage in an informationized environment. Electronic warfare represents another. In contrast to the West, which tends to treat electronic warfare as a distinct discipline, Chinese strategists view it as part of a much larger informationized continuum of competition and thus coordinate its use with other lines of effort in the cyber, air, ground, and maritime realms.[239] Although China has concentrated its development of electronic warfare (EW) capabilities on offensive rather than defensive measures, its location in the General Staff Headquarters demonstrates the high degree of importance the PLA leadership places on EW. Indeed, the PLA views EW as a critical "fourth dimension of combat" that has the potential to "determine the outcome of war."[240] Dominance over the EW realm appears to have surpassed air dominance as the most critical initial goal in conflict, as control over the electronic realm would rightly constrain enemy attempts at controlling the skies—especially if that enemy exhibits a high degree of reliance on electronic systems and communications.[241]

The thinking behind this strategy, conceived in the United States as Anti-Access/Area Denial (A2AD), applies to a number of sensing capabilities developed by China in recent years. But as China's modernization efforts progress, the defensive nature of the A2AD construct may cloud the offensive applicability of many of the technologies currently under development. As the PLA Air Force (PLAAF) continues to introduce "new and upgraded types of combat and support aircraft," including two stealth systems and a fifth-generation aircraft designed to compete with the F-35, the service has begun to morph into one capable of "mounting offensive operations at extended range in a high threat environment."[242] The transformation has included adding advanced EW and intelligence-collection aircraft, such as the J-16D, which mimics the American EA-18G Growler in its design for suppressing air defense.[243] That offensive component, combined with an increasing array of land-, sea-, and space-based sensors, makes for a communications- and intelligence-collection infrastructure that supersedes those of its neighbors in volume if not capability. No nation operating in the East and South China Seas can ignore these considerations when weighing potential conflict with China.

Consistent with the goal of projecting power further and more effectively throughout the globe, China has ramped up exports of indigenously produced defense equipment and technology and increased investments in the development of defense-related technologies in China and abroad. In the past, a concentration on lower-end systems and a lack of innovation hampered China's indigenous defense industry. Xi Jinping set out to change that. In May 2017 China launched a new "innovation-directed development strategy" that aims to transform China from a technological follower to an innovator and eventually to the most technologically advanced nation in the world by 2050.[244] Beijing appears to realize that, as its economic growth begins to sputter, it must enact major civil reforms and increase exports to create and maintain an internationally competitive defense industrial base. Plans to overhaul the country's research-and-development system and for greater civil-military integration are underway as part of this ambitious goal, as is opening many Chinese defense firms to public investment.[245]

Meanwhile, China has deepened and broadened its current defense-export customer base, complementing its international economic investments. Between 2007 and 2016, China surpassed the United States as the primary weapons supplier to Pakistan; arms deals with the country—which consist of diesel submarines, a jointly developed fighter jets, and myriad smaller systems—now comprise 35 percent of China's arms exports.[246] Arms transfers are just one component of China's blossoming friendship with Pakistan, where it has invested $46 billion in infrastructure projects as part of its China-Pakistan Economic Corridor initiative.[247] As the United States continues to expand its defense and economic relationship with India, Beijing has presented itself as an attractive alternative strategic partner to Islamabad.[248]

China also uses this strategy of coupling economic investments with defense exports to build good will outside Asia, most notably in Africa, which accounted for 22 percent of China's defense exports in 2016.[249] Most African countries have purchased weapons systems from Beijing, including artillery, antitank systems, armored fighting vehicles, and various aircraft and watercraft.[250] Between 2011 and 2013, China invested $13.9 billion per year in African countries, making it the largest single source of financing for infrastructure-development projects on the continent.[251] Although the geostrategic motivations behind China's interests in Africa remain unclear, the investments have motivated African countries to maintain positive relations with Beijing. Gambia and São Tomé and Príncipe, longtime friends of Taiwan, switched their allegiances to Beijing after formally recognizing the "one China" principle in recent years.[252]

Although increasingly based on indigenous technology, Beijing's defense exports have thus far lagged behind those of the West and Russia in terms of technological advancement and durability, and its defense industrial base is not equipped to handle the scale or caliber of production that more sophisticated systems require.[253] In addition to reforms to the military research-and-development program, China has endeavored to improve its high-end manufacturing capabilities via several development plans aimed at the defense and aerospace sector.[254] The plans, if successful, will integrate emerging manufacturing capabilities and knowledge from state-owned and private enterprises in the fields of cloud computing, the Internet of Things, and aircraft manufacturing.[255] China has certainly shown the ability to expand and improve indigenous defense-production capabilities in the past; the rise in quality of its unmanned aerial vehicle production and expansion of its capacity provide a key example.[256] The enduring success of continued capacity-expansion efforts, however, remains to be seen. Each relies not only on investments in human and industrial capital but also on ample defense funding, which China's leaders recognize is unsustainable.[257]

Conclusions

Each of Beijing's multiple lines of effort—whether legal or economic, or in cyberspace, outer space, or the maritime realm—provide it with an expanding array of options to arrange in a strategically auspicious manner. Beyond the public statements indicating an intention to regain primacy in the East and South China Sea, what China will do with this arrangement of leverage points remains to be seen. Yet there is reason to believe that China's vision of the future involves only minimal involvement with the West and only then, ideally, from a position of power.

At the end of the Second World War, both Chiang Kaishek and Mao Zedong proclaimed the end to the Century of Humiliation, a period of Chinese history when Western powers subjugated and exploited China. Although their paths to prosperity differed considerably, resentment toward Western powers was a central rallying point that each leader fomented among the population. Autonomy from the West remains a central goal of the Chinese state to this day. Although the lessons of the Century of Humiliation remain a subject of debate, one lesson seems uncontroversial: autonomy is much easier to maintain from a position of strength than from a position of weakness. Although China grew complacent under the Ming dynasty, it had no doubt learned this lesson long before its modern encounters with the West.

The details of China's history reveal less about its current approach to international affairs than does an appreciation of the benefits that historical perspective bestows on its current leaders. Shih may be uniquely Chinese, but the aphorisms and lessons that led to its development derive from many cycles of wars and battles lost and won, from positions of strength and weakness. *People's war* may represent a distinctly Chinese fusion of Marxist-Leninist and Confucian thought, but the primacy of domestic harmony is not a lesson learned by the Chinese alone. Unrestricted warfare may not have analogues elsewhere in the world, but it derived from carefully observing the dominant power, a practice that each of the actors described in this book share in common. With time comes wisdom.

China's position as an inferior power for the past few centuries did not dispel that wisdom. If anything, China's weakness necessitated that it carefully observe the limitations of its potential foes to identify areas of comparative advantage. At first glance, the revolution in military affairs seemed to reinforce the unassailable strength of the U.S. military, but China correctly observed the implications of this doctrinal shift in a manner that would have been impossible for the force that experienced it firsthand. America's creation of networks and precision weapons reduced casualty rates and made the prospect of war more palatable for a population whose resolve to sacrifice for military ends had grown thin. But rather than changing the nature of war, the RMA merely shifted the decisive factors of victory from the realm of the physical battlefield to the one of knowledge. Whereas the free flow of knowledge in America is one of its greatest strengths, the controlled flow of knowledge is essential to winning war—this was the case even before the RMA. The success of the three warfares and other techniques that layer multiple lines of effort toward achieving a specific goal depends on the careful coordination of knowledge. Authoritarian regimes have a distinct advantage in creating and maintaining such systems.

Yet wisdom alone cannot ensure that a civilization will thrive or survive in the future. Nor does it lend itself well to rapid change. Past periods of rapid economic growth in China have disproportionately benefited coastal ports, a pattern that continues to this day. Respect for tradition, inculcated into Chinese youth from a young age and pervasive throughout society, also stifles the kind of innovation that Beijing seems to believe it can foster with the stroke of a pen. Likewise, centuries of separation between the military and civil society will complicate Beijing's dreams of civil-military integration, and the tradition of a strong central authority in Beijing will limit the dynamism of the country's economy. With age also comes an increased reliance on youth, and here too China's age—demographically speaking—may prove problematic if it becomes old before it becomes rich.[258] Indeed, many analysts believe that these are modern China's halcyon days, a period of prosperity before the weight of its problems overwhelms Beijing. Strategy alone, no matter how shrewd, will not be able to solve these challenges.

Time will tell. For now, however, it is clear that China's leaders see a path forward to restore the country's place in the world. Restoring the old order will require ousting any challenger to Beijing's authority from its historic sphere of influence, and this may ultimately mean conflict with the United States—though the nature of conflict may look very different than it has in the past. Thus far, China's pursuit of strategic advantage through the three warfares, maneuvering in cyberspace and outer space, and economic investments have conformed to a bloodless, informationized war that creates advantage without resorting to combat. As the ancient Chinese strategists taught, however, such ways are often useful only to a point, and China seems intent on developing a fighting force that is without rival in its neighborhood if not the world.

A simple analogy illuminates the different ways that America and China see strategy and international competition. China sees strategy like water rolling down the face of a rock. To determine how the water will flow, one must chisel a path in the rock. America sees strategy like a hammer hitting a nail. A nail is of little use until it has been placed on wood. Once there, the hammer can slam it into place. China has spent centuries learning how to chisel with precision, whereas America has spent decades building a more powerful hammer while neglecting its choice of wood. To better compete with China, America must learn that the characteristics of the wood—which in this analogy would represent the strategic environment—are as important to carpentry as the quality of the hammer and the caliber of the nail. Rather than exhausting itself repeatedly by slamming nails back into place as they dislodge themselves from flimsy wood, America must ensure that it chooses the right nails and selects a firmer foundation to hold the nails in place.

4

The United States

Conceptualizing Competition Short of War

Unlike the other cases in this book, the United States began not as the manifestation of a particular people and its relation to a specific place but as an idea rooted in principles of liberty and laissez-faire economics. These principles have clear applicability to many realms of public life, and they also informed America's thinking about its role in the world. The idea of liberty, for instance, animated the westward push of settlers as they pursued lives unencumbered by established interests of the eastern settlements. Support for laissez-faire economics fueled a hunger for new and larger markets with which to trade, a goal that has driven U.S. policy toward Europe and Asia throughout much of its history. These principles also lent a peculiarity to America's relationship with its military forces.

Origins to the American Civil War

In the nation's earliest years, colonial settlers needed to develop ways of survival in their adopted homeland. This required navigating relations not only with far-off colonial overlords but also with other colonies. Relations with the British crown were contentious from the start. Although the colonists could not eliminate reliance on London, many had left for America to minimize the crown's involvement in all aspects of their lives, including religion. They would come to cherish and guard the independence, not just from London but also from other colonies. In light of French, Spanish, Dutch, and Swedish expansionism in North America, English colonists banded together out of necessity, but the differentiated reasons for the founding of each colony did little to develop a common understanding of the world, save for a common sense of threats.

The indigenous population presented the most immediate and pressing challenge. At first, colonists attempted to keep peace with or Christianize Native Americans.[1] The killing of nearly a quarter of Virginia's population by Native Americans in 1622 shattered early notions of peaceful coexistence. With survival at stake, settlers went on the offensive, into the hinterland beyond their coastal settlements. Over time, they developed expertise in low-intensity conflict and negotiated deftly to improve their position. The spread of European diseases further weakened Native American resistance to colonial aims. Thus, by the close of the Second Tidewater War in 1646, Virginians had eliminated any serious "future resistance to white expansion" in the area.[2] The method established by the Virginians was repeated elsewhere in colonial America; when native populations could not be eliminated, they were subjugated or relocated.

Left to provide for their own defense, colonists conscripted militias to defend and extend their frontiers. Early militias mostly conducted offensive operations outside of population centers and often preemptively helped quell civil disturbances closer to home.[3] This contrasted with war-fighting developments in Europe, which were becoming more formalized and limited to conflict between combatants. Colonial conflicts with Native Americans took on a more asymmetric flavor, particularly with respect to differences in capabilities and levels

The United States

of knowledge about local terrain. Moreover, the manner by which Native Americans fought and settled conflict differed from that of the Europeans. Despite the massacre in Virginia in the early 1600s, Native American conceptions of warfare involved less bloodshed and less destruction of property than conflicts initiated by colonists or Europeans.[4] Differing conceptions of property rights no doubt contributed to these conflicting approaches to warfare. Yet because the aim of conflict for the colonists was the defense and expansion of territory, they adopted grander aims than their European counterparts. Rather than limit conflict to sets of armies on known and established territory, warfare became a method to eradicate a problematic population. This early shift, a function of culture as much as necessity, catalyzed what Russell Weigley would later call "a strategy of annihilation."[5]

In his seminal work on American strategy, *The American Way of War*, Weigley traces the historical development of the country's approach to battle and war. Weigley recognized the early American development of skills in low-intensity warfare, or combat and operations involving what we would now call guerrilla tactics (which were then thought of as *petite guerre*). Limited aims, or goals that fall short of the destruction of an adversary's ability to fight and that focus instead on attrition, characterize this approach to warfare. Strategies of annihilation, in contrast, set the complete eradication of an enemy's capabilities as a primary aim. Low-intensity warfare is often pursued by a weaker power out of necessity, as it cannot muster the capabilities necessary to pursue the annihilation of its enemies. Despite the weakness of American colonists relative to their adversaries, Weigley found that their ambitions nonetheless reflected annihilative intentions, even if early Americans lacked the ability to execute their plans.

Some have found room to critique Weigley's claims. Colonial experiences with local terrain and the fighting style of Native Americans may have resulted in an early form of expeditionary warfare rather than a strategy of annihilation expressed through attrition. Antulio Echevarria implicitly makes this point in rejecting Weigley's use of the attrition and annihilation duality.[6] Yet there is room for both interpretations to stand. At the operational level, colonists tried to wear down Native Americans by attrition, but their overall goal—their theory of victory—involved the annihilation of Native Americans, if not from the face of the earth, then at least from areas where colonists sought to settle.[7] In short, the colonists pursued a strategy of annihilation *through* the tactics and operations of attrition warfare.[8]

Because the colonists became more adept at countering the insurgent tactics of various tribes, the strength of the Native American population declined. Decades of a divide-and-conquer approach on the part of European powers weakened whatever cohesiveness existed among Native American tribes, and the devastation wrought by epidemics further diminished their military strength. That adversaries such as France leaned on Native Americans to mitigate their inferior numbers gave further reason for English colonists to eradicate Native Americans from colonial lands. The association between Native Americans and Continental enemies, combined with Anglican sentiments toward Catholics, led prominent colonists to extend their need to eradicate threats of the French and Spanish—the two most serious challengers to Anglo superiority in North America.[9]

In retrospect, it makes intuitive sense that American colonial leaders adopted annihilative strategies toward their adversaries. Their position vis-à-vis their enemies was existential: the very survival of their society (or parts of it) was at stake. Then, as now, calls to fight for survival also served as a recruitment tool. As befitted a people who had fled Europe in part to escape violence, early America held a deep suspicion of permanent military forces. Recruiting quality militiamen proved difficult and was often the preserve of the lowest rungs of society. The rhetoric of survival thus served practical as well as political purposes. The interplay between these two opposing forces—a deep suspicion of the misuses of military power and a military culture given to strategies of annihilation—would echo in the centuries that followed and would obscure the development of a way of competition that incorporated military power but allowed for coexistence with rather than complete eradication of perceived and actual threats.

As the colonists began to seek independence, this paradox would come to influence the conduct of their revolution. At the dawn of the American Revolution, the colonies remained reliant on citizen soldiers, which is to say, on militias and volunteer companies, for their defense. While the militias were well versed in the tactics of petite guerre, or limited war against the Native Americans, the recruitment problems, lack of professionalization, and scant experience with European military science threatened to limit their success in direct conflict with the English.[10] Although press coverage stemming from the opening salvos of the Revolution in Lexington and Concord communicated a sense of American invincibility, militias alone would be insufficient to rid America of its colonial overseers.[11]

Recognizing as much, military leaders, George Washington among them, educated themselves on military strategy. In contrast to London's lack of strategic clarity, Washington maintained a clear vision while maintaining enough operational flexibility to exploit British missteps.[12] This resulted in a dual strategy in which conventional warfare and the tactics of the petite guerre were applied in support of one another, depending on the terrain, the posture of the adversary, and the resources available at the time.[13] Americans were able to achieve their goal of extirpating the British presence from their territory through strategic vision, persistence, and a flexible balancing of conventional and unconventional tactics.

The Revolutionary War made clear the value of a professional military during times of existential crisis, but the appropriate role of the military in times of peace remained unclear. Although the Articles of Confederation provided for a small standing army, at the time of the Constitutional Convention, several years later, only two of the eleven colonies had established any provisions for a standing military in times of peace; most remained silent on the subject.[14] Understanding that the federal coordination of foreign and military policy would be essential for protecting the unity of the new government, the Continental Congress ensured that the federal government, rather than individual states, would decide on matters of military and foreign policy.[15]

Regardless of who controlled the military, the founding fathers were cautious about the power that permanent armed forces could wield in the new republic. One group, led by Thomas Jefferson, questioned the necessity of a permanent federal military. Aside from encounters with the English military, Jefferson and others recognized the vulnerability that a fledgling government would face from an armed and organized military within its midst. Even George Washington, who was hardly a pacifist, bristled at the notion of allowing the military to expand its "coercive powers."[16] Other Federalists argued that the deterrent effect of a permanent military should outweigh such concerns. Alexander Hamilton, for example, pointed out that foreign powers might leverage continued presence along the colonial periphery against America if the young nation did not establish the appropriate means for a common defense.[17] Even James Madison agreed that maintaining the consistent ability to defend the nation would help prevent attacks of opportunity at the hands of foreign powers.[18]

The system of checks and balances established by the U.S. Constitution addressed both concerns by placing the president in command of the armed services but providing Congress with the responsibility for funding it. This hardly resolved the question of the size and role of the military, particularly with respect to federal versus state jurisdiction. George Washington urged Congress to address this issue, which it did in 1792 through the passage of the Uniform Militia Act, but the tension between the liberal society envisioned by the founders and the security needs of the new republic remained. Indeed, the debate about the function and size of the military during times of peace—however one defines it—continues to this day.

Discomfort with a permanent military did not curtail America's expansionist ambitions, nor did it change the way that political and military leaders characterized or perceived threats. On the contrary, Americans continued to describe the defeat of their enemies in absolute terms, even if prudence and constrained resources limited the scope of military engagements. Historian John Shy cites a clear example: in 1790 Benjamin Franklin called for the "extirpation" of the French in Canada for their wickedness.[19] English colonists framed the eviction of Spain and France from other North American territories in similar ways, even though the language of total war was outside the norms of contemporaneous Western conversations about conflict. The ambitions of America's early leaders far exceeded the country's capabilities or, for that matter, those of more established powers.

This tendency overrode a state of affairs that otherwise may have incentivized the development of an American way of competition. As discussed in chapter 1, powers that view themselves as weak or face existential threats develop ways to exploit the weaknesses of stronger powers. Although at a tactical level the United States became adept at this, methods to undermine enemy strengths failed to permeate America's approach to strategy. When new crises arose, leaders used the rhetoric of annihilation, framing threats as existential to build the will to counter them. There were practical reasons for this: the constant need to annihilate potential and actual threats bolstered the Federalist argument that the young nation required a permanent standing military. But the rhetoric also matched reality. The founders never conceived of a role for the American military in maintaining strategic gains outside of war—the military would be used to annihilate enemies, not to compete with them outside of combat.

A strong and centralized organ to coordinate what we would now call diplomatic, informational, and economic tools of statecraft would have mitigated such rigidity. The period before independence is replete with examples of the use of these mechanisms on both the domestic and foreign fronts. The Secret Committee of the Second Continental Congress, for example, not only funded domestic propaganda efforts but also sent emissaries to France to covertly shape diplomatic outcomes to America's advantage. Benjamin Franklin himself may have engineered Britain's willingness to end the war with its colonies by using liaisons with the British Secret Service to "tumble France into war against Britain."[20] Yet the founders held deep suspicions about the potential future uses of such mechanisms. To constrain the executive branch, they not only granted Congress the power of the purse, they also charged it with conducting oversight. Although this decision served as a check on executive actions, it also subjected executive activities to the changing whims of Congress, and, above all, to the need to produce tangible and measurable results. Because congressional turn-over occurred every two years, long-term programs needed to produce measurable results soon after their inception. These early decisions ensured that short-term strategies would, as a general rule, trump longer-term ones in the American system.

In addition to America's strategic inclinations and system of government, two other factors impeded the development of a competitive tradition short of war. The first is geography. Although *manifest destiny* did not enter the American lexicon until later, the country's founders and frontiersmen alike understood the promise that westward expansion held for the young nation.[21] The vast potential of the country insulated its population from the concerns of the rest of the world; the

The United States

avoidance of entanglement in foreign contests was a goal to which few other nations had the luxury to aspire. Because of its distance from its most formidable adversaries, the United States defaulted to a position of neutrality in world affairs and therefore never had the need to develop the continuous threat-mitigation methods that the less-isolated powers discussed in this book pursued as a matter of survival. Because of geography, it could dip its toe into world affairs more or less when it chose to do so. Through a combination of reactive diplomacy and spurts of military campaigns followed by settlement, America pursued expansion not to shape the behaviors of its adversaries but for its own sake.

The second factor relates to the reasons for America's founding. The founders designed the U.S. Constitution to bind nationalist sentiments with imperial ones, thereby protecting the longevity of what Alexander Hamilton and James Madison called a "republican empire."[22] The ambition of these aims is clear when one considers that, at the time of its founding, the United States hardly had a well-developed sense of nationalism, let alone the instruments of state necessary to defend it. While the new nation would be free from the hierarchies and autocracies common in the old world, it would not shy away from aspirations to greatness; the expansive potential of the idea of America was unlimited and applicable far beyond the frontiers of the founding colonies.

But what would an empire with republican characteristics look like? Humanistic ideas and principles would supplant geopolitical calculations as the fountainhead of empire building. America's founders sought to create an empire in the mold of Rome—a nation that would be bound through adherence to common principles and an inclination to include more territory and people within the social contract. The Democratic-Republicans and Federalists disagreed about the extent to which power should be centralized in the new republic, and many details, particularly regarding the power of the president, would take many years to resolve (if they ever were). Yet both groups shared a vision of empire based on the unifying ideals of liberty, one that would hold equal standing in the world as the nations of Europe.[23]

There were some among the founders—particularly Alexander Hamilton—who were less confident about the power of ideals and principles to protect the nation from outside threats. The Federalists expressed their belief in the importance of a capable standing military in their treatises of 1789.[24] To the Federalists, divisions among the states could create opportunities for foreign powers to undermine the unity of the country, and the establishment of a federally controlled standing military of sufficient size to deter foreign meddling would mitigate these risks. Whereas the Federalists took a realistic view of international affairs, particularly with respect to relations with England, the Democratic-Republicans, led by Jefferson, held a more idealistic vision of the future. In addition to viewing revolutionaries in France as kindred spirits, they believed that the "national unity" forged by the nation's founding principles would support an "extending [of] the boundaries of the European system . . . that would eliminate the causes and pretexts of war."[25] These ideas would promulgate not through force but through example and diplomacy. Each vision tended to appeal to two very different groups: Hamilton and the Federalist's views corresponded with the mercantile, urban elite along the East Coast and the Jeffersonian Democratic-Republican view with the "agrarian masses."[26]

Over time, Hamilton's vision would influence the development of America's institutions, and Jefferson's would leave its mark on America's relations with other states. Expansionism based on ideas rather than territory paired easily with strategies of annihilation: time and again, American leaders refer to countervailing ideas outside America as a threat to the American way of life. But a principled and moralistic view of expansion also impeded the development of a way

The United States

of competition. Competitive strategies succeed not because of annihilative fervor or moral outrage but because of careful calculations, realpolitik, and a sober comparison of one's resources as compared to those of their adversary. In other words, competitive strategies succeed because of an approach to international relations, prevalent also in eighteenth-century European courts, that the founders rejected. The very founding of America was an explicit rebuttal to the amoral, calculating, and power-maximizing approach to the world that lies at the core of successful competitive strategies.

These ideas thus became a common reference point—if not justification—for military engagements in the centuries that would follow. Americans would come to view the validity of foreign engagements done in their name through a lens of morality that many of its adversaries did not share. Wars would be waged, expansionism would occur, countless limited engagements would transpire, and an empire would slowly emerge in the name of defending and evangelizing the ideas that inspired the foundation of the American experiment. Whereas other nations engaged in conflict to maximize their power, America rejected this form of statecraft from the beginning. Even if its conquests expanded its power, the impetus for pursuing them was a moral one.

The heady days of the founding soon gave way to addressing external and internal demands for governance. The need to secure recognition of independence, the competing claims on territory on the North American continent, and the exhausted state of the post-revolutionary American military spurned a period of creativity in American statecraft that would echo through the centuries that followed. Working with their Federalist allies in Congress, Washington and Adams oversaw the establishment of a small standing army, of mandated service in militias, and of a small permanent navy.[27] Yet the lack of resources available to the first two American presidents necessitated a limited approach to war in which many slights from Spain and Britain were overlooked in favor of treaties and reprisals against adversarial property. Indebtedness and resource limitations constrained every tool of national power available to the new republic, yet survival necessitated navigating diplomatic intrigues and crises of varying degrees with Barbary pirates, England, the Netherlands, and France.[28]

If creative statecraft borne out of necessity characterized the first decade of America's existence, the election of Thomas Jefferson marked a growing realization that attempts at neutrality could undermine American interests. Although he held a deep suspicion of Great Britain's intentions and appreciated revolutionary developments in France, Jefferson recognized the limitations that America would encounter in its pursuit of equal status with established European powers.[29] He remained suspicious of the role that the military could play in bolstering American credibility and gravitas: upon ascending to the presidency, he restricted the size of the standing army and halted Federalist plans to establish a powerful navy.[30] Nevertheless, he maintained a keen perception of the threat that European land claims in North America represented to American interests and of the central role that commerce played in the nation's security. Securing America's ability to continue its expansion led his administration to purchase the Louisiana Territory from France, and the desire to establish maritime security—along with the need to gain international respect—led him to engage in the first of America's wars off the coast of North Africa.[31]

The altercations now known as the Barbary Wars were an initial test of America's resolve to assert its national interests independent of European powers. Although previous administrations had paid tribute to North African city-states for protection, Jefferson calculated that the cost of military action would be less than tribute payments. In addition, a swift intervention would have the added benefit of "demonstrating sovereignty" to European and American audiences.[32] To assuage

The United States

critics in his own Democratic-Republican Party who viewed wars as requiring actions that would "threaten the principles of the Republic," he framed military action as *jus ad bellum*, or a "just war," which was, actually, an affirmation of those same principles. Although America's military performance in the Barbary Wars was not without issue, the engagement resulted in securing America's free passage through the Mediterranean and solidified the permanent regional presence of the American Navy. Further, it also established a precedent wherein the president would leverage the nation's founding ideas as a justification for military action outside of declared war.[33]

The lack of discipline among American troops in the Barbary Wars, along with rising tensions with England, led Jefferson to approve the longstanding Federalist plan to establish a military academy at West Point. Though military academies hardly held appeal to Jefferson's Democratic-Republican counterparts, his founding of the institution allowed him to leave his mark on its curricular orientation. For a president who held sympathies with the French and antipathy toward the British, West Point would not teach cadets in the English style. Whereas England embraced the idea of *martial genius*, the curriculum of West Point took a scientific approach to warfare, rooted in the teachings of Antoine-Henri Jomini and the geometric concepts of German theorist Heinrich Dietrich von Bülow.[34] Orienting the military academy toward the sciences—which the English thought were of little use for general officers—would lay the predicate for a "scientific" approach to warfare, rooted in mathematics, measurements, and metrics, that would color the approach of generations of American military leaders.

Despite overseeing the foundation of West Point, Jefferson remained skeptical of military engagement. Even as Britain continued to insult the sovereignty and dignity of the United States, Jefferson expressed a preference for a "peaceful means of addressing injustice," such as diplomacy or economic statecraft.[35] When the Chesapeake-Leopard Affair enflamed anti-

British sentiment to a point where nonresponse was politically infeasible, he closed off trade with both Britain and France via the Embargo of 1807.[36] Given America's economic reliance on trade, the embargo was counterproductive: its small economy as compared to France and Britain meant that the United States would bear the brunt of the policy's costs. The embargo reduced America's resource base at a time when preparations for war may have deterred further British meddling; furthermore, it exposed the limits of America's power when the country proved unable to enforce an unpopular economic policy.[37]

Tensions with Britain continued to worsen under Jefferson's successor, James Madison, who considered "expanding economic warfare" against Britain through an invasion of Canada, which was far weaker than the United States.[38] A combination of this and other factors, the aim of securing maritime and economic concessions from Britain foremost among them, led Congress to declare war against Britain in 1812.

Judged by the objective of securing concessions, the war that followed was a failure—the concluding Treaty of Ghent mentioned no economic concessions on the part of Britain and returned the situation to the antebellum status quo. Militarily, however, the war allowed the young nation to refine its approaches and identify areas for improvement. It provided important lessons for use in training curricula, crystallized a new sense of American nationalism, and mitigated trans-Atlantic threats in a manner that would allow the United States to focus on expansion and consolidation in the decades to follow.

In the period between the War of 1812 and the Civil War, debates about the roles of the militia and the standing army continued. Smarting from the burning of Washington during the War of 1812, however, Congress saw fit to provide for a regular and expansible force with a professionalized officer corps. Toward the end of the antebellum era, a school of American strategic thought, rooted in Jomini's interpretation of Napoleon's campaigns, began to emerge from West Point.[39]

The United States

Captain Henry Halleck, a lecturer at West Point, produced the first true American treatise on strategy, *Elements of Military Art and Science*. In defining strategy as "the art of directing masses on decisive points, or the hostile movement of armies beyond the range of cannon," Halleck incorporated both the concentrated application of mass and subtler maneuvers outside the main theater of operations, what we might call *shaping operations* in today's parlance, into his vision of the proper conduct of war.[40] His chapter on the all-encompassing nature of conflict expands upon this point and also delineates "means of redress, short of actual war," ideally taken before the commencement of conflict. He calls for an assessment of the political and ideological characteristics of a target population, its civil-military relations, and its "passive means of resistance."[41] Halleck understood that war was more than combat; it was an expression of the will of opposing peoples drawn together in conflict across a number of modalities.

At first glance, Halleck's observations of the social, political, economic, and geographic aspects of war reflect an understanding of international competition not unlike those described in the previous chapters in this book. Yet it would be inaccurate to describe Halleck's observations as the foundation of an American way of competition. Although they reflect a broad understanding of the components of competition short of war, the object of understanding these factors was still for the scientific execution of warfare. In other words, these factors were not delineated as targets of attack and manipulation themselves; they were identified as elements of what we might today call *preparation of the battlespace*. This distinction between competition and preparation for combat would come to define the American military's approach to international competition. In many respects, Halleck's treatise foreshadowed later military doctrines that would treat military operations outside of combat as merely a prelude to decisive battle.

At the political level, the aim of settling previously unexploited frontiers, shared by successive presidential administrations during this period, fostered a golden age of expansionism. Although an isolationist, nonexpansionist caucus did exist, the general consensus called for nonintervention in European affairs to allow for expansionism elsewhere.[42] This orientation was most evident in the Monroe Doctrine, which expanded America's articulated interests to the entirety of the Western Hemisphere to the exclusion of Europe. The successive military engagements, and outsized persona, of Andrew Jackson added to the nationalistic fervor that characterized the first half of the nineteenth century.[43]

America had begun to find its footing as a nation. Its military remained unprepared for the internecine conflict to come, and its understanding of warfare remained confined to battlefield outcomes. But its success in annihilating the threat of Native Americans and against a foreign power in Mexico under Jackson's leadership had transformed the military into an effective tool of American power. The country's explosive population and economic growth not only fueled self-respect within American society but also forced other countries to interact with America on equal terms.[44] On the eve of the Civil War, America had proven its mettle in battle, risen to outpace the development of many European nations, and found its purpose through territorial, economic, and demographic expansionism.

American Civil War to the Second World War

America's newfound confidence, in retrospect, has an air of naïveté. Its military had demonstrated effectiveness, but the size of the standing army—sixteen thousand troops at the eve of the Civil War—did not square with the country's ambitions or territorial expanse.[45] Its military had rejected the push toward total war as practiced by Napoleon and had instead embraced the Enlightenment thinking of Jomini, with its emphasis on science and engineering in the approach to warfare. Although Americans viewed the War of 1812 as evidence of their ability to succeed against an existential threat, Britain had not actually dedicated much of its might toward the effort, and America had not escaped without substantial cost. It had annihilated Native Americans, but it had not yet encountered a peer competitor. This overconfidence explains the exuberance of the public at the beginning of the Civil War, not unlike the excitement European nations would feel as they entered the First World War fifty years later.

The Civil War may not initially seem relevant to the formulation of America's way of competing outside of war. While it is challenging to draw lessons from internal conflicts and apply them to international competition, the manner by which the Union and Confederate militaries engaged with one another provides a window into American strategic thinking that would characterize America's approach to later conflicts. The methods that each side used to shape the strategic environment outside of and alongside combat are also germane to this study.

West Point graduates made up the leadership cadre of both the Confederate and Union sides, making the War a contest of intellectual peers. Though the Confederacy held undeniable geographic advantages, the north possessed a superior manufacturing base and a larger population. Confederate generals thus pursued a strategy of exhaustion with the primary goal of wearing down the will of the Union to fight, and political leaders sought to win the support of foreign powers to their cause.[46] Northern generals were more focused on geographic objectives, and Northern politicians on maintaining the neutrality of foreign powers.[47] Unlike the wars of America's past, the Civil War was the manifestation of competing and wholly opposed ideas; the involvement of the civilian population was thus inevitable and unprecedented, regardless of the military's chosen emphasis on science. For the Union to win, it would need to not only defeat the opposing military on the battlefield but also quash a noncompatible ideology that had taken root within the population.

Manipulating public perceptions proved key to waging an ideological war. Both the Federals and Confederates engaged in espionage, leaks to the press, and propaganda. Each side recruited spies from various social backgrounds, often women, in order to convey secret messages, apprise military leadership of tactics and plans, spread disinformation, and conduct industrial espionage. Whereas the Union, both bureaucratically through the Secret Service and legally through the suspension of *habeus corpus* at the war's outbreak, was able to coordinate its responses at a national level, convictions about state's rights led the Confederacy to implement a more piecemeal approach. At times, the fruits of an intelligence officer's labors would make their way to the newspapers, which would tip off both the public and the enemy to sensitive plans.[48] Although the ability of either government to harness the power of propaganda remained limited during the Civil War, the ideological camps in the press and intellectual spheres associated with each government attempted to sway public opinion through the use of abolitionist and antiabolitionist publications and cartoons depicting political caricature.[49] In each of these cases, the relative governmental and demographic centralization of the Union gave it a distinct edge.

The clear advantage enjoyed by the Union in the realm of covert influence did not bleed over into the political realm. From an administrative standpoint, Congress established a Joint Committee on the Conduct of War to oversee the wartime operations of the military. The body did more to demonstrate members' ignorance about the military than to exert pressure on the executive branch.[50] Diplomatically, the Union remained fearful that Confederate efforts to woo foreign powers into recognizing or supporting the South would succeed. The fact that there was "no inexpensive means available to Europe to achieve the liberation of the South" compelled old-world powers to respect the North's blockade of the Confederate States.[51] A mixture of tenacity, patience, will, and military acumen eventually resulted in a Union victory, but the entire effort was ad hoc by today's standards. The United States had yet to develop a way for coordinating all of the tools of national power at its disposal.

The transformation of America's approach to foreign policy from dynamic if disorganized to process-oriented and technocratic began with organizational and bureaucratic developments in the decades following the Civil War. Several factors contributed to this change. First, as the expansion of the American economy enabled by the Industrial Revolution and the previous years of territorial acquisitions began to bear fruit, leaders began to search outside the United States for markets for their growing surplus of goods.[52] In turn, the permanent foreign interests of the United States began to expand, and commercial interests became increasingly intertwined with foreign policy.

Second, the expansion of the military's roles (though not yet size) in American life—from Reconstruction to over a thousand combat engagements with Native Americans—cemented it as a permanent fixture in society.[53] Doctrinally, as the Prussian *landwehr* rose in prominence and gained international admiration, so too did Prussian ideas begin to influence the American military. Already adept at the scientific approach to warfare outlined by Jomini, American military officers became influenced by the ideas of Carl von Clausewitz, whose observations emphasized the political—and therefore the social and economic—purposes, complexities, and resources of combat. By the end of the century, Alfred Thayer Mahan, in this theory of naval power, demonstrated the historical use of naval forces for protecting national interests outside of war. The U.S. Navy played a decisive role in American operations in the Caribbean and the Pacific. As the navy found its footing (the Naval War College and the General Board were founded during this period), the army went through a period of unpreparedness and stagnation. The Dodge Commission, launched in response to the lack of coordination and cooperation during the Spanish-American War, led to the establishment of a General Staff composed of line officers through which the Secretary of the Army would exercise authority.[54] The General Board and the General Staff—and the Joint Army and Navy Board that bridged them—enabled strategy formulation and continuity within the services for the first time.

Third, despite the country's territorial expansion, its population became increasingly centralized, which also consolidated capital—and power. The federal government expanded its employment ranks, which tipped the balance of power within the foreign-affairs bureaucracy from the field to Washington and then to an emerging policy elite atop the nation's executive branch.[55] The economic power of the nation, combined with improvements to its military, educational, and bureaucratic institutions, embodied a system of power expansion that equaled if not superseded that available to its international rivals. A simultaneous convergence between religious and secular elements of society created popular support for extending American political, economic, social, and spiritual beliefs to populations across the globe.[56]

Thus, by the early 1900s America possessed the motivation, ability, and will to expand its influence far beyond the Continental empire envisioned by the country's founders. The idealistic motivations and the expansionist imperative cemented during the founding of the nation would now take flight on a global scale.

The means and ways of foreign policy had expanded in ambition and scope. But what of the ends? The Progressive Era marked a shift in American understanding of the universal applicability of the social compact—that "legitimate government requires the consent of the governed." Whereas President Grover Cleveland viewed annexation by force as legitimate only "by consent or as . . . necessitated by dangers threatening American life and property," progressives viewed the enjoyment of liberty as a function of a society's level of civilization and viewed America as having a moral obligation to civilize less advanced societies.[57] Thus as America was developing the capabilities and capacities necessary to protect and advance its global interests, its understanding of the natural rights of all people shifted to one of an obligation to prepare other societies to take on the mantle of liberty.

This shift from a universal understanding of natural rights, hard-won and clarified only several decades prior during the Civil War, to a messianic outlook squared America's increasing involvement in the affairs of foreign nations with its hardwired understanding of the right to self-determination.[58] Moreover, it allowed the United States to continue to view itself as a peaceful nation whose involvement in foreign matters was paternalistic, not jingoistic. A vision of foreign engagement crystalized in which American military intervention would extend access to the promise of liberty, benefiting other societies as much as America. The evangelistic outlook forged during the Progressive Era also fueled an idealism that American involvement could render war itself obsolete. This idealism was quite evident, for example, in President Woodrow Wilson's determination to "end power politics" in exchange for collective security and a peaceful "reformation of the international system."[59] In short, Wilson sought to extend American power by serving as the world's diplomat-in-chief.

The outbreak of war between European powers in 1914 was an opportunity to create a grand deal that would position America as a beneficent power. Thus, despite his fears that a German victory would represent a grave danger to the world's democracies, Wilson was initially reluctant to take sides. Once the United States entered the war in 1917, Wilson outlined the goals of his decision in his famous "Fourteen Points" speech. Although Europeans may have seen Wilson's perspective as the exercise of great-power politics with a more pleasing patina, the goals outlined in the speech—freedom of navigation, free trade, and the primacy of rules and international law—would echo in America's approach to the world for the rest of the twentieth century.[60]

Had Wilson been more willing to take sides with like-minded democracies early in the conflict, much of the fighting that took place between 1914 and 1917 may have been avoided. Still, the military was not in a position to contribute decisively to the conflict in the earlier years of his term. Naval shipbuilding and support elements, the army, and National Guard were not funded in a manner to allow for successful combat in Europe until the National Defense Act and Navy Act of 1916. Congress did not pass its landmark appropriations bill to jumpstart American military aviation until after the declaration of war in July 1917.[61] By 1917, the rhetorical characterization of German militancy as an existential threat to the world of democracy left American leaders with few options but a direct application of force against the Germans along the Western Front.

This harsh reality, as it happened, aligned with the growing influence of Clausewitz in military circles, whose view of war as an "act of violence intended to compel our opponent to fulfill our will" nested into the rhetoric of the Wilson administration. As was the case in previous wars, it was an ideal that provided the motivation: in this case, "securing peace," or, as Elliott Abrams observed, an "expansion of liberty."[62] The stakes had risen, but the prospect of defending its principles—or, colloquially, its "way of life"—still motivated the United States more than hard strategic considerations alone.

Leaving rhetoric aside, the United States was not in an existential crisis in 1917. Unlike the Civil War, or even the Spanish-American War, the First World War took place far away from American soil; German victory represented a potential existential threat, not an imminent one. Wilson had succeeded in creating a new theory of security, one in which the protec-

The United States

tion of American interests would be ensured through foreign engagement.[63] Yet because the defense of "interests" did not in any immediate sense equate to a fight for survival, America was not sufficiently motivated before or during the war to change the manner by which it approached conflict. That period of growth would take place after the war.

Following an initial attempt at collective security through the ill-fated League of Nations, the belligerents of the First World War once again began to prepare for future conflict. For the United States, the interwar period marked a time of strategic uncertainty and limited resources. Both Clausewitz and Jomini influenced reflections on the First World War and on the best way forward: the military sought to develop the means to apply concentrated mass in conflict in a more scientific manner to produce a more decisive result if called to combat again.[64] Despite the ambiguous international political situation, military leaders focused on the capabilities of potential enemies—all of which were mechanizing their forces and developing sophisticated approaches to combined arms. Civilian research emerged as an important supplement to, if not replacement for, military weapons research, while the military focused its resources on educating a new generation of leaders and developing contingency plans for future conflicts.[65] Military applications of new technology developed alongside the mechanization of civilization that was changing all aspects of American life. Thus, even though the United States trailed both its former allies and enemies in military spending throughout the interwar period, rapid innovation still transformed combat disciplines, from amphibious and naval surface warfare to communications and combined arms.[66]

Despite these innovations, the military remained quite separate from the rest of society during the interwar period. As Samuel Huntington explains in his discussion of interwar civil-military relations, differences between the military and civilians trace back to the country's founding tension between militarism and liberalism.[67] In the 1920s and 1930s, as the military was emphasizing loyalty over strict obedience within its professional ranks, society was drifting toward relativism and a greater emphasis on individuality. Given the horrors of the First World War, the business pacifism that first developed in the 1800s seemed even more relevant in the interwar period, and despite an effort to inject liberal arts into the service academies, the military remained skeptical of the ideas and philosophies taking root in civilian educational institutions. It took a critical perspective on the utility of liberal initiatives such as the League of Nations and the Kellogg-Briand Pact and retained its view of world politics and humanity as driven fundamentally by self-interest.

The First World War demonstrated the decisiveness of societal will in combat, leading to new ways of thinking about how to affect the psychology of enemy soldiers and citizens. British military officer and historian J. F. C. Fuller, for example, recognized the psychological power of the tank to instill fear and paralysis in enemy combatants and postulated that this effect was more valuable than any physical destruction it might bring to bear.[68] During the interwar period, the imagined uses of air power shifted from casualty reduction to a tool for inflicting fear and destruction en masse: strategic bombing emerged as a way to obliterate the morale of a mobilized population.[69] Government propaganda efforts provided an additional tool to wage a psychological or "public relations" war at a population-wide scale, whether at home or on the front lines.[70]

As the 1920s gave way to the 1930s, the failures of Versailles became more apparent, and the seriousness of perceived security threats to the United States continued to rise. The League of Nations could do little to mitigate the rise of the National Socialist party in Germany, to counter the ideological appeal of communism, or to contain Japanese ambitions in East Asia. As domestic propaganda and subversive activities once again raised concern in Washington, President Franklin Delano Roosevelt used his executive authority to place the FBI in charge of domestic intelligence, which was expanded in the mid-1930s at the behest of the Department of State. By the late 1930s, Roosevelt succeeded in wresting much of the historical authority for intelligence collection from the Department of State by establishing the Interdepartmental Intelligence Conference, which would oversee "and coordinate all espionage, counterespionage and sabotage investigations involving the federal government."[71]

The outbreak of war in Europe in 1939 sparked a long debate about whether the United States should join in. Although Roosevelt justified overturning the 1935 Neutrality Act by noting both the danger it posed to seaborne commerce and the need to stand with other democracies, many Americans were content to remain as neutral as possible. The attack on Pearl Harbor rendered much of this debate moot. The question shifted from whether to where, when, and how the United States would enter the war.

During the interwar period, the U.S. military devised a series of war plans for a range of contingencies; the most well developed of these was Plan Orange, for war with Japan. Though Japan would receive a swift response for its actions and a war to follow, dealing with the situation in Europe, specifically the threat to democracies posed by Hitler, became the top priority. The military quickly repackaged its hypothetical plans to better square them with current circumstances. The varied perspectives represented by the president, Congress, and society made room for military expertise to determine much of the conduct of the war to come.

This point deserves additional consideration. Once the United States decided to go to war, civilian leaders dropped their critiques of the militarization of democracy and looked to military leaders to plan and execute combat operations. This clean and sudden division of authority had no prior precedent, but no prior conflict had demanded so much from its population so quickly. And no prior conflict had found the military so intellectually prepared to wage war and a civilian population so mentally and temperamentally ill-equipped to understand the requirements of the coming conflict. The military would run the war in accordance with the intentions of the commander-in-chief and the will of the American people. But the military would become the supported organization of society, rather than the reverse, as was the case during times of peace.

According to Samuel Huntington, this rapid passage of authority from civilians to the military reflected a binary understanding of war and peace, characteristic of the American liberal democratic tradition.[72] During times of peace, including the interwar period, the military was pushed to the side as civilian decision-makers pursued the national interest through diplomacy and economic statecraft. With war now on the horizon, civilian leaders—including those in Congress—abdicated their leadership of the nation's direction and decisions to military leaders to achieve victory through an annihilation of enemy forces. That the object of victory had evolved from the destruction of a foreign military to the destruction of a foreign society did little to change this traditional separation between the civilian and military realms.

With the armed forces in charge of American war strategy and society coalescing behind it, the U.S. military also took the lead on what may be called *grand strategy*. When the Joint Chiefs of Staff struggled to find direction from policymakers, for example, they "furnished themselves" with political guidance and took responsibility for economic and social policies that typically would have been handled by the State Department had it not been so ill-prepared to support a war effort.[73] Roosevelt, Harry Hopkins, and the Joint Chiefs made the major foreign policy and strategy decisions with little input from other intergovernmental departments and representatives. On the domestic front, the Office for Emergency Management was established to manage and coordinate the government's wartime mobilization and production efforts and to intercede between the military and the rest of the government. These efforts included propaganda, economic warfare, and industrial planning. Beyond the water's edge, however, the military established primacy over America's interactions with allies and enemies alike for the duration of the war.

America's approach to wartime civil-military relations contrasted with the approach taken by its allies, and these differences manifested in distinct visions of a path to victory.[74] Whereas the Americans pushed for direct confrontations with Germany via an application of "mass and concentration," the British were more interested in combining a blockade, bombing, subversive activities, and propaganda to wear at Germany's will to fight and were content to allow the Soviet Union to conduct the heavy lifting on the Eastern Front.[75] Even as the Americans and Soviets argued to pursue Operation Overlord, Churchill continued to advocate for operations against Germany in the Mediterranean and elsewhere along the strategic periphery. In the end, the pincer movement on Germanys' east and west flanks, supported by the superior resource bases of the Soviet Union on one side and the Anglo-Americans on the other, doomed Germany to lose the war.

Although an analysis of the tactical and operational decisions made during the Second World War are beyond the scope of this work, two additional developments during the war bear relevance to this study. First, the British indirect approach rubbed off on the American military and catalyzed the development of what would become America's primary institutions for shaping strategic outcomes short of war: the special forces and the intelligence community. Beginning with small cells called Jedburgh teams, American military officers worked with their British and French counterparts to establish an unconventional warfare capability behind the front lines in Europe.[76] Elsewhere in Europe, Underwater Demolition Teams emerged to neutralize enemy ordnance. In the Pacific Theater, General Frank Merrill, relying on then-novel airdrops for supplies, employed Chinese troops to take a key Japanese base, and in North Africa, the newly formed First Ranger Battalion previewed how the United States would come to deploy elite infantry units at the front lines of conflicts in the decades to come.[77]

In June 1941 FDR approved the creation of an office for the "coordination of strategic information," led by psychological and special-warfare visionary William J. Donovan.[78] American intelligence operations were concentrated in Europe, with Allen Dulles at the Office of Strategic Services (oss) Bern outpost and the aforementioned Jedburghs leading the way. Although discussed less, American operatives also established a sophisticated propaganda strategy through the use of radio-based information and entertainment and penetrated the Third Reich using German-speaking exiles.[79] While Americans developed a network of human sources, the British supplied the allies with reliable signals intelligence from Bletchley Park. The traditions, tradecraft, and relationships established during the Second World War laid a foundation for permanent organizations that would, after the war, dedicate themselves to American efforts below the threshold of combat.

Second, the advent of the nuclear age would forever alter international strategic dynamics. Although nuclear weapons were developed outside traditional strategic channels, their use added an exclamation point at the end of a worldwide contest of societal will and mobilization. Total war no longer required the complete destruction of a society through armies, strategic bombing, and naval blockades. The terrifying destruction wrought by a single weapon could now bring about total victory. For the first time, a weapon existed whose destructive potential was so vast that preventing its use became more important than its use.[80] Although the United States won the race to employ the weapon for the first time, other countries were not far behind. Atomic weaponry at once rendered the push toward total war, which had consumed the industrialized world, irrational and made the continuation of this trend impossible.

By the end of the Second World War, America had evolved from a rag-tag experiment to a world power. Certain American characteristics, however, remained consistent over the centuries. For one, although the object of expansion had shifted from the acquisition of territory to the promulgation of American ideals and principles, the expansionist imperative that had animated American leaders from the founding of the country remained. Now America would have the opportunity to serve as the primary architect of a world order that would not only boost its own economic and security prospects but also produce similar benefits for much of the rest of the world. While still suspicious of foreign involvement, America, feeling the obligations of power and moral certitude, would now attempt to extend Jefferson's ideals throughout the world.

A second characteristic is that military and civilian realms remained differentiated, with civilian tools of power taking the lead in times of peace and military ones in times of war. This is not to say that the military fell into disuse for policy purposes outside of war—the U.S. Navy in particular evolved to secure sea lanes for American commerce. But as evidenced by the accession of authority at the beginning of the Second World War, America retained a sharp distinction with respect to which organ of government served the other based on whether the country had declared war. In times of peace, employment of economic and diplomatic tools staved off involvement in foreign conflicts and expanded America's overseas commercial interests. Though the methods and stakes changed over the centuries, the military was still trusted to annihilate America's enemies in times of war.

These two factors would create challenges and opportunities for the United States in the decades to follow. The compelling nature of America's ideas, buttressed by its outsized power, tied the Western world together in the continued struggle against authoritarianism. But those same ideas would also be applied in ways that would undermine the long-term sustainability of the world order that America had created.

The separation of civilian and military life would dissolve in some ways and harden in others, but the underlying differences in approach and cultural orientations between American society and its armed forces would preclude the establishment of a unified orientation toward international competition. The false dichotomy between peace and war, along with the delicate balance of civil-military relations that hung upon the distinction, would continue to flummox America's leaders, and drawn-out conflicts would draw into question the efficacy of the strategy of annihilation.

But for a moment in 1945, with American primacy unquestioned, all of these concerns were beside the point. America had always defined itself with respect to other nations—the very founding of the country was a rebuke of past traditions in exchange for a new vision. Now, other countries would define themselves with respect to America. For the first time, America had an opportunity to test whether the ideals and principles enshrined in its Constitution were palatable and applicable to the entire world.

Contemporary Short-of-War Competition

There was, of course, one major roadblock to this rosy outcome: the Soviet Union. The United States had much more leverage in negotiating the terms of peace than it had had after the First World War. But the Soviet Union, which bore the brunt of allied losses, also held sway at the negotiating table, both in the absence and in the presence of the United States. In what has become known as the percentages agreement, Churchill and Stalin discussed a scheme, without President Roosevelt, at the Moscow Conference of 1944 to carve the world into

separate spheres of influence: one for the victorious democracies and another for the Soviet Union.[81] At the other major
peace conferences, the demands of democracy undermined
America's bargaining position. At Tehran, President Roosevelt
recused himself from the question of Poland's future due to
Polish-American interests in his upcoming election, and in preparing for Yalta, American diplomats underscored that Stalin
would have the luxury of speaking for himself rather than for
the people he represented.[82] As in conflicts past, the United
States either failed to grasp the consequentiality of the negotiations underway or assumed the possibility if not probability
of future cooperation with the Soviet Union. Either way, the
Allies had rid the world of fascism, but the brand of authoritarianism espoused by Stalin would remain.

The dangers of this new reality were not entirely evident at
war's end. Between 1945 and 1946, the United States reduced the
size of its standing army from over eight million active troops
to under two million, even with the forthcoming and foreseeable increase to its peacetime worldwide responsibilities.[83]
The U.S. government disbanded the Office of War Information within two weeks of peace with Japan. Although President Harry S. Truman became convinced of the need to retain
the intelligence analysis and operations capacity established
by the oss during the war, others in the executive branch and
in Congress saw little need to maintain this functionality in in
the newfound era of peace.[84] The advent of the atomic bomb
served as a rationale for a drawdown that was in fact quite typical of America's tendency to dismantle military and intelligence functions at the end of a war—and one called for by the
American people.[85] Having only recently facilitated the founding of the United Nations and the Bretton Woods system of
international monetary management, few had the stomach to
consider the possibility of future conflict.

Not all believed that the international institutions established at the end of the Second World War would be suffi-

cient to curtail threats to American national security. When the U.S. Department of Treasury inquired of the U.S. Embassy in Moscow in early 1946 why the Soviets seemed uninterested in the newly established mechanisms of international economic governance, Deputy Head of Mission George F. Kennan responded with his Long Telegram. The memorandum detailed the Kremlin's deeply held sensitivity to "capitalist encirclement," and characterized the Soviet psyche as one "highly sensitive to the logic of force" and "impervious to the logic of reason."[86] Although Kennan was hardly the first to recognize the fundamental incompatibility of free-market capitalism with authoritarian communism, his telegram was a wake-up call. Soviet actions toward Turkey and Greece since the end of the war gave further gave pause to the idea that Moscow would become a cooperative partner of the West.

The growing specter of a communist threat served as a backdrop to ongoing conversations between the Truman administration and Congress about how to restructure national tools of power to suit America's postwar position and priorities. In March 1947, Truman delivered an address to Congress in which he outlined the necessity of supporting Greece and Turkey in light of Soviet pressure against their governments.[87] This first piece of the Truman Doctrine initialized the policy of containment. Later that year, the National Security Act of 1947 would provide the organizational mechanisms within the U.S. government to coordinate a sustained response to Soviet attempts at expansionism; the Marshall Plan and the formulation of NATO would serve similar purposes at an intergovernmental scale. The intertwined perception of an existential threat to both the American way of life and to its security compelled the Truman administration to innovate and reform.

The National Security Act of 1947 was a landmark piece of legislation. Devised in response to coordination problems that FDR and Truman witnessed during the Second World War, the act reorganized and centralized the execution of American national-security policy. If America's Gilded Age leaders saw a need to build and expand the national bureaucracy to better address America's changing position in the world, the Truman administration found that same bureaucracy unwieldy, with a tendency to operate at cross-purposes and to impede, rather than aid, the effective execution of national strategy. The passage of the act served a number of interests. President Truman gained an efficiency in executing command that had previously eluded him. Seasoned practitioners gained a permanent and direct line of influence to the president, which reduced the likelihood that any one individual could exercise outsized influence on national-security decision-making, as had occurred with the arrangement that Harry Hopkins had enjoyed with FDR.[88] The military and intelligence worlds all received assurance about the permanence of their institutions, and Congress was able to point to a concrete accomplishment that would aid in the implementation of containment.

Realizing the potential of these new structures would require strategic direction and budgetary courage. That came in two parts. First, the National Security Council Directive 10/2 created the office of special projects at the newly formed Central Intelligence Agency, which was granted authority to conduct covert operations "during times of peace."[89] Furthermore, the directive provided for coordination of covert activities with the Joint Chiefs of Staff during times of war, charged the new office with the conduct of economic warfare, and detailed the scope of allowable activities, including "preventive direct action," "sabotage," and "support to anti-communist elements in threatened countries of the free world." For the first time in its history, the United States had authorized the systematic conduct of covert and subversive activities aimed at a specific threat during a time of peace. Yet it had also enshrined a dichotomy between peace and war that would lead the military to focus its many resources on crises that resulted in combat and to section off covert activities from the rest of the foreign policy bureaucracy. These self-created seams between civilian and military covert activities and between covert and overt realms of foreign policy would prove problematic throughout the Cold War and beyond.

These seams were somewhat smoothed over, however, due to the publication of a strategic framework to guide all the government's anti-Soviet activities two years later. In 1950, the National Security Council released NSC-68, a classified memo that presented President Truman with several options for countering and defeating the threat posed by the Soviet Union. After outlining recent actions of the Soviet Union, the memorandum presented four possible strategic responses— maintaining the same course, isolation, war, or a "rapid build-up of political, economic, and military strength in the free world."[90] Although the prospect of a massive military buildup was politically unpalatable to the president and many in Congress, the memorandum presented the final course as the most sensible. The increased resource requirements, however, were hardly the most audacious aspect of this strategy. When viewed in combination with the National Security Act of 1947, the United States had developed a government-wide strategy for coordinating all available tools of national power across competitive domains.

Per NSC 10/2, the Central Intelligence Agency would take the lead on covert operations. Nevertheless, some within the military set forth to build upon the lessons in unconventional and psychological warfare learned during the Second World War. In addition to establishing a joint training center for psychological and unconventional warfare at Fort Benning, for example, the U.S. Army provided initial training materials to the CIA's Office of Policy Coordination. Most within the military, however, were happy to wash their hands of the "dirty tricks" and otherwise unsavory aspects of competition short of war.[91] Military training before Korea thus focused on how unconventional and guerrilla warfare could aug-

The United States

ment conventional military endeavors, rather than on how those efforts themselves might independently achieve policy objectives.

NSC-68 was a blueprint for American strategy for the duration of the Cold War. Yet even with structural realignment and a clear direction, another factor would influence the strategy's success: political will. For starters, America's leaders and the public alike had yet to grapple with the enormity of their new responsibilities on the world stage. As Elliott Abrams observed, the first challenge of implementing the strategy became one of "matching the new American responsibilities with a willingness to assume them."[92] The authors of NSC-68 recognized this and contrasted the challenge that America would face with the relative ease of decision-making enjoyed by the Soviets:

> The full power which resides within the American people will be evoked only through the traditional democratic process: This process requires, firstly that sufficient information regarding the basic political, economic, and military elements of the present situation be made publicly available so that an intelligent popular opinion may be formed. . . . The democratic way is harder than the authoritarian way because, in seeking to protect and fulfill the individual, it demands of him understanding, judgment, and positive participation in the increasingly complex and exacting problems of the world. . . . It is obvious that dissent among us can become a vulnerability.[93]

The United States thus faced systemic constraints on its conduct of war that the Soviet Union did not. The open nature of democracy, as well as the checks and balances built into the American system, precluded the establishment of the full range of capabilities and efficient command-and-control structures enjoyed by the Soviet state. The Soviet concepts of *maskirovka*, or deception, and *provokatsiya*, or provocation, could not be practiced by the United States against internal and external targets as in the Soviet Union, owing to the rights provided citizens in the U.S. Constitution and the Bill of Rights.[94] The authors of NSC-68 balanced many considerations—the protection of American values, public opinion, the balance of power between the executive and legislative branches, varied interests within the federal bureaucracy—all while countering the command-and-control structure of a comparatively streamlined authoritarian regime.[95]

The authors of NSC-68 were prescient about the limitations of a democracy engaged in an ongoing competition with an autocratic regime. Yet in 1950 the question of political will was hardly at the forefront.[96] The Soviet Union had successfully tested an atomic weapon in 1949, and many in the United States and elsewhere feared an existential crisis in which the survival not just of America but of the entire planet was at stake. Even without the immediate disclosure of NSC-68 to the public, current events created a sufficient reservoir of public support for a military buildup and a more assertive approach to foreign policy. Convincing policy intellectuals, Congress, and the president of the need to increase budgetary resources for competition with the Soviet Union in a time of peace proved more difficult.[97] Had North Korea not invaded U.S.-backed South Korea later that year, the United States may never have mustered the political will to implement the fourth option outlined in NSC-68.

The invasion seemed to push the contest for the Korean peninsula beyond the competitive space "short of war," a phrase that George Kennan had devised and that the fourth option of NSC-68 meant to convert into acceptable policy. When viewed as a proxy for the heated contest between the United States and Russia, however, the Korean War was, in fact, "short of war": although many would die in gruesome combat, the two superpowers would not come into direct confrontation during the conflict. New tools of diplomatic engagement, namely the United Nations, helped provide the Truman administration cover and support for its coming involvement in the war. The decision to engage hinged on a theory that the loss of a democratic country would create a domino effect and diminish the ability of the United States to contain the spread of communism elsewhere.[98] The conflict, like the other proxy wars fought between the United States and the Soviet Union in the coming decades, thus represented a subordination of war to a larger strategy, one whose ideological objectives were unachievable through fighting alone.

Volumes have been written on the Korean War, and this author will not attempt to duplicate the excellent work already available on the subject.[99] The lack of success in Korea, however, is attributable to several factors: the clash between Truman and MacArthur that resulted in the latter's dismissal, the entry of the People's Republic of China into the war and the outsized manpower that it dedicated to support the North Korean cause, the war weariness of the American people, and the lack of readiness on the part of a recently transformed national-security establishment to conduct a coordinated campaign against a more numerous adversary. For the purposes of this study, this last point deserves some elaboration.

The roles and responsibilities of the national-security bureaucracy did not yet, in practice, reflect the intent or the requirements spelled out in the National Security Council directives of the prior years. Although the Joint Chiefs of Staff were, by law, only to perform a military function, in practice they also held sway over a number of political and administrative decisions.[100] This had the effect of not only undermining civilian authority—as demonstrated by the Truman and MacArthur tussle over conducting air raids in China—but also distracting the military from consolidating its own operational abilities. Nowhere was this more evident than in the military's readiness to conduct psychological and special operations. An urgent memorandum from the Secretary of the Army sent at the beginning of the Korean War underscored the lack of preparedness of psychological warfare, and the first formal unconventional warfare group, the Tenth Special Forces Group, was not established until 1952.[101] As a result, psychological and unconventional warfare officers arrived in Korea untrained and unprepared to support the conventional effort.

Although Korea showed the United States the limitations of its current abilities to conduct covert and what would become known as "special operations" activities during wartime, it also solidified relationships between NATO partners. Europe, more than Asia, remained the primary concern of military planners: the U.S. Army established the Psychological Warfare Center at Fort Bragg to develop a "guerrilla capability in Europe" more than to contribute to the ongoing conflict in Korea (meanwhile, the United States had also increased its ground forces commitment in Europe, from one to five army divisions).[102] Interest in psychological and unconventional warfare, however, would wane under the Eisenhower administration, whose New Look policies favored massive-retaliation capabilities driven by strategic weapons, not ground forces. The U.S. Army thus faced a reduction in manpower, shrinking from about 1.5 million troops in 1953 to 900,000 by 1958.[103] The Psychological Warfare Center narrowly survived these cuts, but by 1956 it was repurposed as the Special Warfare Center and School in order to accommodate a wider range of disciplines with a reduced staff.

While the military focused on developing massive-response capabilities, the Eisenhower administration turned to the CIA and the Department of State to develop and implement operations to deter and dissuade the Soviet Union. Under the leadership of Director of Central Intelligence Allen Dulles, the CIA experienced a golden age of covert operations to complement its growing analytic acumen.[104] Eisenhower, a former general, understood the potential of the CIA in both shaping and reporting on foreign developments and saw using it as a way to avoid a costly war. Eisenhower reestablished the capabilities of the Office of War Information into the U.S. Information Agency, thereby elevating public-diplomacy efforts to the same level of importance as other tools of foreign policy. Mindful of the cost of these operations, he also oversaw CIA efforts to enlist the private sector in the propagation of patriotic and anticommunist narratives, including journalistic outlets and civil-society organizations.[105] Although the ability of the government to intrude in private society remained limited by the Constitution, Eisenhower established the tools necessary to wage an information war on an enemy that had already shown a willingness to do so both in the United States and in Europe.

The two tracks established by Eisenhower—wherein the military acted as a deterrent force and the CIA and U.S. Information Agency took the lead on measures short of war—worked well as long as the United States remained at peace. By the time John F. Kennedy took power in 1961, however, the effectiveness of Eisenhower's two-track policy to prevent the outbreak of war was unclear. Many within and outside the government had criticized New Look policies as overlooking the many different forms of conflict that the Cold War could produce and pointed to American interventions in Lebanon and Taiwan as evidence.[106] World events also brought forth the need to develop flexible-response options. The Communist world had begun to fracture into multiple instantiations, with some calling for more freedom and others advancing competing forms of government. Decolonization had sparked a massive increase in the number of democracies, yet their fragility made for uncertain futures. Meanwhile, dynamics had also shifted in the first world. Europe had largely rebounded from its postwar economic low, and the degree to which it would defer to American policy became less clear. The Soviet Union took advantage of this uncertain environment by testing the new president's mettle, first with respect to the status of Berlin and then in Cuba.

Soon after the disastrous attempt to invade Cuba at the Bay of Pigs, which had highlighted the vulnerability of CIA forces acting alone, the Kennedy administration issued National Security Action Memoranda 57. This directive extended the responsibility for covert action to the Defense Department, with the CIA in a "supporting role" for operations that required "significant numbers of military personnel" or "military equipment which exceed normal CIA-controlled stocks."[107] In effect, this decision meant that both CIA and the Defense Department would need to prepare to engage, in some way or form, in counterinsurgency and unconventional warfare operations. Kennedy's establishment of Special Forces underscored the key role that soldiers would now play in American activities that, though sometimes involving combat, nonetheless occupied the space between war and peace.

Of the many mistakes and misjudgments that characterized the Vietnam War, one of the least discussed is the impact that it had on America's competitive strategies short of war. Prior to the influx of conventional troops, U.S. Army Special Forces attempted to stanch the flow of Vietnamese villagers to the Viet Cong by organizing and supporting civil society in local villages. The CIA-backed mission met with considerable success and may have prevented hundreds of thousands of villagers from joining the Communist insurrection.[108] These same villagers, however, were a primary source of troops for conventional-force missions in Vietnam. Following the assassination of President Kennedy, these missions were largely disbanded or repurposed into local reconnaissance units.

Special Operations Forces and the Central Intelligence Agency continued to play an important role in Vietnam. Psychological operations were employed extensively: the Strategic Hamlet Program established the base for later theories of counterinsurgency; the Navy SEALs notched their first contributions to covert missions; and the raid at Son Tay foreshadowed the "hyperconventional" raids that would later define the popular conception of Special Operations Forces. Other joint Defense and CIA programs, such as the Phoenix program, gained a darker reputation with accusations of targeted assassinations of civilians.[109] Whether this reputation was deserved or not—the Phoenix program was instrumental in dismantling the Viet Cong infrastructure, or shadow government—the perpetuation of negative stories regarding the Phoenix program and the military's level of professionalism contributed to the rapid decline of public support for the war, particularly among the left.[110] As America's social fabric unraveled during the tumultuous upheavals of the late 1960s and 1970s, Vietnam became one of a number of reasons that people began to lose trust in their government.

Vietnam provides a case study in the ineffectiveness of counterinsurgency and unconventional warfare in the absence of a credible threat or willingness to escalate. As will be discussed shortly, reactions to Vietnam would eventually return the military from its detour into prewar shaping operations and strategies of attrition to the more natural American tendency to focus on the domination of its adversaries in combat. From a public and political perspective, Vietnam marked an end to the days when the press was a reliable ally in the government's public-diplomacy efforts. This would lead different politicians down roads of cautiousness or secretiveness—neither of which would help resolve the public-opinion problem. Thus, while the military shied away from what Liddell Hart characterized as the "indirect approach," the American public became more suspicious of the intentions behind the government's foreign policies. These concurrent developments undermined America's ability to develop competitive strategies below the threshold of war, particularly those to counter the active measures of the Soviet Union.

The American people were eager for a new direction, and their dissatisfaction with the status quo created a ripe opportunity for foreign policy innovation.[111] In February 1970 President Nixon provided a speech to Congress outlining a new foreign policy direction for his administration. In his remarks, he declared the "end of the post-war period" and emphasized the importance that partnerships with friendly nations, negotiations, and a sustained but practical orientation toward continued American strength would play in his approach to international relations.[112] He also noted the "shattered" state of the international Communist community and implied that exploiting these fissures would bolster America's position in the world. A policy of containment, he suggested, was no longer relevant: America would need to emphasize the interests that each nation had in maintaining international peace and use diplomacy and strength as tools to nudge the international balance of power in America's favor.

Consolidation of power in the White House sped up these shifts in emphasis. Efforts of line agencies to counter propaganda, employ economic warfare, and use the military to shape the strategic landscape were de-emphasized in the 1970s. Although Soviet propaganda activities were still monitored by the U.S. Information Agency, for example, interest in countering Soviet disinformation declined (despite its growing distribution network, as discussed in the chapter on Russia), and the president dismissed the output of the CIA in favor of the advice of Henry Kissinger.[113] Pledges to reduce America's overseas commitments, combined with the military's transition to an all-volunteer force, resulted in a dramatic reduction in the size of the military and its overseas presence. The "strength" component of Nixon's plan would manifest in the development of new technologies and operational concepts rather than by committing large numbers of American troops to fight foreign wars.[114]

The shift in approach pursued by the Nixon administration represented a new form of American competition, one more rooted in the realpolitik of old-world politics than in a desire to manage and oversee the world's affairs. This differentiated Nixon from his immediate predecessors and the strategy outlined in NSC-68, which provided for a massive build-up in expenditures in an effort to contain the spread of communism. Even though the bureaucratic machinery of competition decreased in relevance under his watch, Nixon attempted to set the scene for great-power politics to unfold in a more orderly, more predictable, less expensive, and less dangerous manner.

The policy of détente and the centralization of power in the White House yielded major accomplishments. Its discordance with American foreign policy traditions, however, led Congress to constrain the Nixon administration. On the plus side, the president and his staff adroitly played Russia and China against each other by reestablishing relations with the latter to prompt better relations with the former. With respect to the Soviets, Nixon negotiated landmark arms-control treaties, such as the Anti-Ballistic Missile Treaty through the Strategic Arms Limitation Talks. There is also evidence to suggest that, as a result of the warming of relations, the Soviet Union reduced its use of active measures, such as propaganda and subversion, during the Nixon years.[115]

Strategic calculations, however, also led to a de-emphasis if not rejection of values that had long guided American foreign policy. For example, the administration minimized concerns over human rights and democracy promotion in favor of relying on regional strongmen to maintain international stability. In addition to diminishing America's moral authority, support to authoritarian regimes and the secrecy borne from centralization resulted in Congressional backlash. The War Powers Resolution attempted to limit presidential authority to engage in military actions without informing Congress, and changes to the Foreign Assistance Act and the subsequent Harkin Amendment passed after Nixon's resignation, limited the government's ability to provide assistance to serial violators of human rights. The circumstances of Nixon's resignation did little to ensure the survival of détente. Although the Nixon administration understood the cold realities of great-power politics, it could not so easily avoid the structural realities of the American system.

Due to backlash against Nixon, America soon faced the opposite problem of allowing its values to overtake its grasp on the reality of its place in the world. Later in the 1970s, Jimmy Carter was elected on a platform of putting values and principles at the center of America's foreign policy concerns. This about-face from the priorities of the Nixon administration created myriad other problems as America began to appear weak on the global stage. The fact that the military had atrophied during the 1970s further contributed to such perceptions: although the 1970s marked a period of doctrinal innovation and adroit planning for the future by the U.S. military, a reduction in end strength and the decline of special-operations units weakened America's ability to deter its enemies. Carter's most notable contribution to the military was the creation of Delta Force, a small group of special-operations soldiers that held the mandate of countering terrorism.[116] Yet even this decision led to problems when Delta Force attempted to rescue American personnel held hostage in Iran: Operation Eagle Claw was called off before it started due to a deadly helicopter collision in the Iranian desert. If realpolitik was unsavory to the American people, the sight on television of impotence at the hand of Iranian revolutionaries was unacceptable.

Ronald Reagan came into office with a completely different set of assumptions and ideas about the Soviet Union. As Thomas Mahnken notes, he "rejected the notion that the Soviet Union was a permanent fixture in the international system, and rather thought of it as a 'temporary aberration . . . [which] is contrary to human nature.'"[117] Thus, unlike the administrations of the 1960s and 1970s, which strayed from the typical American tendency to view the annihilation of its enemies as the ultimate goal, Reagan understood that American strategy would not succeed unless its theory of victory included the eradication of the ideology that drove the Soviet Union.

The United States

Reagan began his ideological war against the Soviet Union by issuing National Security Decision Directive (NSDD) 75, which called for the promotion of change within the Soviet Union to a "more pluralistic political and economic system."[118] The directive goes on to list how each component of national power should contribute to the "shap[ing of] the Soviet environment." Here too, the Reagan administration departed from its predecessors by recognizing the comprehensive view of competition held by the Soviets and specifying how military deterrence, economic warfare, and political warfare could undermine Soviet standing both within its own borders and throughout the world. Rather than sidestepping the bureaucracy under his command, Reagan sought to enlist the activities of each agency and department toward the accomplishment of his grand strategy.

The Reagan administration also parted from past administrations by recognizing that Soviet influence activities amounted to something more than propaganda: they represented a war being waged against the United States in real time. In a 1984 speech to the Central Intelligence Agency, for example, Reagan highlighted the threat of Soviet "active measures," which were "designed to subvert and deceive, to 'disinform' the public opinion upon which our democracies are built."[119] Defining the problem this way unlocked input from—and a role for—an expanded number of additional agencies beyond the U.S. Information Agency. Reagan's CIA director William Casey also understood the comprehensive nature of the Soviet threat. In a 1985 speech, Casey outlined how the Soviet Union weaved together many methods, including political-influence operations, disinformation, forgeries, and front organizations, to create specific campaigns tied to their political and strategic interests.[120] From an implementation standpoint, experts worked across agency lines to combat the Soviet approach: the Active Measures Working Group, for example, mitigated the effectiveness of Soviet disinformation campaigns by exposing Soviet covert collaboration with various media and civil-society organizations.[121] The broad strategic guidance provided in Reagan's NSDDs and the selection of personnel who shared his vision fostered a cooperation among various departments that would have been difficult if not impossible without White House leadership.

On the economic front, NSDD-75 called for the U.S. government to avoid economic policies that might aid the Soviet Union, to minimize Western dependence on Soviet goods and, conversely, to foster Soviet dependencies on those of the West. But the most daunting economic test posed by the Reagan administration to the Soviets came in the form of a massive military buildup. Between 1980 and 1988, America's military spending more than doubled. Much of this increase went to expanding America's global power-projection capabilities, including equipment, supplies, military construction, and both airlift and sealift capabilities.[122] Meanwhile, the Strategic Defense Initiative, a program designed to protect the United States from incoming intercontinental ballistic missiles, threatened to undermine Soviet abilities to strike the mainland United States. Leaving the program's technical feasibility aside, the initiative posed a significant economic challenge to the Soviets, as the cost of countering it would have forced Moscow to cut domestic spending at a time when its resource base was already spread thin.[123]

The injection of funds into the Defense Department allowed the military to implement many of the doctrinal reforms and modernization plans that had been percolating since the 1970s. In addition, the passage of the Goldwater-Nichols Act in 1986 fundamentally changed the command structure of the U.S. military and set the stage for the increased cooperation among the services that would transpire in later conflicts. Despite the significant increase in expenditures and emphasis on AirLand Battle, which emphasized preparations for near-peer conflict, U.S. military engagements took on a limited nature in the 1980s.[124]

The United States

Yet had the military engaged directly with the Soviet Union, the increased flexibility, the streamlining of command, and the improved technical prowess that stemmed from the military reforms of the 1980s, including the Goldwater-Nichols Act, would have increased its chances of success. It's reasonable to assume that this fact was not lost on Moscow.

Although the precise causality of the Soviet Union's fall remains the subject of debate, Reagan's contribution to the development of a way of American competition is clear. Whereas NSC-68 marked a stroke of strategic brilliance, America's postwar institutions were not yet mature enough to achieve the framework's full potential. Eisenhower's New Look helped develop the capabilities of the young Central Intelligence Agency and expanded the deterrent power of the American military, but it also failed to fully address the manner by which the adversary approached its competition with America. And whereas the realpolitik of détente yielded a number of important breakthroughs in international relations and streamlined America's foreign policy actions, its failure to account for structural realities of the American system and its underutilization of the many tools of power that lay outside of the West Wing limited its success.

Ronald Reagan combined an understanding of the enemy with a comprehensive strategy to undermine its power. Whether that led to the collapse of the Soviet Union or not, it demonstrated that the United States is, in fact, able to implement a comprehensive system of competition, one that remains aligned with its principles and that brings all tools of national power to bear against a formidable foe.

Old Techniques, New World Disorder

In November 1989, America awoke to find that the Berlin Wall—the very symbol of the Iron Curtain—would no longer separate West and East Germany. That moment marked the beginning of the end of the Cold War understanding of the world, not only because of the coming disintegration of the Soviet Union. In an instant, the United States found itself without a near-peer adversary in world affairs. For the better part of the decade to come, many in the United States began to consider the victory over communism not just as a signifier of the superiority of Western ideas but also as an opportunity to make permanent America's newfound position in world affairs.

That the United States would soon find itself engaged in its first conventional conflict since Vietnam did little to attenuate America's confidence. On the contrary, the Persian Gulf conflict allowed America to demonstrate the transformation that its military had undergone since Vietnam. Through the use of modern equipment, such as the Abrams tank, Bradley Fighting Vehicle, Patriot missile, and Apache helicopter, and soldiers trained to employ these systems, America suffered only 148 casualties during Operation Desert Storm, as opposed to more than twenty thousand for the Iraqis.[125] The use of air power also proved consequential if not decisive in Desert Storm, particularly in facilitating the rapid pace of victory over the Iraqi military.[126] The use of increasingly networked and precise systems led some to argue that the United States had ushered in a revolution in military affairs; other countries took notice, but in unpredictable ways.

As discussed in chapter 3, the People's Liberation Army noticed the dramatic difference in casualty counts between American and Iraqi forces. It noted that the use of technology enabled this impressive feat but also noticed that many of the technologies employed—especially precision-guided munitions—were employed operationally in order to reduce casualties. This insight hinted at a deeper shift that had occurred within the U.S. military.

The commanders of Desert Storm came of age in the Vietnam war, when troop casualties fomented discord at home and left America's political leadership with little choice but to withdraw forces. Technology, if used adroitly, could allow the United States to use its military in the pursuit of national objectives while minimizing the blow to political will that high casualty rates would entail. Novel technologies allowed a rapid domination of the adversary that would reduce the political cost of going to war.

Although this approach made sense from a military standpoint, and certainly yielded results, it also distracted from the changing nature of international conflict. The need for the U.S. military to achieve rapid dominance over a conventional enemy was decreasing while the need to counter the advances of weaker adversaries was increasing. As discussed throughout this chapter, the development of military doctrine has rarely intersected with national strategic realities. Just as America had begun to develop a comprehensive strategy toward competing with an enemy outside of combat, the need to go to combat arose. As America's experience in Desert Storm demonstrated, the military was far more interested in achieving rapid results than it was in developing skills to win over populations or to limit an adversary's strategic maneuverability. Those tasks had been the priority of civilian agencies, and America's experience in Vietnam did not encourage military leaders to change that status quo. This de-emphasis of "phase zero" operations was implicitly codified in *Joint Publication 3-0*, which directed the military to place the bulk of its effort on domination in combat.[127] Yet world events did not comport with these thrusts toward the rapid domination of conventional adversaries. And as the 1993 downing of a UH-60 Black Hawk helicopter in Mogadishu demonstrated, for all of its power, the United States remained vulnerable to dedicated if inferior actors.

In fairness, the focus on one type of enemy was not the fault of the military alone. Although the 1960s concept of flexible response once again became relevant in the 1990s, policymakers did not feel the same level of urgency to prioritize numerous military-response options as did their historical counterparts. The "peace dividend" that came with the fall of the Soviet Union translated into lower military budgets in the 1990s, and the idea of *unipolarity* suggested that, because it had won the ideological war, America would not need to adapt to the tactics of its enemies. Military and policy leaders alike began to assume that America would be able to set the terms of its military engagements; the incident in Somalia was viewed as an unfortunate aberration from this new norm. Funding to intelligence agencies dropped precipitously.[128] The military still needed to protect America from existential threats, which the new doctrine of rapid domination addressed. But investments in activities, much less a strategy, to address challenges before they arose seemed beside the point—America had won the competition.

That fleeting assumption belied the activities of Islamist extremist groups who, halfway around the globe, catalogued America's weaknesses and devised a plot to attack the country on its own soil. Following the involvement of the CIA with the mujahideen against the Soviets in the 1980s, political leaders of the 1990s de-emphasized American involvement there, even as the Taliban took power. The attacks of September 11, 2001, forever shattered the conclusion that the United States would no longer need to worry about serious challenges to its power.

Aimless Competition: America since 9/11

Within days of September 11, 2001, the United States responded to al-Qaeda by sending missiles and Special Operations Forces to their encampments in the remote reaches of Afghanistan. Thus began the longest conflict engagement in American history, one that continues to this day. The perpetrators of the 9/11 attacks predicted that the United States would react to the acts of terrorism committed on its own soil with military force and viewed America's inevitable involvement in a drawn-out conflict as a shortcut to diminishing its power.

Nevertheless, the United States remained confident that its military primacy would not face a serious challenge. When the George W. Bush administration decided to invade Iraq, confidence that the military would quickly oust Saddam and that Americans would be greeted as liberators overshadowed planning for the country's postinvasion stabilization. Even without launching military operations on multiple fronts, America's power relative to that of its adversaries was decreasing. As countries outside of America's traditional allies began to reap the benefits of involvement with the international economic system, they began investing in sophisticated military capabilities of their own. They observed the manner by which America approached war and began to deploy or accelerate methods of competition that undermined America's standing in the world and with its own public. With the distraction of Iraq and Afghanistan, America's competitive approaches developed during the Cold War that could mitigate these developments remained a low priority.

Even had this not been the case, the number and variety of potential adversaries had grown, as had the number of competitive mediums. This stymied the development of strategic clarity that existed during the age of bipolarity. The belief that America had won the final ideological war against authoritarianism minimized the perceived threat posed by potential near-peer challengers. Such a threat, if it were to occur, seemed very far off, whereas the threat posed by Islamic extremism required immediate action. Furthermore, the short-term nature of the American political cycle rewarded actions that could conclude, or at least bear fruit, during one administration. Although eliminating successive leaders of terrorist cells could not eliminate the threat posed by Islamism, it could at least provide quantifiable success in a way that competitive strategies would not.

As the United States began to shift its priorities towards counterterrorism, the lack of investment in the tools of the indirect approach began to hinder overseas operations. It was not until the adoption of the *Counterinsurgency Field Manual* and, later, the surge, that the situation in Iraq began to turn around. That the military required a reminder of its long history of engaging in insurgencies and counterinsurgencies demonstrates how little value the discipline had enjoyed since Vietnam. The surge marked a turning point in the conflict in that commanders in the field were finally given the tools required to complete the now drawn-out affair of ridding Iraq of an insurgency that had metastasized to urban areas. The fact that such resources were provided only after persistent pleas by field commanders shows the extent to which political will had constrained the president.

Political will, or lack thereof, would influence the way that Americans considered the next contenders for the office of the presidency. Rightly sickened by the atrocities committed by a few servicemembers in Iraq and tired of a conflict that had gone on longer than anyone had foreseen, Americans elected a candidate who promised a more hopeful future that would leave the baggage of the Iraq war behind. Following his election, President Obama embarked on setting the United States on a new path, where policies that he saw as reckless were exchanged for careful and pragmatic ones.

The security demands on the sole remaining superpower, however, did not relent because of one election. Thus, the new president devised a way for addressing America's security concerns while maintaining a distance from the decisions of his immediate predecessor. As had become common among American presidents, President Obama turned to Special Operations Forces, often acting covertly, to fill the gap between his rhetoric and the realities of America's interests in the international system. The pace of special-operations missions increased and resulted in high-profile raids such the one that resulted in the death of Osama bin Laden in Pakistan. Yet they also resulted in many less-noticed missions throughout the Middle East, enough to draw into question whether the administration was using all the tools of national security at its disposal in a coordinated and strategic way.

To coordinate strategy, a clear strategy must first exist. Whereas the Obama administration recognized the ongoing nature of national-security challenges more than many of his detractors expected, his administration nonetheless was unable to complete a national-security strategy that addressed the drivers of these challenges. Specificity and decisiveness made way for platitudes and generalities, leaving the government aimless. Moreover, as power became increasingly concentrated in the White House, senior officials became engrossed in operational-level decisions, distracting if not blinding them from the kind of broader analysis and coordination that only the White House could drive.[129]

This resulted in strategic blind spots. Although many in the national-security and intelligence communities had for years warned of China's tendency to manipulate international legal and economic norms, for example, the administration—despite the rhetoric of the "pivot to Asia"—continued to pursue policies to incentivize China to change its behavior rather than punitive measures to constrain that country's advances. The administration also called the use of chemical weapons in Syria a "red line" that, if crossed, would result in decisive American action. The credibility of such threats, however, rang hollow to Assad, and chemical weapons were indeed used against the Syrian people. The administration also laughed off concerns about the intentions of Russia; meanwhile, Russia not only pursued a steady modernization of its military but also began to experiment with online tools of disinformation. All these developments could have been foreseen; indeed, they were, but handling all the details related to each development proved too much for one concentrated organ in the White House to handle.

Meanwhile, as the recovery from the economic fallout of the late 2000s recession exacerbated the ongoing shift of human and economic capital to a small subset of urban areas, many in the rest of the country began to distrust the intentions of America's education class. The privileged parts of America found few reasons to change a status quo that for the most part was working for them. In the realm of international relations, these differing perspectives manifested, on the one hand, in skepticism for continued American leadership in international affairs, as the benefits of that had grown opaque, and, on the other hand, a broad elite consensus that America's fundamental role in the international system should remain unchanged. The crisis at home was existential for part of the American public and merely a speed bump for many others.

These two dynamics played out within the Trump administration, a subject that this book will not attempt to explore in any depth. The United States produced a National Security Strategy that reflected the challenges that the United States currently faces; one both broadly applicable yet also specific enough to leave little doubt as to the main drivers of national-security threats. The Joint Chiefs of Staff, along with individual services, recognized the need to move past the rapid-dominance strategies of the 1990s and the singular focus on counterterrorism that dominated the first decade of the twenty-first century and to prepare the military to fight in a number of contingencies, of which many may not involve combat at all.[130] Yet the mercurial style of the Trump administration did little to guide the national-security bureaucracy on a clear path toward implementing the recommendations contained within its strategy and doctrinal documents.

Despite all this, larger questions underlay the ephemerality of any one presidential administration. First, it will take far more than a few well-considered documents to develop a coherent American way of competition. Given the penchant for strategies of annihilation so embedded within the American conception of war, America has succeeded in cases when its adversaries pose an existential threat to its existence—whether existence is defined by survival, ideology, or way of life. Contemporary America cannot seem to agree on who the enemy is or to what degree each threat may be existential. Part of this is due to the manner by which America's competitors choose to compete—not through direct, obvious ways but through subtle actions that chip away at America's strategic position over time. Devising a strategy to contain such threats would be difficult enough in the most unified of times, as demonstrated by the Cold War. In a time when the focus of national discourse is more on internal enemies than external ones, it may prove impossible.

The United States also faces a deeper question. Expansion has driven American policy throughout much of its history. Westward exploration and the concept Manifest Destiny first propelled Americans across the continent, annihilating native populations and challenges from European and neighboring countries in its wake. The Monroe Doctrine and the acquisition of overseas territories in the Pacific established America as an empire with holdings and interests far beyond the natural limits of its geography. America continued this tradition, albeit in an abstract way, through the pursuit of "just wars" that defended and expanded the application of its ideas on governance and economics, first to Europe and Asia and later to allied nations across the globe. The unacceptability of fascist and communist expansion unified government leaders and the American public alike.

With the fall of the Soviet Union, it seemed as though American ideas had finally won. However naïve it may look in retrospect, it is understandable that intellectuals and leaders alike reveled in the possibilities of an America that did not have a clear and existential adversary for the first time in memory. That impression has proven to be an illusion. Though the number and variety of challenges to American security has increased since the end of the Cold War, America has in the past shown its ability to innovate and adapt to changing security dynamics. Unlike before, however, it is no longer clear how, or for what purpose, America will expand. The success of alternative governance models and the erosion of the meaning of democracy by those who govern in a manner that is anything but democratic has undermined America's sense of ideological superiority. Whereas foreign lands may not offer freedom, they offer economic and human development on a scale that America currently does not have the political ability to achieve. Young Americans question the superiority of the American way of life, and many older Americans seem content to retreat into the nostalgia of how they imagine America once was rather than dedicate the resources required to build for the future.[131] Until America is able to regain its confidence and overcome its divisions, the struggle to harness an effective means of competition will continue. America will remain powerful. But the central role that political will plays in the American system will, for the foreseeable future, encourage its complacency.

The United States

Conclusions

This work will conclude where it began: with the question of efficacy. For all of America's power, the efficacy of its strategies has declined since the end of the Cold War. This book has shown that the rise of other powers is a symptom rather than a cause of this phenomenon. What is the cause? Examining the current mismatch between America's strategic predispositions and its declining reservoir of political and social will compared to those of its adversaries will provide clues to the answer.

This book has endeavored to demonstrate how America's understanding of warfare contrasts with that of its adversaries. It has validated Russell Weigley's thesis that the United States is predisposed to strategies of annihilation, meaning that it looks to eradicate adversaries rather than develop long-term methods to dilute their influence. It has further demonstrated that other nations possess different strategic predispositions. Russia, Iran, and China have developed methods to diminish America's territorial and ideological influence through the manipulation of various forms of information and have integrated multiple tools of national power into their efforts. Though all are modernizing military technology and have developed comparative advantages in certain areas with respect to America, their success lies primarily in how they integrate efforts across the diplomatic, military, informational, and economic realms. Competing on these terms will require changing America's understanding of international competition, expanding its understanding of warfare, and enhancing the country's ability to employ tools in various combinations as international threat dynamics evolve.

In contrast to Russia, China, and Iran, the political and social will to engage in international competition has declined in America (and also in the West more generally). Whereas the strategic predispositions of Russia, China, and Iran are less reliant on social and political will, these countries nevertheless harbor relatively strong reservoirs of both. The West suffers from the opposite scenario, with strategic predispositions highly reliant on human agency (or, in its collective form, social will) and political will and dwindling supplies of both. Successive American strategy documents, whether specific and prescriptive or anodyne and diagnostic, rarely take into account the importance of social and political will to success. Although developing formal strategies is an important step to initiating change, a typical American strategy document, if it discusses ends, ways, and means at all, assumes the ability to muster support within the federal bureaucracy and in the public writ large.

The current moment demonstrates the flaws in this assumption. America may no longer be at the apex of its power relative to other nations, yet by most every metric it retains a sizeable lead over the militaries and economies of its adversaries. Since the end of the Cold War, the United States has developed a series of strategies to retain the territorial and soft influence that it has spent decades building. Yet these areas are precisely where America's adversaries continue to make strides at its expense. This is because revisionist actors in the international system have observed America, identified the blind spots created by its power and strategic predisposition, and adapted. Their comparative comfort with ambiguity and ability to align various tools of national power have proved useful as adversaries reduce the relevance of America's comparative strengths, particularly in the realm of information and ideas.

The United States positioned ideas and information as the currency of the current age of international competition. The internet, net-centric warfare and now informationized warfare, and the rules-based international order all trace their origins to American ingenuity to some degree. Confidence in the superiority of American ideas, bolstered by the end of the Cold War, however, has caused many leaders to overlook the need to reconfigure their approach. On the one hand, the United States continues to champion the liberal values of its founding; on the other hand, it has grown suspicious of outsiders and less confident in the efficacy of its own systems. Although it shifted the decisive realm of competition from combat to information, America's capability and capacity to dominate the information space has decreased. Assessing adversarial approaches will provide clues to how Washington might begin the process of balancing against its adversaries, a necessary step to improving the efficacy of its strategies. Increased efficacy would, in turn, improve the confidence of Americans in their own government and mitigate recent declines in political and social will.

Through different means, Russia, China, and Iran are each challenging the status quo of the rules-based international order by expanding their spheres of influence—in terms of both territory and ideology—through the use and manipulation of information (information defined here as any data available to alter perceptions of power). As the most powerful actor within the international system, the United States is the most logical target for any actor that wishes to disrupt international power balances or to increase its own influence. Despite the many advantages enjoyed by the United States when competing against its adversaries, Russia, China, and Iran each share similar advantages in their attempts to expand their own influence at America's expense.

First, each has demonstrated the ability and inclination to develop and employ long-term strategies. In a practical sense, Russia, China, and Iran face few of the impediments to taking a long-term view that the United States does. Each has developed a system of governance not only unencumbered by frequent, fair, and free elections but also characterized by a vanguard that, in some way or other, formulates and perpetuates the state's interests beyond the tenure of any one leader. The Iranian Revolutionary Guard, the Chinese Communist Party, and the intelligence and security apparatus in Russia that stretches back to the tsarist period define and protect the interests of the state by permeating their respective societies. The American national security bureaucracy is charged with a similar role. But its comparative fragmentation and the limitations placed on it by the U.S. Constitution prevent any one part of this vanguard, if it can be called that, from protecting national interests both within and outside the country. Furthermore, it is, by design, responsive rather than impervious to the shifting priorities of each successive presidential administration. In terms of strategic predispositions, Russia, China, and Iran have many more centuries of experience to draw from than does America. During that time, the vanguard in each state has developed a cogent understanding not only of the building blocks of international power but also of how to knock them down or build them back up from scratch. The value of long-term strategies is more apparent when short-term strategies prove inadequate.

This orientation toward long-term strategies goes hand in hand with the second advantage, an understanding that armed conflict is but one facet of international competition and not necessarily the most decisive one. This more holistic understanding of competition allows space for methods other than combat to create decisive and lasting strategic impacts; it also incentivizes cross-functional approaches to security dilemmas and provides the basis for expanded cooperation between government and other elements of society. Whether this mindset echoes through ancient and recent strategic aphorisms, as is the case with China, or in the kleptocratic exploitation of national assets as in Russian and Iran, recognizing the multipronged nature of international competition allows for the creation of policies that limit, delay, or avoid armed conflict.

The United States has implemented grand strategies in the past, particularly during the Cold War. However, the quantity and variety of threats in the international system presents an obstacle preventing the emergence of a similar strategy today. The United States continues to focus on ways to ensure military superiority in combat yet fails to provide similar support to devising ways of diplomatic, economic, and broader technological superiority, thus ceding much of the space below the threshold of armed conflict to its adversaries.

Third, while America's adversaries generally enjoy fewer financial resources, their comparative flexibility with the alignment, distribution, and employment of those resources provides them with a distinct advantage in protracted competition. Although Russian, Chinese, and Iranian internal decision-making processes are far from perfect, the ability of each of these nations to align various bureaucracies toward a common goal allows for a concentration of effort that the United States government, by design, does not possess. The centralized decision-making process of authoritarian regimes facilitates iterative responses to changing conditions, and the broad patronage networks and other informal mechanisms of control exercised by Beijing, Moscow, and Tehran act as further lubricant. Whereas the rigid nature of America's national-security funding system and the clear distinctions between private and public enterprises exist for important ethical and constitutional reasons, they also prevent the United States from competing on the same footing as nations that do not share the same constraints.

In the past several years, American policymakers have become more aware of these challenges. The National Security and National Defense Strategies of 2017–18 both recognize the need to broaden the definition of competition and to incorporate all tools of national power into strategic responses to America's enemies. Yet because these advantages manifest at not only the strategic but the operational and tactical levels as well, America must also consider deeper changes to its approach. At the operational level, the military has amended its doctrine to include guidance for shaping and competing short of war. However, these efforts have taken place independent of interagency partners. Moreover, doctrinal guidance is generally just that. As the evolution of American strategy outlined in this work demonstrates, changing the military's approach to warfare often requires decades of dedication, the forcing mechanism of an existential threat, or both.

At a theoretical level, addressing these gaps will require recognizing that the currencies of power in international relations have coalesced into the realm of perceptions shaped by information and data manipulation. The dichotomous view of power as either hard, generally having to do with military power, or soft, having to do with diplomacy, economics, and information, no longer maps to the reality of how nations seek advantage in the world system. Strategies from the Cold War era, which also addressed a shift in the spectrum of power in international relations, provide a useful catalyst for thinking about the current primacy of information in determining the balance of power. Whereas scholars of the nuclear age used the destructive power of atomic weaponry as the impetus for their efforts, today's scholars might use the diffusion of destructive capabilities in the information realm as a starting point to understand the dynamics that drive power and perceptions of power globally.

At a practical level, policy and decision-makers should recognize the integrated nature of the current threat landscape and develop policy reforms and programs that reflect the agile yet centralized characteristics of America's adversaries. What follow are a few proposals to help lay the groundwork for a less complacent, more responsive American national security apparatus.

Need for Comprehensive Long-Term Strategies

Despite only periodic success at developing and implementing grand strategies, the United States has developed a number of long-term strategies to assess and react to foreign threats. The Pentagon established the Office of Net Assessment in 1973 to "develop and coordinate net assessments of the standing, trends, and future prospects of U.S. military capabilities and military potential" in comparison to those of America's adversaries.[1] The Office of Net Assessment, led for most if its existence by the late Andrew Marshall, holds a rightful place of reverence among modern American strategists; however, both its research-focused, diagnostic mandate and its location in the Department of Defense limits its ability to translate its findings into implementable strategies. Nevertheless, the long-term understanding of threat vectors and the intricate connections between societies, economies, and militaries that were a hallmark of Marshall's work remain relevant to this day.

Take the concept of competitive strategies, which Marshall defined as both "inward and outward directed . . . built on one's enduring strengths while seeking to exploit the adversary's enduring weaknesses and vulnerabilities."[2] The competitive-strategies paradigm illustrates the approach that Russia, China, and Iran have taken to diminish American influence. Over time each country has developed an understanding of its internal strengths and weaknesses, assessed those of America, and devised ways to compete on terms that leverage their strengths

Conclusions   243 and mitigate their shortcomings. Competitive strategies are thus a useful guidepost for policymakers and decisionmakers seeking to understand how adversaries pursue strategic advantages below the threshold of armed conflict.

Devising and implementing competitive strategies, however, is much easier said than done. For reasons explained in the introduction and previous chapter, the United States has only successfully employed such methods during periods of perceived existential crisis. In the case of the Cold War, elites *and* the public shared this perception. Without this alignment, decision-makers are likely to focus their efforts on curtailing threats that appear more imminent, if not consequential. In order to ensure the prolonged application of resources and attention that competitive strategies require, strategists must overcome this constraint.

Assuming that threat perceptions do align, the success of a competitive strategy relies upon the accuracy of internal and external assessments and a solid understanding of the nature of the game between two adversaries.[3] Here too, the United States faces significant challenges. Internally, public and elite opinions about America's role in the world have diverged, and perceptions of America's strengths and weaknesses have coalesced along partisan lines. Perceptions of external actors have followed a similar pattern. These issues present little challenge to the policy agenda of any one president, but they damage the ability to maintain a coherent competitive strategy across administrations.[4] More optimistically, the praise that the 2017 National Security Strategy received from across the political spectrum indicates a growing consensus about the nature of the game. Consensus, however, does not always equate with correctness; misunderstanding any of the elements of success may increase the likelihood of conflict rather than decrease it.[5] Moreover, the strategy has yet to prove successful in implementation, and the duration of the current enthusiasm for it remains to be seen.

Conclusions

Enhancing the endurance of a particular strategy will require augmenting the ability of current institutions to enable implementation across administrations or the creation of new institutions. The Office of Net Assessment is neither equipped nor mandated to conduct this task, and its focus on the Department of Defense may lead to analyses that discount tools of national power that reside outside of the department. Although past successful grand strategies such as those in the early years of the Cold War emanated from the Department of State, they only began to guide the efforts of the entire government once adopted and codified by presidential directives at the National Security Council.

Past attempts by Congress to develop strategy proved vulnerable to political vicissitudes and funding; statutory and advisement authorities alone are insufficient to guide the direction of policy.[6] Yet Congress does have the ability to impose reporting requirements on the bodies that it oversees and to guide and direct funding to specific programs. In addition to requiring many regular reports from the Departments of Defense and State, for example, Congress may rely upon the Congressional Research Service to collect information about particular executive policies and programs, and Congress occasionally requests National Intelligence Estimates to determine the intelligence community's collective view of a particular issue. With respect to a long-term-strategy document, however, it is unclear which body Congress would direct to create such a document. Congress's funding authority, provided by the Constitution, is essential to effective oversight of the executive branch. Funding directives are a tool of implementation, however, not of strategy creation. Congress does retain the ability to shape, limit, and define the mandates of the executive-branch organs under its purview. Amendments to the statute that mandated the National Security Council, for example, could help reorient elements of the body away from policy implementation and toward the production of strategies with extended outlooks. Yet such an adjustment would do little to protect the implementation of strategies over multiple presidential administrations.

Presidents enjoy broad authority to set the course of American foreign policy and strategy, and presidential willingness to exert this authority has increased in recent decades. Broad interpretations of the inherent power of the presidency and a number of other authorities designed to allow presidents flexibility in times of crisis have expanded the tools by which presidents may determine the direction of policy initiatives.[7] Operationally speaking, the executive bodies within the White House created during the administration of Franklin Roosevelt, including the National Security Council, coordinate the execution of presidential directives throughout the federal bureaucracy. Because few presidents enter office with a background in strategy formulation, they often must rely on staff to produce a strategic expression of presidential intent. The frequent turnover of staff, particularly following the election of a new president, constrains the ability of the NSC to execute whole-of-government or whole-of-society strategies over multiple administrations.

This should change. Although it is axiomatic that each president retains the prerogative to adapt and change the government's policy priorities, the absence of an institution or individuals to advise the president on strategic challenges that predate and may succeed his administration represents a critical deficiency in the executive advisory process. Whether through the creation of permanent (vice rotational) positions for civil servants on the National Security Council staff or through the creation of a permanent body for long-term strategy formulation within the Executive Office of the President, the United States needs a mechanism to produce and implement strategies that endure beyond a single administration.

The success of such strategies will hinge upon the ability to generate political will not only within government but also with other elements of civil society. In implementation, the White House should maintain links with private-sector elements that play an important role in contributing to and building American industrial and intellectual capital. For the government, these connections will provide a better understanding of the state of the art of industrial and technological advances, which would inform and unlock new modalities of competition. For private-sector groups, these interactions will provide insight into how the government sees long-term threats and opportunities, allowing them to better anticipate demand. Such an approach is not without historical or recent precedent: both Franklin Roosevelt and Donald Trump engaged with industrial leaders when considering their approaches toward warfare and international competition. Yet the ad hoc and crisis-oriented nature of these engagements limited their scope and impact. Longer-term engagements between formulators of national strategy and industrial leaders, as practiced in different ways in both Finland and Israel,[8] would create synergies between policy and private-sector leaders that will help the government gain an improved understanding of America's strengths and weaknesses.

In addition to industrial links, interested academics should provide input to the formulation of long-term strategies, as their understanding of historical trends and theories will provide sage guidance as the organization attempts to map out the future. Whether conducted through working groups or formalized fellowships, links with the academic community would also help foster the next generation of strategists. Such arrangements are also not without precedent, as academics frequently interact with the U.S. government on a range of issues. Regular and formalized interactions with formulators of long-term strategies would strengthen the bridge between theory and practice. The development of a broader set of feedback mechanisms would mitigate groupthink and enlist outside stakeholders in the success of government strategies.

As the United States faces a number of distributed threats across multiple domains, the timing for these changes is particularly favorable. In practice, individuals or subcomponents of the NSC charged with formulating long-term strategies should take an approach to strategy formulation akin to that of the Office of Net Assessment, but with an orientation toward prescriptive solutions at a society- and government-wide scale rather than toward the diagnosis of future contingencies affecting one department.

The individuals or subcomponents would then face their most formidable challenge: defining and articulating what direction the United States should take in foreign affairs in the decades to come. Should the United States continue what Andrew Bacevich called the "strategy of openness" embedded in its founding documents and historical experience? Should it take a more aggressive, nationalistic approach, embrace its dominant position in global affairs with confidence, and formulate a strategy to maintain it, as Bradley Thayer has argued? Or should it embrace multipolarity and adopt strategies to hedge against the inevitable closure of the gap between its power and those of its competitors, as Christopher Layne has asserted?[9] It may be that a mixture of these approaches, or one not mentioned here, is most appropriate. Regardless of the path chosen, enhancing the mechanisms for long-term planning and implementation in the National Security Council will increase the likelihood that the relevance of a strategy will extend beyond a single presidential administration.

This proposal is not without its challenges: Congress has seen fit to reduce the size of presidential staff in recent years rather than seeking to expand it,[10] and the political setting of the Executive Office of the President makes it an unnatural place to develop and refine long-term strategies. Furthermore, one may argue that mechanisms for the creation of such strategies already exist in spades throughout the United States government. This author is sympathetic to that view, particularly given the State Department's prior role in the formation of grand strategy. It is possible that the policy planning staff of the State Department, for example, could fill the capability gap discussed in the preceding paragraphs. Yet because the National Security Council would need to sign off on any strategy produced by the Department of State, inserting a mechanism for long-term planning into the NSC may still be unavoidable. In the past, gifted State Department employees have developed grand strategies. Yet, just as in combat, waiting for a "genius" to emerge is far less reliable than creating mechanisms to reduce overall risk. The insertion of Platonic philosopher kings into the National Security Council would do just that.

Evolving America's Understanding of Warfare

This work has shown that America is capable of adapting and evolving its understanding of threat environments but that such changes tend to take place during times of existential crisis. Not all challenges, however, bubble up in a way that would elicit a response from senior leaders. Indeed, this work has also shown that America's adversaries deliberately pursue strategies that fall below the crisis threshold that would generate a direct response. America's leaders appear to have recognized this. Shifting the nation's understanding of warfare to get ahead of these challenges, however, rather than simply devising strategies to mitigate them, will require the development of a comprehensive understanding of warfare and competition. A number of hurdles stand in the way.

From a legal standpoint, the current era of cross-domain competition poses important challenges to both international and domestic legal regimes. From an international perspective, this book has detailed the extent to which Russia, Iran, and especially China manipulate international legal structures to advance their interests.[11] The conduct of *lawfare*, which often entails exploiting the letter of the law while disregarding its spirit, uses legal maneuvers to intimidate adversaries while undermining faith in international treaties and justice mechanisms. Creating an effective American mechanism for conducting offensive lawfare in accordance with long-term strategies would be the best defense against these measures. When China, for example, manipulates the UN Convention on the Law of the Seas, the United States should stand ready to not only conduct combined Freedom of Navigation Operations but also deploy other tools of national power to increase the costs of such behavior. The United States and its allies should also devise methods to use the international legal system to preempt or otherwise deter such actions rather than reacting to them after they occur.

Domestic legal vulnerabilities extend into a number of arenas that are beyond the scope of this work, from immigration law to policies that govern foreign direct investment in the United States. That said, loose standards for the registration of foreign corporations operating in the United States provide inroads for American adversaries to establish a foothold, often anonymously.[12] Although the United States should continue to provide a regulatory regime that encourages free and open competition, it should also coordinate the reform of vulnerable legal regimes through the lens of national-security concerns.

Beyond internal vulnerabilities to external threats, American legal regimes also hinder the ability of the United States to respond flexibly to adversarial actions. United States Code Titles 10, 50, and 22, which govern federal appropriations to defense and foreign-affairs-related activities, provide a framework for Congressional oversight of executive-branch activities. This funding regime limits the activities in which each agency may engage. While this system simplifies oversight, it also creates seams between the efforts of various organizations. For example, U.S. Title 10 and Title 50, which respectively cover the armed forces and the conduct of national security (including covert intelligence activities), specify different requirements and limitations on the activities that they fund, regardless of how each may fit into a wider strategy. The differences between these authorities and Title 22, which funds activities of the Department of State, are even greater—both in terms of scope and scale.[13] Whereas Russia, China, and Iran may shift various activities and human resources within their bureaucracies as requirements dictate, the inflexibility of U.S. Code and the oversight structure that it supports inhibits the United States from responding in kind. Congressional action could revise the sections of U.S. Code that govern funding and oversight for activities that advance America's competitive stance to eliminate or at least reduce the impact of these visible seams.

Beyond Congress, many other parts of the U.S. government must also adjust to the evolving international strategic landscape. Culturally and historically speaking, executive-branch leadership and coordination cells have oriented themselves to solving crises as they emerge rather than anticipating and shaping environments that produce such crises in the first place. While an orientation toward crisis response provides the flexibility and agility otherwise lacking in the broader executive branch, these benefits often come at the expense of a coherent approach to strategy and the acceptance of an increased risk of surprise.[14] For example, Chinese cyberattacks against the Office of Personnel Management followed a series of other data breaches that failed to trigger a crisis-level response from the United States government. As adversaries test and prod to determine the threshold that would produce a response from the United States, many otherwise preventable losses may occur.

This orientation toward crisis response sets the tone throughout the federal bureaucracy. In the Department of Defense, for example, the recently reformed phasing model in *Joint Publication 3-0* minimized the importance of shaping and risk-mitigation efforts and concentrated effort on dominating adversaries.[15] In the U.S. Intelligence Community, serving a rotation in a crisis-response or warning center has become a rite of passage as much as a stepping-stone to credibility and career advancement. Like America's broader approach to strategic efficacy, crisis-response efforts appeal to Clausewitzian edicts about the importance of individual genius and promise tidy, rapid solutions to situations that often only represent one scene in a multiact play. It is little wonder why crisis response appeals; it is also not surprising why the approach has proved inadequate to understanding, much less winning, ongoing international competitions. A separate insight from Clausewitz may prove more instructive for international competition short of war: that conflict is akin to a wrestling match, where each wrestler identifies and seizes upon even the most minute advantage throughout the duration of the interaction.[16]

Encouraging strategically grounded yet agile operational and tactical approaches will require more than just doctrinal reform, though efforts along these lines—such as the Joint Concept for Integrated Campaigning—are an important first step.[17] The Department of Defense must also incentivize the development of skills that are useful in deterring and mitigating the short-of-war threats that America's adversaries pose. Additionally, Special Operations Forces should continue to develop innovative and scalable techniques and encourage soldiers to consider the impact of their actions on the diplomatic, informational, and economic domains of competition, rather than thinking of the military as a siloed tool of national power. Finally, the Pentagon must resist thinking of new technologies as a panacea to mitigating future threats but consider the dynamics of the new competitive domains that these technologies create and ensure supremacy in preexisting ones. Interagency input and coordination will be critical to ensure that military responsibilities do not bleed over into those of civilian agencies. Reorienting American bureaucracies from relying on a singular genius to activating multiple

Conclusions

inputs in a dynamic and competitive environment will require flexibility, cross-domain collaboration, and amended incentive structures.

Leaving bureaucratic dynamics aside for the moment, the U.S. government must develop an external argument that communicates the nature of international competition and the role that all stakeholders play in improving America's resiliency and competitiveness. Although foreign and defense policy animates only a small fraction the American electorate, public perceptions, particularly when negative, often cloud presidential domestic and foreign policy agendas (the Vietnam War and the torture performed at Abu Ghraib prison in Iraq serve as two obvious examples).[18] Corrosion of public trust—whether from external sources or the actions of the U.S. government—undermines the foundations of America's approach to global affairs. Yet negative perceptions should not preclude the government from articulating the strategy behind its actions, or, when missteps occur, from admitting mistakes and refocusing the conversation on the enduring value of global engagement.

Creating an environment in which each facet of American society has a stake in the outcome of the nation's grand strategy will take time and may require new mechanisms. As mentioned in the previous section, some countries have achieved this through formal programs that create links between public- and private-sector leaders. America may seek to emulate these programs. The foundation of these programs, however, is often a preexisting relationship formed through national service or conscription that is out of step with current political and cultural realities in the United States. In the years since the end of the draft, the gulf in understanding between those who have served in the military and those who have not has expanded and led to differing conceptions of the purpose and relevance of the state itself. For example, the disconnect between innovators in one of the nation's most important economic centers—Silicon Valley—and the national-security establishment has led to many missed opportunities for collaboration and investment that, in the past, served as one of America's greatest strengths.[19] Bridging these divides will require an injection of flexibility into an otherwise formulaic and lengthy acquisition process, as well as a clear articulation of how international business practices that counter American interests may undermine a company's long-term viability. At a more grassroots level, a more flexible and creative approach to the use and composition of the reserve component of the U.S. Armed Forces may further cross-pollinate otherwise independent spheres of American life.

Winning the competition underway will require more than just savvy governance. It will require nothing less than a whole-of-nation approach, one that the United States has not undertaken since the Second World War but has successfully developed at several other points in its history. Historically, American strategic innovation has been driven by geopolitical ambiguity.[20] Recognizing the shifting nature of competition in our own era—and diagnosing the most important agents of change in American government, civil society, and the private sector—could well lead to innovations and adjustments that will perpetuate America's place in the world for generations to come.

Adoption, Alignment, and Implementation

Assuming the development of a coherent long-term strategy and a domestic environment more conducive to international competition, the U.S. government will face additional challenges in realizing its aims. First, various stakeholders may interpret even a well-articulated strategy differently. The government will need to devise strategies to align the mechanisms of power at its disposal in a way that still facilitates innovation and, in the words of the National Defense Strategy, "operational unpredictability." Only if the first two hurdles are overcome will the government then face its most daunting challenge: implementation.

Writing a National Security Strategy requires balancing concision with broad applicability to a wide variety of government institutions. However sophisticated the strategy may be, different departments and subcomponents within each will interpret it through the lens of their own institutional interests. This is inevitable and not necessarily negative, as the process may foster creative thinking about how to wield each tool of national power to maximum effect. Conversely, varied interpretations may also impede the implementation of presidential intent and serve as a rhetorical tool to justify outmoded operational approaches.

The most recent National Security Strategy, for example, heralds a return to an era of great power competition and provides a clear picture of the methods that China, Russia, and rogue states (i.e., North Korea and Iran) pursue to attain strategic advantages at America's expense. Because America has oriented itself toward domination at the expense of noncombat tactics, the risk existed that the recommendations would be interpreted through that orientation. That is exactly what has transpired. One of the primary contributors to the National Defense Strategy (NDS) testified to Congress that "the once overwhelming U.S. conventional military advantage vis-à-vis . . . major powers has eroded and will continue to erode" and that the United States must refocus away from "shaping" missions and "prioritize readying for major war against China or Russia."[21] Although America's conventional-force advantage has indeed eroded and preparing for combat does deter other nations from pushing the United States into armed conflict, the dichotomy between shaping operations and deterrence is false. This seemingly small elision of the important role of the military in creating strategic advantage outside of combat nonetheless created room for service chiefs to train their focus on near-peer combat scenarios rather than the messy and less quantifiable reality of how America's adversaries pursue their interests. The NDS also opens the door to this line of thinking by stating that the "surest way to prevent war is to be prepared to win one."[22] Yet even this statement fails to recognize that the war is already well underway, albeit in an unfamiliar form. Preparing to win a future war and devising ways to win a current competition require different resources, approaches, tools, and implementation strategies.

At the operational level, the military's development of the Joint Concept for Integrated Campaigning and ongoing conversations about multidomain battle are important steps toward injecting the "operational unpredictability" called for in the NDS into the application of American military power. Because these concepts are military-focused, however, they do little to align other tools of national power into similarly broad and flexible operating paradigms. While the National Security Council will take the lead on interagency integration, strategy documents set the foundation for functional and regional strategies relevant to each tool of national power, help induce interagency cooperation, and set the boundaries and parameters by which the success of implementation will be judged.[23] The successes of the Active Measures Working Group established to counter Soviet actions short of war in the 1980s provides an important case in point.[24]

Because the national-security bureaucracy is organized to take instruction from the president, the preferences and leadership of the president are the most consequential factors in the success of a particular foreign policy approach. This is true both from the perspective of the public—which views foreign policy more or less as a function of the presidency—and the government itself.[25] Yet because the public tends to place a higher value on the domestic-policy agendas of presidential candidates than on foreign policy platforms, strategic acumen tends not to rank highly in qualities that Americans require of their presidents. Likewise, presidents have little incentive to focus their energy on foreign policy when they could achieve more recognition from directing those energies toward domestic reforms. The concentration of foreign policy power in the chief executive thus presents two faces. On one hand, it may aide in strategic alignment; on the other hand, it may undermine strategic implementation, particularly if the leadership style of the president is mercurial or impulsive. Here again we see that the American system is built around the agency of an individual; the hope is that democratic mechanisms will select a genius. When this does not occur, or if the president's genius lies in domains outside of strategy and foreign policy, the efficacy of long-term strategies becomes endangered.

The Trump administration provides a vivid case study of this built-in risk. Policy decisions made at a bureaucratic level following the release of President Trump's National Security and Defense Strategies gave reason for optimism that the Departments of State, Treasury, and Commerce and the intelligence agencies would align with the statements made in the NSS. Serious capability gaps remained, particularly in the realm of response mechanisms to cross-functional threats (e.g., when China used its economic leverage to carve out new security advantages in South and Southeast Asia or when Moscow used cyberattacks against Kiev to undermine faith in governmental institutions far afield from Ukraine). Nevertheless, there was a noticeable change in the way that bureaucratic Washington viewed and dealt with Russia, China, and Iran following the release of the strategies.

Despite this apparent alignment, the words and actions of the president often contradicted the policy positions taken by those within his own administration, and subordinate officials also contradicted the president.[26] While such unpredictability creates a deterrent effect of its own, it also complicates the implementation of a government-wide approach to the "strategic predictability" as called for in the National Defense Strategy. These circumstances highlight the centrality of presidential leadership to the successful execution of foreign policy in the American system—as well as the limitations of the efforts to constrain or otherwise circumvent the intentions of the commander-in-chief. Each time the United States has effectively executed grand strategy—whether under Franklin Roosevelt, Richard Nixon, or Ronald Reagan—the president served as a primary advocate of the strategy to the American people and supported its implementation through national-security directives and decisions.

Although reforms to the National Security Council could create avenues for the implementation of strategy outside of presidential actions, the president's jurisdiction over the organization would limit its ability to do so. In the American system, strategic efficacy is reliant upon presidential leadership; there is no substitute for it. Questions of leadership style as well as foreign policy inclinations should thus occupy a more central place in the national conversation when selecting each successive president, and Congress should discuss mechanisms that could mitigate a lack of vision or, at the very least, ensure that presidential advisors possess the technical experience required to provide sage advice.

Looking Forward

The United States faces many structural and cultural impediments to developing long-term strategies, adapting its understanding of warfare, and aligning all the tools of national power into a comprehensive approach to international competition. Its predisposition toward strategies of domination has fed an expansionist imperative, first in the realm of territory and then in the realm of ideas. Despite the decreasing relevance and effectiveness of this approach, America has become complacent with the status quo and reluctant to adjust to the shifting terms of competition. The sad truth is that it may take a national crisis to jolt America's leadership into action. In the meantime, however, the United States may take a number of steps to mitigate the gains of its adversaries.

With respect to its power, the United States must rethink and recalibrate how and when it responds to adversarial behaviors. For the time being, its power is unmatched. It possesses a civil society and economy that, though difficult to harness, is the envy of the world. First and foremost, it must reconsider the threshold that determines whether it will respond in kind to adversarial behavior. As weaker powers, Russia, China, and Iran have found many ways to increase their strategic advantages without provoking a response. The United States should work to confuse this calculus by responding swiftly and unpredictably to provocations. To be clear, this is not a call to deploy masses of troops when, say, China manipulates international organizations to its advantage. Rather, it is a call to develop a nuanced and variable response capacity that imposes costs on adversaries and blurs the discernibility of the response threshold. The United States has many tools at its disposal to do this, from the selective use of offensive cyberattacks to the support of foreign dissident groups and a more strategic use of the U.S. Agency for Global Media. It will also be critical to enlist allies and partners in a response architecture that leverages the comparative advantages of each state to further impose costs and eliminate the perception of any response threshold. The potential of the combined application of American power and that of its allies and partners is without match.

Mustering the political will to apply it is a more formidable challenge. This book has detailed a number of methods that could reduce the complacency of American society, but the impetus for change must come from the top. The advent of information dominance as the most decisive realm of competition, as the Chinese observed, has its origin in the casualty aversion of American society. Fortunately, many if not most of the tools of international competition short of war do not result in casualties. The battle that a president wishing to implement competitive strategies will face, then, is not one of sacrificing American lives; it is one of convincing the American people of their nation's greatness, of eschewing moral relativism and pursuing the national interest without apology or hesitation. In this battle of ideas, every aspect of society must participate in the protection of its way of life. In this sense there is hope: the United States has a long history of engaging in world affairs because of the value that its citizens place on freedom and liberty. Looking ahead, the challenge will be to demonstrate how the actions of adversarial nations impact individual Americans. The emergence of a "genius" in the form of presidential leadership may well be the only way that this broader realization will occur.

In the end, this work has come full circle: the central importance of the individual "genius" may well be unavoidable as the West pursues strategic efficacy. Yet waiting for this individual to appear should not preclude a deeper understanding of adversarial strategies and how they differ from our own, nor should it blind us to the shifting realities of the international system or prevent our ability to devise effective countermeasures to balance revisionist powers. At the very least, such measures will mold the context in which the "genius" will create efficacy; they may also obviate the need to rely on the arrival of an individual savior at all. The absence of a genius should not prevent the exercise of power to protect America's national interests. Waiting for a genius to produce efficacy while adversaries achieve it may be the most inexcusable and avoidable example of complacency of all.

NOTES

Preface

1. Brooks, *How Everything Became War*.

2. There are exceptions to this rule, such as the idea of systemic operational design. Perhaps because the exceptions require a dynamic and fluid reaction to adversarial behavior—something difficult to achieve at a military or government-wide level in a democratic system like the United States—these concepts have not received widespread attention outside of the small and comparatively agile special-operations community. Wass de Czege, "Systemic Operational Design," 2–12.

Introduction

1. Jullien, *Treatise on Efficacy*, 1–14.

2. Machiavelli, *Prince*, 79–82; for context, see Carr, *Twenty Years' Crisis, 1919–1939*, 63.

3. For example, the utility of the Idea is demonstrated in Aristotle's discussion of the varying definitions of happiness. Although he questions whether there can be a universal definition of the term, he nonetheless recognizes that men are motivated by it, regardless of how they define it. Therefore, one can conclude that ideas have utility even if they are conceived of differently. Aristotle, *Nichomachean Ethics*, Book 1.4, 7.13; Ball, "Theory and Practice"; Lobkowicz, *Theory and Practice*.

4. Jullien, *Treatise on Efficacy*, 2–3.

5. The emphasis on human agency contrasts with the approach of non-Western cultures, such as that of China, which connects theory and practice through objects and positioning rather than through exceptional human beings.

6. More recently, Carl Jung placed archetypes at the center of his understanding of the subconscious, and archetypes are used as romantic narratives by countermodernist movements that seek to return society to an idealized, less complex period. See Lewin, *Jung on War*; Spektorowski, "Intellectual New Right."

7. Machiavelli, *Prince*, 79–82.

8. Clausewitz, *On War*, 100–112.

9. Rogers, "Clausewitz, Genius, and the Rules."

10. Weigley, *American Way of War*, 82; Shy, "Jomini," 146.

11. Jomini, *Art of War*, 29–30, 53–55.

12. Guerlac, "Vauban: Impact of Science"; Earle, "Adam Smith," 64–90, 217–61; Kollars, "Genius and Mastery."

13. Liddell Hart, *Strategy*, 23–142, 162, 294–95, 328–29.

14. For a discussion on the importance of capability perceptions to effective deterrence, see Schelling, *Arms and Influence*, 1–34.

15. Lohaus, "Missing Shade of Gray"; Cohen, "Constraints on America's Conduct."

16. Bellin, "Reconsidering Robustness."

17. Dahl, "Concept of Power," 202–3.

18. Little, *Balance of Power in International Relations*, 36–49, 110–11, 113–17, 157, 271; Morgenthau, Thompson, and Clinton, *Politics among Nations*, 216–20.

19. Haas, "Balance of Power"; Kaufman, Little, and Wohlforth, *Balance of Power*, 1–3.

20. Mearsheimer, *Tragedy of Great Power Politics*, 29–54.

21. Doran and Parsons, "War and the Cycle"; Doran, *Politics of Assimilation*, 1–61.

22. A more convincing case was later made by Paul Kennedy, who included economics as an explanatory variable that fueled competitive cycles. Yet because his argument is largely rooted in grand strategy, it is of limited utility for the more strategy- and operations-focused plane of this work. See Kennedy, *Rise and Fall*.

23. Some of the most enduring texts from this period include Rosecrance, "Bipolarity, Multipolarity, and the Future"; Waltz, "Stability of Bipolar World," 881–909; Morgenthau, Thomnpson, and Clinton, *Politics among Nations*; Keohane and Nye, *Power and Interdependence*; Gilpin, *War and Change*, 156–210.

24. Waltz, "Stability of Bipolar World," 881–909; Waltz, *Theory of International Politics*, 116–28.

25. Waltz, *Theory of International Politics*, 116–28, as discussed in Kaufman, Little, and Wohlforth, *Balance of Power*, 8–10.

26. Mearsheimer, *Tragedy of Great Power Politics*; Walt, "Alliance Formation," 4–8; Layne, "War on Terrorism," 106.

27. Paul, *Asymmetric Conflicts*, 3–37, 86–106, 126–66.

28. Schelling, *Arms and Influence*, 260–86.

29. Schelling, *Arms and Influence*, xiii.

30. Schelling, *Arms and Influence*, 35–91, 99, 135, 142–43, 164.

31. George and Simons, *Limits of Coercive Diplomacy*, 8.

32. Less daylight is between these two approaches than first meets the eye, as Lawrence Freedman discusses in *Strategic Coercion*, which builds upon the foundation laid out by Schelling and George. Freedman points out the differing conceptions of the relationship between force and diplomacy outlined by George and Schelling. He also identifies the limitations of using the military for diplomatic purposes: diplomacy is better for communicating specific demands, for one, and, second, the effectiveness of military threats hinges on credibility, which becomes more difficult to attain when an imbalance, or asymmetry, of power exists between two competitors. See Freedman, *Strategic Coercion*, 15–36.

33. This lack of interest was temporary, as Freedman's 1998 work attempts to show. However, at the time, thoughts related to unipolarity pervaded, if not everywhere, at least in the halls of power in Washington. This idea will be developed further in the next section of the text. See Freedman, *Strategic Coercion*.

34. Snyder, "Soviet Strategic Culture."

35. Creighton, *English National Character*, 7; Colbert, *National Character vs. National Security*, 3; Chenevix, *Essay upon National Character*, 1–2; Smith, "Economic Security," 518; Ginsberg, "National Character," 188; Wolfers, "'National Security,'" 67.

36. Johnston, "Thinking about Strategic Culture," 32–64; Gray, "National Style in Strategy," 21–47; Jones, "Soviet Strategic Culture"; Klein, "Hegemony and Strategic Culture," 133–48.

37. Johnston, "Thinking about Strategic Culture," 37–38.

38. Johnston, "Thinking about Strategic Culture," 37–39, 41–42, 46–47; Gray, "Strategic Culture as Context," 51–56, 62; Johnston, "Strategic Cultures Revisited," 521–22.

39. One could, after all, classify anything and everything as "context."

40. Johnston, "Strategic Cultures Revisited."

41. Booth, "Strategic Culture," 25–28; Booth, *Strategy and Ethnocentrism*, 20–31, 63–93. Such problems may impede accurate intercultural understanding more generally, as Edward Said discussed. See Said, *Orientalism*, 1–9.

42. Scobell, *China and Strategic Culture*.

43. Gray, "Out of the Wilderness," 221–41.

44. See, for example, Stanley, "Iranian Strategic Culture," 137–56; Eisenstadt, "Strategic Culture of Islamic Republic"; Lord, "American Strategic Culture," 269–93; Lord, "American Strategic Culture in Small Wars;" Giles, "Israel's Strategic Culture," 97–116; Adamsky, "From Israel with Deterrence," 157–84.

45. All the case studies in this book will develop these conceptions in greater detail.

46. Weigley, *American Way of War*, xiv.

47. Rothstein, *Afghanistan and Troubled Future*, 95.

48. Attrition-based strategies do not fare well against adversaries that temporally or geographically "become less . . . defined, and more . . . dispersed." Luttwak, "Notes on Low-Intensity Warfare," 14.

49. Luttwak, "Notes on Low-Intensity Warfare," 14.

50. Szabo, *Operational Issues*, 14–20; Breen, *American Insurgents, American Patriots*, 185–206; Bossenbroek, *Boer War*; Lomperis, *From People's War*, 30–84.

51. Hoffman, *Conflict in 21st Century*; Mattis and Hoffman, "Future Warfare," 18–19; Hoffman, "Preparing for Hybrid Wars," 57–61. From the Romans to Napoleon's Peninsular campaign, and from the Great Game between Russia and Britain in South Asia to Japan's experience in Northern China during the Second World War, hybrid threats have stymied hegemons throughout history. See Murray and Mansoor, *Hybrid Warfare*. For a discussion of insurgency during the Great Game, see Noyce, *England, India, and Afghanistan*.

52. Goldwater-Nichols Department of Defense Reorganization Act of 1986, Pub L. No. 99–443, 111, 10 (1986). http://history.defense.gov/Portals/70/Documents/dod_reforms/Goldwater-NicholsDoDReordAct1986.pdf.

53. For a discussion of conventional commander hostility toward SOF in the lead-up to the Goldwater-Nichols Act, see Lohaus, *Precarious Balance*, 3–30.

54. Joint Chiefs of Staff, *Joint Publication 3–0*, 2011.

55. The reliance of successive presidential administrations in the first twenty years of the twenty-first century on SOF to achieve an increasing number of foreign-policy objectives cannot be explained by political temptations alone. SOF has also become a tool of first choice for objectives that in the past may have been assigned to the wider military or to the Department of State. The demand for its skills has increased as the threat environment has changed. See Robinson, "Future of Special Operations," 6; Turse, "Special Ops Surge."

56. Toynbee, *Study of History*, 41; Goffart, "Rome, Constantinople," 275–77; Goldsworthy, *How Rome Fell*, 405–15; Heather, *Fall of Roman Empire*.

57. Friedberg, *Weary Titan*.

58. Kennedy, *Rise and Fall*, 533.

59. Peden, "Suez and Britain's Decline."

60. Waley-Cohen, "Militarization of Culture," 278–95.

1. Russia

1. Ermarth, *Russia's Strategic Culture*, 4; Kaplan, *Revenge of Geography*, 154–87.

2. The popular national shame and the resulting appeal of heroic military figures such as Mikhail Skobelev during this period cemented familiar archetypes of Russian society, which parallel the modern appeal of the revanche and Putin among the Russian masses.

3. Kagan and Higham, *Military History of Tsarist Russia*, 137–39.

4. Sherr, *Hard Diplomacy and Soft Coercion*, 545.

5. Ermarth, *Russia's Strategic Culture*, 6–7.

6. Ermarth, *Russia's Strategic Culture*, 6–7.

7. The messianic outlook manifested not just externally, through conquest and imperial expansion, but also internally, where it rationalized and undergirded new sets of tools for population control. For a detailed overview of the ambitions and outlook of Russian tsars and their messianic outlook toward expansionism, see Johnson, *Third Rome*; For further details about Russia's internal social control mechanisms during the tsarist period, see Squire, *Third Department*.

8. Leighton, *Soviet Propaganda*, 11.

9. Squire, *Third Department*, 1–2.

10. Deacon, *History of Russian Secret Service*, 86; Fischer, *Okhrana*, 1–5.

11. Lenin, *What Is to Be Done?*, 31–53; Pipes, *Russian Revolution*, 358–61.

12. Freemantle, KGB, 21.

13. Lenin did not read Clausewitz until later in life, but he did, according to historian Richard Pipes, share the latter's view of war as peace's "dialectical corollary." When considered alongside his other views about the universal potential of the Communist movement, however, one could reasonably find Lenin's views of war to be more expansive and encompassing than those typically possessed by Western strategists. Later Soviet strategists, particularly as they prepared the Soviet Union for war, would explore these contrasting views further. See Pipes, *Russian Revolution*, 349; quotation from Shultz and Godson, *Dezinformatsia*, 1–2.

14. Shelley, *Policing Soviet Society*, 14–15.

15. Carter, *Russian Nationalism*, 149.

16. Svechin, *Strategy*, 85.

17. Though Western Europe served as an intellectual wellspring for early Soviet thinkers, Lenin and his successors recognized that Western thought could not apply directly to Russia. Ultimately, the Soviets infused their empirical study of the military art with communist ideology and integrated the idea of progressive history with that of the international mission of the Soviet state. See Glantz, *Soviet Military Operational Art*, 1–15.

18. Blackstock, *Secret Road to World War Two*, 14.

19. Weinstein and Vassiliev, *Haunted Wood*, 4.

20. Schrecker, "Soviet Espionage in America," 359.

21. Weinstein and Vassiliev, *Haunted Wood*, 22–23; Sibley, *Red Spies in America*, 13.

22. Weinstein and Vassiliev, *Haunted Wood*, 37. The authors widely reference information that they gleaned from the KGB archives in Moscow. In this case, they reference File 17643, vol. 1, p. 64. For an illuminating overview of the intelligence history of the Russian consulate in San Francisco, see Dorfman, "Secret History."

23. New York was chosen as the initial intelligence headquarters, in part because it was easier to blend into New York's cultural milieu than relatively homogenous Washington and in part because the base of commercial contacts from which the Soviets would launch their intelligence network was centered on New York.

24. Weinstein and Vassiliev, *Haunted Wood*, 37.

25. Sibley, *Red Spies in America*, 14–17.

26. In 1940, for example, J. Edgar Hoover reported that he had arranged for undercover agents to infiltrate major American industrial firms such as Standard Oil to monitor Russian business deals. Prior to the 1940, the U.S. House of Representatives was the main governmental organization calling for a critical view of Communists in America. As early as 1918, the House of Representatives established special committees charged with investigating the threat of communism. See Hoover to Watson; Sibley, *Red Spies in America*, 18–19. Despite the sometimes alarmist findings of the congressional investigations, they garnered little reaction from the press and the public. See *New York Times*, "Reds Brought 20,000 Weapons"; for the blasé reaction of the press, see *Baltimore Sun*, "Red Herring Report."

27. Yet even these efforts were met by skepticism from the press and the general public, even in light of the sometimes alarmist findings of the committee. See *New York Times*, "Reds Brought 20,000 Weapons;" *Baltimore Sun*, "Red Herring Report."

28. Haynes, Klehr, and Vassiliev, *Spies*, 371.

29. See messages 669, 670, 721, 1775, 1609, 1621, 1623, 1017 and 1022 from U.S. Army Signal Intelligence Service, "Venona Project."

30. See messages 1711, 777–781, 1261, 1274, 990, and 1843 from U.S. Army Signal Intelligence Service, "Venona Project."

31. See message 812 from U.S. Army Signal Intelligence Service, "Venona Project."

32. Benson, "Venona Historical Monograph #2," 2–4.

33. Birman, *Secret Incomes*; Sibley, *Red Spies in America*, 93.

34. Sibley, *Red Spies in America*, 95. At the time of the request in 1942, the B-29 was still in the prototype stage of development; Willis, "Warplane Classic."

35. Lyotov, "Lenin's Ideas on Defending Socialism," 16–19; Lenin, *What Is to Be Done?* See also Selznick, *Organizational Weapon*, 4–12.

36. Svechin, *Strategy*, 91–101.

37. Stoecker, *Forging Stalin's Army*, 143–49.

38. Glantz, *Soviet Military Deception*, 3.

39. Examples abound of the use of *maskirovka* in the decades that follow to manipulate the perceptions of both domestic and foreign audiences. See Glantz, *Soviet Military Deception*, 1–39; Shea, "Post-Soviet Maskirovka," 63–67.

40. For an example of the tactical focus of America political warfare plans, see Office of Strategic Services, "Outline Plan for Political Warfare."

41. Schwartz, *Political Warfare*, 98–99.

42. Schwartz, *Political Warfare*, 102.

43. At the end of the Second World War, Assistant Secretary of State for Public Affairs William Benton fought to maintain a functional public diplomacy capability in the State Department against protests from Congress. His

efforts were constrained, however, by budgetary realities. See Schwartz, *Political Warfare*, 99–100; Benton, "Beginning of Russian Broadcasts."

44. U.S. Information Agency Office of Research, "Soviet Psychological Warfare Activities."

45. U.S. Information Agency, *Communist Propaganda*.

46. Declassified cables from the U.S. Army Signal Corp and National Security Agency revealed a highly detailed account of the establishment of these networks during and immediately following the war. Of the voluminous literature written on this topic from both primary and secondary sources, interested parties may wish to begin with Benson and Warner, *Venona*; Haynes, Klehr, and Vassiliev, *Spies*; Weinstein and Vassiliev, *Haunted Wood*.

47. Orlov, *Soviet Intelligence*.

48. Shultz and Godson, *Dezinformatsia*, 12–14.

49. Central Intelligence Agency, "Soviet Capabilities for Deception, 1."

50. Dodd, "Confusion of the West," 1.

51. Kennan to Secretary of State. Also see later in this chapter and the chapter on the United States for a more detailed discussion of American thinking about the Soviet Union.

52. Trotsky, *Third International after Lenin*, 158. Trotsky's words drew from those of Lenin, who reflected on the inseparability between words, actions, and organizations in 1901. See Lenin, *What Is to Be Done?* For further reading, see Selznick, *Organizational Weapon*.

53. Gorbachev, *Perestroika*, 140.

54. Twining, "Soviet Strategic Culture," 182–83.

55. Shultz and Godson, *Dezinformatsia*, 40. Although the specific motivations of the politburo with respect to active measures remain unknown in the West, Shultz and Godson summarize observed outcomes of active measures and help explain the goals and importance of the organizations conducting them.

56. Kramer, "Role of the CPSU International Department," 430–32; Schapiro, "International Department of the CPSU," 41–55.

57. Shultz and Godson, *Dezinformatsia*, 17–33. As the authors note, streamlining of the organizational structure for the conduct of active measures was a function of the Soviet Union's increased power after the Second World War and the end of the Stalinist purges. See also Kux, "Soviet Active Measures and Disinformation"; Kramer, "Role of the CPSU International Department," 431–32.

58. Kramer, "Role of the CPSU International Department," 429–446; Schapiro, "International Department of the CPSU," 41–55; Shultz and Godson, *Dezinformatsia*, 21–25; Leighton, *Soviet Propaganda*, 21–23.

59. Shultz, "Soviet Use of Surrogates," 32–42; Adams, "Incremental Activism," 614–630; Schapiro, "International Department of the CPSU," 429–446. In the 1950s, many international front organizations were operating in Western Europe, but most of these were expelled in the early 1960s. See U.S. Information Agency, *Communist Propaganda*; Shultz and Godson, *Dezinformatsia*,

111–14. Shultz and Godson define *political warfare* as the use of "both overt and covert measures, including diplomacy and negotiations, to influence politics and events in foreign countries," a definition to which this book adheres.

60. Adams, "Incremental Activism," 622–24; Schapiro, "International Department of the CPSU," 43.

61. Adams, "Incremental Activism," 626.

62. Shultz, "Soviet Use of Surrogates," 37–39; Adams, "Incremental Activism," 616–17.

63. Adams, "Incremental Activism," 614.

64. U.S. Information Agency Office of Research, *External Information*, 127; U.S. Information Agency, *Communist International Radio*, 4, as quoted in Shultz and Godson, *Dezinformatsia*, 27; U.S. Information Agency, "Soviet Gray Broadcasting," 1–2.

65. Office of Research, *Machinery of Soviet Propaganda*, 1; Barghoorn, *Soviet Foreign Propaganda*, 244–50; Leighton, *Soviet Propaganda*, 20.

66. Casey, "Soviet Use of Active Measures," 1.

67. Kux, "Soviet Active Measures," 24.

68. Casey, "Soviet Use of Active Measures," 2.

69. U.S. Department of State, *Soviet Influence Activities*, ix–x.

70. Shultz and Reese, *Turmoil and Triumph*, 997–98, as quoted in Lamb and Schoen, *Deception, Disinformation, and Strategic Communication*, 6.

71. Andrew, *Sword and the Shield*, xxx.

72. Andrew, *Sword and the Shield*, 426.

73. Andrew, *Sword and the Shield*, 466; Shultz and Godson, *Dezinformatsia*, 133–49.

74. For information about KGB pressure on the Finnish press and government, see Salminen, *Silenced Media*; regarding the recruitment of a Danish journalist, see Andrew, *Sword and the Shield*, 428.

75. Although decrypts from the Venona files link White to the Soviets with a high level of confidence, debate continues as to the level of his cooperation and willingness to aid the KGB. For material arguing his guilt, see Romerstein and Breindel, *Venona Secrets*, 29–54; Adams, "Trial of Harry Dexter White." For an argument that sheds doubt on these claims, see Craig, *Treasonable Doubt*.

76. See Cline and Alexander, *Terrorism*; Library of Congress, "KGB Active Measures."

77. Federal Research Division, "KGB Active Measures"; O'Halpin, *Defending Ireland*, 322–23.

78. Kux, "Soviet Active Measures," 20; Rid, "Disinformation," 2; Library of Congress, "KGB Active Measures."

79. Gorbachev's eventual attempts to transition the Soviet military to a "defensive posture" in 1990, for example, seemed to undermine its very raison d'être. See Mikolashek, "New Defensive Doctrine," 26–33.

80. Gaidar, *State and Evolution*, 5.

81. Rousso, "Russia's Transformation," 107–9.

82. Interview with Russian diplomat, Russian embassy to the United States April 10, 2017.

83. Russian Federation Ministry of Foreign Affairs, "Foreign Policy Concept."

84. Czuperski et al., "Distract, Deceive, Destroy," 1, 22; Treisman, "Why Putin Took Crimea," 47–54.

85. Reuters, "Russia Moves Nuclear-Capable Missiles into Kaliningrad."

86. Conley et al., "Russian Soft Power"; Hedenskog and Larsson, "Russian Leverage," 6–7; Grigas, *Legacies, Coercion and Soft Power*, 1; Sherr, *Hard Diplomacy and Soft Coercion*, 17–18.

87. Quinlivan, "Russia's Military."

88. Breedlove, "NATO's Next Act," 97.

89. Soldatov and Borogan, *New Nobility*, 30–34.

90. Morris, "Grading Gerasimov."

91. Kofman, "Russian Hybrid Warfare"; Hoffman, *Conflict in 21st Century*, 7–11.

92. McDermott, "Learning from Today's Wars," 98.

93. Lohaus and Jermilavicius, "Proceedings of AEI/ICDS Workshop." The contrasting Western and Russian understandings of state mobilization illustrates the potential confusion created by mischaracterization of adversarial behavior. See Monaghan, *Russian State Mobilization*, 7–14.

94. Giles, *Russia's "New" Tools*, 6–9; "Russia Gets Its Own SOCOM"; Marsh, *Russian Special Operations*, 19–21.

95. Interview with Russian diplomat, Russian embassy to the United States.

96. Bershidsky, "Putin's Rejection of the West"; Interview with Russian diplomat, Russian embassy to the United States.

97. Beard, "Putin Signs Decree."

98. Interview with Russian diplomat, Russian embassy to the United States.

99. Pynnöniemi and Rácz, "Fog of Falsehood," 33–41; Weiss, "Revealed."

100. O'Neil, "Bowling Alone."

101. Lohaus and Jermilavicius, "Proceedings of AEI/ICDS Workshop."

102. This was particularly true in the U.S. intelligence community. See Northam, "Intelligence Community Rethinks Strategy."

103. Soldatov and Borogan, *Red Web*, 65–84, 172, 225.

104. For an overview of reflexive control theory, its development, and application to Soviet and Russian conceptions of warfare, see Thomas, "Russia's Reflexive Control Theory"; Chotikul, *Soviet Theory of Reflexive Control*.

105. Thomas, "Russia's Reflexive Control Theory," 242.

106. Soldatov and Borogan, *Red Web*, 223; Segal, *Hacked World Order*, 233.

107. U.S. Army, *"Little Green Men,"* 15.

108. For a useful summary of Russian cyber operations, see Buchanan and Sulmeyer, "Russia and Cyber Operations."

109. Foxall, "Putin's Cyber War," 4–9; Chen, "Agency."

110. Foxall, "Putin's Cyber War," 4–9; For an overview of Russia's first major operation in the cyber domain, which was directed at Estonia in the lead-up to the "Bronze Night" demonstrations in 2007, see Segal, *Hacked World Order*, 60–66.

111. Allan, "Attribution Issues in Cyberspace."

112. Greenberg, "Russia's Test Lab for Cyberwar."

113. Note that NotPetya was a revamped version of a previously used malware known as Petya. See Perlroth, Scott, and Frenkel, "Cyberattack Hits Ukraine"; Da Silva, "Russia Behind Global Cyber Attack"; Shymkiv, "Ukraine," panel discussion, Future in Review Conference, Park City UT, October 11, 2017.

114. Maurer, "Cyber Proxies," 80–86.

115. Segal, *Hacked World Order*, 65.

116. Grierson, Obordo, and Elgot, "Ransomware Attacks"; Miller, Nakashima, and Entous, "Obama's Secret Struggle."

117. Regarding Putin's denial of involvement with Fancy Bear and other "patriotic hacking" groups, see Rudnitsky, Micklethwait, and Riley, "Hack Was a Public Good." Regarding Fancy Bear targets and modus operandi, see FireEye, *APT28*; CrowdStrike, "Who Is Fancy Bear?"; Nakashima, "Russian Government Hackers."

118. National Intelligence Council, *Assessing Russian Activities*, 1.

119. Brodkin, "Microsoft Shuts Down Phishing Sites."

120. Segal, *Hacked World Order*, 219–20; Nocetti, "Contest and Conquest," 117–18.

121. Nocetti, "Contest and Conquest," 114.

122. Entous, Nakashima, and Jaffe, "Kremlin Trolls Burned"; Pomerantsev, *Nothing Is True.*

123. T & R Productions LLC and ANO TV-Novosti, "Registration Statement," 2; Pisnia, "Why Has RT Registered?."

124. Aron, "Kremlin's Propaganda Campaign."

125. Pynnöniemi and Rácz, "Fog of Falsehood," 71–78.

126. Pynnöniemi and Rácz, "Fog of Falsehood," 92–105.

127. Pynnöniemi and Rácz, "Fog of Falsehood," 75–78.

128. Taylor, "'Novorossiya,' the Latest Concept."

129. Basora and Fisher, "Putin's 'Greater Novorossiya.'"

130. Lohaus and Jermilavicius, "Proceedings of AEI/ICDS Workshop."

131. For an example of one of these alleged agents, see Propaganda Relief Collective, "Kremlin's Voice: Johan Bäckman."

132. Klein, "Russia's New Military Doctrine," 2.

133. Marcu, "Russian Propaganda in the Facebook Age."

134. Metelitsa, "Oil and Natural Gas Sales."

135. Eurostat, "Energy Production and Imports."

136. Rapoza, "Europe Devises Energy Security Measures"; TASS Russian News Agency, "Russia's Gas Pipelines"; Lang, "Russia-German Pipeline."

137. Richter, "How Will Crimea Change Relations?"; International Energy Agency, "Emergency Response Systems," 132, 137; International Institute for Strategic Studies, "Europe," 102.

138. Schmitt, "Poland, Hungary, and the Czech Republic," 12–18.

139. International Energy Agency, "Emergency Response Systems," 137.

140. Braw, "Finland's Mysterious Nuclear Investor"; Interviews with security experts in Helsinki, Finland, November 16, 2015; Than, "Special Report."

141. MacFarquhar, "How Russians Pay to Play"; Dennison and Pardijs, "Europe's Insurgent Parties," 4, 12; *Guardian*, "Czech Republic Claims War."

142. Rohac, Zgut, and Györi, *Populism in Europe*, 6; Orenstein, "Putin's Western Allies"; Foster, "Russia Accused of Clandestine Funding"; Sharkov, "Far-Right MEP Accused"; Higgins, "Russia Taps Foot Soldiers"; Juhász et al., *I Am Eurasian*, 24.

143. Schmitt, "Poland, Hungary, and the Czech Republic," 25–26.

144. Sharkov, "Poland Jails Colonel"; Foy, "Zmiana Party Urges Embrace"; Agence France-Presse, "Poland Detains Pro-Kremlin Leader."

145. Kreko et al., "Marching Towards Eurasia," 37, 40; Rohac, Zgut, and Györi, *Populism in Europe*, 12; Klapsis, *Unholy Alliance*, 26; Kreko and Szabados, "Russia's Far-Right Friends."

146. Reuters, "Baltics Can Keep Lights on If Russia Turns off the Gas"; Directorate-General for Economic and Financial Affairs, *Member States' Energy Dependence*, 102, 158.

147. Directorate-General for Economic and Financial Affairs, *Member States' Energy Dependence*, 167–71; Hoellerbauer, "Baltic Energy Sources."

148. Grigas, "Legacies, Coercion and Soft Power," 1–2.

149. Conley, "Russia's Influence on Europe," 29. Russia's trade with the EU represented 48.5 percent of the latter's total trade volume in 2014, making policies that directly target Russia economically risky.

150. With respect to France, see Walt, "Le Pen Is Doubling Down"; Gude, *Russia's 5th Column*; Gatehouse, "Marine Le Pen." Le Pen is not the only French politician that has cultivated ties with Putin: 2017 presidential candidate Francois Fillon also had financial ties with the Kremlin and enjoyed support from Russian media. See also Fouquet, "Fillon Slips Further"; Smith, "Le Pen Visits Putin"; Barnett et al., "Kremlin's Trojan Horses." With respect to Germany, see Hille and Chazan, "Russia Adds Germany's AfD"; Amann and Lokshin, "Moscow's Fifth Column"; Oltermann and Soloveitchik, "Russian Minority Could Boost Far Right"; Center for Investigative Reporting, "Rise of New German Right." With respect to the UK Independence Party's support for Russia, see Dennison and Pardijs, "Europe's Insurgent Parties." With respect to Austria and Italy, see Smale, "Austria's Far Right"; Sharkov, "Putin's United Russia"; Phillips, "Leader to Meet Putin."

151. Wesslau, "Putin's Friends in Europe"; Gotev, "MEPs Draw Map."

152. Eurostat, "Main Origin of Primary Energy."

153. Eurostat, "Nuclear Energy Statistics."

154. European Commission, "Russia"; Wagstyl, "Merkel Sharpens Attack."

155. Higgins, "Finger Pointed at Russians"; Marusic, "Did Moscow Botch a Coup?."

156. Lavinder, "Russia Ramps Up Influence."

157. Lohaus and Jermilavicius, "Proceedings of AEI/ICDS Workshop," 3–5; Interviews with security experts in Helsinki, Finland, November 16, 2015; Pynnöniemi and Saari, "Hybrid Influence."

158. The line between information campaigns and active measures is often difficult to draw. Two Swedish academics provide a useful distinction: public diplomacy, according to them, bleeds into active measures when information campaigns are designed to "hamper the target country's ability to generate public support in pursuing its policies." See Kragh and Åsberg, "Russia's Strategy for Influence."

159. On the right, Russia has engaged with the Nordic Resistance, most notably at a Swedish identitarian conference held by the group in Sweden in 2015. See Shekhovtsov, "Russian Fascist Militants." The views of Nordic Resistance are mirrored by Swedish author and Wikileaks representative in Russia Israel Shamir. See Gibney, "Can We Trust Julian Assange?." Meanwhile, on the left, Russia has found sympathetic mouthpieces in legacy Cold War anti-war and anti-imperialist organizations, especially via the editorial section of the widely circulated newspaper *Aftonbladet*. See Pynnöniemi and Rácz, "Fog of Falsehood," 194; Kragh and Åsberg, "Russia's Strategy for Influence," 30–32.

160. International Energy Agency, "Emergency Response Systems," 419; International Monetary Fund, "Direction of Trade Statistics."

161. Keyton, "Swedish Island Likely to Reject"; Reuters, "Sweden Drops Objections."

162. Standish, "Why Is Finland Able?."

163. Pynnöniemi and Saari, "Hybrid Influence."

164. Aro, "Troll Magnet"; Jantunen, "Problem with Finland." Both women are excellent researchers on Russian information warfare in their own right and are worth reading. See, for example, Jantunen, *Infosota* (in Finnish); Aro, "Cyberspace War" (in English).

165. Propaganda Relief Collective, "Kremlin's Voice."

166. Reuters, "Croatian Investor"; Martikainen, Saari, and Pynnöniemi, "Neighbouring an Unpredictable Russia."

167. Braw, "Back to the Finland Station"; Interviews with security experts in Helsinki, Finland, November 16, 2015 (Aapo Cederberg et al.).

168. Zakharova, "Брифинг Официального Представителя" ["Official representative briefing"]; Interview with Russian diplomat, Russian embassy to the United States.

169. Russia's ability to do so was greatly enhanced by its decision in the early 2000s to focus on bilateral relations with former Soviet States rather than

on multilateral forums such as the Commonwealth of Independent States. Bilateral relations provided Russia with much more leverage over individual actors than would be possible if pursued through a multilateral framework. See Hedenskog and Larsson, "Russian Leverage," 20–24.

170. Gerrits and Bader, "Russian Patronage." See also Hedenskog and Larsson, "Russian Leverage," 25.

171. Trenin, "Georgian-Russian Crisis."

172. Kofman et al., *Lessons from Russia's Operations*, 20–22.

173. Lohaus and Jermilavicius, "Proceedings of AEI/ICDS Workshop"; Kononczuk, "Ukraine."

174. Bentzen and Dietrich, "Belarus."

175. Ministry of Foreign Affairs, Republic of Belarus, "Foreign Trade of Belarus"; Belarus's reliance on Russia may be underplayed by these numbers. IMF data from 2016 suggests a much higher level of reliance on Russia for exports and imports. See International Monetary Fund, "Direction of Trade Statistics."

176. Miller, "Belarus and Failure."

177. Seddon, "Belarus's Lukashenko Slams Russia"; Mackinnon, "Russia's Propaganda Machine"; Vesti, "Потребительский сектор стран ЕАБР" ["The consumer sector of EDB countries"]; Vesti, "Белоруссия получила российский кредит" ["Belarus received a Russian credit"].

178. Seddon, "Belarus's Lukashenko Slams Russia"; Grove, "Russia and Belarus."

179. Grove, "Russia and Belarus."

180. For an excellent overview of Russia's connections and affinity with alternative election monitoring groups, see Shekhovtsov, *Russia and the Western Far Right*, 101–31.

181. Marchesano, "Election Observation," 265; Fawn, "Battle over the Box," 1133–53.

182. Hyde, "Quality of Monitoring," 160.

183. Marchesano, "Election Observation," 263; Hyde, "Quality of Monitoring," 159; Shekhovtsov, *Russia and the Western Far Right*, 104–5; Kupchinsky, "CIS."

184. Shekhovtsov, *Russia and Western Far Right*, 109.

185. The organization has also adopted the name the CIS-*Europe* Monitoring Organization (emphasis added), according to its website. However, the use of this term has yet to be universally adopted either on the website or in related literature.

186. Popescu, "Russia's Soft Power Ambitions," 2; The firm's founder, Aleksey Kochetkov, has grown close to far-right groups in Russia and Europe over time. See Shekhovtsov, *Russia and Western Far Right*, 103–13.

187. Shekhovtsov, *Russia and Western Far Right*, 106; Hedenskog and Larsson, "Russian Leverage," 26–27.

188. In 2011, for example, the group's report on Estonian parliamentary elections drew into question whether the process "fully conformed to the stan-

dards and requirements imposed on modern democratic states," a conclusion that contrasted sharply with that of OSCE-ODIHR. Following the 2014 Maidan Crisis in Ukraine, the organization issued a report, *Ukraine after Euromaidan: Democracy Under Fire*, that highlighted the allegedly democratic nature of Crimea's annexation and Russia's historic claims to Eastern Ukraine, using the Novorossiya narrative. In another attempt to co-opt the language of liberal democracy, CIS-EMO cited international human-rights law in a 2017 presentation to OSCE-ODIHR to chastise the Baltic states for "discriminating" against "non-citizens" (likely a euphemism for Russian-speaking nationals). See Shekhovtsov, *Russia and Western Far Right*, 107; Semenov, "Issues of Discrimination"; Bedritskiy, Kochetkov, and Byshok, "Ukraine after Euromaiden," 107–30, 197–210.

189. Political scientist Susan Hyde argues that maintaining the appearance of adhering to this norm is important enough to dedicate considerable resources to it. Her description of the methods by which authoritarian regimes manipulate perceptions of electoral processes is particularly valuable. See Hyde, "Quality of Monitoring," 158–59.

190. For a recent example, see Byrnes, *Response to Russia's Criticism*.

191. When exercised in its highest form, disinformation creates a circumstance similar to Gary Schaub's definition of *compellence*: "the use of threats by one actor to induce change in the behavior of another actor by persuading the target that the probable costs of continuing its current behavior will exceed the probable costs of altering it in the direction desired by the actor issuing the compellent threat." See Freedman, *Strategic Coercion*, 4.

192. U.S. Department of State, *Soviet Influence Activities*, 7–11.

193. U.S. Department of State, *Soviet Influence Activities*, 11–14.

194. Higgins, "Faith Combines with Firepower."

195. Garrard and Garrard, *Russian Orthodoxy Resurgent*, 47–54.

196. Papkova, *Orthodox Church and Russian Politics*, 14; Freeze, *Russian Orthodoxy and Politics*, 1–8.

197. Blitt, "Russia's 'Orthodox' Foreign Policy."

198. For example, President Medvedev explicitly outlawed Jehovah's Witnesses and Scientology from practicing in Russia, claiming that they represented a "western weapon of mass destruction" aimed at subverting Russia's unity. See Blitt, "Russia's 'Orthodox' Foreign Policy," 370–71.

199. Papkova, *Orthodox Church and Russian Politics*, 44.

200. Zarakhovich, "Putin's Reunited Russian Church."

201. Papkova, "Role of Russian Orthodox Church"; Blitt, "Russia's 'Orthodox' Foreign Policy," 364.

202. Blitt, "Russia's 'Orthodox' Foreign Policy"; Soroka, "Putin's Patriarch."

203. Soroka, "Putin's Patriarch."

204. Maida, *Online and on All Fronts*; Kirillova, "Russian Church Serves Kremlin"; Movsesian, "Clash of Traditions."

205. Bennetts, "Putin Brings God." The imprisonment of members of the feminist rock band Pussy Riot is perhaps the most well-known example of this crackdown on dissent. See BBC News, "Pussy Riot."

206. For a comprehensive view of the internal political dynamics of the Russian Orthodox Church, see Papkova, *Orthodox Church and Russian Politics*. In their work describing the resurgence of the Russian Orthodox Church, Garrard and Garrard usefully remind readers that the church, having never undergone a Reformation, sees its followers as "true believers" and followers of "Catholicism and its spin-off, Protestantism," as "to some degree" false. See Garrard and Garrard, *Russian Orthodoxy Resurgent*, 37–38.

207. Higgins, "Faith Combines with Firepower."

208. Lever, "Romania Has Lowest Proportion"; de Cristian, "Russia's Silent Threat."

209. Kirillova, "Russian Church Serves Kremlin."

210. Martens, "Russian Military Modernization," 1; Nichol, *Russian Military Reform*, 4–7.

211. Gouré, "Face the Facts."

212. Pifer, "Pay Attention, America"; Dunford, "Gen. Dunford's Remarks"; Patterson, "Russia's Warfare Capabilities."

213. TASS Russian News Agency, "2018 State Arms Procurement"; TASS Russian News Agency, "Russian State Armaments Program."

214. BBC News, "Crimea Crisis"; Isachenkov, "Putin."

215. Martens, "Russian Military Modernization," 4.

216. Martens, "Russian Military Modernization," 1; Fisher, "Russian Troops Welcomed."

217. Martens, "Russian Military Modernization," 5.

218. Martens, "Russian Military Modernization," 5.

219. Pifer, "Pay Attention, America."

220. Gady, "Sarmat ICBMs."

221. Pifer, "Pay Attention, America."

222. Reuters, "Russia Moves Nuclear-Capable Missiles."

223. Martens, "Russian Military Modernization," 5.

224. Appel, "The 'Near-Abroad' Factor."

225. For an excellent summary of the development of Russian special operations forces, see Marsh, *Russian Special Operations*.

226. Bukkvoll, "Russian Special Operations Forces," 15.

227. Bukkvoll, "Russian Special Operations Forces," 17.

228. Peterson, "Ukraine's Frozen Front"; Bukkvoll, "Russian Special Operations Forces," 19.

229. Bartles, "GRU Utilization," 53; Gibbons-Neff, "Ukrainian Special Forces Fight."

230. Organization for Security and Cooperation in Europe, Treaty on Open Skies; U.S. Department of State, New Strategic Arms Reduction Treaty.

231. Tomkins, "NATO Interception."

232. Peker, "Russia Violated Airspace"; Klikushin, "'NATO Airspace.'"

233. Reuters, "Two British Jets Dispatched"; Tomlinson, "More Russian Spy Planes"; Gady, "Japan Scrambles Fighter Jets"; Reuters, "Sweden Protests."

234. Rosen, "Russia's Submarine Activity."

235. Braw, "Submarine Intruders."

236. Tomlinson, "Russian Spy Ship Spotted." Martinez, "Russian Bombers Intercepted."

237. Pynnöniemi and Rácz, "Fog of Falsehood," 75; Miller et al., "An Invasion," 32.

238. U.S. Army, *"Little Green Men,"* 23–32.

239. U.S. Army, *"Little Green Men,"* 43.

240. Fitzpatrick, "RBC Publishes Report"; Hawk, Deiss, and Watson, "Russian Mercenaries."

241. Tsvetkova, "Exclusive"; Interview with Russian diplomat, Russian embassy to the United States, May 10, 2017.

242. Kabanenko, "Zapad 2017"; Sutyagin, "Zapad-2017."

243. RadioFreeEurope RadioLiberty, *Power Projection*; Brzezinski and Varangis, "NATO-Russia Exercise Gap."

244. Brzezinski and Varangis, "NATO-Russia Exercise Gap"; Sputnik News, "Russian Baltic Fleet."

245. Dobbins et al., *Extending Russia*, 47–90.

246. Nikolskaya and Tétrault-Farber, "Russia's GDP Growth"; Benedictow, Fjærtoft, and Løfsnæs, "Oil Dependency," 400–428.

247. Dobbins et al., *Extending Russia*, 47–267.

2. Iran

1. Amanat and Vejdani, *Iran Facing Others*, 175.

2. Amanat and Vejdani, *Iran Facing Others*, 5.

3. Hovannisian and Sabagh, *Persian Presence*, 4–5.

4. Hovannisian and Sabagh., *Persian Presence*, 6; Busse, "Iran under the Buyids," 250–304.

5. Clawson and Rubin, *Eternal Iran*, 2.

6. Rubin, *Strategies Underlying Iranian Soft Power*.

7. Amanat and Vejdani, *Iran Facing Others*, 3–11.

8. Momen, *Introduction to Shi`i Islam*, 183.

9. Eisenstadt, "Iran Primer."

10. Rahnema, *Superstition as Ideology*, 184–95.

11. *Ahadith* is the plural form of *hadith*, a record of the sayings and customs of Muhammad and his companions.

12. Rahnema, *Superstition as Ideology*, 184–95, 200–54. Rahnema also describes how former president Mahmoud Ahmadinejad leveraged this heritage to his advantage.

13. The Buyids predate the Safavids as the first Shi'ite dynasty in Iran but did not seek to convert preexisting Sunni and Christian populations as the Safavids did. Thus, it was not until the Safavids that Shi'ism gained the prominence in Iran familiar to modern observers. See Busse, "Iran under the Buyids," 287–88; Lewis, "'Abbāsids."

14. Tor, "Islamisation of Iranian Kingly Ideals," 115.

15. Ansari, *Perceptions of Iran*, 82–83.

16. Ward, *Immortal*, 91–115.

17. Mozaffari, *Forming National Identity*, 20–21, 64–87.

18. Ironically, this historical reawakening was driven in part by Western-led excavations of ancient Persian sites. See Mozaffari, *Forming National Identity*, 33–63.

19. Ward, *Immortal*, 211.

20. Bruno, Bajoria, and Masters, "Iran's Revolutionary Guards"; Oxford Islamic Studies Online, s.v. "Sipah-I Pasdaran-I Inqilab-I Islami."

21. Rubin, *Strategies Underlying Iranian Soft Power*.

22. Towfighi, *Persian Empire to Islamic Iran*, 9–20.

23. Rubin, "Iran Has Never Started a War?"; Pearl, "If Iran Had Nuclear Weapons"; McInnis and Gilmore, *Iran at War*, 12.

24. Bruno, Bajoria, and Masters, "Iran's Revolutionary Guards."

25. McInnis and Gilmore, *Iran at War*, 11–25.

26. American Enterprise Institute, Iran Shaping Operations Workshop, "Participant Discussions" (unpublished manuscript available upon request).

27. For a recent discussion of the extensive economic interests enjoyed by the IRGC, see Lob and Habibi, "Battle in Iran."

28. Nader, "The Revolutionary Guards."; Wehrey et al., *Rise of the Pasdaran*, xiv, 9; Golkar, *Captive Society*, 52. For an excellent baseline discussion of the Basiji, see Katzman, *Warriors of Islam*.

29. Golkar, *Captive Society*, xvi, 7.

30. O'Hern, *Iran's Revolutionary Guard*, 70–73; Montagne, "Evolution of Iran's Revolutionary Guard."

31. Tehran has long cultivated ties to ideologically likeminded groups in Latin America. For a recent appraisal of these activities, see Kredo, "Iran Expanding Terror Network."

32. Eisenstadt, "Strategic Culture of Islamic Republic," 12–26.

33. Eisenstadt assigns a double meaning to the word *moral*, in that it pertains to both the state of mind of combatants (as in morale) and ethical considerations. Both meanings are critical to Iran, as opposed to America's approach. In addition to placing an emphasis on higher-end capabilities, America also values rational approaches to warfare over moral ones. The United States uses morality as a rationale for action, whereas others may use logic as a rationale for decisions that have moral motivations. See Weigley, *American Way of War*.

34. Quran 8.

35. Golkar, "Iran's Revolutionary Guard," 53.

36. Sinha and Campbell Beachy, "Timeline on Iran's Nuclear Program"; Broad, "Iran Shielding Its Nuclear Efforts."

37. Hannah, "Iran Deal's Ticking Time Bomb."

38. Krauss, "War in the Gulf."

39. Lohaus, "Special Operations Forces."

40. For an overview of the doctrinal challenges faced by the U.S. military in responding to insurgency in Iraq and the subsequent period of doctrinal adjustment, see Sepp, "U.S. Counterinsurgency Capability in Iraq," 217–30.

41. Lee, *Iran's Influence in Iraq*, 5–20; Felter and Fishman, *Iranian Strategy in Iraq*, 6–11; Eisenstadt, Knights, and Ali, *Iran's Influence in Iraq*.

42. Borger, "U.S. Intelligence Fears"; International Crisis Group, *Iraq Backgrounder*, 16–17.

43. Wing, "History of Dawa Party."

44. Initially, the extent to which Iran would take advantage of this historic opportunity was hotly debated. See, for example, Aslan et al., "Emerging Shia Crescent."; Barzegar, "Iran and Shiite Crescent," 87–99; Black, "Fear of Shia Full Moon"; *Economist*, "Shia Crescendo"; Trofimov, "After Islamic State."

45. Naylor, "In Syria's Aleppo."

46. Sabet and Safshekan, *Soft War*, 3, 7.

47. Sabet and Safshekan, *Soft War*; Adelkhah, "Iran Integrates 'Soft War.'"

48. National Democratic Action Society of Bahrain members, in discussion with the author, January 13, 2007. For information on how this dynamic plays out vis-a-vis Gulf States' developing sense of nationalism, see Partrick, *Nationalism in the Gulf States*, 26–28.

49. Mohseni, *Islamic Awakening*, 1–4.

50. American Enterprise Institute, Iran Shaping Operations Workshop, "Participant Discussions" (unpublished manuscript available upon request).

51. For additional material on *taqiyya*, see Campo, *Encyclopedia of Islam*, 264, 323, 386, 680.

52. Quran 8:9–19 and 66. For example, verse 8:66 reads, "Now, Allah has lightened [the hardship] for you, and He knows that among you is weakness. So if there are from you one hundred [who are] steadfast, they will overcome two hundred. And if there are among you a thousand, they will overcome two thousand by permission of Allah."

53. Overt sectarian incitement is generally left to second-party proxies.

54. Agence France Press, "Over 40% of Iranians"; National Council of Resistance in Iran, "Iran: Regime Admits."

55. Esfandiari, "Iranians and Their Satellite Dishes."

56. BBC News, "BBC Persian Audiences Nearly Double."

57. Wojcieszak, Brouillette, and Smith, *Practices of Iranian Diaspora*, 6; BBG Watch, "Gallup Iran Survey"; Wojcieszak, Smith, and Enayat, *Iranians Reach for News*, 15.

58. Wojcieszak, Smith, and Enayat, *Iranians Reach for News*, 12.

59. Open Source Center, *Iran's State-Run TV IRIB*.

60. Azizi, "TV Chief Bring IRIB, Rouhani Closer?."

61. Malek, "Al-Alam's Game."

62. Telhami, "Most-Feared News Network."

63. Alkawthar TV Channel, "Who Are We?."

64. Sedarat, "Satellite TV News, Serials."

65. Coutrix, "Press TV: A Slick Propaganda Tool."

66. Yardley and Kumar, "Kashmir Erupts"; Sonne and Fassihi, "Channel Loses British License."

67. Azizi, "Iran Is Spending More."

68. Islamic Development Organization, "Soft War Reasons."

69. Though in this instance the official's reference to *the system* meant the international media, Iranians also view the system as their own institutions, which are similarly vulnerable to the same forces. See, for example, Wehrey et al., "Iran's Nuclear Threat."

70. ABNA is but the tip of the iceberg of activities in which the Ahl al-Bayt World Organization has involved itself; more on this organization is included in the "Religious Influence" section.

71. Tabnak News, "ABNA Site Was Filtered."

72. Golkar, "Militant Clergy."

73. Golkar, "Militant Clergy."

74. Almustafa University, "List of Agreements"; Library of Congress, "Iran's Ministry of Intelligence," 1.

75. Lanzillo, "Iran and the Green Movement."

76. American Enterprise Institute, Iran Shaping Operations Workshop, "Participant Discussions" (unpublished manuscript available upon request).

77. Shalal-Esa, "Iran Strengthened Cyber Capabilities."

78. Iran Media Program and ASL19, "Supreme Council of Cyberspace"; Fassihi, "Iran's Censors Tighten Grip."

79. Iran Media Program and ASL19, "Supreme Council of Cyberspace"; PressTV, "Iran Should Boost Passive Defense."; *Jerusalem Post*, "'Passive Defense' Plan."

80. Jones, "Cyber Warfare."

81. Thompson, "Iranian Cyber Attack."

82. See, for example, Berman, *Cyber Threats*.

83. Berman, "Fallout Ploy"; Jones, "Cyber Warfare."

84. These tools were a mix of indigenously developed ones and some developed in the West, as discussed in Kagan and Stiansen, *Growing Cyberthreat from Iran*, v. For a discussion of Iran's expanding network of targets, see Jones, "Cyber Warfare."

85. Perlroth, "Cyberespionage Attacks"; Berman, "Fallout Ploy."

86. Kagan and Stiansen, *Growing Cyberthreat from Iran*, 11.

87. Newman, "Hack Brief."

88. American Enterprise Institute, Iran Shaping Operations Workshop, "Participant Discussions" (unpublished manuscript available upon request); Duggan, "Special Warfare in Cyberspace"; Frenkel, "Iranian Authorities Block Access."

89. Felter and Fishman, *Iranian Strategy in Iraq*, 22–57.

90. Felter and Fishman, *Iranian Strategy in Iraq*, 22–57.

91. Suwaidi, *Iran and the Gulf*, 163.

92. Pollock and Ali, "Iran Gets Negative Reviews."

93. Interview with Shi'a community leaders, January 2017, Manama, Bahrain. This situation has provided Iran with a ready-made opportunity to showcase the plight of regional Shi'ites, which, in a vicious cycle, further mobilizes Shi'ites in other countries to support those in Bahrain. See Press tv, "Bahrainis Hold Nationwide Rallies."

94. Habeeb, *Middle East in Turmoil*, 34; Partrick, *Nationalism in Gulf States*, 2; Interview with government officials and academics, Abu Dhabi, January 2017.

95. Wehrey, "Shiite Problem."

96. Graham, "Sheikh Nimr al-Nimr."

97. Stratfor, "Iran's Ties."

98. Mamouri, "Leaked Cables."; Azizi, "Iran Is Spending More."

99. Buchta, "Tehran's Ecumenical Society," 351.

100. Buchta, "Tehran's Ecumenical Society," 351.

101. See Hamshahri Online, "Introduction to World Assembly"; Ahl al-Bayt World Assembly, "Home"; Qara'ati, *Commentary Prayer*, xv–xvi.

102. Khamenei, "Leader's Speech."; Islamic Republic News Agency, "Supreme Leader."

103. Wehrey, "Ominous Divide"; Groisman, "Gulf Shi'ites Paying Religious Tax."

104. Wilson, "Lebanese Wary."

105. Rudner, "Hizbullah Terrorism Finance"; Bartels, "Strategic Goods Provision," 33–34.

106. Rubin, *Strategies Underlying Iranian Soft Power.*

107. Levitt, "Charitable Organizations and Terrorist Financing"; U.S. Department of Treasury, "Iran's Support for Terrorism."

108. Peterson, "Iran Steps Up Recruitment."

109. *Aharq Al-Awsat*, "In the Name of Charity."

110. Rubin, *Strategies Underlying Iranian Soft Power*; *Economist*, "Why Iran"; Borger and Tait, "Financial Power."

111. U.S. Department of the Treasury, "Treasury Designates Iranian Entities."

112. Islamic Republic of Iran, *Collection of Laws.*

113. Iran Tour, "Free Trade Zones in Iran"; U.S. Department of Treasury, "Iran's Support for Terrorism."

114. Khamenei, "Year of Economy of Resistance."

115. Smyth, "Deciphering Iranian Leader's Call."

116. Khajehpour, "Decoding Iran's 'Resistance Economy.'"

117. Rubin, "Strategies Underlying Iranian Soft Power"; Sadjadpour, *Battle of Dubai*.

118. For additional detail on IRGC involvement in conflict zones, see the section "Military Shaping Operations."

119. Jafarzadeh, "Revolutionary Guards' Financial Empire."

120. Katzman, *Iran Sanctions*, 33–37.

121. Katzman, "Iran Sanctions," 33; Meier and Weiser, "Court Halts U.S. Seizure."; U.S. Department of the Treasury, "Continuing Illicit Finance Threat." As Anna Fifield describes, as a critical node in the international *hawala* system, the UAE frequently serves as a transshipment point for these funds. Whether inadvertently or intentionally, however, Western companies were not entirely innocent of conducting business with Iranian banks and faced fines of hundreds of millions of dollars as a result. See Fifield, "Iranians Are Avoiding Sanctions"; Raphaeli, "Violations of Iranian Sanctions"; U.S. Government Accountability Office, "Sanctions Adversely Affected Iranian Economy."

122. American Enterprise Institute, Iran Shaping Operations Workshop, "Participant Discussions" (unpublished manuscript available upon request).

123. Kennedy, *Rise and Fall*.

124. *Capability* is a quantifiable means, whereas *capacity* is the ability to use such means, which encompasses factors like political will and tactical acumen.

125. Cordesman and Toukan, "Iran and Gulf Military Balance."

126. Cordesman and Toukan, "Iran and Gulf Military Balance"; Cenciotti, "Iran Unveils New UCAV."

127. Haghshenass, *Iran's Asymmetric Naval Warfare*.

128. Daoud, "Meet the Proxies"; Jafarzadeh, "Revolutionary Guards' Financial Empire"; National Council of Resistance of Iran, U.S. Office, *Iran Fuels Syria War*; Nadami, "Iran's Afghan and Pakistani Proxies"; Bucci, *Iran's Power Projection Capability*; Interview with Fifth Fleet command staff, January 13, 2017 (notes available upon request).

129. Cordesman, "Iran's Revolutionary Guards."

130. See, for example, Levitt, "Iran and Hezbollah"; Levitt, *Hezbollah: Global Footprint*, 131–32; Levitt, "Hezbollah: A Case Study."

131. For a detailed account of this period, see Navias and Hooton, *Tanker Wars*.

132. See, for example, Keck, "Iran's Mass Producing Submarines"; Jamieson, "Iran Navy Produces Armed Copy"; Cordesman and Toukan, "Iran and Gulf Military Balance." Only recently has Iran discussed efforts to project naval power outside of its immediate environs, and its statements have thus far not been met with serious action. See Ben Taleblu and Megahan, "Iran's Maritime Mirage"; Adelkhah, "Three Strategies."

133. Interview with Fifth Fleet command staff; CBS News, "Iranian Boats in 'Unsafe' Encounter." For example, Iran frequently threatens to close the Strait

of Hormuz, through which one-third of all sea-based oil shipments transit each year, based on what it sees as mistreatment by the United States and its Gulf Cooperation Council (GCC) allies on the high seas. Miscalculations could result in situations that support Iran's rhetoric.

134. Martinez, "U.S. Fires on Persian Gulf Boat"; Starr et al., "10 U.S. Sailors in Custody."

135. Cunningham, "Iran Holds Military Exercises."

136. Jain, "World According to Ahmadinejad."

137. Donovan, et al., "Iran News Round Up."

138. Reuters, "Iran May Seek Naval Bases."

139. McInnis, "Iran's Military."

140. Gady, "Sarmat ICBMs"; McGarry, "Russia Finishes Delivery."

141. Golkar, "Iran's Revolutionary Guard," 53.

3. China

1. Sawyer, *Seven Military Classics*, 17–18.

2. Johnston, *Cultural Realism*, 59. For alternative viewpoints, see Feng, *Chinese Strategic Culture*, 3–4.

3. See, for example, Sawyer, *Seven Military Classics*, 126, 133, 135, 158, 161, 182–83, 186; Jullien, *Treatise on Efficacy*, 46–60. For a review of other works related to the Chinese way of war, see Scobell, "Chinese Way of War?."

4. Sun, *Art of Warfare*, 111.

5. Sun, *Art of Warfare*, 113.

6. Swaine and Tellis, *Interpreting China's Grand Strategy*, 23.

7. Di Cosmo, *Military Culture in Imperial China*, 23–44; Sawyer, *Seven Military Classics*, 17. As Andrew Wilson points out, *The Art of Warfare* frequently equates the general "to god and his soldiers to mindless automatons." See Mahnken and Blumenthal, *Strategy in Asia*, 122.

8. Jullien, *Treatise on Efficacy*, 120–52.

9. Jullien, *Propensity of Things*, 11–18.

10. Sawyer, *Seven Military Classics*, 207.

11. Sun, *Art of Warfare*, 120; Kissinger, *On China*, 30.

12. Sawyer, *Seven Military Classics*, 165; Sun, *Art of Warfare*, 120. This perception of frictionless motion toward an end contrasts starkly with the Clausewitzian concept of friction, which suggests that strategic motion results in bursts from pent-up energy.

13. Pillsbury, *Hundred-Year Marathon*, 36.

14. Yutang, *Importance of Living*, 442.

15. Pillsbury, *Hundred-Year Marathon*, 43–44.

16. Kissinger, *On China*, 30.

17. Sawyer, *Seven Military Classics*, 301.

18. Sawyer, *Seven Military Classics*, 353.

19. Sawyer, *Seven Military Classics*, 56–57.

20. Johnston, *Cultural Realism*, 122.

21. Sun, *Art of Warfare*, 111.

22. Johnston, *Cultural Realism*, 122.

23. Sawyer, *Seven Military Classics*.

24. Swaine and Tellis, *Interpreting China's Grand Strategy*, 25, 29.

25. Swaine and Tellis, *Interpreting China's Grand Strategy*, 25–27.

26. Wang, *Harmony and War*, 34.

27. Fairbank, "Chinese Military Experience," 7–9; Boylan, "Chinese Cultural Style of Warfare," 345.

28. Zhang, "Confucian Foreign Policy Traditions," 197–218; Wang, *Harmony and War*, 147. See also Dotson, *Confucian Revival in Propaganda*.

29. Wang, *Harmony and War*, 34–76.

30. Waldron, *Great Wall of China*, 30–51.

31. Waldron, *Great Wall of China*, 144.

32. Yu, *Han China: A Study*, 36–60. Indeed, the Mandarin word for China, 中國 (*zhonggou in pinyin*) translates to "middle kingdom," reflecting China's view of itself at the center of known realms.

33. Fairbank and Têng, "Ch'ing Tributary System," 135–246.

34. Katzenstein, *Sinicization and Rise of China*; Sinicization attempts were even undertaken by the Mongols of the Yuan dynasty, both within their own territory and in territory they conquered, such as Yunnan. See Yang, *Between Winds and Clouds*, 147–63; for examples of Sinicization attempts during the Qing dynasty, see Ho, "In Defense of Sinicization," 123–55.

35. Tsiang, "China and European Expansion," 1–18, as quoted by Fairbank and Têng in "On the Chi'ing Tributary System," presented at the London School of Economics, n.d.

36. See, for instance, Zhou, "Equilibrium Analysis of Tributary System," 147–78.

37. Zhou, "Equilibrium Analysis of Tributary System," 147–78.

38. Pillsbury, *Hundred-Year Marathon*, 45; Kissinger, *On China*, 20.

39. Wang, *Harmony and War*, 147.

40. Rongxia, "Zheng He's Voyages."

41. Wang, *Harmony and War*, 151–80.

42. Waley-Cohen, "Militarization of Culture," 278–95.

43. Waley-Cohen, *Culture of War*, 3–7.

44. Roberts, *Concise History of China*, 206–7.

45. Leung, *Essentials of Modern Chinese History*, 59–61.

46. Guillermaz, *Chinese Communist Party*, 22–23.

47. Gregor and Chang, "Marxism, Sun Yat-Sen," 54–79.

48. Sun, *Fundamentals of National Reconstruction*, 76–83.

49. Gregor and Chang, "Nazionalfascismo and Revolutionary Nationalism," 25–33; Gregor and Chang, "Marxism, Sun Yat-Sen," 66–78; Bedeski, "Tutelary State," 314.

50. Fairbank, *United States and China*, 276–79.

51. Fairbank, *United States and China*, 287.

52. Cook, *Mao's Little Red Book*, 136–37.

53. In "On Protracted War," Mao discussed the relationship between politics and war as he understood it: "When politics develops to a certain stage beyond which it cannot proceed by the usual means, war breaks out to sweep the obstacles from the way. . . . When the obstacle is removed and our political aim attained, the war will stop." See Mao, *Selected Works*, vol. 2, 152–53; Clausewitz, *On War*, 87.

54. Mao, *War and Strategy*, 2–3; Cook, *Mao's Little Red Book*, 23–42, 271.

55. Mao, *War and Strategy*, 19–22.

56. Cook, *Mao's Little Red Book*, 87; Mao, *War and Strategy*, 26.

57. Cook, *Mao's Little Red Book*, 95–98.

58. For further information about Mao's application of ancient Chinese strategic thought, see Jullien, *Propensity of Things*, 34.

59. Cook, *Mao's Little Red Book*, 79–80.

60. Mao spoke extensively about the importance of battlespace preparation. He states that "all organizational works and struggles before the outbreak of hostilities are undertaken as preparations for war," for example, and emphasizes the importance of preparing for the worst while not neglecting the possibility of engaging in more limited forms of war. See Cook, *Mao's Little Red Book*, 87; Mao, *War and Strategy*, 4.

61. Yufan and Zhihai, "China's Decision," 94–99.

62. Hunt, "Beijing and Korean Crisis," 457–59.

63. Kissinger, *On China*, 133.

64. Yufan and Zhihai, "China's Decision," 112–14; Stueck, *Korean War*, 111–12.

65. Barnouin and Changgen, *Zhou Enlai*, 148; Yufan and Zhihai, "China's Decision."

66. Stueck, *Korean War*, 360–70. Though China was unable to wage a people's war in Korea along the lines that Mao had during previous conflicts, his strategy in Korea still demonstrated the primacy of mass as compared to technological means in early PRC strategic thinking. See Wang, "China's Evolving Strategic Doctrine," 1042–43.

67. Fairbank, *United States and China*, 462–70.

68. Huisken, "People's Republic of China," 36–37.

69. Roberts, *Concise History of China*, 293–95; Wang, "China's Evolving Strategic Doctrine," 1042–43.

70. Chase and Chan, "China's Evolving Strategic Deterrence," 117; Wang, "China's Evolving Strategic Doctrine," 1048–50.

71. Wang, "China's Evolving Strategic Doctrine," 1048–55.

72. Shambaugh, "China's Military Views World," 52–79.

73. Johnston, "China's New 'Old Thinking,'" 23–42; Shambaugh, "China's Military Views World," 55.

74. Breslin, "China's Emerging Global Role," 52–54; Zhao, *"China's Power"*, 251–70.

75. Zhao, *"China's Power,"* 251–70.

76. Chase and Chan, "China's Evolving Strategic Deterrence," 117.

77. The ancient Chinese devised a term for such posturing: "hiding [a] dagger behind [a] smile," which meant to charm and ingratiate oneself with enemies to gain their trust and then later to move against them in secret. See the work of Tang-dynasty poet Bai Juyi, as quoted in Verstappen, *Thirty-Six Strategies*.

78. Cheng, "Chinese Lessons"; Newmyer, "Revolution in Military Affairs," 483–504; Liang and Wang, *Unrestricted Warfare*, 1–5.

79. Biddle, *Military Power*, ix, 4.

80. Liang and Wang, *Unrestricted Warfare*, 4, 43.

81. Liang and Wang, *Unrestricted Warfare*, 18.

82. Jullien, *Treatise on Efficacy*, 150.

83. Newmyer, "Revolution in Military Affairs"; Liang and Wang, *Unrestricted Warfare*, 19, 30, 43; Chase and Chan, "China's Evolving Strategic Deterrence," 122–23, 126–29.

84. Fravel, "Evolution of China's Military Strategy," 84–86.

85. Liang and Wang, *Unrestricted Warfare*, 14–15.

86. Liang and Wang, *Unrestricted Warfare*, 87, 94–95; Newmyer, "Revolution in Military Affairs," 493; Chase and Chan, "China's Evolving Strategic Deterrence," 118–19; Fravel, "Evolution of China's Military Strategy," 84–85.

87. Liang and Wang, *Unrestricted Warfare*, 113–15.

88. As Sun Tzu put it, one should "attack the enemy where he is unprepared . . . appear where unexpected." See Verstappen, *Thirty-Six Strategies*, 9.

89. Scobell, "China and Strategic Culture," 16–20.

90. Scobell, "China and Strategic Culture," 12–14, 16–17.

91. Gady, "China's Air Force"; Fisher, "China's Beihang Unmanned Aircraft."

92. Halper, *China: Three Warfares*, 27–28.

93. Fravel, "China's Changing Approach," 8.

94. Shen, "Study of PLA's Three Warfares," 11.

95. Halper, *China: Three Warfares*, 14–15.

96. Stokes and Hsiao, *Political Warfare with Chinese Characteristics*; Stokes, "CMC Political Work Department." Reportedly the PLA learned the value of political warfare as a formal discipline from the Soviets, but in an informal sense, the Chinese were already predisposed to this type of work (as described elsewhere in this chapter). Stokes, "CMC Political Work Department," 3.

97. Sun, *Art of Warfare*, 119–20. An alternative translation reads "the interplay between direct and indirect methods generates countless tactics." Verstappen, *Thirty-Six Strategies*, 35.

98. Cheng, "Winning without Fighting," 1; Thomas, "Chinese Psychological Warfare," 3.

99. Thomas, "Chinese Psychological Warfare," 7.

100. Guo, *Psychological Warfare Knowledge*, 14; Lee, "China's 'Three Warfares,'" 198–221.

101. Though China views Taiwan as a renegade province and the United States has repeatedly reaffirmed its support of the "one China" policy, Taiwan is addressed separately from the domestic-audience target in the three warfares doctrine, so it will likewise be treated separately in this report.

102. Holslag, *China's Coming War*, 93; Republic of China Tourism Bureau, "Visitor Arrivals by Residence."

103. Hammond, "China's Relations with Taiwan," 1.

104. Holslag, *China's Coming War*, 93–94.

105. American Enterprise Institute, Chinese Three Warfares Workshop, "Participant Discussions."

106. American Enterprise Institute, Chinese Three Warfares Workshop, "Participant Discussions"; Holslag, *China's Coming War*, 93–94.

107. Roy, *Taiwan's Threat Perceptions*, 1–4.

108. Huang, "Chinese Trolls Jumped Firewall"; Republic of China Tourism Bureau, "Visitor Arrivals by Residence"; Smith, "China Is Using Tourism."

109. Jensen, "China's Psychological War."

110. American Enterprise Institute, Chinese Three Warfares Workshop, "Participant Discussions"; Interview with senior Japanese security official, May 2017 (available upon request).

111. Matsumura, "China Waging Psychological Warfare."

112. Stokes, "Hostile Neighbors"; Panda, "Pacific Rim States"; Xinhua, "China Welcomes More Japanese Investments."

113. Xie, "How Did China Lose South Korea?"; Han, "South Korea Seeks to Balance."

114. Clark, "Lips and Teeth," 52–54; Interview with South Korean officials and academics, May 2016 (available upon request); Buchman, "Chinese Sanctions Could Influence."

115. Ministry of Foreign Affairs, People's Republic of China, "Statement on China's Territorial Sovereignty."

116. National Institute for Defense Studies, *East Asian Strategic Review*, 136–62; American Enterprise Institute, Chinese Three Warfares Workshop, "Participant Discussions"; Nguyen, "Resurgence of China-Vietnam Ties." In the case of the Philippines, this shift has come with a concurrent cooling of Manila's relations with the United States, as demonstrated by the reversal of the Subic Bay submarine-basing decision in the Philippines and the campaign rhetoric of President Rodrigo Duterte.

117. Joy-Perez and Scissors, "Close Look at OBOR."

118. Farchy et al., "One Belt, One Road"; Thant, "Why Burma Must Reset."

119. Mao, *War and Strategy*, 2–3; Mao, "Speech on Propaganda Work"; Dotson, "Confucian Revival in Propaganda."

120. Shambaugh, "China's Propaganda System," 48–50.

121. Xu and Albert, "Media Censorship in China." More than a dozen government organizations are responsible for censorship standards, the main one being the Communist Party's Central Propaganda Department (CPD). The government radio, film, and television producers are accountable to the CPD to ensure they're promoting the CCP's messages.

122. American Enterprise Institute, Chinese Three Warfares Workshop, "Participant Discussions"; McElroy, "Chinese Media Warns of War." For a contemporary example of Chinese efforts to influence political elites through personal incentives, see Craig, Becker, and Drucker, "Jared Kushner Chases Chinese Deal."

123. PWC, China Entertainment and Media Outlook, 32–33, 66.

124. Edney, Globalization of Chinese Propaganda, 6.

125. Nelson, CCTV's International Expansion; Reuters, "CCTV Launches Global Media Network."

126. Shambaugh, "China's Propaganda System," 30–47.

127. Shambaugh, "China's Propaganda System," 27.

128. International Media Support, Danish National Commission for UNESCO, and Copenhagen Business School, "Growth of Media in China," 15; Shambaugh, "China's Soft-Power Push," 99.

129. Shambaugh, "China's Propaganda System," 53.

130. Keith, "Internet in China"; Boehler, "Two Million 'Internet Opinion Analysts.'"

131. Shambaugh, "China's Propaganda System," 25–26.

132. Bandurski, "Me-Media."

133. Bandurski, "Me-Media."

134. Li, "Find Out Territory."

135. Gao, Ingram, and Kee, Global Media, 111.

136. Gao, Ingram, and Kee, Global Media, 111

137. Lai and Lu, China's Soft Power, 117.

138. Shambaugh, "China's Soft-Power Push," 99.

139. See, for example, Hu, Economic Leverage; Lorber, "Economic Coercion."

140. See, for example, Cole, "China Intensifies Disinformation"; Gonzalez, "Propaganda from China and Russia?." For more information on Russian disinformation campaigns, see the Russia chapter in this series.

141. Stokes, "CMC Political Work Department."

142. For additional details about the PLA's work in these fields, see the work of Mark Stokes, including Stokes and Hsiao, Political Warfare with Chinese Characteristics and Stokes, "CMC Political Work Department."

143. Cole, "China Intensifies Disinformation Campaign."

144. American Enterprise Institute, Chinese Three Warfares Workshop, "Participant Discussions."

145. American Enterprise Institute, Chinese Three Warfares Workshop, "Participant Discussions."

146. Huang, "China Is Making Life Hard."

147. Kim et al., *South Korean Attitudes on China*; Interview with *Dong-A Ilbo* journalists, Seoul, May 2017.

148. *Japan Times*, "China Opposes Pact."; Cossa, "Japan–South Korea Relations"; Interview with *Dong-A Ilbo* journalists, Seoul, May 2017; Interview with South Korean officials and academics, May 2016; Son, "Seoul Proposes GSOMIA."

149. Feldman, *Law in Politics*, 207; Besson, "Authority of International Law," 343–80.

150. Halper, *China: Three Warfares*, 48–49.

151. Ford, *Mind of Empire*, 5, 9, as quoted in Halper, "China: The Three Warfares," 47–48.

152. Ford, *Mind of Empire*, 49, 51.

153. Halper, *China: Three Warfares*, 48–49.

154. Cheng, "Winning without Fighting."

155. Halper, *China: Three Warfares*, 50.

156. For a discussion about how common law lends itself to an instrumentalist approach, see Kittrie, *Lawfare*, 32–33.

157. Liang and Wang, *Unrestricted Warfare*, 51, 55.

158. Liang and Wang, *Unrestricted Warfare*, 129–30; Halper, *China: Three Warfares*, 50–51.

159. Bhattacharya, *Intellectual Property Rights*; Morrison, *China-U.S. Trade Issues*.

160. Brown, "Calculated Ambiguity"; Jamandre, "PH Protests."

161. Kittrie, *Lawfare*, 190.

162. Cheng, *Cyber Dragon*, 186–87.

163. Kittrie, *Lawfare*, 162, 165.

164. Halper, *China: Three Warfares*, 56–57.

165. Halper, *China: Three Warfares*, 51; Nankivell, "China's Use of Lawfare," 427.

166. Ministry of Foreign Affairs, People's Republic of China, "Statement on China's Territorial Sovereignty" as quoted in Gewirtz, *Limits of Law*, 2–3.

167. Ku, "China's Weak Legal Argument."

168. Reuters, "More than 40 Countries"; Ku, "China's Weak Legal Argument."

169. Pedrozo, *China's Active Defense Strategy*, 4.

170. This approach is consistent with ideas of transformation embedded in Chinese strategic culture and also with the incrementalism advocated for by Mao Zedong and his intellectual predecessors. See Tsou, *Cultural Revolution*; Huang, "Chinese Military Doctrine," 140; Jullien, *Treatise on Efficacy*, 49–50.

171. Kittrie, *Lawfare*, 167.

172. President Duterte mentioned that the Chinese were "willing to go to war" if the Philippines insisted on enforcing the findings of the tribunal. See Villamor, "Xi Warned Philippines."

173. McDevitt, *South China Sea*, ii; Yeo, "China Upgrades Military Infrastructure."

174. Center for Strategic and International Studies, "China's Continuing Reclamation"; Garton Ash, "Islands for Civilian Use."

175. Rinehart and Elias, "China's Air Defense Identification Zone," i.

176. Hsu, *Zone Intended to Provide Flexibility*.

177. Holmes, "Thinly Veiled Grab"; Lee, "China's Declaration."

178. United Nations, *United Nations Treaties*; Bourbonnière and Lee, "Legality of Deployment," 873–901.

179. Bourbonnière and Lee, "Legality of Deployment," 880–81.

180. Bourbonnière and Lee, "Legality of Deployment," 876.

181. Maogoto and Freeland, "Final Frontier," 21; Wortzel, "Space Warfare," 112–37; United Nations, "United Nations Treaties," 4; Bourbonnière and Lee, "Legality of Deployment," 890–91.

182. Cheng, "China's Military Role in Space," 57–60. Concerns raised by these developments were further heightened by America's withdrawal from the Anti-Ballistic Missile Treaty in 2001. See Maogoto and Freeland, "Final Frontier," 1–4.

183. Wortzel, "Space Warfare"; Kumar, "China Conquers Fourth Territory."

184. Cheng, "China's Military Role in Space," 61–62. The fact that the Chinese space program is consistently led by members of the PLA is nontrivial evidence of the military's continued interest in the utility of space on the battlefield. See Maogoto and Freeland, "Final Frontier," 5.

185. For a discussion of the development of norms with respect to cyberspace, and China's views in particular, see Austin, "International Legal Norms."

186. Liu et al., "Letter from Permanent Representatives"; Hsu and Murray, *International Law in Cyberspace*; McKune, "Analysis of International Code."

187. White House, *International Strategy for Cyberspace*, 3.

188. Huang and Mačák, "Rule of Law in Cyberspace"; Hsu and Murray, *International Law in Cyberspace*.

189. Wee, "China's New Cybersecurity Law."

190. KPMG China IT Advisory Practice, "China's Cybersecurity Law."

191. Inkster, "Conflict Foretold," 7–28.

192. Segal, "China, International Law, and Cyberspace."

193. Kittrie, *Lawfare*, 28–39, 191–96.

194. McLeary, "Chinese Military Modernization."

195. Gertz, "Chinese Military Revamps Cyber Warfare."

196. Chase and Chan, *China's Evolving Approach*, vii, 14–17.

197. This approach is consistent with how Chinese think of deterrence more generally. Chinese deterrence, which incorporates aspects of what Thomas Schelling characterizes as "compellence" and "coercion," lends itself well to integrated and active measures. See Chase and Chan, *China's Evolving Approach*, 2–5; Schelling, *Arms and Influence*, xi, 72.

198. PLA Academy of Military Science, *Science of Military Strategy*, 194, as quoted in Chase and Chan, *China's Evolving Approach*, 17.

199. Whittle, "Global Cyber Treaty."

200. Lindsay, *China and Cybersecurity*, 22–33; Finkle, "Hacker Group in China."

201. Lindsay, *China and Cybersecurity*; Kostadinov, "GhostNet—Part 1."

202. FireEye, *Redline Drawn*; CrowdStrike, *Global Threat Report 2019*.

203. American Enterprise Institute, Chinese Three Warfares Workshop, "Participant Discussions." Beijing had infiltrated the networks of thirty Taiwanese government agencies by 2003, including the Defense Ministry, the Election Commission, and the National Police Administration. In 2005 the Taiwanese National Security Council "was targeted with socially engineered e-mails" that contained malicious code. See Krekel, *Capability of China*, 67–70; Spade, *Information as Power*, 4.

204. American Enterprise Institute, Chinese Three Warfares Workshop, "Participant Discussions."

205. American Enterprise Institute, Chinese Three Warfares Workshop, "Participant Discussions."

206. For summaries of these activities, which are too extensive to be covered in detail here, see Clarke and Knake, *Cyber War*, 47–62; Rogin, "Chinese Cyber Attacks."

207. Adams, "OPM Hack Is Far Worse"; Gertz, "F-35 Secrets."

208. Harold, "U.S.-China Cyber Agreement"; Kumar, "Obama, Xi Reach Agreement."

209. Thomas, "Nation-State Cyber Strategies," 6.

210. Thomas, "Nation-State Cyber Strategies," 7.

211. U.S. Department of Defense, *Military and Security Developments*, i.

212. Blanchard and Martina, "China's Xi Says"; U.S. Department of Defense, "Military and Security Developments," 1.

213. Cordesman and Kendall, *Chinese Strategy*, 38; Saunders, et al., *Xi Remakes the PLA*, 114.

214. U.S. Department of Defense, *Military and Security Developments*, 1–3.

215. U.S. Department of Defense, *Military and Security Developments*, 1–3.

216. Kiselycznyk and Saunders, "Civil-Military Relations," 6.

217. Information Office of the State Council of the People's Republic of China, "China's Military Strategy," 4.

218. Erickson, "Sweeping Change in China's Military."

219. Information Office of the State Council of the People's Republic of China, "China's Military Strategy"; U.S. Department of Defense, *Military and Security Developments*, 4; International Institute for Strategic Studies, "Asia," 2016, 221.

220. The tone of these documents may have been purposefully moderated to match the level of rhetoric used by American leaders toward China during the Obama administration. See Cordesman and Kendall, *Chinese Strategy*, 24–30.

221. Halper, *China: Three Warfares*, 27–38.

222. U.S. Department of Defense, *Military and Security Developments*, 58; Information Office of the State Council of the People's Republic of China, "China's Military Strategy," 4.

223. Kristensen and Norris, "Chinese Nuclear Forces, 2016," 205.

224. U.S. Department of Defense, *Military and Security Developments*, 1, 22–26, 38; Kristensen and Norris, "Chinese Nuclear Forces, 2016," 205.

225. Kristensen and Norris, "Chinese Nuclear Forces, 2016," 205.

226. Information Office of the State Council of the People's Republic of China, "China's Military Strategy," 4.

227. U.S. Department of Defense, *Military and Security Developments*, 33; Cordesman and Kendall, *Chinese Strategy*, 194.

228. U.S. Department of Defense, *Military and Security Developments*, 34.

229. Cordesman and Kendall, *Chinese Strategy*, 197; U.S. Department of Defense, *Military and Security Developments*, 25–26; Information Office of the State Council of the People's Republic of China, "China's Military Strategy," 3.

230. Erickson, "China's First Aircraft Carrier"; Louth, Taylor, and Tyler, *Defence Innovation and UK*, 9–12.

231. Louth, Taylor, and Tyler, *Defence Innovation and UK*, 9; Yung, *China's Capabilities Trajectory*; International Institute for Strategic Studies, "Asia," 2016, 225.

232. U.S. Department of Defense, *Military and Security Developments*, 25–26; Ju and Clover, "Chinese Military Base."

233. Peck, "Carriers May Be Obsolete."

234. Morris, "New 'Normal.'"

235. American Enterprise Institute, Chinese Three Warfares Workshop, "Participant Discussions"; Morris, "New 'Normal.'"

236. Erickson and Kennedy, "China's Maritime Militia."

237. For an overview of the history of fishing vessels, international law, and war, see Kraska and Monti, "Law of Naval Warfare," 456–65.

238. Kraska and Monti, "Law of Naval Warfare," 465–67.

239. Pomerleau, "China's Electronic Warfare Tactics"; U.S. Department of Defense, *Military and Security Developments*, 65.

240. Raud, *China and Cyber*, 23; U.S. Department of Defense, *Military and Security Developments*, 65.

241. Cordesman and Kendall, *Chinese Strategy*, 153–54.

242. International Institute for Strategic Studies, "Asia," 2016, 223.

243. Roblin, "America Should Fear"; Lin and Singer, "China Builds Its Own."

244. International Institute for Strategic Studies, "Asia," 2017, 260.

245. International Institute for Strategic Studies, "Asia," 2017, 260–62.

246. Fleurant et al., *Trends in International Arms Transfers*, 2; Blachfield, Wezeman, and Wezeman, "Major Arms Transfers"; Sethi, "China behind Pak's Growing Confidence."

247. Johnson, "Expanded Chinese-Operated Pakistani Port."

248. Manuel, "Growing Alliance"; Small, *China-Pakistan Axis*.

249. Fleurant et al., *Trends in International Arms Transfers*, 4.

250. International Institute for Strategic Studies, "Asia," 2016, 21.

251. Du Plessis, "China's African Infrastructure Projects," 3.

252. Ramzy, "China Resumes Diplomatic Relations"; Ives, "Nation Severs Ties."

253. International Institute for Strategic Studies, "Asia," 2017, 261.

254. International Institute for Strategic Studies, "Asia," 2017, 259–62; Cheung et al., *Planning for Innovation*, 3–4.

255. Cheung et al., "Planning for Innovation," 3–5.

256. Chase et al., *"China's Development of Unmanned Systems."*

257. International Institute for Strategic Studies, "Asia," 2017, 261–62.

258. *Economist*, "China's Achilles Heel."

4. The United States

1. Shy, "American Military Experience," 212; Higginbotham, "Early American Way of War," 233–34; Hope, *Scientific Way of War*, 18. For a discussion of the paternalistic view of Native Americans held by European settlers, see Sheehan, *Savagism and Civility*.

2. Millett and Maslowski, *For the Common Defense*, 14.

3. Shy, "American Military Experience," 212; Millett and Maslowski, *For the Common Defense*, 7, 18; Grenier, *First Way of War*, 260–96; Black, "Defining a New Empire," 14–15.

4. Millett and Maslowski, *For the Common Defense*, 11–13; Lee, "Early American Ways of War," 271–73; Lee, "Peace Chiefs and Blood Revenge," 701–41.

5. Higginbotham, "Early American Way of War," 231; Weigley, *American Way of War*, xiv, 19–20.

6. Echevarria, *Reconsidering American Way of War*, 9–12.

7. Onuf, *Jefferson's Empire*, 16.

8. As James Kiras notes, the Delbrückian dichotomy was similarly rejected by other military thinkers, including Mao Tse-Tung. One must also consider the context in which Delbrück formulated his dichotomy; European warfare and colonial-indigenous conflict were altogether different in terms of means, ways, and ends. See Kiras, *Special Operations and Strategy*, 72.

9. Shy, "American Military Experience," 214–15.

10. Millett and Maslowski, *For the Common Defense*, 18–19; Hope, *Scientific Way of War*, 21–22; Shy, "American Military Experience," 213; Cohen, "Militia Era (1775–1830)," 8–10.

11. Fleming, *Strategy of Victory*.

12. Weigley, *American Way of War*, 19–39; Higginbotham, "Early American Way of War," 235–36; Millett and Maslowski, *For the Common Defense*, 59, 67–

12. For details on how and when Washington adapted his strategic approach to the British, see Fleming, *Strategy of Victory*.

13. Shefveland, "Dual Strategy," 105–12.

14. *Federalist*, no. 24 (Hamilton).

15. Black, "Defining a New Empire," 16.

16. Merriam, "Political Theory of Jefferson," 36–37; Millett and Maslowski, *For the Common Defense*, 92–93.

17. *Federalist*, no. 24 (Hamilton).

18. *Federalist*, no. 41 (Madison); Read, "'Our Complicated System,'" 452–75.

19. Shy, "American Military Experience," 214–15. For an overview of the limited-war mentality that pervaded early American military thought (in contrast to bellicose rhetoric), see Stuart, *War and American Thought*, 182–83.

20. Miller, *Spying for America*, 34–37, 48–53.

21. For example, Thomas Jefferson, when facing the cessation of Louisiana from Spain to France during his presidency twenty years later, recognized the move as a threat to American expansionism and therefore to its national security. See Gruver, *American Nationalism, 1783–1830*, 143.

22. Larkin, *American School of Empire*, 1, 15–20. For more on the founding fathers' views of America as an empire, see *Federalist*, no. 1 (Hamilton). See also Hendrickson, "First Union," 35–37; Van Alstyne, *Rising American Empire*, 3.

23. Onuf, *Jefferson's Empire*, 53–61.

24. Cunningham, *Jefferson vs. Hamilton*, 115.

25. Black, "Defining a New Empire," 17–18; Onuf, *Jefferson's Empire*, 60.

26. Kaplan, *Entangling Alliances with None*, 1472; Millett and Maslowski, *For the Common Defense*, 100.

27. Millett and Maslowski, *For the Common Defense*, 97–100; Hope, *Scientific Way of War*, 27–35.

28. Russell Weigley argues that the crisis precipitated by conflicting American reactions to the French Revolution caused the formulation of a more coherent, organized, and unified articulation of the nation's foreign and defense policy. See Weigley, *American Way of War*, 42; Cunningham, *Jefferson vs. Hamilton*; Onuf, *Jefferson's Empire*; Miller, *Spying for America*, 57; Stuart, *War and American Thought*, 88–9; Kaplan, *Entangling Alliances with None*, 1138, 1200–1390; McColley, *Federalists, Republicans, and Foreign Entanglements*, 17–19.

29. Kaplan, *Entangling Alliances with None*, 12–13.

30. Weigley, *American Way of War*, 41–52; Black, "Defining a New Empire," 17–18.

31. Stuart, *War and American Thought*, 98–99.

32. Leeman, "War without Declaration," 164–65, 167; Stuart, *War and American Thought*, 104.

33. Stuart, *War and American Thought*, 104; Fisher, "Scholarly Support for Presidential Wars" 590–607; Fisher, *Presidential War Power*.

34. Hope, *Scientific Way of War*, 34–44.

35. Hellenbrand, "Not 'To Destroy,'" 523–49; Jefferson, *"Writings of Thomas Jefferson,"* xi, 288–90, 294–96.

36. Horsman, *Causes of War of 1812,* 64–94.

37. White, "Embargo"; Heaton, "Erosion of Economic Warfare," 32–37, 38–45.

38. Black, "International Context of War of 1812," 6–8; Gutzman, *Madison and Making of America,* 318–19. The extent to which the invasion of Canada motivated Congress to declare war on Britain in 1812 remains the subject of debate. See Hacker, "Desire for Canadian Land," 46–52; Pratt, "Land Hunger Thesis Challenged," 53–57; Hickey, *Forgotten Conflict,* 1, 66–69.

39. Weigley, *American Way of War,* 82–83.

40. Halleck, *Elements of Military Art and Science.*

41. Halleck, *Elements of Military Art and Science,* 35–60.

42. Fensterwald, "Anatomy of 'Isolationism' and Expansionism. Part 1," 112.

43. Weeks, *Building the Continental Empire,* 30–64; Hettle, *Peculiar Democracy,* 1–11.

44. Weeks, *Building the Continental Empire,* 53–56.

45. Robertson, *Military Strategy in Civil War,* 11.

46. Gallagher, *Confederate War,* 115–16; Current, "God and Strongest Battalions," 15.

47. Instructions and dispatches to foreign emissaries at the outset of the war reveal the essential nature of preventing foreign intervention in the war. See U. S. Department of State, "Message of the President," 37–51, 71–181, 195–256. For a summary of these and later efforts to maintain political neutrality, see Donald, *Why the North Won,* 50–57. With respect to the challenge to the Union posed by the daunting geography of the Confederate States, see Stewart, *American Military History,* vol. 1, 203.

48. Keithly, "Intelligence Sesquicentennial," 53–66.

49. Lively, "Propaganda Techniques," 99–106; Smith, "Union Propaganda," 26–32.

50. Tap, *Over Lincoln's Shoulder,* 8, 193–208.

51. Graebner, "Northern Diplomacy and European Neutrality," 58–80.

52. Williams, Bacevich, and Gardner, *Tragedy of American Diplomacy,* 24–25; Sarkesian, *America's Forgotten Wars,* 51.

53. Weigley, *American Way of War,* 156–60; Stewart, *American Military History,* vol. 1, 307–16, 325–45.

54. Hewes, *From Root to McNamara,* 3–12; Weigley, *American Way of War,* 200; Gutiérrez and Neiberg, "Elusive Lesson," 137–54.

55. Skowronek, *Building a New American State,* 3–11; Beisner, *Old Diplomacy to the New,* 78–85; Williams, Bacevich, and Gardner, *Tragedy of American Diplomacy,* 6–7.

56. Williams, Bacevich, and Gardner, *Tragedy of American Diplomacy,* 59–89.

57. This understanding contributed to the social, political, and religious consensus discussed earlier. See Grant, "Taft on America and Philippines,"

121–50. Quote of Grover Cleveland, as cited by Grant, is in Cleveland, "Message to Congress," 1260.

58. In other words, "the Progressive rejection of the doctrines of equality and individual natural rights was essential to justify the new foreign policy of imperialism." See Grant, "Taft on America and Philippines," 130.

59. Kennedy, *Will to Believe*, 43.

60. Wilson, "Fourteen Points."

61. National Defense Act of 1916, Pub. L. No. HR 12766, 39 Stat. 166 (1916); Navy Act Pub. L. No. HR 15947, 39 Stat. 556 (1916); Aviation Act, Pub. L. No. HR 5326, 40 Stat. 243 (1917).

62. Wilson, *Papers of Woodrow Wilson*; Abrams, *Security and Sacrifice*, 66.

63. Abrams, *Security and Sacrifice*, 66.

64. Weigley, *American Way of War*, 212.

65. For a discussion of the color plans developed by the U.S. military during the interwar period, see Matloff and Snell, *Strategic Planning for Coalition Warfare*; Weigley, *American Way of War*, 245–48, 313–16. For an overview of developments in military education during the interwar period, see Huntington, *Soldier and State*, 294–303.

66. For a detailed overview of interwar military innovation, see the authoritative text on the topic: Murray and Millet, *Military Innovation*, 300–416.

67. Huntington, *Soldier and State*, 289–314.

68. Fuller, *Conduct of War, 1789–1961*, 241–42, 256.

69. Murray and Millet, *Military Innovation*, 99–101, 331; Meilinger, "Trenchard and 'Morale Bombing,'" 243–70.

70. With respect to the development of battlefield propaganda, see Laurie, "'Chanting of Crusaders,'" 457–82. Domestic propaganda efforts were also coordinated by civil society organizations, which sought to undermine German communications aimed at influencing Americans and rally society to provide material aid to the war effort. See, for example, National Security League, "General Pershing Says"; National Special Aid Society, "Fight German Propaganda"; *Popular Science Monthly*, "Trinkets and Jewels," 560. See also Holsti, "Public Opinion and Foreign Policy," 440, from which the quotation in the noted sentence is derived.

71. Batvinis, *Origins of FBI Counterintelligence*, 68, as quoted in Schaefer et al., "History of Domestic Intelligence," 25. See also Troy, *Donovan and CIA*, 5–14.

72. Huntington, *Soldier and State*, 315–22; Matloff, "Allied Strategy in Europe," 367–70.

73. Huntington, *Soldier and State*, 323; For a detailed list of the extensive reorganizations to the federal bureaucracy performed by Roosevelt following the declaration of war, see Schmeckebier, "Organization of Executive Branch," 482–91.

74. For discussion on these differences, see Matloff, "Allied Strategy in Europe," 678–83.

75. Matloff, "Allied Strategy in Europe," 684–85; Glantz, "Soviet Military Strategy," 116–17.

76. Jones, "Freeing France," 4; Lewis, *Jedburgh Team Operations*, 3.

77. Paddock, *U.S. Army Special Warfare*, 21–23; Ogburn, "Merrill's Marauders," 39–40; Center of Military History, *Merrill's Marauders*, 22.

78. For a complete history of the founding of the oss, see Troy, *Donovan and cia*, 24–153.

79. For an in-depth overview of American covert operations in Europe, based largely on research from the American and German national archives, see Mauch, *Shadow War against Hitler*.

80. Freedman, "First Two Generations of Nuclear Strategists," 735.

81. Churchill, "Percentages Agreement"; Churchill, *Second World War*, vol. 6, 196–97. The extent to which the "percentages agreement" was intended for postwar spheres of influence remains unclear, as does Stalin's level of interest in the agreement. See Resis, "Churchill-Stalin Secret," 368–87.

82. Thompson, Memorandum to Dunn; Lukas, "Polish American Congress," 39–53; Harbutt, *Yalta 1945*, 183–224.

83. Bertinetti and Bonin, "Greatest Generation's Army," 176.

84. Troy, *Donovan and cia*, 287–349, 461–70.

85. Weigley, *American Way of War*, 368.

86. Kennan, Telegram to Secretary of State; X [Kennan] "Sources of Soviet Conduct."

87. Truman, "Address before Congress."

88. Troy, *Donovan and cia*, 347–48; Kasten Nelson, "Truman and National Security Council," 361. For an overview of Hopkins's outsized role in the Roosevelt administration, see McJimsey, *Harry Hopkins*.

89. National Security Council, "Directive on Office of Special Projects.".

90. Executive Secretary, *Report to National Security Council*.

91. Paddock, *U.S. Army Special Warfare*, 69; Shultz and Godson, *Dezinformatsia*, 14; Godson, *Intelligence Requirements for 1980's*, 1–11, 79, 193–207.

92. Abrams, *Security and Sacrifice*, 75.

93. Executive Secretary, *Report to National Security Council*, 23–24.

94. See the chapter on Russia for more information about these concepts. For more information on provokatsiya in a contemporary context, see Ennis, "Russian Media."

95. For a longer discussion on these issues, see Nye, "Systematic Problems," 210–12.

96. White, "Seeing Red"; Quester, "Origins of Cold War," 648–51.

97. For an excellent analysis of the context in which nsc-68 was drafted, see May, *American Cold War Strategy*, 1–14; Popescu, *Emergent Strategy*, 54.

98. Stueck, *Korean War*, 42–46.

99. See, for example, Stueck, *Korean War*; Fehrenbach, *This Kind of War*; Brands, *General vs. President*.

100. Huntington, *Soldier and State*, 432.

101. Paddock, *U.S. Army Special Warfare*, 89–104.

102. Center of Military History, *American Military History*, 574.

103. Center of Military History, *American Military History*, 575–81; Kretchik, *U.S. Army Doctrine*, 167.

104. Rudgers, "Origins of Covert Action," 259-60; Laurie, "Evolution of the CIA," 2–7.

105. Laville, "Committee of Correspondence; Parry-Giles, "Eisenhower Administration's Conceptualization," 263–76; Parry⊠Giles, "Camouflaged' Propaganda," 146–67; Jeffreys-Jones, *CIA and American Democracy*, 38.

106. Center of Military History, *American Military History*, 622–23; Rudgers, "Origins of Covert Action," 260–63.

107. Bundy, National Security Action Memoranda 57.

108. Adams, *US Special Operations Forces*, 84–85.

109. For an excellent analysis of the Phoenix program, see Moyar and Summers, *Phoenix and Birds of Prey*, 219–32, 353–65.

110. As the war dragged on, Democrats who were "more informed" viewed the war more negatively than those who were "less informed"; for Republicans, the opposite was true. See Berinsky, *In Time of War*, 113–18; Krebs, *Narrative and US National Security*, 245–57. For a deeper argument discussing these issues, see Lewy, *America in Vietnam*.

111. Brenner, "Problem of Innovation," 255–94.

112. Nixon, *Foreign Policy for the 1970s*.

113. See, for example, U.S. Information Agency Office of Research, *Machinery of Soviet Propaganda*; U.S. Information Agency Office of Research, *Soviet Propaganda Vulnerabilities*; Helgerson, "Intelligence Support for Nixon."

114. Stewart, *American Military History*, vol. 2, 379–82.

115. Kux, "Soviet Active Measures," 20; Rid, *Disinformation: A Primer*, 2.

116. Kretchik, *U.S. Army Doctrine*, 193–204; Stewart, *American Military History*, vol. 2, 374–97. With respect to the creation of Delta Force, see Bowden, *Guests of Ayatollah*, 138; Tucker and Lamb, "Restructuring Special Operations Forces."

117. Mahnken, "Reagan Administration's Strategy," 405; Gaddis, *Cold War*, 217.

118. Clark, "National Security Decision Directive 75," 75.

119. Sulc, *Active Measures, Quiet War*. For two examples of the growth in understanding of the nature of the Soviet threat exhibited during this period, see National Security Council, "NSDD 77"; National Security Council, "NSDD 277."

120. Casey, "Soviet Use of Active Measures."

121. Lamb and Schoen, *Deception, Disinformation, and Strategic Communications*, 10.

122. White House, "Office of Management and Budget," table 8.7; Gelb, "Reagan's Military Budget."

123. Suri, "End of the Cold War," 65.

124. Fondacaro, *AirLand Battle and* SOF, 1–3, 5, 11.

125. Stewart, *American Military History*, vol. 2, 404–27.

126. Keaney and Cohen, *Gulf War Air Power*. For a contrasting view, see Press, "Myth of Air Power," 5–44.

127. Fish, "Painting by Numbers"; Lohaus, "New Blueprint for Competing."

128. Nelsen, "U.S. Intelligence Budget," 195–203.

129. Wittaker, Smith, and McKune, *National Security Policy Process*, 16, 19–20; Rozen, "Obama's NSC Takes Power"; DeYoung, "Obama White House."

130. White House, *National Security Strategy*; U.S. Department of Defense, *Summary of 2018 National Defense Strategy*; Joint Chiefs of Staff, *Joint Concept for Integrated Campaigning*.

131. Foa and Mounk, "Danger of Deconsolidation," 5–17; Mellor and Rehr, *Baby Boomers*, 8–26; Norris and Inglehart, *Cultural Backlash*, 331–64.

Conclusions

1. U.S. Department of Defense, *Defense Directive 5111.11*.

2. Watts, "Barriers to Acting Strategically," 47.

3. Rosen, "Competitive Strategies," 22–26.

4. Walton, *Grand Strategy and Presidency*, 8, 98–119.

5. Rosen, "Competitive Strategies." For an argument outlining the risks of applying competitive strategies against Russia, see Rovner, "Competitive Strategies against Russia."

6. Miller, *Spying for America*, 34–37; Garvey and Sheffner, *Congress's Authority to Influence*; Grimmett, *Foreign Policy Roles*.

7. Fisher, *Presidential Power in National Security*.

8. Interviews with national security officials, Tel Aviv, Israel, July 2016 and Helsinki, Finland, November 2016. Both Finland and Israel engage leaders of industry in the formulation of national-security policies and programs. Although the circumstances of each country differ significantly from the United States— each has conscription, and each is relatively small and homogenous—these interactions help align private and public understandings of strategic challenges in a manner that mimics the advantages of nondemocracies.

9. Bacevich, *American Empire*, 3; Layne and Thayer, *American Empire: A Debate*, 41, 62, 93.

10. Cancian, *Limiting Size of* NSC *Staff*.

11. For more detailed descriptions of lawfare, see Kittrie, *Lawfare*; Sari, "Legal Resilience."

12. Vittori, "Anonymous Shell Companies"; Sharman, "Shopping for Anonymous Shell Companies," 127–40.

13. For a useful overview of the jurisdiction of each Title, see Boyle, "Fact Sheet."

14. Marshall, "Long-Term Competition."

15. Joint Chiefs of Staff, *Joint Publication 3-0*, 2011; Joint Chiefs of Staff, *Joint Publication 3-0*, 2017; Fish, "Painting by Numbers"; Lohaus, "Special Operations Forces."

16. Clausewitz, *On War*; Walton, *Grand Strategy and Presidency*, 124.

17. Joint Chiefs of Staff, *Joint Concept for Integrated Campaigning*.

18. Although the extent to which public opinion constrains presidential decision-making is the subject of considerable debate, the public reaction to the Vietnam War—and later to Operation Iraqi Freedom—demonstrated that public opinion did in fact matter to presidents, particularly if negative opinions were sustained over years. See Holsti, "Public Opinion and Foreign Policy," 439–66; Voeten and Brewer, "Public Opinion," 809–30.

19. Tiku, "Line between Big Tech and Defense,"; Olney, "Rift between Silicon Valley and Pentagon"; Krepinevich, "Why No Transformation?."

20. Trubowitz, Goldman, and Rhodes, *Politics of Strategic Adjustment*, 4–5, 305, 316.

21. Colby, *National Defense Strategy*, 4–8. Ironically, the testimony mentions "gray zone" conflict and recognizing the folly of pursuing strategies of domination against a near-peer, yet it seems to limit its operational scope to the commencement of combat hostilities. For a relevant discussion of shaping operations and their importance for strategic competition, see Braun and Allen, "Shaping Defense Strategy."

22. U.S. Department of Defense, *Summary of 2018 National Defense Strategy*, 5.

23. One way of enhancing this mechanism may be to introduce a director of national security operations into the National Security Council staff, as discussed by Martin, *Enhancing American Interagency Integration*. See also Carafano and Weitz, *Mismanaging Mayhem*, 247.

24. Lamb and Schoen, *Deception, Disinformation, and Strategic Communications*, 8–11, 97–115.

25. Potter, "Presidential Leadership," 88–89.

26. William, "Trump Renews Attacks"; Watkins, "Trump Chastises Intel Chiefs"; Phillip, "Trump Undercuts His Aides."

BIBLIOGRAPHY

Manuscripts and Archives

Benson, Robert Louis. "Venona Historical Monograph #2." National Security Agency, 1996. Box 2, 457/190/37/3/4. National Archives, College Park MD.

Benton, William. Benton to Stone, memorandum, January 6, 1947. "On the Beginning of Russian Broadcasts." Charles Thayer Papers, Box 5, Folder "Voice of America." Harry S. Truman Presidential Library, Independence MO.

Bundy, McGeorge. "National Security Action Memoranda 57: Responsibility for Paramilitary Operations," June 28, 1961. JFLNSF-330-007-p0001. John F. Kennedy Presidential Library, Boston MA. https://www.jfklibrary.org /asset-viewer/archives/JFKNSF/330/JFKNSF-330-007.

Churchill, Winston. "Percentages Agreement." October 1944. National Archives of the United Kingdom. https://images.nationalarchives.gov.uk/assetbank -nationalarchives/action/viewFullSizedImage?id=30941&size=800.

Hoover, John Edgar. Memorandum to Major General Edwin M. Watson. October 25, 1940. Franklin Delano Roosevelt Presidential Library, Hyde Park NY. https://www.fdrlibrary.org/documents/356632/390886/cti.00linternment .pdf/ff7d0d4f-a9f3-499c-b2b7-95cf6bea345b.

Kennan, George. Telegram to the Secretary of State. February 22, 1946. George Washington University National Security Archive, Washington DC. http:// nsarchive2.gwu.edu//coldwar/documents/episode-1/kennan.htm.

Library of Congress. *Iran's Ministry of Intelligence and Security: A Profile*. Federal Research Division. Washington DC: Library of Congress, December 2012. http://www.parstimes.com/history/mois_loc.pdf.

———. "KGB Active Measures—Russia / Soviet Intelligence Agencies." Country Studies—Soviet Union. Library of Congress, 1989. https://fas.org/irp /world/russia/kgb/su0523.htm.

National Security Council. "NSDD 77 Management of Public Diplomacy Relative to National Security." Series: National Security Decision Directives (NSDDs), 1981–1989: 1983. https://catalog.archives.gov/id/6879676.

———. "NSDD 277 National Policy and Strategy for Low Intensity Conflict." Series: National Security Decision Directives (NSDDs), 1981–1989: 1987. https://catalog.archives.gov/id/6879854.

National Security League. "General Pershing Says: 'We Will Smash the German Line in France, If You Smash the Hun Propaganda at Home.'" Poster, n.d., ca. 1914. US 4319. Hoover Institution Archives, Stanford University. https://digitalcollections.hoover.org/objects/37541/general-pershing-says -we-will-smash-the-german-line-in-fran?ctx=f3906d02-ef12-4a7a-b9ca -6b2e521d5242&idx=2.

National Special Aid Society. "Fight German Propaganda by Joining the Patriotic Penny to Help Our Well, Sick or Wounded Soldiers and Sailors." Poster, n.d., ca. 1917. US 5837, Hoover Institution Archives, Stanford University. https://digitalcollections.hoover.org/objects/39423/fight-german -propaganda-by-joining-the-patriotic-penny-to-he?ctx=f3906d02-ef12 -4a7a-b9ca-6b2e521d5242&idx=1.

Office of Research. *The Machinery of Soviet Propaganda*. Series: Special Reports, 1953–1997. U.S. Information Agency, 1972. RG 0306, Entry P160: Special Reports, 1953–1997, S-2–71. National Archives 2, College Park MD.

Thompson, Llewellyn. Memorandum by Llewellyn E. Thompson Jr., of the Division of Eastern European Affairs, to Dunn, the Assistant Secretary of State for European, Far Eastern, Near Eastern, and African Affairs. In *Foreign Relations of the United States*, vol. 5. Diplomatic Papers, 1945, Europe: Union of Soviet Socialist Republics 1945. Washington DC: United States Department of State. http://digicoll.library.wisc.edu/cgi-bin/FRUS/FRUS-idx?type =turn&entity=FRUS.FRUS1945v05.p0826&id=FRUS.FRUS1945v05&isize =M&q1=yalta%20declaration, accessed December 17, 2018.

U.S. Army Signal Intelligence Service. "The Venona Project." RG 457/190/37/3/4, Boxes 2–3, National Archives 2, College Park MD.

U.S. Central Intelligence Agency. "Soviet Capabilities for Deception." May 28, 1957. Series: National Intelligence Estimates and Related Reports and Correspondence, 1950–1985, SNIE 100-2-57. National Archives, College Park MD. https://catalog.archives.gov/id/7326937.

U.S. Information Agency. *Communist Propaganda: A Fact Book 1957–1958*. Washington DC: U.S. Government Printing Office, 1958.

———. "Soviet Gray Broadcasting: 'Radio Peace and Progress,'" memorandum, March 8, 1971. RG 0306, Entry P160: Special Reports, 1953–1997, S-2–71. National Archives 2, College Park MD. https://catalog.archives .gov/id/5684041.

U.S. Information Agency Office of Research. *Communist International Radio Broadcasting in 1980*. Series: Research Memoranda, 1963–1999: 1963.

———. *The External Information and Cultural Relations Programs of the Union of Soviet Socialist Republics*. Washington DC, 1973.

———. *The Machinery of Soviet Propaganda*. Series: Special Reports, 1953–1997, 1972.

———. *Soviet Propaganda Vulnerabilities*. Series: Special Reports, 1953–1997, 1973.

———. "Soviet Psychological Warfare Activities." February 1, 1953. RG 0306, Entry A1 1008: Reports and Studies; 1949–1953, Box 2. National Archives, College Park MD.

White, John Kenneth. "Seeing Red: The Cold War and American Public Opinion." Paper presented at the Cold War International History Conference. National Archives, College Park MD, September 1998. https://www.archives.gov/research/foreign-policy/cold-war/conference/white.html.

Published Works

Abrams, Elliott. *Security and Sacrifice: Isolation, Intervention, and American Foreign Policy*. Indianapolis IN: Hudson Institute, 1995.

Adams, Jan S. "Incremental Activism in Soviet Third World Policy: The Role of the International Department of the CPSU Central Committee." *Slavic Review* 48, no. 4 (1989): 614–30. https://doi.org/10.2307/2499786.

Adams, Michael. "Why the OPM Hack Is Far Worse Than You Imagine." *Lawfare* (blog), March 11, 2016. https://www.lawfareblog.com/why-opm-hack-far-worse-you-imagine.

Adams, Thomas K. *US Special Operations Forces in Action: The Challenge of Unconventional Warfare*. New York: Routledge, 2001.

Adams, Tom. "The Trial of Harry Dexter White: Soviet Agent of Influence." Master's thesis, University of New Orleans, 2004. http://scholarworks.uno.edu/cgi/viewcontent.cgi?article=1181&context=td.

Adamsky, Dmitry "Dima." "From Israel with Deterrence: Strategic Culture, Intra-War Coercion and Brute Force." *Security Studies* 26, no. 1 (2017): 157–84.

Adelkhah, Nima. "Iran Integrates the Concept of the 'Soft War' into Its Strategic Planning." *Terrorism Monitor*, June 12, 2010, 7–9. https://jamestown.org/wp-content/uploads/2010/06/TM_008_46.pdf?x87069.

———. "The Three Strategies behind Iran's Projection of Naval Power." *Terrorism Monitor*, November 4, 2011. https://jamestown.org/program/the-three-strategies-behind-irans-projection-of-naval-power/.

Ahl al-Bayt World Assembly, "Home." http://ahl-ul-bayt.org/en/, accessed July 27, 2017.

Allan, Collin. "Attribution Issues in Cyberspace." Scholarly Paper. Social Science Research Network, Rochester NY, November 25, 2013.

Alkawthar TV Channel. "Who Are We?" [Translated]. https://translate.google.com/translate?hl=en&sl=ar&u=https://www.alkawthartv.com/&prev=search&pto=aue, accessed December 16, 2016.

Agence France-Presse. "Poland Detains Pro-Kremlin Party Leader for 'Spying.'" *Guardian*, May 19, 2016. http://www.theguardian.com/world/2016/may /19/poland-detains-pro-kremlin-party-leader-mateusz-piskorski-spying.

——. "Over 40% of Iranians Watch Illegal TV Channels." *Your Middle East*, August 28, 2013. http://www.yourmiddleeast.com/news/over-40-of-iranians -watch-illegal-tv-channels_17467.

Almustafa University. "List of Agreements," February 28, 2017. http://en.miu .ac.ir/index.aspx?fkeyid=&siteid=4&pageid=35782.

Amanat, A., and F. Vejdani, eds. *Iran Facing Others: Identity Boundaries in a Historical Perspective*. New York: Palgrave Macmillan, 2012.

Amann, Melanie, and Pavel Lokshin. "Moscow's Fifth Column: German Populists Forge Ties with Russia." *Der Spiegel*, April 27, 2016. http://www .spiegel.de/international/germany/german-populists-forge-deeper-ties -with-russia-a-1089562.html.

Andrew, Christopher. *The Sword and the Shield: The Mitrokhin Archive and the Secret History of the KGB*. New York: Basic, 2000.

Ansari, Ali M. *Perceptions of Iran: History, Myths and Nationalism from Medieval Persia to the Islamic Republic*. London: I. B. Tauris, 2014.

Appel, Hilary. "The 'Near-Abroad' Factor: Why Putin Stands Firm over Ukraine." *National Interest*, May 23, 2014. http://nationalinterest.org/feature/the-near -abroad-factor-why-putin-stands-firm-over-ukraine-10517.

Aristotle. *Nichomachean Ethics*, 350 AD. http://classics.mit.edu/Aristotle /nicomachaen.html.

Aro, Jessikka. "My Year as a Pro-Russia Troll Magnet: International Shaming Campaign and an SMS from Dead Father." *Yle Kioski* (blog), September 11, 2015. http://kioski.yle.fi/omat/my-year-as-a-pro-russia-troll-magnet.

——. "The Cyberspace War: Propaganda and Trolling as Warfare Tools." *European View* 15, no. 1 (June 1, 2016): 121–32. https://doi.org/10.1007 /s12290-016-0395-5.

Aron, Leon. "The Kremlin's Propaganda Campaign and Russia's Regression." *American Enterprise Institute* (blog), U.S. October 24, 2013. https://www.aei .org/articles/the-kremlins-propaganda-campaign-and-russias-regression/.

Asharq Al-Awsat. "In the Name of Charity, Iran Recruits Iraqi Women." February 4, 2016. https://eng-archive.aawsat.com/asharq-al-awsat-english /news-middle-east/in-the-name-of-charity-iran-recruits-iraqi-women.

Aslan, Reza, Dale Eickelman, Noah Feldman, Lisa Anderson, Steven Cook, Ray Takeyh, Ethan Bronner, Fouad Ajami, Vali Nasr, and Richard Haass. "The Emerging Shia Crescent: Implications for the Middle East and U.S. Policy." Paper presented at The Emerging Shia Crescent Conference, New York, June 5, 2006. http://i.cfr.org/content/meetings/emerging_shia_cresenct _summary.pdf.

Austin, Greg. "International Legal Norms in Cyberspace: Evolution of China's National Security Motivations." In *International Cyber Norms:*

Legal, Policy, & Industry Perspectives, edited by Anna-Maria Osula and Henry Röigas, 171–201. Tallinn, Estonia: NATO Cooperative Cyber Defense Center of Excellence, 2016. https://ccdcoe.org/uploads/2018/10 /InternationalCyberNorms_Ch9.pdf.

Azizi, Arash. "Can Iran's New TV Chief Bring IRIB, Rouhani Closer?." *Al-Monitor*, November 16, 2014. https://www.al-monitor.com/pulse/originals /2014/11/iran-irib-sarafraz-press-tv.html.

———. "Iran Is Spending More Money on Culture, but Where's the Account-ability?." *Al-Monitor*, January 27, 2016. https://www.al-monitor.com/pulse /originals/2016/01/iran-budget-bill-rouhani-cultural-spending-ministry.html.

Bacevich, Andrew J. *American Empire: The Realities and Consequences of U.S. Diplomacy*. Cambridge MA: Harvard University Press, 2002.

Ball, Terence. "Theory and Practice: An Examination of the Platonic and Aris-totelian Conceptions of Political Theory." *Western Political Quarterly* 25, no. 3 (1972): 534–45. https://doi.org/10.2307/446967.

Bandurski, David. "The Me-Media of Mass Manipulation." *Media Beat, China Media Project* (blog), September 2, 2014. http://chinamediaproject.org /2014/09/02/me-media-the-mass-line-and-mass-manipulation/.

Barghoorn, Frederick Charles. *Soviet Foreign Propaganda*. Princeton NJ: Princ-eton University Press, 2016.

Barnett, Alina Polyakova, Marlene Laruelle, Stefan Meister, and Neil. "The Kremlin's Trojan Horses." Atlantic Council. http://www.atlanticcouncil .org/publications/reports/kremlin-trojan-horses, accessed January 27, 2017.

Barnouin, Barbara, and Yu Changgen. *Zhou Enlai: A Political Life*. Hong Kong: Chinese University Press, 2006.

Bartles, Chuck. "Detailed Description of Russian GRU Utilization in Eastern Ukraine." United States Army, Foreign Military Studies Office. OE *Watch* 5, no. 9 (2015): 1–54.

Barzegar, Kayhan. "Iran and the Shiite Crescent: Myths and Realities." *Brown Journal of World Affairs* 15, no. 1 (2008): 87–99.

Basora, Adrian A., and Aleksandr Fisher. "Putin's 'Greater Novorossiya'—The Dismemberment of Ukraine." Foreign Policy Research Institute, May 2, 2014. https://www.fpri.org/article/2014/05/putins-greater-novorossiya -the-dismemberment-of-ukraine/.

Batvinis, Raymond J. *The Origins of FBI Counterintelligence*. Annotated ed. Lawrence: University Press of Kansas, 2007.

BBC News. "BBC Persian Audiences Nearly Double in Iran despite Continued Censorship." April 2, 2013. http://www.bbc.co.uk/mediacentre/latestnews /2013/persian-arabic-audiences-rise.

———. "Crimea Crisis: Russian President Putin's Speech Annotated." March 19, 2014. http://www.bbc.com/news/world-europe-26652058.

———. "Pussy Riot: The Story So Far." December 23, 2013. http://www.bbc .com/news/world-europe-25490161.

BBG *Watch* (blog), "Broadcasting Board of Governors—The Gallup Iran Survey." June 30, 2012. http://bbgwatch.com/bbgwatch/broadcasting-board -of-governors-the-gallup-iran-survey/.

Beard, Nadia. "Putin Signs Decree Approving Russia's State Cultural Policy." *Calvert Journal*. https://www.calvertjournal.com/articles/show/3494/putin -signs-decree-approving-russias-state-cultural-policy, accessed October 30, 2020.

Bedeski, Robert E. "The Tutelary State and National Revolution in Kuomintang Ideology, 1928–31." *China Quarterly*, no. 46 (June 1971): 308–30.

Bedritskiy, Alexander, Alexey Kochetkov, and Stanislav Byshok. "Ukraine after Euromaiden: Democracy Under Fire." Nizhny Novgorod, Russia: Commonwealth of Independent States–Election Monitoring Organization, 2015. http://www.cis-emo.net/sites/default/files/imagesimce/after _euromaidan.pdf.

Beisner, Robert L. *From the Old Diplomacy to the New: 1865–1900.* 2nd ed. Arlington Heights IL: Wiley-Blackwell, 1986.

Bellin, Eva. "Reconsidering the Robustness of Authoritarianism in the Middle East: Lessons from the Arab Spring." *Comparative Politics* 44, no. 2 (January 1, 2012): 127–49. https://doi.org/10.5129/001041512798838021.

Benedictow, Andreas, Daniel Fjærtoft, and Ole Løfsnæs. "Oil Dependency of the Russian Economy: An Econometric Analysis." *Economic Modelling* 32 (May 1, 2013): 400–428. https://doi.org/10.1016/j.econmod.2013.02.016.

Bennetts, Marc. "Putin Brings God, and Potential Jail Time for Atheists, to Russia." *Washington Times*, http://www.washingtontimes.com/news/2016/apr /4/vladimir-putin-patriarch-kirill-alliance-puts-athe/, accessed December 16, 2016.

Benson, Robert Louis, and Michael Warner, eds. *Venona: Soviet Espionage and the American Response 1939–1957.* Washington DC: National Security Agency and Central Intelligence Agency, 1996.

Ben Taleblu, Behnam, and Patrick Megahan. "Iran's Maritime Mirage." Cipher Brief, January 3, 2017. https://www.thecipherbrief.com/article /exclusive/middle-east/irans-maritime-mirage-power-projection-through -conventional-means.

Bentzen, Naja, and Christian Dietrich. "Belarus: A Repressed Economy." European Parliament Think Tank, March 2016. https://www.europarl.europa .eu/thinktank/en/document.html?reference=EPRS_ATA(2016)579068.

Berinsky, Adam J. *In Time of War: Understanding American Public Opinion from World War II to Iraq.* Chicago: University of Chicago Press, 2009.

Berman, Ilan. *Cyber Threats from China, Russia, and Iran: Protecting American Critical Infrastructure.* Before Committee on Homeland Security (2013). https://www.gpo.gov/fdsys/pkg/CHRG-113hhrg82583/html/CHRG -113hhrg82583.htm.

———. "Fallout Ploy: Iran's Cyberwarfare Contingency Plan." *Foreign Affairs*, January 11, 2016. https://www.foreignaffairs.com/articles/iran/2016-01-11 /fallout-ploy.

Bershidsky, Leonid. "Putin's Rejection of the West, in Writing." *Bloomberg View*, April 4, 2014. https://www.bloombergview.com/articles/2014-04 -04/putin-s-rejection-of-the-west-in-writing.

Bertinetti, Scott and John A. Bonin. "Searching for the Greatest Generation's Army in 1950." In *Drawdown: The American Way of Postwar*, edited by Jason W. Warren, 175–89. New York: New York University Press, 2016.

Besson, Samantha. "The Authority of International Law—Lifting the State Veil." *Sydney Law Review* 31 (2011): 343–80.

Bhattacharya, Celia. *Intellectual Property Rights: Violations in China*. Washington DC: The International Economics Study Center, April 2001. http:// internationalecon.com/v1.0/ch25/china/bhattacharya.pdf.

Biddle, Stephen. *Military Power: Explaining Victory and Defeat in Modern Battle*. Princeton NJ: Princeton University Press, 2010.

Birman, Igor. *Secret Incomes of the Soviet State Budget*. Leiden, Netherlands: M. Nijhoff, 1981.

Blachfield, Kate, Pieter Wezeman, and Siemon Wezeman. "The State of Major Arms Transfers in 8 Graphics." *Commentary/WritePeace* (blog), Stockholm International Peace Research Institute, February 22, 2017, https://www.sipri.org/commentary/blog/2017/state-major-arms-transfers -8-graphics.

Black, Ian. "Fear of a Shia Full Moon." *Guardian*, January 26, 2007. https://www .theguardian.com/world/2007/jan/26/worlddispatch.ianblack.

Black, Jeremy. "Defining a New Empire." In *America, War and Power: Defining the State, 1775–2005*, edited by Lawrence Sondhaus and A. James Fuller, 11–28. New York: Routledge, 2007.

———. "The International Context of the War of 1812." In *The Routledge Handbook of the War of 1812*, edited by Donald R. Hickey and Connie D. Clark, 4–14. New York: Routledge, 2016.

Blackstock, Paul W. *The Secret Road to World War Two: Soviet versus Western Intelligence, 1921–1939*. Chicago: Quadrangle, 1969.

Blanchard, Ben, and Michael Martina. "China's Xi Says to Shake up Military Structure in Reform Push." Reuters, November 26, 2015. http://www.reuters .com/article/us-china-defence-idUSKBN0TF13T20151126.

Blitt, Robert C. "Russia's 'Orthodox' Foreign Policy: The Growing Influence of the Russian Orthodox Church in Shaping Russia's Policies Abroad." *University of Pennsylvania Journal of International Law* 33, no. 2 (2011): 363. https://papers.ssrn.com/sol3/papers.cfm?abstract_id=1725522.

Boehler, Patrick. "Two Million 'Internet Opinion Analysts' Employed to Monitor China's Vast Online Population." *South China Morning Post*, October

3, 2013. https://www.scmp.com/news/china-insider/article/1323529/two
-million-employed-monitor-chinese-public-opinion.

Booth, Ken. "Strategic Culture: Validity and Validation." *Oxford Journal on Good Governance* 2, no. 1 (2005): 25–28.

———. *Strategy and Ethnocentrism*. Teaneck NJ: Holmes & Meier, 1979.

Borger, Julian. "U.S. Intelligence Fears Iran Duped Hawks into Iraq War." *Guardian*, May 24, 2004. https://www.theguardian.com/world/2004/may /25/usa.iraq10.

Borger, Julian, and Robert Tait. "The Financial Power of the Revolutionary Guards." *Guardian*, February 15, 2010. https://www.theguardian.com/world /2010/feb/15/financial-power-revolutionary-guard.

Bossenbroek, Martin. *The Boer War*. Translated by Yvette Rosenberg. New York: Seven Stories, 2018.

Bourbonnière, Michel, and Ricky J. Lee. "Legality of the Deployment of Conventional Weapons in Earth Orbit: Balancing Space Law and the Law of Armed Conflict." *European Journal of International Law* 18, no. 5 (November 1, 2007): 873–901.

Bowden, Mark. *Guests of the Ayatollah: The Iran Hostage Crisis: The First Battle in America's War with Militant Islam*. New York: Grove, 2007.

Boylan, Edward S. "The Chinese Cultural Style of Warfare." *Comparative Strategy* 3, no. 4 (January 1, 1982): 341–64. https://doi.org/10.1080 /01495938208402647.

Boyle, Ashley. "Fact Sheet: U.S.C. Title 10, Title 22, and Title 50." American Security Project, August 2012. https://www.americansecurityproject.org /ASP%20Reports/Ref%200073%20-%20U.S.C.%20Title%2010%2C%20Title %2022%2C%20and%20Title%2050.pdf.

Brands, H. W. *The General vs. the President: MacArthur and Truman at the Brink of Nuclear War*. New York: Doubleday, 2016.

Braun, William, III, and Charles D. Allen. "Shaping a 21st-Century Defense Strategy: Reconciling Military Roles." *Joint Forces Quarterly*, April 1, 2014. http://ndupress.ndu.edu/Portals/68/Documents/jfq/jfq-73/jfq-73_52–59 _Braun-Allen.pdf.

Braw, Elisabeth. "Back to the Finland Station." *Foreign Affairs*, June 18, 2015. https://www.foreignaffairs.com/articles/finland/2015-06-18/back-finland -station.

———. "Finland's Mysterious Nuclear Investor." Politico Europe. July 12, 2015. http://www.politico.eu/article/finland-nuclear-investor-russia-investor -reactor-energy/.

———. "Submarine Intruders on Sweden's Coastline." *Carl Lavo: Journalist and Author* (blog), September 29, 2015. http://carllavo.blogspot.com/2015 /09/submarine-intruders-on-swedens-coastline.html.

Breen, T. H. *American Insurgents, American Patriots: The Revolution of the People*. New York: Hill and Wang, 2011.

Breedlove, Philip M. "NATO's Next Act." *Foreign Affairs*, June 13, 2016. https://www.foreignaffairs.com/articles/europe/2016-06-13/natos-next-act.

Brenner, Michael J. "The Problem of Innovation and the Nixon-Kissinger Foreign Policy." *International Studies Quarterly* 17, no. 3 (1973): 255–94. https://doi.org/10.2307/2600371.

Breslin, Shaun. "China's Emerging Global Role: Dissatisfied Responsible Great Power." *Politics* 30 (December 1, 2010): 52–62. https://journals.sagepub.com/doi/abs/10.1111/j.1467-9256.2010.01385.x.

Broad, William J. "Iran Shielding Its Nuclear Efforts in Maze of Tunnels." *New York Times*, January 5, 2010. http://www.nytimes.com/2010/01/06/world/middleeast/06sanctions.html.

Brodkin, Jon. "Microsoft Shuts Down Phishing Sites, Accuses Russia of New Election Meddling." *Ars Technica*, August 21, 2018. https://arstechnica.com/tech-policy/2018/08/microsoft-shuts-down-phishing-sites-accuses-russia-of-new-election-meddling/.

Brooks, Rosa. *How Everything Became War and the Military Became Everything: Tales from the Pentagon*. New York: Simon & Schuster, 2016.

Brown, Peter. "Calculated Ambiguity in the South China Sea." *Asia Times*, December 8, 2009. http://www.ocnus.net/artman2/publish/Defence_Arms_13/Calculated-Ambiguity-in-the-South-China-Sea.shtml.

Bruno, Greg, Jayshree Bajoria, and Jonathan Masters. "Iran's Revolutionary Guards." Council on Foreign Relations, 2013. Updated May 6, 2019. https://www.cfr.org/backgrounder/irans-revolutionary-guards.

Brzezinski, Ian J., and Nicholas Varangis. "The NATO-Russia Exercise Gap." *Atlantic Council* (blog), February 23, 2015. http://www.atlanticcouncil.org/blogs/natosource/the-nato-russia-exercise-gap.

Bucci, Steve. *Iran's Power Projection Capability*. Before Oversight and Government Reform Subcommittee on National Security (2015). https://www.govinfo.gov/content/pkg/CHRG-114hhrg22382/html/CHRG-114hhrg22382.htm, accessed April 20, 2017.Error! Hyperlink reference not valid.

Buchanan, Ben, and Michael Sulmeyer. "Russia and Cyber Operations: Challenges and Opportunities for the Next US Administration." Task Force White Paper. Washington DC: Carnegie Endowment for International Peace, December 13, 2016. http://carnegieendowment.org/2016/12/13/russia-and-cyber-operations-challenges-and-opportunities-for-next-u.s.-administration-pub-66433.

Buchman, Brandi. "Experts Say Chinese Sanctions Could Influence North Korea." *Courthouse News Service* (blog), March 22, 2017. https://www.courthousenews.com/experts-say-chinese-sanctions-influence-n-korea/.

Buchta, Wilfried. "Tehran's Ecumenical Society (Majma' al-Taqrīb): A Veritable Ecumenical Revival or a Trojan Horse of Iran?." In *The Twelver Shia in Modern Times: Religious Culture and Political History*, edited by Rainer Brunner and Werner Ende, 333–54. Leiden, Netherlands: Brill, 2001.

Bukkvoll, Tor. "Russian Special Operations Forces in Crimea and Donbas." *Parameters* 46, no. 2 (Summer 2016): 13–21.

Busse, Heribert. "Iran under the Buyids." In *From the Arab Invasion to the Saljuqs*. Vol. 4 of *The Cambridge History of Iran*, edited by R. N. Frye, William Bayne Fisher, Richard Nelson Frye, Peter Avery, John Andrew Boyle, Ilya Gershevitch, Peter Jackson, Charles Peter Melville, Laurence Lockhart, and Gavin Hambly. Cambridge, UK: Cambridge University Press, 1975.

Byrnes, Kate. *Response to Russia's Criticism of ODIHR Election Observation*. U.S. Mission to the OSCE. Before Permanent Council, Vienna, April 27, 2017. http://www.osce.org/permanent-council/324276?download=true.

Campo, Juan Eduardo. *Encyclopedia of Islam*. New York: Infobase, 2009.

Cancian, Mark. *Limiting Size of NSC Staff*. Washington DC: Center for Strategic and International Studies, July 1, 2016. https://csis-website-prod.s3 .amazonaws.com/s3fs-public/publication/160902_Limiting_Size_NSC _Staff.pdf.

Carafano, James Jay, and Richard Weitz, eds. *Mismanaging Mayhem: How Washington Responds to Crisis*. Westport CT: Praeger, 2007.

Carr, Edward Hallett. *The Twenty Years' Crisis, 1919–1939: An Introduction to the Study of International Relations*. 45th ed. Basingstoke, UK: Harper Perennial, 1964.

Carter, Stephen. *Russian Nationalism: Yesterday, Today, Tomorrow*. New York: Palgrave Macmillan, 1990.

Casey, William. "Soviet Use of Active Measures." *Current Policy*, no. 761 (November 1985): 1–4. Washington DC: United States Department of State Bureau of Public Affairs.

CBS News. "Iranian Boats in 'Unsafe' Encounter with U.S. Surveillance Ship," March 6, 2017. http://www.cbsnews.com/news/iran-fast-boats-unsafe -encounter-usns-invincible-spy-ship-strait-of-hormuz/.

Cenciotti, David. "Iran Unveils New UCAV Modeled on Captured US RQ-170 Stealth Drone." *Aviationist*, October 2, 2016. https://theaviationist .com/2016/10/02/iran-unveils-new-ucav-modeled-on-captured-u-s-rq -170-stealth-drone/.

Center for Investigative Reporting. "The Rise of the New German Right." Podcast. Reveal.org, September 16, 2017. https://www.revealnews.org/episodes /the-rise-of-the-new-german-right/.

Center for Strategic and International Studies. "Update: China's Continuing Reclamation in the Paracels." Asia Maritime Transparency Initiative, February 8, 2017. https://amti.csis.org/paracels-beijings-other-buildup/.

Center of Military History. *American Military History*. Washington DC: United States Army, 1989. https://history.army.mil/books/AMH/amh-toc.htm.

———. *Merrill's Marauders*. Superintendent of Documents, Washington DC: United States Army, 1945. http://www.history.army.mil/books/wwii /marauders/marauders-fw.htm.

Chase, Michael S., and Arthur Chan. *China's Evolving Approach to "Integrated Strategic Deterrence."* Santa Monica CA: RAND, 2016. http://www.rand.org /content/dam/rand/pubs/research_reports/rr1300/rr1366/rand_rr1366.pdf.

———. "China's Evolving Strategic Deterrence Concepts and Capabilities." *Washington Quarterly* 39, no. 1 (Spring 2016). https://www.tandfonline .com/doi/full/10.1080/0163660X.2016.1170484.

Chase, Michael S., Kristen Guinness, Lyle J. Morris, Samuel K. Berkowitz, and Benjamin Purser. *Emerging Trends in China's Development of Unmanned Systems.* Santa Monica CA: RAND, 2015. https://www.rand.org/pubs /research_reports/RR990.html.

Chen, Adrian. "The Agency." *New York Times,* June 2, 2015. http://www.nytimes .com/2015/06/07/magazine/the-agency.html.

Chenevix, Richard. *An Essay upon National Character: Being an Inquiry into Some of the Principal Causes Which Contribute to Form and Modify the Characters of Nations in the State of Civilisation.* London: James Duncan, Paternoster-Row, 1832.

Cheng, Dean. "Chinese Lessons from the Gulf Wars." In *Chinese Lessons from Other Peoples' Wars.* Edited by Andrew Scobell, David Lai, and Roy Kamphausen, 153–200. Carlisle PA: U.S. Army Strategic Studies Institute, 2011.

———. "China's Military Role in Space." *Strategic Studies Quarterly,* Spring 2012: 55–77.

———. *Cyber Dragon: Inside China's Information Warfare and Cyber Operations.* Westport CT: ABC-CLIO/Greenwood, 2016.

———. "Winning without Fighting: Chinese Legal Warfare." Washington DC: Heritage Foundation, May 21, 2016. https://www.heritage.org/asia/report /winning-without-fighting-chinese-legal-warfare.

Cheung, Tai Ming, Thomas Mahnken, Deborah Seligsohn, Kevin Pollpeter, Eric Anderson, and Fan Yang. *Planning for Innovation: Understanding China's Plans for Technological, Energy, Industrial and Defense Development.* Washington DC: U.S.-China Economic and Security Review Commission, September 18, 2015. https://www.uscc.gov/research/planning-innovation -understanding-chinas-plans-technological-energy-industrial-and-defense.

Chotikul, Diane. *Soviet Theory of Reflexive Control in Historical and Psychocultural Perspective: A Preliminary Study.* Monterey CA: Naval Postgraduate School, July 1986. https://calhoun.nps.edu/bitstream/handle/10945 /30190/soviettheoryofre00chot.pdf?sequence=1.

Churchill, Winston. *The Second World War: Triumph and Tragedy.* Vol. 6. Boston: Houghton Mifflin, 1953.

Clark, Trevor. "Lips and Teeth: Chinese-North Korean Trade and Foreign Direct Investment Impact." In *SAIS US-Korea 2012 Yearbook,* 52–54. Washington DC: U.S.-Korea Institute at SAIS, 2012.

Clark, William P. "National Security Decision Directive 75." The White House, January 17, 1983. https://fas.org/irp/offdocs/nsdd/nsdd-75.pdf.

Clarke, Richard A., and Robert Knake. *Cyber War: The Next Threat to National Security and What to Do About It.* New York: Harper Collins, 2010.

Clausewitz, Carl von. *On War.* Indexed ed. Translated by Michael Eliot Howard and Peter Paret. Princeton NJ: Princeton University Press, 1989.

Clawson, P., and M. Rubin. *Eternal Iran: Continuity and Chaos.* New York: Palgrave Macmillan, 2005.

Cleveland, Grover. "Message to Congress, December 18, 1893." In *Hawaiian Islands: Report of the Committee on Foreign Relations, United States Senate*, vol. 2, 1253–66. Washington DC: Government Printing Office, 1894.

Cline, Ray S., and Yonah Alexander. *Terrorism: The Soviet Connection.* New York: Crane, Russak, 1984.

Cohen, Eliot A. "Constraints on America's Conduct of Small Wars." *International Security* 9, no. 2 (Fall 1984): 151–81.

Cohen, Raphael S. "The Militia Era (1775–1830)." In *Demystifying the Citizen Soldier*, 8–10. Santa Monica CA: RAND, 2015. https://www.jstor.org/stable/10.7249/j.ctt19rmdcb.11.

Colbert, Christopher R. *National Character vs. National Security: Conflict in the Making?* Carlisle Barracks PA: U.S. Army War College, 2011. https://apps.dtic.mil/dtic/tr/fulltext/u2/a552995.pdf.

Colby, Elbridge. *Implementation of the National Defense Strategy.* Before the U.S. Senate Armed Services Committee (2019). https://www.armed-services.senate.gov/imo/media/doc/Colby_01-29-19.pdf.

Cole, J. Michael. "China Intensifies Disinformation Campaign against Taiwan." *Taiwan Sentinel*, January 19, 2007. https://sentinel.tw/china-disinformation-tw/.

Conley, Heather. "Russia's Influence on Europe." In *Global Forecast 2015*, edited by Craig Cohen, Josiane Gabel, and J. Stephen Morrison, 28–31. Washington DC: Center for Strategic and International Studies, 2014. https://www.csis.org/analysis/russia%E2%80%99s-influence-europe.

Conley, Heather, Theodore Gerber, Lucy Moore, and Mihaela David. "Russian Soft Power in the 21st Century: An Examination of Russian Compatriot Policy in Estonia." Center for Strategic and International Studies, August 2011. http://csis.org/files/publication/110826_Conley_RussianSoftPower_Web.pdf.

Cook, Alexander C. *Mao's Little Red Book: A Global History.* New York: Cambridge University Press, 2014.

Cordesman, Anthony. "Iran's Revolutionary Guards, the Al Quds Force, and Other Intelligence and Paramilitary Forces." Working Paper, August 16, 2007. https://csis-prod.s3.amazonaws.com/s3fs-public/legacy_files/files/media/csis/pubs/070816_cordesman_report.pdf.

Cordesman, Anthony, and Joseph Kendall. *Chinese Strategy and Military Modernization in 2016: A Comparative Analysis.* Washington DC: Center for Strategic and International Studies, December 5, 2016. http://csis-website

-prod.s3.amazonaws.com/s3fs-public/publication/161208_Chinese_Strategy
_Military_Modernization_2016.pdf.

Cordesman, Anthony, and Abdullah Toukan. "Iran and the Gulf Military Balance." Working Paper, n.d. Washington DC: Center for Strategic and International Studies. https://csis-prod.s3.amazonaws.com/s3fs-public /publication/161004_Iran_Gulf_Military_Balance.pdf.

Cossa, Ralph. "Japan–South Korea Relations: Time to Open Both Eyes." Council on Foreign Relations, July 23, 2012. https://www.cfr.org/report/japan -south-korea-relations-time-open-both-eyes.

Coutrix, Stephanie. "Press TV: A Slick Propaganda Tool Against the West." *Global Media Wars* (blog), 2011. http://www.globalmediawars.com.s3-website -us-east-1.amazonaws.com/GMW/archives.jrn.columbia.edu/2010-2011 /globalmediawars.com/indexcc4bcc4b.html?page_id=74.

Craig, R. Bruce. *Treasonable Doubt: The Harry Dexter White Spy Case.* Lawrence: University Press of Kansas, 2004.

Craig, Susanne, Jo Becker, and Jesse Drucker. "Jared Kushner, a Trump In-Law and Adviser, Chases a Chinese Deal." *New York Times,* January 7, 2017. https://www.nytimes.com/2017/01/07/us/politics/jared-kushner-trump -business.html.

Creighton, Mandell. *The English National Character.* Oxford, UK: Clarendon Press Depository, 1896.

CrowdStrike. *Global Threat Report 2019: Adversary Tradecraft and the Importance of Speed.* Palo Alto CA: CrowdStrike, 2019.

———. "Who Is Fancy Bear?." *CrowdStrike* (blog), September 12, 2016. https:// www.crowdstrike.com/blog/who-is-fancy-bear/.

Cunningham, Erin. "Iran Holds Military Exercises in Response to U.S. Sanctions." *Washington Post.* February 4, 2017. https://www.washingtonpost .com/world/iran-holds-military-exercises-in-response-to-us-sanctions /2017/02/04/68d06668-e8bd-11e6-903d-9b11ed7d8d2a_story.html.

Cunningham, Noble E., Jr. *Jefferson vs. Hamilton: Confrontations That Shaped a Nation.* Boston: Bedford/St. Martin's, 2000.

Current, Richard N. "God and the Strongest Battalions." In *Why the North Won the Civil War,* edited by David Herbert Donald, 21–37. New York: Touchstone, 1996.

Da Silva, Chantal. "Russia Was behind Global Cyber Attack, Ukraine Says." *Independent,* July 2, 2017. http://www.independent.co.uk/news/world/europe /russia-cyber-attack-ukraine-petya-telebots-blackenergy-sbu-cadbury -a7819501.html.

Dahl, Robert A. "The Concept of Power." *Behavioral Science* 2, no. 3 (1957): 201–15. https://doi.org/10.1002/bs.3830020303.

Daoud, David. "Meet the Proxies: How Iran Spreads Its Empire through Terrorist Militias." *Tower,* March 2015. http://www.thetower.org/article/meet -the-proxies-how-iran-spreads-its-empire-through-terrorist-militias/.

Deacon, Richard. *A History of the Russian Secret Service*. Rev. ed. London: Grafton, 1987.

De Cristian, Pantazi. "Russia's Silent Threat." *HotNews Romania* (blog), September 4, 2014. http://english.hotnews.ro/stiri-top_news-18034632-russia-39 -silent-threat-the-pillars-kremlin-influence-romanian-domestic-life.htm.

Dennison, Susi, and Dina Pardijs. "The World According to Europe's Insurgent Parties: Putin, Migration and People Power." European Council on Foreign Relations, 2016. https://ecfr.eu/archive/page/-/ECFR_181_-_THE_WORLD _ACCORDING_TO_EUROPES_INSURGENT_PARTIES_NEW.pdf.

DeYoung, Karen. "How the Obama White House Runs Foreign Policy." *Washington Post*, August 4, 2015. https://www.washingtonpost.com/world/national -security/how-the-obama-white-house-runs-foreign-policy/2015/08/04 /2befb960-2fd7-11e5-8353-1215475949f4_story.html.

Di Cosmo, Nicola. *Military Culture in Imperial China*. Cambridge MA: Harvard University Press, 2009.

Directorate-General for Economic and Financial Affairs. *Member States' Energy Dependence: An Indicator-Based Assessment*. Brussels: European Commission, 2013. http://ec.europa.eu/economy_finance/publications/occasional _paper/2013/pdf/ocp145_en.pdf.

Dobbins, James, Raphael S. Cohen, Nathan Chandler, Bryan Frederick, Edward Geist, Paul DeLuca, Forrest E. Morgan, Howard J. Shatz, and Brent Williams. *Extending Russia*. Arlington VA: RAND, 2019. https://www.rand .org/pubs/research_reports/RR3063.html.

Dodd, Thomas J. "The Confusion of the West: An Analysis of Certain Aspects of Communist Political Warfare," vol. S, Docs 87–1, 1–13. Proceedings of the 87th Congress. Paris, France: U.S. Government Printing Office, 1960.

Donald, David Herbert, ed. *Why the North Won the Civil War*. New York: Touchstone, 1996.

Donovan, John C. "Congressional Isolationists and the Roosevelt Foreign Policy." *World Politics* 3, no. 3 (1951): 299–316. https://doi.org/10.2307/2009117.

Donovan, Marie, Paul Bucala, Caitlin Pendleton, and Ali Javaheri. "Iran News Round Up." Critical Threats, September 2, 2016. https://www .criticalthreats.org/briefs/iran-news-round-up/iran-news-round-up -september-2-2016.

Doran, Charles F. *The Politics of Assimilation: Hegemony and Its Aftermath*. Baltimore: Johns Hopkins University Press, 1971.

Doran, Charles F., and Wes Parsons. "War and the Cycle of Relative Power." *American Political Science Review* 74, no. 4 (1980): 947–65. https://doi .org/10.2307/1954315.

Dorfman, Zach. "The Secret History of the Russian Consulate in San Francisco." *Foreign Policy* (blog), December 14, 2017. https://foreignpolicy.com /2017/12/14/the-secret-history-of-the-russian-consulate-in-san-francisco -putin-trump-spies-moscow/, accessed October 30, 2020.

Dotson, John. *The Confucian Revival in Propaganda Narratives of the Chinese Government*. Washington DC: U.S.-China Economic and Security Review Commission, July 20, 2011.

Duggan, Patrick Michael. "Strategic Development of Special Warfare in Cyberspace." *Joint Forces Quarterly* 79, no. 4 (Winter 2015): 46–53. http://ndupress.ndu.edu/Portals/68/Documents/jfq/jfq-79/jfq-79_46-53_Duggan.pdf.

Dunford, Joseph, Jr. "Gen. Dunford's Remarks and Q&A at the Center for Strategic and International Studies" Speech. Washington DC, March 29, 2016. http://www.jcs.mil/Media/Speeches/Article/707418/gen-dunfords-remarks-and-qa-at-the-center-for-strategic-and-international-studi/.

Du Plessis, Rudolf. "China's African Infrastructure Projects: A Tool Reshaping Global Norms." *Policy Insights*, no. 35 (September 2016): 1–13. https://www.jstor.org/stable/resrep25976?seq=1#metadata_info_tab_contents.

Earle, Edward Meade. "Adam Smith, Alexander Hamilton, Friedrich List: The Economic Foundations of Military Power." In *Makers of Modern Strategy from Machiavelli to the Nuclear Age*, edited by Peter Paret, Gordon A. Craig, and Felix Gilbert, 217–61. Princeton NJ: Princeton University Press, 1986.

Echevarria, Antulio J., II. *Reconsidering the American Way of War: US Military Practice from the Revolution to Afghanistan*. Washington DC: Georgetown University Press, 2014.

Economist. "China's Achilles Heel." April 21, 2012. http://www.economist.com/node/21553056.

———. "The Shia Crescendo." March 28, 2015. http://www.economist.com/news/middle-east-and-africa/21647367-shia-militias-are-proliferating-middle-east-shia-crescendo.

———. "Why Iran Is Finding It Hard to Create Jobs." December 5, 2016. http://www.economist.com/blogs/economist-explains/2016/12/economist-explains-4.

Edney, Kingsley. *The Globalization of Chinese Propaganda: International Power and Domestic Political Cohesion*. London: Palgrave Macmillan, 2014.

Eisenstadt, Michael. "Iran Primer: Iran and Iraq." *Frontline*, Tehran Bureau, October 28, 2010. http://www.pbs.org/wgbh/pages/frontline/tehranbureau/2010/10/iran-primer-iran-and-iraq.html.

———. *The Strategic Culture of the Islamic Republic of Iran: Religion, Expediency, and Soft Power in an Era of Disruptive Change*. Middle East Studies Monographs. Quantico VA: Marine Corps University, August 2011. https://www.washingtoninstitute.org/uploads/Documents/pubs/MESM_7_Eisenstadt.pdf.

Eisenstadt, Michael, Michael Knights, and Ahmed Ali. *Iran's Influence in Iraq: Countering Tehran's Whole-of-Government Approach*. Washington DC: Washington Institute for Near East Policy, April 2011. http://www.washingtoninstitute.org/policy-analysis/view/irans-influence-in-iraq-countering-tehrans-whole-of-government-approach.

Ennis, Stephen. "Russian Media and the Art of 'Provokatsiya.'" BBC (blog), June 27, 2013. https://www.bbc.co.uk/blogs/collegeofjournalism/entries/cle6a130-1fcf-3a70-bb9a-d8b245641dea.

Entous, Adam, Ellen Nakashima, and Greg Jaffe. "Kremlin Trolls Burned across the Internet as Washington Debated Options." *Washington Post*, December 25, 2017. https://www.washingtonpost.com/world/national-security/kremlin-trolls-burned-across-the-internet-as-washington-debated-options/2017/12/23/e7b9dc92-e403-11e7-ab50-621fe0588340_story.html.

Erickson, Andrew. "How Does China's First Aircraft Carrier Stack Up?." ChinaPower Project (website), December 9, 2015. http://chinapower.csis.org/aircraft-carrier/.

——. "Sweeping Change in China's Military: Xi's PLA Restructuring." *China Real Time* (blog), *Wall Street Journal*, September 2, 2015. https://blogs.wsj.com/chinarealtime/2015/09/02/sweeping-change-in-chinas-military-xis-pla-restructuring/.

Erickson, Andrew S., and Conor M. Kennedy. "China's Maritime Militia." *Foreign Affairs*, June 23, 2016. https://www.foreignaffairs.com/articles/china/2016-06-23/chinas-maritime-militia.

Ermarth, Fritz W. *Russia's Strategic Culture: Past Present and . . . in Transition?*. Fort Belvoir VA: Defense Threat Reduction Agency, October 31, 2006. https://fas.org/irp/agency/dod/dtra/russia.pdf.

Esfandiari, Golnaz. "Nothing Comes between Iranians and Their Satellite Dishes—Not Even the Police." *RadioFreeEurope RadioLiberty* (blog), March 13, 2012. https://www.rferl.org/a/persian_letters_satellite_dishes_iran_police/24514665.html.

European Commission. "Russia," February 2017. http://ec.europa.eu/trade/policy/countries-and-regions/countries/russia/.

Eurostat. "Energy Production and Imports." http://ec.europa.eu/eurostat/statistics-explained/index.php/Energy_production_and_imports, accessed August 30, 2017.

——. "Main Origin of Primary Energy Imports, EU-28, 2005–2015 (% of Extra EU-28 Imports)." http://ec.europa.eu/eurostat/statistics-explained/index.php/File:Main_origin_of_primary_energy_imports,_EU-28,_2005-2015_(%25_of_extra_EU-28_imports)_YB17.png, accessed September 7, 2017.

——. "Nuclear Energy Statistics." http://ec.europa.eu/eurostat/statistics-explained/index.php/Nuclear_energy_statistics, accessed February 2017.

Executive Secretary of the National Security Council. *A Report to the National Security Council on United States Objectives and Programs for National Security*. Washington DC: National Security Council, April 14, 1950. https://fas.org/irp/offdocs/nsc-hst/nsc-68.htm.

Fairbank, J. K., and S. Y. Têng. "On the Ch'ing Tributary System." *Harvard Journal of Asiatic Studies* 6, no. 2 (1941): 135–246.

Fairbank, John King. *The United States and China*. 4th rev. and enlarged ed. Cambridge MA: Harvard University Press, 1983.

———. "Varieties of the Chinese Military Experience." In *Chinese Ways in Warfare*,1–27. Cambridge MA: Harvard University Press, 1974.

Farchy, Jack, James Kynge, Chris Campbell, and David Blood. "One Belt, One Road." *Financial Times*, September 14, 2016. https://ig.ft.com/sites/special -reports/one-belt-one-road.

Fassihi, Farnaz. "Iran's Censors Tighten Grip." *Wall Street Journal*, March 16, 2012. https://www.wsj.com/articles/SB10001424052702303717304 577279381130395906.

Fawn, Rick. "Battle over the Box: International Election Observation Missions, Political Competition and Retrenchment in the Post-Soviet Space." *International Affairs* 82, no. 6 (November 1, 2006): 1133–53. https://doi.org/10 .1111/j.1468-2346.2006.00592.x.

Federalist, no. 1, Philadelphia PA, 1781 (Alexander Hamilton). http://avalon .law.yale.edu/18th_century/fed01.asp.

———. no 24, Philadelphia PA, 1788 (Alexander Hamilton). https://supreme .findlaw.com/documents/federalist/federalist24.html.

———. no 41. Philadelphia PA, 1788. (James Madison). http://avalon.law.yale .edu/18th_century/fed41.asp.

Fehrenbach, T. R. *This Kind of War: The Classic Korean War History*. 50th anniversary ed. Dulles VA: Potomac, 2001.

Feldman, David. *Law in Politics, Politics in Law*. London: Bloomsbury, 2013.

Felter, Joseph, and Brian Fishman. *Iranian Strategy in Iraq: Politics and "Other Means."* West Point NY: Combating Terrorism Center at West Point, October 13, 2008. https://ctc.usma.edu/wp-content/uploads/2010/06/Iranian -Strategy-in-Iraq.pdf. .

Feng, Huiyun. *Chinese Strategic Culture and Foreign Policy Decision-Making: Confucianism, Leadership and War*. New York: Routledge, 2007.

Fensterwald, Bernard. "The Anatomy of American 'Isolationism' and Expansionism. Part 1." *Journal of Conflict Resolution* 2, no. 2 (1958): 111–39.

Fifield, Anna. "How Iranians Are Avoiding Sanctions." *Financial Times*, April 14, 2008. https://www.ft.com/content/6ca69788-0a48-11dd-b5b1-0000779fd2ac.

Finkle, Jim. "Hacker Group in China Linked to Big Cyber Attacks: Symantec." *Reuters*, September 17, 2013. http://www.reuters.com/article/us-cyberattacks -china-idUSBRE98G0M720130917.

FireEye. *APT28: A Window into Russia's Cyber Espionage Operations?* Milpitas CA: FireEye, 2014. https://www2.fireeye.com/rs/fireye/images/rpt -apt28.pdf.

———. *Redline Drawn: China Recalculates Its Use of Cyberespionage*. Milpitas CA: FireEye, June 2016. https://www.fireeye.com/content/dam/fireeye -www/current-threats/pdfs/rpt-china-espionage.pdf.

Fischer, Ben B. *Okhrana: The Paris Operations of the Russian Imperial Police.* Darby PA: DIANE, 1999.

Fish, Lauren. "Painting by Numbers: A History of the U.S. Military's Phasing Construct." *War on the Rocks,* November 1, 2016. https://warontherocks .com/2016/11/painting-by-numbers-a-history-of-the-u-s-militarys-phasing -construct/.

Fisher, Louis. "The Law: Scholarly Support for Presidential Wars." *Presidential Studies Quarterly* 35, no. 3 (September 1, 2005): 590–607. https://doi .org/10.1111/j.1741-5705.2005W.00266.x.

———. *Presidential Power in National Security: A Guide to the President-Elect.* White House Transition Project Reports. Washington DC: Library of Congress, 2007. https://www.loc.gov/law/help/usconlaw/pdf/presidential -power-national-security.pdf.

———. *Presidential War Power.* Lawrence: University Press of Kansas, 2013. https://muse.jhu.edu/book/39876.

Fisher, Matthew. "Russian Troops Welcomed by Rapturous Crowds in Crimean Port City Balaklava." *National Post of Canada.* March 1, 2014. https:// nationalpost.com/news/russian-troops-welcomed-by-rapturous-crowds -in-crimean-port-city-balaklava#:~:text=BALAKLAVA%2C%20Ukraine %20%E2%80%94%20Crowds%20waving%20Russian,Putin%20to%20send %20troops%20to.

Fisher, Richard D., Jr. "China's Beihang Unmanned Aircraft System Technology Unveils TYW-1 Strike-Capable UAV." *Jane's 360,* November 15, 2017. http://www.janes.com/article/75700/china-s-beihang-unmanned-aircraft -system-technology-unveils-tyw-1-strike-capable-uav.

Fitzpatrick, Catherine A. "RBC Publishes Report Sourced in FSB and Military on Wagner Private Military Contractor with 2,500 Fighters in Syria." *Interpreter,* August 26, 2016. http://www.interpretermag.com/russia-update -august-26-2016/.

Fleming, Thomas. *The Strategy of Victory: How General George Washington Won the American Revolution.* Boston: Da Capo, 2017.

Fleurant, Aude, Pieter Wezeman, Siemon Wezeman, and Nan Tian. *Trends in International Arms Transfers.* Stockholm, Sweden: Stockholm International Peace Research Institute, February 2017. https://www.sipri.org/sites /default/files/Trends-in-international-arms-transfers-2016.pdf.

Flynn, Gregory. *The West and the Soviet Union: Politics and Policy.* London: Palgrave Macmillan, 1990.

Foa, Roberto Stefan, and Yascha Mounk. "The Danger of Deconsolidation." *Journal of Democracy* 27, no. 3 (July 2016): 5–17. http://www.journalofdemocracy .org/sites/default/files/Foa%26Mounk-27-3.pdf.

Fondacaro, Steve. *AirLand Battle and SOF: A Proposal for an Interim Doctrine for Joint Special Operations.* Fort Leavenworth KS: School of Advanced

Military Studies, May 15, 1989. http://www.dtic.mil/dtic/tr/fulltext/u2
/a215563.pdf.

Ford, Christopher A. *The Mind of Empire: China's History and Modern Foreign Relations*. Reprint ed. Lexington: University Press of Kentucky, 2015.

Foster, Peter. "Russia Accused of Clandestine Funding of European Parties as US Conducts Major Review of Vladimir Putin's Strategy," *Telegraph*, January 16, 2016. http://www.telegraph.co.uk/news/worldnews
/europe/russia/12103602/America-to-investigate-Russian-meddling-in
-EU.html.

Fouquet, Helene. "Fillon Slips Further in France as Canard Reports Putin Ties." *Bloomberg*, March 21, 2017. https://www.bloomberg.com/news/articles/2017
-03-21/france-s-fillon-earned-54-000-fixing-putin-meeting-canard-says.

Foxall, Andrew. "Putin's Cyber War: Russian Statecraft in the Fifth Domain." Henry Jackson Society, May 2016. www.stratcomcoe.org/download/file
/fid/5212.

Foy, Henry. "Poland's Pro-Russian Zmiana Party Ugres Embrace of Putin." *Financial Times*, March 16, 2016. https://www.ft.com/content/a088379e
-cbdb-11e4-beca-00144feab7de.

Fravel, Taylor. "China's Changing Approach to Military Strategy: The Science of Military Strategy from 2001 and 2013." In *China's Evolving Military Strategy*, edited by Joe McReynolds, 40–73. Washington DC: Brookings Institution, 2016.

———. "The Evolution of China's Military Strategy: Comparing the 1987 and 1999 Editions of Zhanlüexue." In *China's Revolution in Doctrinal Affairs: Emerging Trends in the Operational Art of the Chinese People's Liberation Army*. Edited by James Mulvenon and David Finkelstein, 79–99. Washington DC: Chinese People's Liberation Army, 2002.

Freedman, Lawrence. "The First Two Generations of Nuclear Strategists." In *Makers of Modern Strategy: From Machiavelli to the Nuclear Age*, edited by Peter Paret, 735–778. National Defense University. Princeton NJ: Princeton University Press, 1986.

———. *Strategic Coercion: Concepts and Cases*. Oxford, UK: Oxford University Press, 1998.

Freemantle, Brian. *KGB: Inside the World's Largest Intelligence Networks*. New York: Henry Holt, 1988.

Freeze, Gregory L. *Russian Orthodoxy and Politics in the Putin Era*. Washington DC: Carnegie Endowment for International Peace, February 9, 2017. http://carnegieendowment.org/2017/02/09/russian-orthodoxy-and-politics
-in-putin-era-pub-67959.

Frenkel, Sheera. "Iranian Authorities Block Access to Social Media Tools." *New York Times*, January 3, 2018. https://www.nytimes.com/2018/01/02
/technology/iran-protests-social-media.html.

Friedberg, Aaron L. *The Weary Titan: Britain and the Experience of Relative Decline, 1895–1905*. Princeton NJ: Princeton University Press, 1989.

Fuller, J. F. C. *The Conduct of War, 1789–1961: A Study of the Impact of the French, Industrial, and Russian Revolutions on War and Its Conduct*. New York: Da Capo, 1992.

Gaddis, John Lewis. *The Cold War: A New History*. New York: Penguin, 2006.

Gady, Franz-Stefan. "China's Air Force Can Now Launch Long-Range, Precision Strikes." *Diplomat*. October 15, 2015. https://thediplomat.com/2015/10/chinas-air-force-can-now-launch-long-range-precision-strikes/.

———. "Japan Scrambles Fighter Jets to Intercept 3 Russian Strategic Bombers." *Diplomat*, January 26, 2017. http://thediplomat.com/2017/01/japan-scrambles-fighter-jets-to-intercept-3-russian-strategic-bombers/.

———. "First Serial-Produced RS-28 Sarmat ICBMs to Enter Service in Russia in 2021." *Diplomat*, February 3, 2020. https://thediplomat.com/2020/02/first-serial-produced-rs-28-sarmat-icbms-to-enter-service-in-russia-in-2021/.

Gaidar, Yegor. *State and Evolution: Russia's Search for a Free Market*. Seattle: University of Washington Press, 2011.

Gallagher, Gary W. *The Confederate War*. Cambridge MA: Harvard University Press, 1999.

Gao, Jia, Catherine Ingram, and Pookong Kee. *Global Media and Public Diplomacy in Sino-Western Relations*. New York: Routledge, 2016.

Garrard, John, and Carol Garrard. *Russian Orthodoxy Resurgent: Faith and Power in the New Russia*. Princeton NJ: Princeton University Press, 2008.

Garton Ash, Timothy. "South China Sea Islands Are Only for Civilian Use, Says Chinese General." *Guardian*, October 16, 2015. https://www.theguardian.com/world/2015/oct/17/south-china-sea-islands-are-only-for-civilian-use-says-chinese-general.

Garvey, Todd, and Daniel Sheffner. *Congress's Authority to Influence and Control Executive Branch Agencies*. Washington DC: Congressional Research Service, December 19, 2018. https://fas.org/sgp/crs/misc/R45442.pdf.

Gatehouse, Gabriel. "Marine Le Pen: Who's Funding France's Far Right?." *BBC News*, April 3, 2017. http://www.bbc.com/news/world-europe-39478066.

Gelb, Leslie H. "Reagan's Military Budget Puts Emphasis on a Buildup of U.S. Global Power." *New York Times*, February 7, 1982, sec. U.S. https://www.nytimes.com/1982/02/07/us/reagan-s-military-budget-puts-emphasis-on-a-buildup-of-us-global-power.html.

George, Alexander L., and William E. Simons. *The Limits of Coercive Diplomacy*. Nashville TN: Westview, 1994.

Gerrits, Andre, and Max Bader. "Russian Patronage over Abkhazia and South Ossetia: Implications for Conflict Resolution." *East European Politics* 32, no. 3 (July 19, 2016): 297–313.

Gertz, Bill. "Chinese Military Revamps Cyber Warfare, Intelligence Forces." *Washington Free Beacon* (blog), January 27, 2016. http://freebeacon.com

/national-security/chinese-military-revamps-cyber-warfare-intelligence
-forces/.

———. "Top Gun Takeover: F-35 Secrets Now Showing up in China's Stealth
Fighter." *Washington Times*, March 13, 2014. http://www.washingtontimes
.com/news/2014/mar/13/f-35-secrets-now-showing-chinas-stealth-fighter/.

Gewirtz, Paul. *Limits of Law in the South China Sea*. Washington DC: Brookings
Institution, May 2016. https://www.brookings.edu/wp-content/uploads
/2016/07/Limits-of-Law-in-the-South-China-Sea-2.pdf.

Gibbons-Neff, Thomas. "Inside the Ukrainian Special Forces Fight against
Separatists—and Their Own Government." *Washington Post*, November
12, 2015. https://www.washingtonpost.com/news/checkpoint/wp/2015/11
/12/for-ukraines-special-forces-a-war-of-misuse-and-ill-supply/.

Gibney, Alex. "Can We Trust Julian Assange and WikiLeaks?." Opinion, *New
York Times*, August 8, 2016. https://www.nytimes.com/2016/08/08/opinion
/can-we-trust-julian-assange-and-wikileaks.html.

Giles, Gregory. "Continuity and Change in Israel's Strategic Culture." In *Strategic Culture and Weapons of Mass Destruction*. Initiatives in Strategic
Studies: Issues and Policies, edited by Jeannie Johnson, Kerry Kartchner,
and Jeffrey Larsen, 97–116. New York: Palgrave Macmillan, 2009. https://
doi.org/10.1057/9780230618305_7.

Giles, Keir. *Russia's "New" Tools for Confronting the West: Continuity and Innovation in Moscow's Exercise of Power*. London: Chatham House, March
21, 2016. https://www.chathamhouse.org/publication/russias-new-tools
-confronting-west.

Gilpin, Robert. *War and Change in World Politics*. 1981. Reprint, Cambridge,
UK: Cambridge University Press, 1983.

Ginsberg, M. "National Character." *British Journal of Psychology* 32, no. 3 (January 1942): 183–205.

Glantz, David M. *Soviet Military Operational Art: In Pursuit of Deep Battle*.
London: Routledge, 1991.

———. "Soviet Military Strategy during the Second Period of War (November 1942–December 1943): A Reappraisal." *Journal of Military History* 60,
no. 1 (1996): 115–50. https://doi.org/10.2307/2944451.

———. *Soviet Military Deception in the Second World War*. New York: Routledge, 1989.

Godson, Roy. *Intelligence Requirements for the 1980's: Covert Action*. Washington DC: National Strategy Information Center, 1980.

Goffart, Walter. "Rome, Constantinople, and the Barbarians." *American Historical Review* 86, no. 2 (1981): 275–306. https://doi.org/10.2307/1857439.

Goldsworthy, Adrian. *How Rome Fell: Death of a Superpower*. New Haven CT:
Yale University Press, 2010.

Golkar, Saeid. *Captive Society: The Basij Militia and Social Control in Iran*. New
York: Columbia University Press, 2015.

———. "Iran's Revolutionary Guard: Its Views of the United States." *Middle East Policy* 21, no. 2 (June 1, 2014): 53–63. https://doi.org/10.1111/mepo.12070.

———. "Militant Clergy—The Future of Shia Islam?." *Foreign Policy* (blog), July 28, 2016. https://lobelog.com/militant-clergy-the-future-of-shia-islam/.

Gonzalez, Mike. "Are You Reading Propaganda from China and Russia?." *Federalist*, April 19, 2016. http://thefederalist.com/2016/04/19/authoritarian -regimes-send-westerners-agitprop-to-inflame-far-left-far-right/.

Gorbachev, Mikhail S. *Perestroika: New Thinking for Our Country and the World.* Cambridge, UK: Harper Collins, 1987.

Gotev, Georgi. "MEPs Draw Map of Pro- and Anti-Russian Countries in the EU." *Euractiv* (blog), November 25, 2016. https://www.euractiv.com/section /global-europe/news/meps-draw-map-of-pro-and-anti-russian-countries -in-the-eu/.

Gouré, Dan. "Face the Facts: Russia's Military Is Modernizing into a Lethal Fighting Force." *National Interest.* May 17, 2016. http://nationalinterest .org/blog/the-buzz/face-the-facts-russias-military-modernizing-lethal -fighting-16234.

Graebner, Norman A. "Northern Diplomacy and European Neutrality." In *Why the North Won the Civil War*, edited by David Herbert Donald, 58– 80. New York: Touchstone, 1996.

Graham, David A. "Sheikh Nimr Al-Nimr and the Forgotten Shiites of Saudi Arabia." *Atlantic*, January 5, 2016. https://www.theatlantic.com/international /archive/2016/01/nimr-al-nimr-saudi-arabia-shiites/422670/.

Grant, John. "William Howard Taft on America and the Philippines: Equality, Natural Rights, and Imperialism." In *Toward an American Conservativism: The Birth of Constitutional Conservatism during the Progressive Era*, edited by Joseph Postell and Jonathon O'Neill, 121–50. London: Palgrave Macmillan, 2013.

Gray, Colin. "National Style in Strategy: The American Example." *International Security* 6, no. 2 (Fall 1981): 21–47.

———. "Out of the Wilderness: Prime Time for Strategic Culture." In *Strategic Culture and Weapons of Mass Destruction*. Initiatives in Strategic Studies: Issues and Policies, edited by Jeannie Johnson, Kerry Kartchner, and Jeffrey Larsen, 221–41. New York: Palgrave Macmillan, 2009.

———. "Strategic Culture as Context: The First Generation of Theory Strikes Back." *Review of International Studies* 25 (1999): 49–69.

Greenberg, Andy. "How an Entire Nation Became Russia's Test Lab for Cyberwar." *Wired*, June 20, 2017. https://www.wired.com/story/russian-hackers -attack-ukraine/.

Gregor, A. James, and Maria Hsia Chang. "Marxism, Sun Yat-Sen, and the Concept of 'Imperialism.'" *Pacific Affairs* 55, no. 1 (1982): 54–79.

———. "Nazionalfascismo and the Revolutionary Nationalism of Sun Yat-Sen." *Journal of Asian Studies* 39, no. 1 (1979): 21–37.

Grenier, John. *The First Way of War: American War Making on the Frontier, 1607–1814*. Cambridge, UK: Cambridge University Press, 2005.

Grierson, Jamie, Rachel Obordo, and Jessica Elgot. "Ransomware Attacks: Putin Says Russia Is Not Responsible—As It Happened." *Guardian*, May 15, 2017. http://www.theguardian.com/technology/live/2017/may/15/ransomware -attacks-uk-government-defends-investment-in-security-live.

Grigas, Agnia. *Legacies, Coercion and Soft Power: Russian Influence in the Baltic States*. London: Chatham House, August 2012. http://www.chathamhouse .org/sites/files/chathamhouse/public/Research/Russia%20and%20Eurasia /0812bp_grigas.pdf.

Grimmett, Richard F. *Foreign Policy Roles of the President and Congress*. Washington DC: Congressional Research Service, June 1, 1999. http://nsp_intro.golearnportal.org/rawmedia_repository/65e78775 972271272638fflc8dcee27e.pdf.

Groisman, Maayan. "Gulf Shi'ites Paying Religious Tax to Iran Are Funding Terror, Sunni Campaign Says." *Jerusalem Post*, May 4, 2016. http://www .jpost.com/Middle-East/Iran-News/Gulf-Shiites-paying-religious-tax-to -Iran-are-funding-terror-Sunni-campaign-says-453052.

Grove, Thomas. "Russia and Belarus Hold Joint Drills, and Tensions Emerge." *Wall Street Journal*, September 19, 2017. https://www.wsj .com/articles/russia-and-belarus-hold-joint-drills-and-tensions-emerge -1505813405.

Gruver, Rebecca Brooks. *American Nationalism, 1783–1830: A Self-Portrait*. New York: Putnam Group, 1970.

Guardian. "Czech Republic Claims Propaganda War by Russia and Sets Up Counter-Effort." October 21, 2016. https://www.theguardian.com/world /2016/oct/21/czech-republic-claims-propaganda-war-by-russia-and-sets -up-counter-effort.

Gude, Ken. *Russia's 5th Column*. Washington DC: Center for American Progress, July 28, 2017. https://www.americanprogress.org/issues/security/reports /2017/03/15/428074/russias-5th-column/.

Guerlac, Henry. "Vauban: The Impact of Science on War." In *Makers of Modern Strategy from Machiavelli to the Nuclear Age*, edited by Peter Paret, Gordon A. Craig, and Felix Gilbert, 64–90. Princeton NJ: Princeton University Press, 1986.

Guillermaz, Jacques. *A History of the Chinese Communist Party*. Singsby, UK: Methuen, 1968.

Guo, Yanhua. *Psychological Warfare Knowledge*. Beijing: National Defense University Press, 2005.

Gutiérrez, Edward A., and Michael S. Neiberg. "The Elusive Lesson: US Army Unpreparedness from 1898 to 1938." In *Drawdown: The American Way of Postwar*, edited by Jason W. Warren, 137–54. New York: New York University Press, 2016.

Gutzman, Kevin R. C. *James Madison and the Making of America*. New York: St. Martin's Griffin, 2013.

Haas, Ernst B. "The Balance of Power: Prescription, Concept, or Propaganda." *World Politics* 5, no. 4 (1953): 442–77. https://doi.org/10.2307/2009179.

Habeeb, William Mark. *The Middle East in Turmoil: Conflict, Revolution, and Change*. Westport CT: ABC-CLIO/Greenwood, 2012.

Hacker, Louis. "The Desire for Canadian Land." In *The Causes of the War of 1812: National Honor or National Interest?*, edited by Bradford Perkins, 46–52. New York: Holt, Rinehart and Winston, 1962.

Haghshenass, Fariborz. *Iran's Asymmetric Naval Warfare*. Washington DC: Washington Institute for Near East Policy, September 2008. https://www .washingtoninstitute.org/uploads/Documents/pubs/PolicyFocus87.pdf.

Halleck, Henry Wager. *Elements of Military Art and Science: Or, Course of Instruction in Strategy, Fortification, Tactics of Battles, &c. Embracing the Duties of Staff, Infantry, Cavalry, Artillery, and Engineers*. 3rd ed. London: D. Appleton, 1846.

Halper, Stefan. *China: The Three Warfares*. Washington DC: Office of Net Assessment, May 2013. https://cryptome.org/2014/06/prc-three-wars.pdf.

Hammond, Rupert. *Recent Developments in China's Relations with Taiwan and North Korea*. Before the U.S.-China Economic and Security Review Commission (2014).

Hamshahri Online. "Introduction to the World Assembly of Ahl al-Bayt (AS)." [Translated]. http://www.hamshahrionline.ir/details/84506, accessed July 27, 2017.

Han, Suk-hee. "South Korea Seeks to Balance Relations with China and the United States." Council on Foreign Relations, November 2012. https://www .cfr.org/report/south-korea-seeks-balance-relations-china-and-united -states.

Hannah, John. "Defusing the Iran Deal's Ticking Time Bomb." *Foreign Policy* (blog), July 18, 2016. https://foreignpolicy.com/2016/07/18/defusing-the -iran-deals-ticking-time-bomb/.

Harbutt, Fraser. *Yalta 1945: Europe and America at the Crossroads*. Cambridge, UK: Cambridge University Press, 2010.

Harold, Scott Warren. "The U.S.-China Cyber Agreement: A Good First Step." *TheRANDblog* (blog), August 1, 2016. https://www.rand.org/blog/2016/08 /the-us-china-cyber-agreement-a-good-first-step.html.

Hawk, J., Daniel Deiss, and Edwin Watson. "Russian Mercenaries in Syria and around the World." *South Front* (blog), January 28, 2017. https://southfront .org/russian-mercenaries-in-syria-and-around-the-world/.

Haynes, John Earl, Harvey Klehr, and Alexander Vassiliev. *Spies: The Rise and Fall of the KGB in America*. New Haven CT: Yale University Press, 2009.

Heather, Peter. *The Fall of the Roman Empire: A New History of Rome and the Barbarians*. Oxford, UK: Oxford University Press, 2007.

Heaton, Herbert. "The Erosion of Economic Warfare." In *The Causes of the War of 1812: National Honor or National Interest?*, edited by Bradford Perkins, 32–45. New York: Holt, Rinehart and Winston, 1962.

Hedenskog, Jakob, and Robert Larsson. "Russian Leverage on the CIS and the Baltic States." Swedish Defence Research Agency, June 2007. http://www.foi.se/ReportFiles/foir_2280.pdf.

Helgerson, John L. "Intelligence Support for Richard M. Nixon (U)." Central Intelligence Agency, January 1, 1996. https://www.cia.gov/library/readingroom/docs/1996-01-01.pdf.

Hellenbrand, Harold. "Not 'To Destroy but to Fulfill': Jefferson, Indians, and Republican Dispensation." *Eighteenth-Century Studies* 18, no. 4 (1985): 523–49. https://doi.org/10.2307/2739008.

Hendrickson, David C. "The First Union: Nationalism versus Internationalism in the American Revolution." In *Empire and Nation: The American Revolution in the Atlantic World*, edited by Eliga H. Gould and Peter S. Onuf, 35–53. Reprint ed. Baltimore MD: Johns Hopkins University Press, 2015.

Hettle, Wallace. *The Peculiar Democracy: Southern Democrats in Peace and Civil War.* Athens GA: University of Georgia Press, 2001.

Hewes, James E. *From Root to McNamara: Army Organization and Administration, 1900–1963.* Washington DC: Center of Military History, U.S. Army, 1975.

Hickey, Donald R. *The War of 1812: A Forgotten Conflict.* Rev. ed. Urbana: University of Illinois Press, 2012.

Higginbotham, Don. "The Early American Way of War: Reconnaissance and Appraisal." *William and Mary Quarterly* 44, no. 2 (1987): 230–73. https://doi.org/10.2307/1939664.

Higgins, Andrew. "Finger Pointed at Russians in Alleged Coup Plot in Montenegro." *New York Times*, November 26, 2016. https://www.nytimes.com/2016/11/26/world/europe/finger-pointed-at-russians-in-alleged-coup-plot-in-montenegro.html.

———. "In Expanding Russian Influence, Faith Combines with Firepower." *New York Times*, September 13, 2016. http://www.nytimes.com/2016/09/14/world/europe/russia-orthodox-church.html.

———. "Intent on Unsettling EU, Russia Taps Foot Soldiers from the Fringe." *New York Times*, December 24, 2016. https://www.nytimes.com/2016/12/24/world/europe/intent-on-unsettling-eu-russia-taps-foot-soldiers-from-the-fringe.html.

Hille, Kathrin, and Guy Chazan. "Russia Adds Germany's AfD to Contacts Book of European Populists." *Financial Times.* February 21, 2017. https://www.ft.com/content/d78bd9b8-f833-11e6-9516-2d969e0d3b65.

Ho, Ping-Ti. "In Defense of Sinicization: A Rebuttal of Evelyn Rawski's 'Reenvisioning the Qing.'" *Journal of Asian Studies* 57, no. 1 (1998): 123–55. https://doi.org/10.2307/2659026.

Hoffman, Frank. *Conflict in the 21st Century: The Rise of Hybrid Wars*. Arlington VA: Potomac Institute for Policy Studies, December 2007. http://www.potomacinstitute.org/images/stories/publications/potomac_hybridwar_0108.pdf.

———. "Preparing for Hybrid Wars." *Marine Corps Gazette* 91, no. 3 (March 2007): 57–61.

Holmes, James. "China's East China Sea ADIZ Represents a Thinly Veiled Grab for Sovereignty." *National Interest*, April 21, 2017. http://nationalinterest.org/feature/chinas-east-china-sea-adiz-represents-thinly-veiled-grab-20298.

Holslag, Jonathan. *China's Coming War with Asia*. Hoboken NJ: John Wiley & Sons, 2015.

Holsti, Ole R. "Public Opinion and Foreign Policy: Challenges to the Almond-Lippmann Consensus Mershon Series: Research Programs and Debates." *International Studies Quarterly* 36, no. 4 (1992): 439–66. https://doi.org/10.2307/2600734.

Hope, Ian C. *A Scientific Way of War: Antebellum Military Science, West Point, and the Origins of American Military Thought*. Lincoln: University of Nebraska Press, 2015.

Horsman, Reginald. *The Causes of the War of 1812*. Auckland, New Zealand: Pickle Partners, 2018.

Hovannisian, Richard G., and Georges Sabagh, eds. *The Persian Presence in the Islamic World*. Cambridge, UK: Cambridge University Press, 1998.

Hsu, Kimberly. *Air Defense Identification Zone Intended to Provide China Greater Flexibility to Enforce East China Sea Claims*. Washington DC: U.S.-China Economic and Security Review Commission, January 14, 2014.

Hsu, Kimberly, and Craig Murray. *China and International Law in Cyberspace*. Washington DC: U.S.-China Economic and Security Review Commission, May 6, 2014.

Hu, Yifan. *Economic Leverage, the Key to a Rising China's New Foreign Affairs Strategy*. Washington DC: Peterson Institute for International Economics, September 2013. https://www.piie.com/sites/default/files/china/files/2013/09/Economic-leverage_the-key-to-a-rising-Chinas-new-foreign-affairs-strategy.pdf.

Huang, Alexander Chieh-cheng. "Transformation and Refinement of Chinese Military Doctrine: Reflection and Critique on the PLA's View." In *Seeking Truth from Facts*, edited by James C. Mulvenon and Andrew N. D. Yang, 131–40. Santa Monica CA: RAND, 2001.

Huang, Echo. "China Is Making Life Hard for South Korea Because of an Antimissile System in over 40 Petty Ways." *Quartz* (blog), February 26, 2017. https://qz.com/917366/china-is-making-life-hard-for-south-korea-because-of-the-thaad-antimissile-system-in-over-40-petty-ways/.

Huang, Zheping. "Chinese Trolls Jumped the Firewall to Attack Taiwan's President and Military on Facebook." *Quartz* (blog), January 3, 2017. https://qz.com/876614/chinese-trolls-jumped-the-firewall-to-attack-taiwans-military-and-president-tsai-ing-wen-on-facebook/.

Huang, Zhixiong, and Kubo Mačák. "Towards the International Rule of Law in Cyberspace: Contrasting Chinese and Western Approaches." *Chinese Journal of International Law* 271, no. 16, (May 17, 2017): 1–43. https://ore.exeter.ac.uk/repository/bitstream/handle/10871/31902/Huang%20and%20Ma%20%E1k%20(2017)%20pre-print.pdf;jsessionid=5CBC68B4117DFB174B7C385F0504AC3B?sequence=5.

Huisken, Ron, ed. "The People's Republic of China: Early Foreign and Security Policy Choices." In *Introducing China, The World's Oldest Great Power Charts Its Next Comeback*, vol. 176, 31–68. Canberra, Australia: ANU, 2010.

Hunt, Michael H. "Beijing and the Korean Crisis, June 1950–June 1951." *Political Science Quarterly* 107, no. 3 (1992): 453–78.

Huntington, Samuel P. *The Soldier and the State: The Theory and Politics of Civil-Military Relations*. Rev. ed. Cambridge MA: Belknap, 1981.

Hyde, Susan D., ed. "The Quality of Monitoring and Strategic Manipulation: Why Election Monitoring Became an International Norm." In *The Pseudo-Democrat's Dilemma*, 158–84. Ithaca NY: Cornell University Press, 2011. http://www.jstor.org/stable/10.7591/j.ctt7z647.10.

Inkster, Nigel. "Conflict Foretold: America and China." *Survival: Global Politics and Strategy* 55, no. 5 (October 1, 2013): 7–28.

Information Office of the State Council of the People's Republic of China. "China's Military Strategy." Edited by Zhang Tao. May 26, 2015. http://eng.mod.gov.cn/DefenseNews/2015-05/26/content_4586748.htm.

International Crisis Group. *Iraq Backgrounder: What Lies Beneath*. Amman/Brussels: International Crisis Group, October 2002.

International Energy Agency. "Emergency Response Systems of Individual IEA Countries." In *Energy Supply Security 2014*. Paris: International Energy Agency, 2014. https://www.iea.org/media/freepublications/security/EnergySupplySecurity2014_TheCzechRepublic.pdf.

International Institute for Strategic Studies. "Europe." *Military Balance* 116, no. 1 (2016): 55–162. https://doi.org/10.1080/04597222.2016.1127564.

———. "Asia." *Military Balance* 116, no. 1 (2016): 211–306. http://dx.doi.org/10.1080/04597222.2016.1127567.

———. "Asia." *Military Balance* 117, no. 1 (2017): 237–350. https://doi.org/10.1080/04597222.2017.1271212.

International Media Support, Danish National Commission for UNESCO, and Copenhagen Business School. *The Growth of Media in China—And Its Impact on Political and Economic Development in China*. Copenhagen, Denmark: International Media Support, 2008. https://

www.mediasupport.org/wp-content/uploads/2012/11/ims-growth-china
-2008.pdf.

International Monetary Fund. "Direction of Trade Statistics." International
Monetary Fund, 2017. http://data.imf.org/?sk=9D6028D4-F14A-464C
-A2F2-59B2CD424B85&sId=1500660911120.

Iran Media Program and ASL19. "The Supreme Council of Cyberspace: Cen-
tralizing Internet Governance in Iran." *Iran Media Program of the Annenberg School of Communications, University of Pennsylvania* (blog), April
8, 2013. https://asl19.org/en/blog/2013-04-09-the-supreme-council-on
-cyberspace-centralizing-internet-governance-in-iran.html.

Iran Tour. "Free Trade Zones in Iran." http://irantour.org/Iran/Free-Trade
-Zones.html, accessed January 3, 2017.

Isachenkov, Vladimir. "Putin: New Nuclear Weapons to Enter Duty in
Next Few Years." Associated Press, May 18, 2018. https://apnews.com
/88c351c63b8d4ed8930e5670895880f0.

Islamic Development Organization. "Soft War Reasons against Islamic Republic of Iran," January 2, 2010. http://old.ido.ir//en/en-a.aspx?a=1388101204.

Islamic Republic of Iran. *Collection of Laws and Regulations Related to Free
Trade, Industrial and Special Economic Zones.* Translated by Yaghoob
Javadi. 3rd Ed. Tehran: Legal Department of the Iranian Presidential
Office, 2017. https://investiniran.ir/Portals/0/410.pdf.

Islamic Republic News Agency. "Supreme Leader Receives Islamic World
Elites." August 17, 2015. http://www.irna.ir/en/News/81722520/.

Ives, Mike. "A Small African Nation Severs Ties with Taiwan, and Beijing
Applauds." *New York Times*, December 22, 2016. https://www.nytimes.com
/2016/12/22/world/asia/china-taiwan-sao-tome-principe.html.

Jafarzadeh, Alireza. "Iran, Terrorism and the Rise of the Revolutionary Guards'
Financial Empire." Fox News, March 8, 2017. https://www.foxnews.com
/opinion/iran-terrorism-and-the-rise-of-the-revolutionary-guards
-financial-empire.

Jain, Ash. "The World According to Ahmadinejad." *Weekly Standard*, September 23, 2011. http://www.npr.org/2011/09/23/140735581/weekly-standard
-according-to-ahmadinejad.

Jamandre, Tessa. "PH Protests China's '9-Dash Line' Spratlys Claim." *Malaya*.
April 19, 2011. English ed. https://web.archive.org/web/20110419050124
/http://www.malaya.com.ph/apr14/news4.html.

Jamieson, Alastair. "Iran Navy Produces Armed Copy of Bladerunner 51
Speedboat." *Telegraph*, August 11, 2010. http://www.telegraph.co.uk/news
/worldnews/middleeast/iran/7938334/Iran-navy-produces-armed-copy
-of-Bladerunner-51-speedboat.html.

Jantunen, Saara. *Infosota*. Helsinki: Otava, 2015.

———. "The Problem with Finland." *UpNorth* (blog), July 29, 2016. https://
upnorth.eu/the-problem-with-finland/.

Japan Times. "China Opposes Japan–South Korea Military Intelligence-Sharing Pact." November 24, 2016. National ed. http://www.japantimes.co.jp /news/2016/11/24/national/china-opposes-japan-south-korea-military -intelligence-sharing-pact/.

Jefferson, Thomas. *The Writings of Thomas Jefferson.* Vol. 11. Edited by Andrew Adgate Lipscomb and Albert Ellery Bergh. Washington DC: Thomas Jefferson Memorial Association, 1903. http://hdl.handle.net/2027/hvd .32044004577722.

Jeffreys-Jones, Rhodri. *The CIA and American Democracy.* 3rd ed. New Haven CT: Yale University Press, 2003.

Jensen, Aaron. "China's Psychological War on Taiwan." *National Interest,* April 7, 2016. http://nationalinterest.org/feature/chinas-psychological-war-taiwan-15700.

Jerusalem Post. "Iran Setting up 'Passive Defense' Plan." July 4, 2008. http://www .jpost.com/Iranian-Threat/News/Iran-setting-up-passive-defense-plan.

Johnson, Kay. "Expanded Chinese-Operated Pakistani Port on $46bn Economic Corridor 'Almost Ready.'" Reuters, April 12, 2016. http://www.reuters.com /article/pakistan-china-ports-idUSL3N17F3FT.

Johnson, Matthew Raphael. *The Third Rome: Holy Russia, Tsarism and Orthodoxy.* 2nd ed. Washington DC: Foundation for Economic Liberty, 2004.

Johnston, Alastair I. "China's New 'Old Thinking': The Concept of Limited Deterrence." *International Security* 20, no. 3 (1995): 5–42.

——— . *Cultural Realism: Strategic Culture and Grand Strategy in Chinese History.* Princeton NJ: Princeton University Press, 1995.

——— . "Strategic Cultures Revisited: Reply to Colin Gray." *Review of International Studies* 25 (1999): 519–23.

——— . "Thinking about Strategic Culture." *International Security* 19, no. 4 (Spring 1995): 32–64.

Joint Chiefs of Staff. *Joint Concept for Integrated Campaigning.* Arlington VA: U.S. Department of Defense, March 16, 2018. https://www.jcs.mil/Portals /36/Documents/Doctrine/concepts/joint_concept_integrated_campaign .pdf?ver=2018-03-28-102833-257.

——— . *Joint Publication 3–0: Joint Operations.* Arlington VA: U.S. Department of Defense, January 17, 2017. https://www.jcs.mil/Portals/36/Documents /Doctrine/pubs/jp3_0ch1.pdf?ver=2018-11-27-160457-910.

——— . *Joint Publication 3–0: Joint Operations.* Arlington VA: U.S. Department of Defense, August 2011. https://www.hsdl.org/?view&did=685338.Error! Hyperlink reference not valid.

Jomini, Baron Antoine-Henri. *The Art of War.* Radford, VA: Wilder, 2008.

Jones, Benjamin F. "Freeing France: The Allies, the Resistance, and the Jedburghs." Ph.D. Dissertation, University of Kansas, 2008. https://apps.dtic .mil/dtic/tr/fulltext/u2/a488406.pdf.

Jones, Benjamin F. "Freeing France: The Allies, the Resistance, and the Jedburghs." PhD diss., University of Kansas, 2008. http://search.proquest

.com.ezp-prod1.hul.harvard.edu/docview/230668589/abstract
/141D7C7A541500345F1/2?accountid=11311.

Jones, David. "Soviet Strategic Culture." In *Strategic Power: USA/USSR*, edited by Carl G. Jacobsen, 35–49. London: Palgrave, Macmillan, 1990.

Jones, Sam. "Cyber Warfare: Iran Opens a New Front." *Financial Times*, April 26, 2016. http://www.ft.com/intl/cms/s/0/15e1acf0-0a47-11e6-b0f1-61f222853ff3.html#axzz47b5op8ks.

Joy-Perez, Cecilia, and Derek Scissors. "A Close Look at OBOR Reveals Overstated Gains." White paper. American Enterprise Institute, Washington DC, May 16, 2017. https://www.aei.org/research-products/report/a-close-look-at-obor-reveals-overstated-gains/.

Ju, Sherry Fei, and Charles Clover. "Chinese Military Base Takes Shape in Djibouti." *Financial Times*, July 12, 2017. https://www.ft.com/content/bcba2820-66e1-11e7-8526-7b38dcaef614.

Juhász, Attila, Lóránt Györi, Péter Krekó, and András Dezsö. *I Am Eurasian: The Kremlin Connections of the Hungarian Far Right*. Budapest, Hungary: Political Capital Policy Research & Consulting Institute and Social Development Institute, March 2015. https://cz.boell.org/sites/default/files/pc_sdi_boll_study_iameurasian.pdf.

Jullien, François. *The Propensity of Things: Toward a History of Efficacy in China*. Translated by Janet Lloyd. New York: Zone, 1999.

———. *A Treatise on Efficacy: Between Western and Chinese Thinking*. Translated by Janet Lloyd. Honolulu: University of Hawaii Press, 2004.

Kagan, F., and R. Higham. *The Military History of Tsarist Russia*. London: Palgrave Macmillan, 2016.

Kagan, Frederick, and Tommy Stiansen. *The Growing Cyberthreat from Iran: The Initial Report of Project Pistachio Harvest*. Washington DC: American Enterprise Institute Critical Threats Project and Norse Corporation, April 2015. https://www.aei.org/wp-content/uploads/2015/04/Growing-Cyberthreat-From-Iran-final.pdf.

Kaplan, Lawrence S. *Entangling Alliances with None: American Foreign Policy in the Age of Jefferson*. Kent OH: Kent State University Press, 1987.

———. "Jefferson, the Napoleonic Wars, and the Balance of Power." *The William and Mary Quarterly* 14, no. 2 (1957): 196–217. https://doi.org/10.2307/1922110.

Kaplan, Robert D. *The Revenge of Geography: What the Map Tells Us about Coming Conflicts and the Battle against Fate*. New York: Random House, 2013.

Kasten Nelson, Anna. "President Truman and the Evolution of the National Security Council." *Journal of American History* 72, no. 2 (1985): 360–78. https://doi.org/10.2307/1903380.

Katzenstein, Peter J. *Sinicization and the Rise of China: Civilizational Processes Beyond East and West*. New York: Routledge, 2013.

Katzman, Kenneth.. *Iran Sanctions*. Washington DC: Congressional Research Service, December 2, 2011.

———. *The Warriors of Islam: Iran's Revolutionary Guard*. Boulder CO: Westview, 1993.

Kaufman, S., R. Little, and W. Wohlforth, eds. *Balance of Power in World History*. Basingstoke, UK: Palgrave Macmillan, 2007.

Keaney, Thomas A., and Eliot A. Cohen. *Gulf War Air Power Survey Summary Report*. Fort Belvoir VA: Defense Technical Information Center, January 1, 1993. https://doi.org/10.21236/ADA273996.

Keck, Zachary. "Eyeing Gulf Shipping, Iran's Mass Producing Submarines." *Diplomat*. September 28, 2013. http://thediplomat.com/2013/09/eyeing -gulf-shipping-irans-mass-producing-submarines/.

Keith, James R. "The Internet in China: A Tool for Freedom or Suppression?." Before the US-China Economic and Security Review Commission (2006). https://2001-2009.state.gov/p/eap/rls/rm/61275.htm.

Keithly, David M. "Intelligence Sesquicentennial: Testament of Bleeding War." *Journal of Strategic Security* 8, no. 3 (2015): 53–66.

Kennedy, Paul. *The Rise and Fall of the Great Powers: Economic Change and Military Conflict from 1500 to 2000*. New York: Random House, 1989.

Kennedy, Ross. *The Will to Believe: Woodrow Wilson, World War I, and America's Strategy for Peace and Security*. Kent OH: Kent State University Press, 2009.

Keohane, Robert O., and Joseph S. Nye Jr. *Power and Interdependence*. 4th ed. Boston: Pearson, 2011.

Keyton, David. "Swedish Island Likely to Reject Renting Space to Russia." Associated Press, December 14, 2016. https://apnews.com/article /c3acff76ef47484f9df8537756ae8800.

Khajehpour, Bijan. "Decoding Iran's 'Resistance Economy.'" *Iran Pulse* (blog), February 24, 2014. http://www.al-monitor.com/pulse/originals/2014/02 /decoding-resistance-economy-iran.html.

Khamenei, Ali. "The Year of the Economy of Resistance: Action and Implementation." *Khamenei.Ir* (blog), March 20, 2016. http://english.khamenei .ir/news/3544/The-Year-of-the-Economy-of-Resistance-Action-and -Implementation.

———. "Leader's Speech to Members of Ahlul Bayt World Assembly and Islamic Radio and TV Union." August 17, 2015. http://english.khamenei.ir /news/2109/Leader-s-speech-to-members-of-Ahlul-Bayt-World-Assembly -and-Islamic.

Kim, Jiyoon, Karl Friedhoff, Kang Chungku, and Lee Euicheol. *South Korean Attitudes on China*. Seoul: Asan Institute, July 2014. http://en.asaninst.org /contents/south-korean-attitudes-on-china/.

Kiras, James D. *Special Operations and Strategy: From World War II to the War on Terrorism*. New York: Routledge, 2006. http://www.routledge.com /books/details/9780415459495/.

Kirillova, Kseniya. "How Russian Church Serves Kremlin Propaganda." *Euro-maidan Press*, December 15, 2015. http://euromaidanpress.com/2015/12/15 /how-russian-church-serves-kremlin-propaganda/.

Kiselycznyk, Michael, and Phillip Saunders. "Civil-Military Relations in China: Assessing the PLA's Role in Elite Politics." *China Strategic Perspectives*, no. 2 (August 2010): 1–30.

Kissinger, Henry. *On China*. London: Penguin, 2012.

Kittrie, Orde F. *Lawfare: Law as a Weapon of War*. Oxford, UK: Oxford University Press, 2016.

Klapsis, Antonis. *An Unholy Alliance: The European Far Right and Putin's Russia*. Brussels: Wilfried Martens Centre for European Studies, 2015. https://www .martenscentre.eu/sites/default/files/publication-files/far-right-political -parties-in-europe-and-putins-russia.pdf.

Klein, Bradley S. "Hegemony and Strategic Culture: American Power Projection and Alliance Defence Politics." *Review of International Studies* 14 (1988): 133–48.

Klein, Margarete. "Russia's New Military Doctrine: NATO, the United States, and the 'Colour Revolutions.'" *SWP Comments*, February 2015. https://www .swp-berlin.org/fileadmin/contents/products/comments/2015C09_kle.pdf.

Klikushin, Mikhail. "Russia Declares There's No Such Thing as 'NATO Airspace.'" *Observer* (blog), February 8, 2016. http://observer.com/2016/02 /russia-declares-theres-no-such-thing-as-nato-airspace/.

Kofman, Michael. "Russian Hybrid Warfare and Other Dark Arts." *War on the Rocks*, March 11, 2016. https://warontherocks.com/2016/03/russian -hybrid-warfare-and-other-dark-arts/.

Kofman, Michael, Katya Migacheva, Brian Nichiporuk, Andrew Radin, Olesya Tkacheva, and Jenny Oberholtzer. *Lessons from Russia's Operations in Crimea and Eastern Ukraine*. Santa Monica CA: RAND, 2017. https://www .rand.org/pubs/research_reports/RR1498.html.

Kollars, Nina. "Genius and Mastery in Military Innovation." *Survival* 59, no. 2 (March 4, 2017): 125–38. https://doi.org/10.1080/00396338.2017.1302193.

Kostadinov, Dimitar. "GhostNet—Part 1." *Infosec* (blog), April 24, 2013. https:// resources.infosecinstitute.com/topic/ghostnet-part-i/.

KPMG China IT Advisory Practice. "Overview of China's Cybersecurity Law." Beijing: KPMG, February 2017. https://assets.kpmg.com/content/dam/kpmg /cn/pdf/en/2017/02/overview-of-cybersecurity-law.pdf.

Kragh, Martin, and Sebastian Åsberg. "Russia's Strategy for Influence through Public Diplomacy and Active Measures: The Swedish Case." *Journal of Strategic Studies* 40, no. 6 (September 19, 2017): 773–816. https://doi.org /10.1080/01402390.2016.1273830.

Kramer, Mark. "The Role of the CPSU International Department in Soviet Foreign Relations and National Security Policy." *Soviet Studies* 42, no. 3 (1990): 429–46.

Kraska, James, and Michael Monti. "The Law of Naval Warfare and China's Maritime Militia." *International Law Studies* 91, no. 450 (2015): 450–467. http://stockton.usnwc.edu/cgi/viewcontent.cgi?article=1406&context=ils.

Krauss, Clifford. "War in the Gulf: Iran Said to Play Both Sides in Gulf." *New York Times*, January 31, 1991. http://www.nytimes.com/1991/01/31/world /war-in-the-gulf-iran-iran-said-to-play-both-sides-in-gulf.html.

Krebs, Ronald R. *Narrative and the Making of US National Security*. New York: Cambridge University Press, 2015.

Kredo, Adam. "Iran Expanding Terror Network in Latin America." *Washington Free Beacon*, August 23, 2016. http://freebeacon.com/national-security /iran-solidifying-terror-network-latin-america/.

Krekel, Bryan. *Capability of the People's Republic of China to Conduct Cyber Warfare and Computer Network Exploitation*. McLean VA: Northrup Grumman, October 9, 2009. https://nsarchive2.gwu.edu/NSAEBB/NSAEBB424 /docs/Cyber-030.pdf.

Kreko, Peter, and Krisztian Szabados. "Russia's Far-Right Friends." *Risk and Forecast* (blog), March 12, 2009. http://www.riskandforecast.com/post/in -depth-analysis/russia-s-far-right-friends_349.html.

Kreko, Peter, Lorant Gyori, Daniel Milo, Juraj Marusiak, Janos Szeky, and Anita Lencses. "Marching Towards Eurasia: The Kremlin Connections of the Slovak Far-Right." *Political Capital*, 2015. http://www .politicalcapital.hu/wp-content/uploads/PC_Study_Russian_Influence _Slovakia_ENG.pdf.

Krepinevich, Andrew, Jr. "Why No Transformation?." *Joint Force Quarterly* (Autumn/Winter, 1999–2000): 97–101. https://apps.dtic.mil/docs/citations /ADA524173.

Kretchik, Walter E. *U.S. Army Doctrine: From the American Revolution to the War on Terror*. Lawrence: University Press of Kansas, 2011.

Kristensen, Hans, and Robert Norris. "Chinese Nuclear Forces, 2016." *Bulletin of the Atomic Scientists* 72, no. 4 (June 13, 2016): 205–11.

Ku, Julian. "China's Ridiculously Weak Legal Argument against Complying with the South China Sea Arbitration Award." *Lawfare* (blog), June 6, 2016. https://www.lawfareblog.com/chinas-ridiculously-weak-legal-argument -against-complying-south-china-sea-arbitration-award.

Kupchinsky, Roman. "CIS: Monitoring the Election Monitors." RadioFreeEurope/RadioLiberty. https://www.rferl.org/a/1058234.html, accessed October 14, 2017.

Kumar, Anita. "Obama, Xi Reach Anti-Hacking Agreement, but Skepticism Remains." McClatchy News Service. September 25, 2015. http://www .mcclatchydc.com/news/nation-world/national/article36608748.html.

Kumar, Dhawal. "China Conquers the Fourth Territory." *Geospatial World* (blog), December 14, 2010. https://www.geospatialworld.net/article/china -conquers-the-fourth-territory/.

Kux, Dennis. "Soviet Active Measures and Disinformation: Overview and Assessment." *Parameters* 15, no. 4 (Winter 1985): 19–28. http://www.iwp .edu/docLib/20131120_KuxSovietActiveMeasuresandDisinformation.pdf.

Lai, Hongyi, and Yiyi Lu. *China's Soft Power and International Relations.* New York: Routledge, 2012.

Lamb, Christopher, and Fletcher Schoen. *Deception, Disinformation, and Strategic Communications: How One Interagency Group Made a Major Difference.* Washington DC: National Defense University Press, June 2012. http:// ndupress.ndu.edu/Portals/68/Documents/stratperspective/inss/Strategic -Perspectives-11.pdf.

Lang, John. "Russia-German Pipeline May Break Europe's Energy Union." *Oil-Price.Com* (blog), June 24, 2016. http://oilprice.com/Energy/Energy-General /Russia-German-Pipeline-May-Break-Europes-Energy-Union.html.

Lanzillo, Amanda. "Iran and the Green Movement." *Changing Communications* (blog), August 26, 2011. https://changingcommunications.wordpress .com/research/iran-and-the-green-movement/.

Larkin, Edward. *The American School of Empire.* New York: Cambridge University Press, 2016.

Laurie, Clayton D. "'The Chanting of Crusaders': Captain Heber Blankenhorn and AEF Combat Propaganda in World War I." *Journal of Military History* 59, no. 3 (1995): 457–82. https://doi.org/10.2307/2944618.

———. "The Evolution of the CIA: A New President, a Better CIA, and an Old War: Eisenhower and Intelligence Reporting on Korea, 1953." *Studies in Intelligence* 54, no. 4 (December 2010): 1–12 https://www .cia.gov/library/center-for-the-study-of-intelligence/csi-publications /csi-studies/studies/vol.-54-no.-4/pdfs/Laurie-Ike%20and%20Intel -Extract-Annotated.pdf.

Laville, Helen. "The Committee of Correspondence: CIA Funding of Women's Groups, 1952–1967." In *Eternal Vigilance? 50 Years of the CIA*, edited by Rhodri Jeffreys-Jones and Christopher Andrew, 104–21. Portland OR: Frank Cass, 1997.

Lavinder, Kaitlin. "Russia Ramps Up Media and Military Influence in Balkans." Cipher Brief. October 13, 2017. https://www.thecipherbrief.com /article/exclusive/europe/russia-ramps-media-military-influence-balkans.

Layne, Christopher. "The War on Terrorism and the Balance of Power." In *Balance of Power: Theory and Practice*, edited by T. V. Paul, James Wirtz, and Michel Fortmann, 106–11. Redwood City CA: Stanford University Press, 2004.

Layne, Christopher, and Bradley A. Thayer. *American Empire: A Debate.* New York: Routledge, 2006.

Lee, Jaemin. "China's Declaration of an Air Defense Identification Zone in the East China Sea: Implications for Public International Law: ASIL." *American Society of International Law* 18, no. 17 (August 9, 2014). https://www

.asil.org/insights/volume/18/issue/17/china%e2%80%99s-declaration-air
-defense-identification-zone-east-china-sea.

Lee, Sangkuk. "China's 'Three Warfares': Origins, Applications, and Organizations." *Journal of Strategic Studies* 37, no. 2 (February 23, 2014): 198–221.

Lee, Terry. *Iran's Influence in Iraq*. Carlisle Barracks PA: U.S. Army War College, July 6, 2010. https://www.hsdl.org/?view&did=698409.

Lee, Wayne E. "Early American Ways of War: A New Reconnaissance, 1600–1815." *Historical Journal* 44, no. 1 (2001): 269–89.

———. "Peace Chiefs and Blood Revenge: Patterns of Restraint in Native American Warfare, 1500–1800." *Journal of Military History* 71, no. 3 (2007): 701–41.

Leeman, William P. "War without Declaration: The Barbary Wars." In *The Routledge Handbook of American Military and Diplomatic History: The Colonial Period to 1877*, edited by Christos G. Frentzos and Antonio S. Thompson, 164–72. New York: Routledge, 2014.

Leighton, Marian. *Soviet Propaganda as a Foreign Policy Tool*. New York: University Press of America, 1991.

Lenin, V. I. *What Is to Be Done? Burning Questions of Our Movement*. Rev. ed. New York: International, 1969.

Leung, Edwin Pak-Wah. *Modern Chinese History Essentials*. Piscataway NJ: Research & Education Association, 2012.

Lever, Liam. "Romania Has Lowest Proportion of Urban Population in the EU." *Romania Insider* (blog), April 2, 2012. http://www.romania-insider
.com/romania-has-lowest-proportion-of-urban-population-in-the-eu/.

Levitt, Matthew. "Charitable Organizations and Terrorist Financing: A War on Terror Status-Check." Paper presented at Dimensions of Terrorist Financing workshop, University of Pittsburgh, March 19, 2014. http://www
.washingtoninstitute.org/policy-analysis/view/charitable-organizations
-and-terrorist-financing-a-war-on-terror-status-che.

———. "Hezbollah: A Case Study in Global Reach." Lecture presented at Post-Modern Terrorism: Trends, Scenarios, and Future Threats, Herzliya, Israel, September 8, 2003. http://www.washingtoninstitute.org/policy-analysis
/view/hezbollah-a-case-study-of-global-reach.

———. *Hezbollah: The Global Footprint of Lebanon's Party of God*. Washington DC: Georgetown University Press, 2015.

———. "Iran and Hezbollah Remain Hyperactive in Latin America," Interview with Cipher Brief. August 11, 2016. http://www.washingtoninstitute
.org/policy-analysis/view/iran-and-hezbollah-remain-hyperactive-in
-latin-america.

Lewin, Nicholas Adam. *Jung on War, Politics and Nazi Germany: Exploring the Theory of Archetypes and the Collective Unconscious*. London: Karnac Books, 2009.

Lewis, Bernard. "'Abbāsids." In *Encyclopedia of Islam*, edited by P. Bearman, Th. Bianquis, C. E. Bosworth, E. van Donzel, and W. P. Heinrichs. Leiden,

Netherlands: Brill, 2012. http://referenceworks.brillonline.com/entries
/encyclopaedia-of-islam-2/abbasids-COM_0002?s.num=45&s.start=40.

Lewis, S. J. *Jedburgh Team Operations in Support of the 12th Army Group, August 1944*. Fort Leavenworth KS: U.S. Army Command and General Staff College Combat Studies Institute, October 1991. http://usacac.army.mil/cac2 /cgsc/carl/download/csipubs/lewis.pdf.

Lewy, Guenter. *America in Vietnam*. Oxford, UK: Oxford University Press, 1980.

Li, Xiguang. "Find Out the Territory and Position of Ideology." *Communist Party of China News*, August 22, 2014. http://theory.people.com.cn/n/2014 /0822/c112851-25517343.html.

Liang, Qiao, and Xiangsui Wang. *Unrestricted Warfare*. Beijing: PLA Literature and Arts, 1999.

Liddell Hart, B. H. *Strategy: The Indirect Approach*. Washington DC: Pentagon Press, 2012.

Lin, Jeffrey, and P. W. Singer. "China Builds Its Own 'Wild Weasel' to Suppress Air Defenses." *Eastern Arsenal* (blog), *Popular Science*, December 29, 2015. http://www.popsci.com/china-builds-its-own-wild-weasel-to -suppress-air-defenses.

Lindsay, Jon. *China and Cybersecurity: Political, Economic, and Strategic Dimensions*. San Diego: University of California Institute on Global Conflict and Cooperation, April 2012. http://www.bdo3c.f-sc.org/archives /921.pdf.

Little, Richard. *The Balance of Power in International Relations: Metaphors, Myths and Models*. Cambridge, UK: Cambridge University Press, 2007.

Liu, Jieyi, Kairat Abdrakhmanov, Talaibek Kydyrov, Vitaly Churkin, Mahmdamin Mahmadaminov, and Muzaffarbek Madrakhimov. "Letter from the Permanent Representatives of China, Kazakhstan, Kyrgyzstan, the Russian Federation, Tajikistan and Uzbekistan to the United Nations Addressed to the Secretary-General." UN General Assembly, A/69/723. New York: United Nations Press, 2015.

Lively, James K. "Propaganda Techniques of Civil War Cartoonists." *Public Opinion Quarterly* 6, no. 1 (1942): 99–106.

Lob, Eric, and Nader Habibi. "There's a Battle in Iran over the Islamic Revolutionary Guards Corps Business Empire." *Washington Post*, January 5, 2017. https://www.washingtonpost.com/news/monkey-cage/wp/2017/01 /05/theres-a-battle-in-iran-over-the-islamic-revolutionary-guards-corps -business-empire/.

Lobkowicz, Nikolaus. *Theory and Practice: History of a Concept from Aristotle to Marx*. Lanham MD: University Press of America, 1967.

Lohaus, Phillip. "A Missing Shade of Gray: Political Will and Waging Something Short of War." *War on the Rocks*, January 11, 2017. https://warontherocks.com /2017/01/a-missing-shade-of-gray-political-will-and-waging-something -short-of-war/.

———. "A New Blueprint for Competing Below the Threshold: The Joint Concept for Integrated Campaigning." *War on the Rocks*, May 23, 2018. https://warontherocks.com/2018/05/a-new-blueprint-for-competing-below-the-threshold-the-joint-concept-for-integrated-campaigning/.

———. *A Precarious Balance: Preserving the Right Mix of Conventional and Special Operations Forces*. Washington DC: American Enterprise Institute, 2014.

———. "Special Operations Forces (SOF) in the Gray Zone: An Operational Framework for Employing SOF in the Space between War and Peace." *Special Operations Journal* 2, no. 2 (December 15, 2016): 75–91. https://doi.org/10.1080/23296151.2016.1239989.

Lohaus, Phillip, and Tomas Jermilavicius. "Proceedings of AEI/ICDS Workshop on Allied Shaping Operations." In *Beyond Attrition: A Way Forward for Allied Shaping Operations*, 1–10. Unpublished transcript, November 18, 2015 (available upon request).

Lomperis, Timothy J. *From People's War to People's Rule: Insurgency, Intervention, and the Lessons of Vietnam*. Chapel Hill: University of North Carolina Press, 1996.

Lorber, Eric. "Economic Coercion, with a Chinese Twist." *Foreign Policy*, February 28, 2017. http://foreignpolicy.com/2017/02/28/economic-coercion-china-united-states-sanctions-asia/.

Lord, Carnes. "American Strategic Culture." *Comparative Strategy* 5, no. 3 (January 1, 1985): 269–93. https://doi.org/10.1080/01495938508402693.

———. "American Strategic Culture in Small Wars." In *Legal and Moral Constraints on Low-Intensity Conflict*. Vol. 67 of *International Law Studies*, edited by Alberto R. Coll, James S. Order, and Stephen A. Rose, 265–73. Newport RI: United States Naval War College, 1995.

Louth, John, Trevor Taylor, and Andrew Tyler. *Defence Innovation and the UK: Responding to the Risks Identified by the US Third Offset Strategy*. London: Royal United Services Institute, July 11, 2017. https://rusi.org/publication/occasional-papers/defence-innovation-and-uk-responding-risks-identified-us-third-offset.

Lukas, Richard C. "The Polish American Congress and the Polish Question, 1944–1947." *Polish American Studies* 38, no. 2 (1981): 39–53.

Luttwak, Edward. "Notes on Low-Intensity Warfare." *Parameters* 13, no. 4 (December 1983). https://press.armywarcollege.edu/parameters/vol13/iss1/15/.

Lyutov, Ivan. "Lenin's Ideas on Defending Socialism." *International Affairs*, no. 1 (January 1988): 12–19. https://archive.org/stream/dli.bengal.10689.11809/10689.11809_djvu.txt.

MacFarquhar, Neil. "How Russians Pay to Play in Other Countries." *New York Times*, December 30, 2016. https://www.nytimes.com/2016/12/30/world/europe/czech-republic-russia-milos-zeman.html.

Machiavelli, Niccolo. *The Prince.* Edited by Robert M. Adams. 2nd ed. New York: W. W. Norton, 1992.

Mackinnon, Amy. "Why Has Russia's Propaganda Machine Set Its Sights on Belarus?." Coda Story, March 23, 2017. https://codastory.com/disinformation -crisis/information-war/russia-s-propaganda-machine-sets-its-sights-on -belarus.

Mahnken, Thomas. "The Reagan Administration's Strategy toward the Soviet Union." In *Successful Strategies: Triumphing in War and Peace from Antiquity to the Present,* edited by Williamson Murray and Richard Sinnreich, 403–31. Cambridge, UK: Cambridge University Press, 2014.

Mahnken, Thomas, and Dan Blumenthal. *Strategy in Asia: The Past, Present, and Future of Regional Security.* Stanford CA: Stanford University Press, 2014.

Maida, Adam. *Online and on All Fronts: Russia's Assault on Freedom of Expression.* Washington DC: Human Rights Watch, July 18, 2017. https://www .hrw.org/report/2017/07/18/online-and-all-fronts/russias-assault-freedom -expression.

Malek, Alia. "Al-Alam's Game." *Columbia Journalism Review,* July 1, 2007. https://archives.cjr.org/feature/alalams_game.php.

Mamouri, Ali. "Leaked Cables Show Gulf Leery of Shiite Expansion." *Al-Monitor,* June 26, 2015. https://www.al-monitor.com/pulse/originals/2015/06/gulf -fears-shiite-expansion-wikileaks-saudi-arabia-iran.html.

Manuel, Anja. "What to Read into a Growing Alliance between China and Pakistan." *Reuters Blogs* (blog), April 27, 2016. http://blogs.reuters.com /great-debate/2016/04/26/what-to-read-into-a-growing-alliance-between -china-and-pakistan/.

Mao, Tse-Tung. *Problems of War and Strategy.* Peking: Foreign Language Press, 1960.

———. *Selected Works.* Vol. 2. New York: International Publishers, 1954.

———. "Speech at the Chinese Communist Party's National Conference on Propaganda Work," Shanghai, China, March 12, 1957.

Maogoto, Jackson Nyamuya, and Steven Freeland. "The Final Frontier: The Laws of Armed Conflict and Space Warfare." Scholarly Paper. Social Science Research Network, Rochester NY, January 1, 2008. https://papers .ssrn.com/sol3/papers.cfm?abstract_id=1079376.

Marchesano, Francesco. "Election Observation as a Point of Contention between the Russian Federation and ODIHR." In *OSCE Yearbook 2014,* 263–74. Baden-Baden, Germany: Institut für Friedensforschung und Sicherheitspolitik an der Universität Hamburg, 2015. https://ifsh.de/file-CORE /documents/yearbook/english/14/Marchesano-en_S.pdf.

Marcu, Bogdan. "Russian Propaganda in the Facebook Age." *Huffington Post* (blog), July 30, 2016. http://www.huffingtonpost.com/bogdan-marcu /russian-propaganda-in-the_b_11280828.html.

Marsh, Christopher. *Developments in Russian Special Operations: Spetsnaz, SOF, and Russian Special Operations Forces Command.* Ottawa: Canadian Special Operations Forces Command, 2016. http://publications.gc
.ca/collections/collection_2017/mdn-dnd/D4-10-21-2017-eng.pdf.
Marshall, Andrew W. *Long-Term Competition with the Soviets.* Arlington VA: RAND, 1972. https://www.rand.org/pubs/reports/R862.html.
Martens, Maria. "Russian Military Modernization." NATO Parliamentary Assembly Science and Technology Committee, October 2015. www.nato-pa.int
/shortcut.asp?FILE=4193.
Martikainen, Toivo, Sinikukka Saari, and Katri Pynnöniemi. "Neighbouring an Unpredictable Russia: Implications for Finland." Finnish Institute for International Affairs, October 31, 2016. http://www.fiia.fi/en/publication
/629/neighbouring_an_unpredictable_russia/.
Martin, Gregory. *Enhancing American Interagency Integration for the Global War on Terrorism.* Carlisle PA: U.S. Army War College, March 15, 2006. https://www.hsdl.org/?view&did=470248.
Martinez, Luis. "Russian Bombers Intercepted Off Alaska for Second Time this Year." *ABC News,* September 7, 2018. https://abcnews.go.com/International
/russian-bombers-intercepted-off-alaska-time-year/story?id=57671426.
———. "U.S. Fires on Persian Gulf Boat, 1 Dead." *ABC News,* July 16, 2012. http://abcnews.go.com/Blotter/us-navy-fires-ship-persian-gulf-dead/story
?id=16787035.
Marusic, Damir. "Did Moscow Botch a Coup in Montenegro?" *American Interest* (blog), October 31, 2016. http://www.the-american-interest.com/2016
/10/30/did-moscow-botch-a-coup-in-montenegro/.
Matloff, Maurice. "Allied Strategy in Europe, 1939–1945." In *Makers of Modern Strategy from Machiavelli to the Nuclear Age,* edited by Peter Paret, Gordon A. Craig, and Felix Gilbert, 677–702. Princeton NJ: Princeton University Press, 1986.
Matloff, Maurice, and Edwin Snell. *Strategic Planning for Coalition Warfare 1941–1942.* Washington DC: U.S. Army Center of Military History, 1980. https://history.army.mil/books/wwii/SP1941-42/index.htm#Contents.
Matsumura, Masahiro. "China Waging Psychological Warfare in the East China Sea." *Japan Times,* March 13, 2014. http://www.japantimes.co.jp/opinion
/2014/03/13/commentary/japan-commentary/china-waging-psychological
-warfare-in-the-east-china-sea/.
Mattis, James N., and Frank Hoffman. "Future Warfare: The Rise of Hybrid Wars." *Proceedings* 131, no. 11 (November 2005): 18–19.
Mauch, Christof. *The Shadow War against Hitler: The Covert Operations of America's Wartime Secret Intelligence Service.* Translated by Jeremiah Riemer. New York: Columbia University Press, 1999.
Maurer, Tim. "Cyber Proxies and the Crisis in Ukraine." In *Cyber War in Perspective: Russian Aggression against Ukraine,* 79–86. Tallinn, Estonia:

NATO Cooperative Cyber Defense Center of Excellence, 2015. https:// ccdcoe.org/sites/default/files/multimedia/pdf/CyberWarinPerspective _Maurer_09.pdf.

May, Ernest R., ed. *American Cold War Strategy: Interpreting NSC 68*. Boston: Bedford/St. Martin's, 1993.

McColley, Robert. *Federalists, Republicans, and Foreign Entanglements 1789–1815*. Upper Saddle River NJ: Prentice Hall, 1969.

McDermott, Roger. "Learning from Today's Wars: Does Russia Have a Gerasimov Doctrine?." *Parameters* 46, no. 1 (Spring 2016): 97–105.

McDevitt, Michael. *The South China Sea: Assessing U.S. Policy Options for the Future*. Arlington VA: CNA, November 2014. https://www.cna.org/cna _files/pdf/IOP-2014-U-009109.pdf.

McElroy, Damien. "Chinese Media Warns of War with Philippines," *Telegraph*, May 10, 2012. http://www.telegraph.co.uk/news/worldnews/asia/philippines /9258225/Chinese-media-warns-of-war-with-Philippines.html.

McGarry, Brendan. "Russia Finishes Delivery of S-300 Missile Systems to Iran." *Defensetech* (blog), October 14, 2016. https://www.defensetech.org/2016 /10/14/russia-finishes-delivery-s-300-missile-systems-iran/.

McInnis, J. Matthew. "Iran's Military Might Be Getting Ready to Make Some Sweeping Changes." *National Interest*, September 9, 2016. http:// nationalinterest.org/blog/the-buzz/irans-military-might-be-getting-ready -make-some-sweeping-17635.

McInnis, J. Matthew, and Ashton Gilmore. *Iran at War: Understanding Why and How Tehran Uses Military Force*. Washington DC: American Enterprise Institute, December 2016. https://www.aei.org/wp-content/uploads /2016/12/RPT-FP-McInnis-Iran-at-War-final-December-2016.pdf.

McJimsey, George. *Harry Hopkins*. Cambridge MA: Harvard University Press, 1987.

McKune, Sarah. "Analysis of International Code of Conduct for Information Security." *Citizen Lab* (blog), September 28, 2015. https://citizenlab.org /2015/09/international-code-of-conduct/.

McLeary, Paul. "Pentagon: Chinese Military Modernization Enters 'New Phase.'" *Foreign Policy* (blog), May 13, 2016. https://foreignpolicy.com/2016/05/13 /pentagon-chinese-military-modernization-enters-new-phase/.

Mearsheimer, John J. *The Tragedy of Great Power Politics*. New York: W. W. Norton, 2014.

Meier, Barry, and Benjamin Weiser. "Court Halts U.S. Seizure of New York Building Linked to Iran." *New York Times*, July 20, 2016. https://www .nytimes.com/2016/07/21/business/iran-assets-terrorism-appeals-court -ruling.html.

Meilinger, Phillip S. "Trenchard and 'Morale Bombing': The Evolution of Royal Air Force Doctrine Before World War II." *Journal of Military History* 60, no. 2 (1996): 243–70. https://doi.org/10.2307/2944407.

Mellor, M. Joanna, and Helen Rehr. *Baby Boomers: Can My Eighties Be Like My Fifties?*. New York: Springer, 2005.

Merriam, C. E. "The Political Theory of Jefferson." *Political Science Quarterly* 17, no. 1 (1902): 24–45. https://doi.org/10.2307/2140379.

Metelitsa, Alexander. "Oil and Natural Gas Sales Accounted for 68% of Russia's Total Export Revenues in 2013." U.S. Energy Information Administration, July 23, 2014. http://www.eia.gov/todayinenergy/detail.php?id=17231.

Mikolashek, Paul T. "The Soviet Union's 'New Defensive Doctrine' and the Changing Face of Soviet Strategic Culture." U.S. Army War College Study Project, February 20, 1990.

Miller, Chris. "Belarus and the Failure of the Russian World." *American Interest* (blog), April 4, 2017. https://www.the-american-interest.com/2017/04/04/belarus-and-the-failure-of-the-russian-world/.

Miller, James, Pierre Vaux, Catherine Fitzpatrick, and Michael Weiss. *An Invasion by Any Other Name: The Kremlin's Dirty War in Ukraine*. New York: Institute of Modern Russia and *The Interpreter*, September 17, 2015. https://www.imrussia.org/media/pdf/An_Invasion_by_Any_Other_Name.pdf.

Miller, Nathan. *Spying for America: The Hidden History of U.S. Intelligence*. New York: Paragon, 1989.

Miller, Greg, Ellen Nakashima, and Adam Entous. "Obama's Secret Struggle to Punish Russia for Putin's Election Assault." *Washington Post*, June 23, 2017. https://www.washingtonpost.com/graphics/2017/world/national-security/obama-putin-election-hacking/.

Millett, Allan R., and Peter Maslowski. *For the Common Defense*. 3rd ed. New York: Free Press, 2012.

Ministry of Foreign Affairs, People's Republic of China. "Statement of the Government of the People's Republic of China on China's Territorial Sovereignty and Maritime Rights and Interests in the South China Sea." Press Release, July 12, 2016. https://www.fmprc.gov.cn/nanhai/eng/snhwtlcwj_1/t1379493.htm.

Ministry of Foreign Affairs, Republic of Belarus. "Foreign Trade of Belarus in January–June 2017." October 5, 2017. https://mfa.gov.by/en/export/foreign_trade/.

Mohseni, Payam. *The Islamic Awakening: Iran's Grand Narrative of the Arab Uprisings*. Waltham MA: Crown Center for Middle East Studies at Brandeis University, April 2013. https://www.brandeis.edu/crown/publications/meb/MEB71.pdf.

Momen, Moojan. *An Introduction to Shi'i Islam: The History and Doctrines of Twelver Shi'ism*. New Haven: Yale University Press, 1987.

Monaghan, Andrew. *Russian State Mobilization: Moving the Country on to a War Footing*. London: Chatham House, May 2016. https://www.chathamhouse.org/sites/files/chathamhouse/publications/research/2016-05-20-russian-state-mobilization-monaghan-2.pdf.

Montagne, Renee. "The Evolution of Iran's Revolutionary Guard." National Public Radio, April 5, 2007. http://www.npr.org/templates/story/story .php?storyId=9371072.

Morgenthau, Hans J., Kenneth W. Thompson, and David Clinton. *Politics among Nations*. 7th ed. Boston: McGraw-Hill Education, 2005.

Morris, Lyle J. "The New 'Normal' in the East China Sea." *TheRANDblog* (blog), February 27, 2017. https://www.rand.org/blog/2017/02/the-new-normal -in-the-east-china-sea.html.

Morris, Victor. "Grading Gerasimov: Evaluating Russian Nonlinear War Through Modern Chinese Doctrine." *Small Wars Journal* (blog), September 17, 2015. http://smallwarsjournal.com/jrnl/art/grading-gerasimov-evaluating -russian-nonlinear-war-through-modern-chinese-doctrine.

Morrison, Wayne. *China-US Trade Issues*. Washington DC: Congressional Research Service, October 2003.

Movsesian, Mark. "The Clash of Traditions." *Library of Law & Liberty* (blog), July 7, 2017. http://www.libertylawsite.org/2017/07/07/the-clash-of-traditions/.

Moyar, Mark, and Harry G. Summers Jr. *Phoenix and the Birds of Prey: Counterinsurgency and Counterterrorism in Vietnam*. Lincoln NE: Bison, 2007.

Mozaffari, Ali. *Forming National Identity in Iran: The Idea of Homeland Derived from Ancient Persian and Islamic Imaginations of Place*. London: I. B. Tauris, 2013.

Murray, Williamson, and Alan R Millet. *Military Innovation in the Interwar Period*. New York: Cambridge University Press, 1998.

Murray, Williamson, and Peter R. Mansoor, eds. *Hybrid Warfare: Fighting Complex Opponents from the Ancient World to the Present*. New York: Cambridge University Press, 2012.

Nadami, Farzin. "Iran's Afghan and Pakistani Proxies: In Syria and Beyond?." Washington Institute for Near East Policy, August 22, 2016. http://www .washingtoninstitute.org/policy-analysis/view/irans-afghan-and-pakistani -proxies-in-syria-and-beyond.

Nader, Alireza. "The Revolutionary Guards." In *The Iran Primer: Power, Politics, and U.S. Policy*, edited by Robin Wright, 1–5. Washington DC: United States Institute of Peace, 2010. http://iranprimer.usip.org/resource/revolutionary -guards.

Nakashima, Ellen. "Russian Government Hackers Penetrated DNC, Stole Opposition Research on Trump." *Washington Post*, June 14, 2016. https://www .washingtonpost.com/world/national-security/russian-government-hackers -penetrated-dnc-stole-opposition-research-on-trump/2016/06/14/cf006cb4 -316e-11e6-8ff7-7b6c1998b7a0_story.html.

Nankivell, Justin. "China's Use of Lawfare in the South China Sea Dispute." In *China: The Three Warfares*, 427–49. Washington DC: Office of Net Assessment, 2013. https://cryptome.org/2014/06/prc-three-wars.pdf.

National Council of Resistance of Iran, U. S. Representative Office. *How Iran Fuels Syria War: Details of the IRGC Command HQ and Key Officers in Syria.* Washington DC: National Council of Resistance of Iran-U.S. Office, 2016.

———. "Iran: Regime Admits over 40% Iranians View Satellite TV Despite Crackdown." August 28, 2013. http://www.ncr-iran.org/en/news/iran-resistance/14464-iran-regime-admit-over-40-iranians-view-satellite-tv-despite-crackdown.

National Institute for Defense Studies. *East Asian Strategic Review 2015.* Tokyo: Japan Times, 2015.

National Intelligence Council. *Assessing Russian Activities and Intentions in Recent US Elections.* Washington DC: Office of the Director of National Intelligence, January 6, 2017. https://www.dni.gov/files/documents/ICA_2017_01.pdf.

National Security Council. "National Security Council Directive on Office of Special Projects," June 18, 1948. https://history.state.gov/historicaldocuments/frus1945-50Intel/d292.

Navias, Martin S., and E. R. Hooton. *Tanker Wars: The Assault on Merchant Shipping during the Iran-Iraq Crisis 1980–1988.* London: I. B.Tauris, 1996.

Naylor, Hugh. "In Syria's Aleppo, Shiite Militias Point to Iran's Unparalleled Influence." *Washington Post*, November 20, 2016. https://www.washingtonpost.com/world/middle_east/in-syrias-aleppo-shiite-militias-point-to-irans-unparalleled-influence/2016/11/20/2f1a47c2-92cd-11e6-bc00-1a9756d4111b_story.html?utm_term=.3b63cb6873e3.

Nelsen, Harvey. "The U.S. Intelligence Budget in the 1990s." *International Journal of Intelligence and CounterIntelligence* 6, no. 2 (June 1, 1993): 195–203. https://doi.org/10.1080/08850609308435211.

Nelson, Anne. *CCTV's International Expansion: China's Grand Strategy for Media?* Washington DC: Center for International Media Assistance, October 22, 2013.

Newman, Lily Hay. "Hack Brief: Hackers Breach the Ultra-Secure Messaging App Telegram in Iran." *Wired*, August 2, 2016. https://www.wired.com/2016/08/hack-brief-hackers-breach-ultra-secure-messaging-app-telegram-iran/.

Newmyer, Jacqueline. "The Revolution in Military Affairs with Chinese Characteristics." *Journal of Strategic Studies* 33, no. 4 (August 2010): 483–504.

New York Times. "Reds Brought 20,000 Weapons, Fish Committee Is Told." October 9, 1930, 1.

Nguyen, Minh Quang. "The Resurgence of China-Vietnam Ties." *Diplomat*, January 25, 2017. http://thediplomat.com/2017/01/the-resurgence-of-china-vietnam-ties/.

Nichol, Jim. *Russian Military Reform and Defense Policy.* Washington DC: Congressional Research Service, August 24, 2011. https://fas.org/sgp/crs/row/R42006.pdf.

Nikolskaya, Polina, and Gabrielle Tétrault-Farber. "Russia's GDP Growth, at Six-Year High, Raises Question of Durability." Reuters, February 12, 2019. https://www.reuters.com/article/us-russia-economy-gdp-idUSKCN1Q10NO.

Nixon, Richard. *US Foreign Policy for the 1970s: A New Strategy for Peace.* Washington DC: The White House, February 18, 1970. https://history.state.gov/historicaldocuments/frus1969-76v01/d60.

Nocetti, Julien. "Contest and Conquest: Russia and Global Internet Governance." *International Affairs* 91, no. 1 (January 1, 2015): 111–30. https://doi.org/10.1111/1468-2346.12189.

Norris, Pippa, and Ronald Inglehart. *Cultural Backlash and the Rise of Populism: Trump, Brexit, and Authoritarian Populism.* New York: Cambridge University Press, 2019.

Northam, Jackie. "Intelligence Community Rethinks Strategy after Russian Military Moves." Morning Edition. National Public Radio, November 11, 2015. http://www.npr.org/2015/11/11/455577641/intelligence-community-rethinks-strategy-after-russian-military-movements.

Noyce, Frank. *England, India, and Afghanistan.* Cambridge, UK: Cambridge University Press, 2013.

Nye, Joseph. "Systematic Problems: American Policy Toward the Soviet Union." In *The West and the Soviet Union: Politics and Policy,* edited by Gregory Flynn, 194–221. Palgrave Macmillan UK, 1990. https://doi.org/10.1007/978-1-349-20985-9.

Office of Strategic Services. "Outline Plan for Political Warfare for Operation Overlord/Plan for Psychological Warfare Against Germany, Propaganda Objectives and Themes, 1944." Joint Chiefs of Staff and Office of Strategic Services, May 22, 1944. CIA Records Search Tool (CREST) FOIA Database, Central Intelligence Agency. https://www.cia.gov/library/readingroom/docs/CIA-RDP13X00001R000100370007-7.pdf.

Ogburn, Charlton. "Merrill's Marauders: The Truth about an Incredible Adventure." *Harper's,* January 1, 1957.

O'Halpin, Eunan. *Defending Ireland: The Irish State and Its Enemies since 1922.* Oxford, UK: Oxford University Press, 1999.

O'Hern, Steven. *Iran's Revolutionary Guard: The Threat That Grows While America Sleeps.* McLean VA: Potomac, 2012.

Olney, Rachel. "The Rift between Silicon Valley and the Pentagon Is Economic, Not Moral." *War on the Rocks,* January 28, 2019. https://warontherocks.com/2019/01/the-rift-between-silicon-valley-and-the-pentagon-is-economic-not-moral/.

Oltermann, Philip, and Rina Soloveitchik. "How Germany's Russian Minority Could Boost Far Right." *Guardian,* September 22, 2017. http://www.theguardian.com/world/2017/sep/22/how-germanys-russian-minority-could-boost-far-right.

O'Neil, Joseph. "Bowling Alone." *Atlantic*, October 2007. http://www.theatlantic
.com/magazine/archive/2007/10/bowling-alone/306185/.

Onuf, Peter S. *Jefferson's Empire: The Language of American Nationhood.* Char-
lottesville: University of Virginia Press, 2000.

Open Source Center. *Structure of Iran's State-Run TV IRIB.* December 16, 2009.
https://fas.org/irp/dni/osc/iran-tv.pdf.

Orenstein, Mitchell. "Putin's Western Allies," *Foreign Affairs*, August 2, 2017.
https://www.foreignaffairs.com/articles/russia-fsu/2014-03-25/putins
-western-allies.

Organization for Security and Cooperation in Europe. Treaty on Open Skies.
March 24, 1992. https://www.osce.org/files/f/documents/1/5/14127.pdf.

Orlov, Alexander. *The Theory and Practice of Soviet Intelligence.* Articles from
"Studies in Intelligence," 1955–92. Washington DC: Central Intelligence
Agency, 1963. https://catalog.archives.gov/id/7282730.

Oxford Islamic Studies Online, "Sipah-i Pasdaran-i Inqilab-i Islami." Edited by
John L. Esposito. http://www.oxfordislamicstudies.com/article/opr/t125
/e2220, accessed November 4, 2020.

Paddock, Alfred H., Jr. *U.S. Army Special Warfare: Its Origins.* Rev. ed. Lawrence: University Press of Kansas, 2002.

Panda, Ankit. "Pacific Rim States Can (and Will) Move Forward on Trade Without the US." *Diplomat*, November 22, 2016. http://thediplomat.com/2016/11
/pacific-rim-states-can-and-will-move-forward-on-trade-without-the-us/.

Papkova, Irina. *The Orthodox Church and Russian Politics.* Washington DC:
Oxford University Press, 2011.

———. "What Is Really the Role of the Russian Orthodox Church in Russian
Federal Politics?." Lecture at book discussion, Washington DC, November
14, 2011. https://www.wilsoncenter.org/publication/the-orthodox-church
-and-russian-politics.

Parry-Giles, Shawn J. "'Camouflaged' Propaganda: The Truman and Eisenhower Administrations' Covert Manipulation of News." *Western Journal of Communication* 60, no. 2 (June 1, 1996): 146–67. https://doi.org/10
.1080/10570319609374539.

———. "The Eisenhower Administration's Conceptualization of the USIA: The
Development of Overt and Covert Propaganda Strategies." *Presidential
Studies Quarterly* 24, no. 2 (1994): 263–76.

Partrick, Neil. *Nationalism in the Gulf States.* London: London School of Economics Centre for the Study of Global Governance, October 2009. http://
www.lse.ac.uk/middleEastCentre/kuwait/documents/NeilPartrick.pdf.

Patterson, Caitlin. "Russia's Surging Electronic Warfare Capabilities." *Diplomat*, April 19, 2016. http://thediplomat.com/2016/04/russias-surging
-electronic-warfare-capabilities/.

Paul, T. V. *Asymmetric Conflicts: War Initiation by Weaker Powers.* Cambridge,
UK: Cambridge University Press, 1994.

Pearl, Mike. "We Asked Two Military Experts What Would Happen If Iran Had Nuclear Weapons." Vice (website). March 13, 2015. https://www.vice.com /en_us/article/what-would-happen-if-iran-had-nuclear-weapons-772.

Peck, Michael. "New Study Warns Aircraft Carriers May Be Obsolete (Thanks to Russia and China)." *National Interest*, July 14, 2017. http://nationalinterest .org/blog/the-buzz/new-study-warns-aircraft-carriers-may-be-obsolete -thanks-21542.

Peden, G. C. "Suez and Britain's Decline as a World Power." *Historical Journal* 55, no. 4 (December 2012): 1073–96. https://doi.org/10.1017 /S0018246X12000246.

Pedrozo, Stacy. *China's Active Defense Strategy and Its Regional Impact.* Before the U.S.-China Economic and Security Review Commission (2011). Washington DC. https://www.cfr.org/report/chinas-active-defense-strategy -and-its-regional-impact.

Peker, Emre. "Turkey Says Russia Violated Its Airspace Again." *Wall Street Journal*, January 30, 2016. http://www.wsj.com/articles/turkey-says-russia -violated-its-airspace-again-1454171970.

Perlroth, Nicole. "Cyberespionage Attacks Tied to Hackers in Iran." *New York Times Bits* (blog), May 29, 2014. https://bits.blogs.nytimes.com/2014/05 /29/cyberespionage-attacks-tied-to-hackers-in-iran/.

Perlroth, Nicole, Mark Scott, and Sheera Frenkel. "Cyberattack Hits Ukraine then Spreads Internationally." *New York Times*, June 27, 2017. https://www .nytimes.com/2017/06/27/technology/ransomware-hackers.html.

Peterson, Nolan. "Ukraine's Frozen Front: Trench Warfare Like the Somme." *Newsweek*, March 12, 2016. http://www.newsweek.com/ukrain-frozen -front-trench-warfare-somme-435627.

Peterson, Scott. "Iran Steps Up Recruitment of Shiite Mercenaries for Syrian War." *Christian Science Monitor*, June 12, 2016. http://www.csmonitor .com/World/Middle-East/2016/0612/Iran-steps-up-recruitment-of-Shiite -mercenaries-for-Syrian-war.

Phillip, Abby. "Trump Undercuts His Aides by Contradicting Their Statements." *Washington Post*, June 6, 2017. https://www.washingtonpost.com/politics /trump-undercuts-his-aides-by-contradicting-their-statements/2017/06 /06/1ae3155a-4ad2-11e7-9669-250d0b15f83b_story.html.

Phillips, Catherine. "Leader of Italy's Right-Wing Northern League to Meet Putin." *Newsweek*, December 4, 2014. http://www.newsweek.com/putin -meet-italian-opposition-come-january-289178.

Pifer, Steven. "Pay Attention, America: Russia Is Upgrading Its Military." Brookings Institution, February 5, 2016. https://www.brookings.edu/opinions /pay-attention-america-russia-is-upgrading-its-military/.

Pillsbury, Michael. *The Hundred-Year Marathon: China's Secret Strategy to Replace America as the Global Superpower.* New York: Henry Holt, 2015.

Pipes, Richard. *The Russian Revolution.* New York: Vintage, 1991.

Pisnia, Natalka. "Why Has RT Registered as a Foreign Agent with the US?." BBC. November 15, 2017. http://www.bbc.com/news/world-us-canada -41991683.

PLA Academy of Military Science. *The Science of Military Strategy*. 3rd ed. Beijing: Military Science Press, 2013.

Pollock, David, and Ahmed Ali. "Iran Gets Negative Reviews in Iraq, Even from Shiites." *Washington Institute for Near East Policy* (blog), May 4, 2010. https://www.washingtoninstitute.org/policy-analysis/view/iran-gets -negative-reviews-in-iraq-even-from-shiites.

Pomerantsev, Peter. *Nothing Is True and Everything Is Possible: Adventures in Modern Russia*. London: Faber & Faber, 2015.

Pomerleau, Mark. "Breaking Down China's Electronic Warfare Tactics." *C4IS- RNET* (blog), March 22, 2017. http://www.c4isrnet.com/articles/breaking -down-chinas-electronic-warfare-tactics.

Popescu, Ionut. *Emergent Strategy and Grand Strategy: How American Presidents Succeed in Foreign Policy*. Baltimore MD: Johns Hopkins University Press, 2017.

Popescu, Nicu. "Russia's Soft Power Ambitions." *CEPS Policy Briefs*, nos. 1–12 (2006): 1–3.

Popular Science Monthly. "Trinkets and Jewels—Into the Melting Pot to Help Win the War." April 1918.

Potter, Philip B. K. "Presidential Leadership in American Foreign Policy." In *Leadership in American Politics*, edited by Jeffery A. Jenkins and Craig Volden, 88–103. Lawrence: University Press of Kansas, 2018.

Pratt, Julius W. "The Land Hunger Thesis Challenged." In *The Causes of the War of 1812: National Honor or National Interest?*, edited by Bradford Perkins, 53–57. New York: Holt, Rinehart and Winston, 1962.

Press, Daryl G. "The Myth of Air Power in the Persian Gulf War and the Future of Warfare." *International Security* 26, no. 2 (2001): 5–44.

PressTV. "Bahrainis Hold Nationwide Rallies in Support of Top Shia Cleric." January 6, 2017. https://www.presstv.com/detail/2017/01/06/505016/bahrain -sbeikh-isa-qassem.

——. "Iran Should Boost Passive Defense." September 16, 2015. http://www .presstv.com/Detail/2015/09/16/429380/Ayatollah-Seyyed-Ali-Khamenei -Gholamreza-Jalali-passive-defense.

Price, Monroe. "Iran and the Soft War." *International Journal of Communication* 6 (2012): 2397–2415.

Propaganda Relief Collective. "The Kremlin's Voice: Johan Bäckman." *UpNorth* (blog), September 13, 2016. https://upnorth.eu/the-kremlins-voice-johan -backman/.

PWC. *China Entertainment and Media Outlook 2016–2020*. Beijing: PWC China, 2016. https://www.pwccn.com/en/entertainment-media/em-china-outlook -nov2016.pdf.

Pynnöniemi, Katri, and András Rácz. "Fog of Falsehood: Russian Strategy of Deception and the Conflict in Ukraine." Finnish Institute for International Affairs, May 10, 2016. http://www.fiia.fi/en/publication/588/fog _of_falsehood/.

Pynnöniemi, Katri, and Sinikukka Saari. "Hybrid Influence—Lessons from Finland." NATO Review, June 28, 2017. http://www.nato.int/docu/review /2017/Also-in-2017/lessons-from-finland-influence-russia-policty-security /EN/index.htm.

Qara'ati, Muhsin. A Commentary Prayer. Morrisville NC: Lulu, 2014.

Quester, George H. "Origins of the Cold War: Some Clues from Public Opinion." Political Science Quarterly 93, no. 4 (1978): 647–63. https://doi.org /10.2307/2150108.

Quinlivan, James T. "Yes, Russia's Military Is Getting More Aggressive." TheRANDblog (blog), December 2014. http://www.rand.org/blog/2014 /12/yes-russias-military-is-getting-more-aggressive.html.

RadioFreeEurope RadioLiberty. "Power Projection: Comparing NATO and Russian Military Exercises." December 2015. http://www.rferl.org/a/data -visualization-nato-russia-exercises/27212161.html.

Rahnema, Ali. Superstition as Ideology in Iranian Politics: From Majlesi to Ahmadinejad. Cambridge, UK: Cambridge University Press, 2011.

Ramzy, Austin. "China Resumes Diplomatic Relations with Gambia, Shutting Out Taiwan." New York Times, March 18, 2016. https://www.nytimes.com /2016/03/19/world/asia/china-gambia-taiwan-diplomatic-relations.html.

Raphaeli, Nimrod. "Violations of Iranian Sanctions: The Role of Multi-National Banks." MEMRI (Middle East Media Research Institute), October 22, 2013. https://www.memri.org/reports/violations-iranian-sanctions-role-multi -national-banks.

Rapoza, Kenneth. "Europe Devises Energy Security Measures to Reduce Russia Dependence." Forbes Investing (blog), February 9, 2016. https://www .forbes.com/sites/kenrapoza/2016/02/09/europe-devises-energy-security -measures-to-reduce-russia-dependence/?sh=7ba656ce235c.

Raud, Mikk. China and Cyber: Attitudes, Strategies, Organisation. Tallinn, Estonia: NATO Cooperative Cyber Defence Centre of Excellence, August 2016. https://ccdcoe.org/uploads/2018/10/CS_organisation_CHINA_092016 _FINAL.pdf.

Read, James H. "'Our Complicated System': James Madison on Power and Liberty." Political Theory 23, no. 3 (1995): 452–75.

"Red Herring Report." Baltimore Sun, January 18, 1931, 8.

Republic of China Tourism Bureau. "Visitor Arrivals by Residence." Ministry of Transportation and Communication. https://admin.taiwan .net.tw/English/FileUploadCategoryListE003130.aspx?appname= FileUploadCategoryListE003130, accessed April 5, 2017.

Resis, Albert. "The Churchill-Stalin Secret 'Percentages' Agreement on the Balkans, Moscow, October 1944." *American Historical Review* 83, no. 2 (1978): 368–87. https://doi.org/10.2307/1862322.

Reuters. "Baltics Can Keep Lights on If Russia Turns off the Gas." May 7, 2014. https://www.reuters.com/article/us-ukraine-crisis-baltics-analysis-idUSBREA460JN20140507.

———. "China Says More than 40 Countries Support Its Stance on South China Sea Dispute." May 20, 2016. http://www.reuters.com/article/us-southchinasea-china-idUSKCN0YB1EO.

———. "China's CCTV Launches Global 'Soft Power' Media Network to Extend Influence." December 31, 2016. https://www.reuters.com/article/us-china-cctv/chinas-cctv-launches-global-soft-power-media-network-to-extend-influence-idUSKBN14K05N.

———. "Croatian Investor in Finnish Reactor Has Russian-Born Owners." July 7, 2015. https://www.reuters.com/article/us-fennovoima-nuclear-idUSKCN0PH0WG20150707.

———. "Iran May Seek Naval Bases in Yemen or Syria: Chief of Staff." November 27, 2016. http://www.reuters.com/article/us-iran-navy-yemen-syria-idUSKBN13M08M.

———. "Russia Moves Nuclear-Capable Missiles into Kaliningrad." October 8, 2016. http://www.reuters.com/article/us-russia-usa-missiles-confirm-idUSKCN1280IV.

———. "Sweden Drops Objections to Port Striking Nord Stream Deal." January 30, 2017. https://www.reuters.com/article/us-sweden-nordstream/sweden-drops-objections-to-port-striking-nord-stream-deal-idUSKBN15E1RI.

———. "Sweden Protests against Airspace Violation by Russian Planes." September 19, 2014. https://www.reuters.com/article/us-sweden-russia-warplanes-idUSKBN0HE1WM20140919.

———. "Two British Jets Dispatched after Russian Incursion." May 27, 2017. https://www.reuters.com/article/us-britain-jets-idUSKBN18N0H4.

Richter, Jan. "How Will Crimea Crisis Change Czech-Russian Trade Relations?." Radio Praha, March 27, 2014. http://www.radio.cz/en/section/panorama/how-will-crimea-crisis-change-czech-russian-trade-relations.

Rid, Thomas. *Disinformation: A Primer in Russian Active Measures and Influence Campaigns.* Before Senate Select Committee on Intelligence (2017). https://www.intelligence.senate.gov/sites/default/files/documents/os-trid-033017.pdf.

Rinehart, Ian, and Bart Elias. *China's Air Defense Identification Zone (ADIZ).* Washington DC: Congressional Research Service, January 20, 2015. https://fas.org/sgp/crs/row/R43894.pdf.

Roberts, J. A. G. *A Concise History of China.* Cambridge MA: Harvard University Press, 1999.

Robertson, James I., ed. *Military Strategy in the American Civil War*. Signature Conference Series, vol. 3. Richmond VA: Virginia Sesquicentennial of the American Civil War Commission, 2012.

Robinson, Linda. "The Future of Special Operations: Beyond Kill and Capture." *Foreign Affairs* 91, no. 6 (December 2012): 110–18.

Roblin, Sebastien. "Why America Should Fear China's Electronic Warfare Plane." *National Interest*, April 29, 2017. http://nationalinterest.org/blog/the-buzz/why-america-should-fear-chinas-electronic-warfare-plane-20402.

Rogers, Clifford J. "Clausewitz, Genius, and the Rules." *Journal of Military History* 66, no. 4 (2002): 1167–76. https://doi.org/10.2307/3093268.

Rogin, Joshua. "The Top 10 Chinese Cyber Attacks (That We Know Of)." *Foreign Policy* (blog), January 10, 2010. https://foreignpolicy.com/2010/01/22/the-top-10-chinese-cyber-attacks-that-we-know-of/.

Rohac, Dalibor, Edit Zgut, and Lóránt Győri. *Populism in Europe and Its Russian Love Affair*. Washington DC: American Enterprise Institute, January 2017. http://www.aei.org/publication/populism-in-europe-and-its-russian-love-affair/.

Romerstein, Herbert, and Eric Breindel. *The Venona Secrets: Exposing Soviet Espionage and America's Traitors*. Washington DC: Regnery, 2001.

Rongxia, Li. "Significance of Zheng He's Voyages." *Beijing Review*, May 28, 2005.

Rosecrance, R. N. "Bipolarity, Multipolarity, and the Future." *Journal of Conflict Resolution* 10, no. 3 (September 1, 1966): 314–27. https://doi.org/10.1177/002200276601000304.

Rosen, Armin. "U.S. Admiral: Russia's Submarine Activity in the North Atlantic Is at Cold War Levels, but We Don't Know Why." *Business Insider*, February 5, 2016. http://www.businessinsider.com/russias-submarine-activity-in-the-north-atlantic-is-at-cold-war-levels-2016-2.

Rosen, Stephen Peter. "Competitive Strategies: Theoretical Foundations, Limits, and Extensions." In *Competitive Strategies for the 21st Century: Theory, History, and Practice*, edited by Thomas G. Mahnken, 12–27. Redwood City CA: Stanford Security Studies, 2012.

Rothstein, Hy S. *Afghanistan and the Troubled Future of Unconventional Warfare*. Annapolis MD: Naval Institute Press, 2006.

Rousso, Alan. "Russia's Transformation: The Prospects for Democracy." *Brown Journal of World Affairs* 7, no. 1 (Spring 2000): 107–27. http://bjwa.brown.edu/7-1/russias-transformation-the-prospects-for-democracy/.

Rovner, Joshua. "Competitive Strategies against Russia Are Seductive, Dangerous, and Unnecessary." *War on the Rocks*, April 16, 2018. https://warontherocks.com/2018/04/competitive-strategies-against-russia-are-seductive-dangerous-and-unnecessary/.

Roy, Denny. *Taiwan's Threat Perceptions: The Enemy Within*. Honolulu: Asia Pacific Center for Security Studies, March 2003.

Rozen, Laura. "Obama's NSC Takes Power." *Foreign Policy* (blog), March 3, 2009. https://foreignpolicy.com/2009/03/03/obamas-nsc-takes-power/.

Rubin, Michael. "Iran Has Never Started a War?." *Commentary Magazine* (blog), March 16, 2016. https://www.commentarymagazine.com/michael-rubin/iran-never-started-war/.

———. *Strategies Underlying Iranian Soft Power.* Fort Leavenworth KS: Foreign Military Studies Office, 2017. https://www.aei.org/research-products/journal-publication/strategies-underlying-iranian-soft-power/.

Rudgers, David F. "The Origins of Covert Action." *Journal of Contemporary History* 35, no. 2 (2000): 249–62.

Rudner, Martin. "Hizbullah Terrorism Finance: Fund-Raising and Money-Laundering." *Studies in Conflict & Terrorism* 33, no. 8 (July 15, 2010): 700–715. https://doi.org/10.1080/1057610X.2010.494169.

Rudnitsky, Jake, John Micklethwait, and Michael Riley. "Putin Says DNC Hack Was a Public Good, But Russia Didn't Do It." *Bloomberg.* September 2, 2016, sec. Politics. https://www.bloomberg.com/news/articles/2016-09-02/putin-says-dnc-hack-was-a-public-good-but-russia-didn-t-do-it.

Russian Federation Ministry of Foreign Affairs. "Foreign Policy Concept of the Russian Federation." June 28, 2000. https://fas.org/nuke/guide/russia/doctrine/econcept.htm.

Sabet, Farzan, and Roozbeh Safshekan. *Soft War: A New Episode in the Old Conflict between Iran and the United States.* Philadelphia: University of Pennsylvania Annenberg School for Communications, June 2014. https://repository.upenn.edu/cgi/viewcontent.cgi?article=1004&context=iranmediaprogram.

Sadjadpour, Karim. *The Battle of Dubai: The United Arab Emirates and the U.S.-Iran Cold War.* Washington DC: Carnegie Endowment for International Peace, July 27, 2011. https://carnegieendowment.org/2011/07/27/battle-of-dubai-united-arab-emirates-and-u.s.-iran-cold-war-pub-45193.

Said, Edward W. *Orientalism.* New York: Knopf Doubleday, 2014.

Salminen, E. *The Silenced Media: The Propaganda War Between Russia and the West in Northern Europe.* London: Palgrave Macmillan, 1999.

Sari, Aurel. "Legal Resilience in an Era of Gray Zone Conflicts and Hybrid Threats." Working Paper. Exeter Centre for International Law, Exeter, UK. January 14, 2019. https://www.law.upenn.edu/live/files/8987-saripdf.

Sarkesian, Sam C. *America's Forgotten Wars: The Counterrevolutionary Past and Lessons for the Future.* Westport CT: Praeger, 1984.

Saunders, Phillip C., Arthur S. Ding, Andrew Scobell, Andrew N. D. Yang, and Joel Wuthnow, eds. *Chairman Xi Remakes the PLA: Assessing Chinese Military Reforms.* Washington DC: National Defense University Press, 2019.

Sawyer, Ralph D. *The Seven Military Classics of Ancient China.* Boulder CO: Westview, 1993.

Schaefer, Agnes Gereben, Darcy Noricks, Benjamin W. Goldsmith, Genevieve Lester, Jeremiah Goulka, Michael A. Wermuth, Martin C. Libicki, and David R. Howell, eds. "The History of Domestic Intelligence in the United States: Lessons for Assessing the Creation of a New Counterterrorism Intelligence Agency." In *The Challenge of Domestic Intelligence in a Free Society: A Multidisciplinary Look at the Creation of a U.S. Domestic Counterterrorism Intelligence Agency*, 13–48. Santa Monica CA: RAND, 2009. https://www.jstor.org/stable/10.7249/mg804dhs.9.

Schapiro, Leonard. "The International Department of the CPSU: Key to Soviet Policy." *International Journal* 32, no. 1 (March 1, 1977): 41–55. https://doi .org/10.1177/002070207703200103.

Schelling, Thomas C. *Arms and Influence*. New Haven CT: Yale University Press, 2008.

Schmeckebier, L. F. "Organization of the Executive Branch of the National Government of the United States: Changes between November 15, 1941, and March 31, 1942." *American Political Science Review* 36, no. 3 (1942): 482–91. https://doi.org/10.2307/1949626.

Schmitt, Gary. "Poland, Hungary, and the Czech Republic: The Security Record of 'New Europe.'" Washington DC: American Enterprise Institute, November 2016. https://www.aei.org/wp-content/uploads/2016/11/Poland-Hungary -and-the-Czech-Republic.pdf.

Schrecker, Ellen. "Soviet Espionage in America: An Oft-Told Tale." *Reviews in American History* 38, no. 2 (2010): 355–61. https://doi.org/10.1353/rah.0.0207.

Schwartz, Lowell H. *Political Warfare against the Kremlin: US and British Propaganda Policy at the Beginning of the Cold War*. Basingstoke, UK: Palgrave Macmillan, 2009.

Scobell, Andrew. "Is There a Chinese Way of War?." *Parameters* 35, no. 1 (March 1, 2005): 118–22. https://press.armywarcollege.edu/parameters/vol35/iss1/12.

———. *China and Strategic Culture*. Carlisle PA: U.S. Army War College, 2002. https://www.globalsecurity.org/military/library/report/2002/ssi_scobell.pdf.

Sedarat, Firouz. "Satellite TV News, Serials Widen Iranian-Arab Gulf." Reuters, December 14, 2011. http://www.reuters.com/article/us-arabs-iran -television-idUSTRE7BD11Q20111214.

Seddon, Max. "Belarus's Lukashenko Slams Russia over Border Controls." *Financial Times*, February 3, 2017. https://www.ft.com/content/4eeeb5ca -ealf-11e6-893c-082c54a7f539.

Segal, Adam. "China, International Law, and Cyberspace." *Council on Foreign Relations* (blog), October 2, 2012. https://www.cfr.org/blog-post/china -international-law-and-cyberspace.

———. *The Hacked World Order: How Nations Fight, Trade, Maneuver, and Manipulate in the Digital Age*. New York: PublicAffairs, 2016.

Selznick, Philip. *The Organizational Weapon: A Study of Bolshevik Strategy and Tactics*. Santa Monica CA: RAND, January 1952.

Semenov, Alexey. "The Issues of Discrimination of Non-Citizens in the Baltic States." PowerPoint presentation at the Human Dimension Implementation Meeting 2017, Warsaw, September 15, 2017. http://www.cis-emo.net/en/news/issues-discrimination-non-citizens-baltic-states.

Sepp, Kalev I. "From 'Shock and Awe' to 'Hearts and Minds': The Fall and Rise of US Counterinsurgency Capability in Iraq." *Third World Quarterly* 28, no. 2 (2007): 217–30.

Sethi, Abheet. "China behind Pak's Growing Confidence, Supplies 63% of Islamabad's Arms Need." *Hindustan Times*, September 30, 2016. http://www.hindustantimes.com/india-news/china-behind-pak-s-growing-confidence-supplies-63-of-islamabad-s-arms-need/story-fnqRQYRHRRU73kDxmlILdL.html.

Shalal-Esa, Andrea. "Iran Strengthened Cyber Capabilities after Stuxnet: U.S. General." Reuters, January 18, 2013. http://www.reuters.com/article/us-iran-usa-cyber-idUSBRE90G1C420130118.

Shambaugh, David. "China's Military Views the World: Ambivalent Security." *International Security* 24, no. 3 (1999): 52–79.

———. "China's Propaganda System: Institutions, Processes and Efficacy." *China Journal*, no. 57 (January 2007): 25–58.

———. "China's Soft-Power Push." *Foreign Affairs*, June 16, 2015. https://www.foreignaffairs.com/articles/china/2015-06-16/china-s-soft-power-push.

Sharkov, Damien. "Far-Right MEP Accused of Acting as Russian Spy." *Newsweek*, September 26, 2014. http://www.newsweek.com/far-right-mep-accused-acting-russian-spy-273444.

———. "Poland Jails Colonel for Being a Russian Spy." *Newsweek*, May 31, 2016. http://www.newsweek.com/polish-officer-jailed-spying-russia-465017.

———. "Putin's United Russia and Italy's Northern League Sign Cooperation Deal." *Newsweek*, March 6, 2017. http://www.newsweek.com/russias-ruling-party-strikes-cooperation-deal-italian-euroskeptics-564427.

Sharman, J. C. "Shopping for Anonymous Shell Companies: An Audit Study of Anonymity and Crime in the International Financial System." *Journal of Economic Perspectives* 24, no. 4 (December 2010): 127–40. https://doi.org/10.1257/jep.24.4.127.

Shea, Timothy C. "Post-Soviet Maskirovka, Cold War Nostalgia, and Peacetime Engagement." *Military Review* 82, no. 3 (May 1, 2002): 63.

Sheehan, Bernard. *Savagism and Civility: Indians and Englishmen in Colonial Virginia*. Cambridge, UK: Cambridge University Press, 1980.

Shefveland, Kristalyn Marie. "A Dual Strategy: Conventional and Unconventional Warfare." In *The Routledge Handbook of American Military and Diplomatic History: The Colonial Period to 1877*, edited by Christos G. Frentzos and Antonio S. Thompson, 105–12. New York: Routledge, 2014.

Shekhovtsov, Anton. *Russia and the Western Far Right: Tango Noir*. London: Routledge, 2018.

———. "Russian Fascist Militants Give Money to Swedish Counterparts." *Anton Shekhovtsov Blog* (blog), September 19, 2015. http://anton-shekhovtsov .blogspot.com/2015/09/russian-fascist-militants-give-money-to.html.

Shelley, Louise I. *Policing Soviet Society: The Evolution of State Control*. London: Psychology Press, 1996.

Shen, Ming-Shih. "A Study of PLA's Three Warfares—Application Scenarios and Its Inner Logic." PowerPoint presentation, China's Three Warfares Workshop, Taipei, March 24, 2016.

Sherr, James. *Hard Diplomacy and Soft Coercion: Russia's Influence Abroad*. London: Chatham House, 2013.

Shultz, George, and Johnathan Reese. *Turmoil and Triumph: My Years as Secretary of State*. Books on Tape, 1995.

Shultz, Richard. "Soviet Use of Surrogates to Project Power into the Third World." *Parameters* 16, no. 3 (Autumn 1986): 32–42.

Shultz, Richard, and Roy Godson. *Dezinformatsia: Active Measures in Soviet Strategy*. McLean VA: Pergamon-Brassey's, 1984.

Shy, John. "Jomini." In *Makers of Modern Strategy from Machiavelli to the Nuclear Age*, edited by Peter Paret, Gordon A. Craig, and Felix Gilbert, 143–85. Princeton NJ: Princeton University Press, 1986.

———. "The American Military Experience: History and Learning." *The Journal of Interdisciplinary History* 1, no. 2 (1971): 205–28. https://doi.org/10 .2307/202641.

Sibley, Katherine A. S. *Red Spies in America: Stolen Secrets and the Dawn of the Cold War*. Lawrence: University Press of Kansas, 2004.

Sinha, Shreeya, and Susan Campbell Beachy. "Timeline on Iran's Nuclear Program." *New York Times*, March 21, 2013. https://www.nytimes.com /interactive/2014/11/20/world/middleeast/Iran-nuclear-timeline.html.

Skowronek, Stephen. *Building a New American State: The Expansion of National Administrative Capacities, 1877–1920*. Cambridge, UK: Cambridge University Press, 1982.

Smale, Alison. "Austria's Far Right Signs a Cooperation Pact With Putin's Party," *New York Times*, December 19, 2016, sec. Europe. https://www.nytimes .com/2016/12/19/world/europe/austrias-far-right-signs-a-cooperation-pact -with-putins-party.html.

Small, Andrew. *The China-Pakistan Axis: Asia's New Geopolitics*. Oxford: Oxford University Press, 2015.

Smith, Geoffrey. "Le Pen Visits Putin Amid Fears of Russian Interference in French Vote." *Fortune* (blog), August 2, 2017. http://fortune.com/2017/03 /24/putin-french-election-marine-le-pen-russia/.

Smith, George Winston. "Union Propaganda in the American Civil War." *Social Studies* 35, no. 1 (January 1, 1944): 26–32. https://doi.org/10.1080 /00220973.1936.11016899.

Smith, Llewellyn. "Economic Security and Unemployment Insurance." *Economic Journal* 20, no. 80 (December 1910): 513–29.

Smith, Nicola. "China Is Using Tourism to Hit Taiwan Where It Really Hurts." *Time*, November 16, 2016. http://time.com/4574290/china-taiwan-tourism-tourists/.

Smyth, Gareth. "Deciphering the Iranian Leader's Call for a 'Resistance Economy.'" *Guardian*, April 19, 2016. https://www.theguardian.com/world/iran-blog/2016/apr/19/iran-resistance-economy-tehranbureau.

Snyder, Jack. "The Soviet Strategic Culture: Implications for Limited Nuclear Operations." Santa Monica CA: RAND, September 1977. http://www.rand.org/content/dam/rand/pubs/reports/2005/R2154.pdf.

Soldatov, Andrei, and Irina Borogan. *The New Nobility: The Restoration of Russia's Security State and the Enduring Legacy of the KGB*. New York: PublicAffairs, 2011.

——. *The Red Web: The Struggle Between Russia's Digital Dictators and the New Online Revolutionaries*. New York: PublicAffairs, 2015.

Son, H. J. "Seoul Proposes GSOMIA to Beijing." *Dong-A Daily*. October 29, 2016, English ed. http://english.donga.com/Home/3/all/26/770443/1.

Sonne, Paul, and Farnaz Fassihi. "Tehran's TV Channel Loses British License." *Wall Street Journal*, January 21, 2012. http://www.wsj.com/articles/SB10001424052970204616504577172763781772708.

Soroka, George. "Putin's Patriarch." *Foreign Affairs (blog)*, February 11, 2016. https://www.foreignaffairs.com/articles/russian-federation/2016-02-11/putins-patriarch.

Spade, Jayson. *Information as Power: China's Cyber Power and America's National Security*. Carlisle Barracks PA: U.S. Army War College, May 2012. https://www.hsdl.org/?view&did=719179.

Spektorowski, Alberto. "The Intellectual New Right, the European Radical Right and the Ideological Challenge to Liberal Democracy." *International Studies* 39, no. 2 (May 2002): 165–82. https://doi.org/10.1177/002088170203900203.

Sputnik News. "Russian Baltic Fleet Naval Aviation Holds Air Combat Drills," October 30, 2015. https://sputniknews.com/military/201510301029330020-russian-baltic-fleet-aviation-drills/.

Squire, P. S. *The Third Department*. London: Cambridge University Press, 1968.

Standish, Reid. "Why Is Finland Able to Fend Off Putin's Information War?." *Foreign Policy* (blog), March 1, 2017. https://foreignpolicy.com/2017/03/01/why-is-finland-able-to-fend-off-putins-information-war/.

Stanley, Willis. "Iranian Strategic Culture and Its Persian Origins." In *Strategic Culture and Weapons of Mass Destruction*. Initiatives in Strategic Studies: Issues and Policies, edited by Jeanie Johnson, Kerry Kartchner, and Jeffrey Larsen, 137–56. New York: Palgrave Macmillan, 2009.

Starr, Barbara, Jim Sciutto, Jim Acosta, Stephen Collinson, and Tom LoBianco. "10 U.S. Sailors in Iranian Custody." CNN, January 12, 2016. http://www.cnn.com/2016/01/12/politics/10-u-s-sailors-in-iranian-custody/index.html.

State Council Information Office of the People's Republic of China. "China's Military Strategy," May 26, 2015. http://eng.mod.gov.cn/DefenseNews/2015-05/26/content_4586748.htm.

Stewart, Richard W., ed. *American Military History*. Vol. 1, *The United States Army and the Forging of a Nation, 1775–1917*. 2nd ed. Washington DC: United States Army Center of Military History, 2009. https://www.armyupress.army.mil/Portals/7/educational-services/military-history/american-military-history-volume-1.pdf.

——. *American Military History*. Vol. 2, *The United States Army in a Global Era, 1917–2008*. 2nd ed. Washington DC: United States Army Center of Military History, 2010.

Stoecker, Sally W. *Forging Stalin's Army: Marshal Tukhachevsky and the Politics of Military Innovation*. Boulder CO: Routledge, 1998.

Stokes, Bruce. "Hostile Neighbors: China vs. Japan." Pew Research Center, Global Attitudes & Trends, September 13, 2016. https://www.pewresearch.org/global/2016/09/13/hostile-neighbors-china-vs-japan/.

Stokes, Mark. "CMC Political Work Department Influence Operations: Opportunities and Challenges for the United States." PowerPoint presentation, Chinese Three Warfares Workshop, Taipei, March 24, 2016 (available upon request).

Stokes, Mark, and Russell Hsiao. *The People's Liberation Army General Political Department: Political Warfare with Chinese Characteristics*. Arlington VA: Project 2049 Institute, October 14, 2013. https://project2049.net/wp-content/uploads/2018/04/P2049_Stokes_Hsiao_PLA_General_Political_Department_Liaison_101413.pdf.

Stratfor. "Iran's Ties to the Bahraini Opposition," September 27, 2011. https://worldview.stratfor.com/article/irans-ties-bahraini-opposition.

Stuart, Reginald C. *War and American Thought: From the Revolution to the Monroe Doctrine*. Kent OH: Kent State University Press, 1982.

Stueck, William. *The Korean War*. Princeton NJ: Princeton University Press, 1997.

Sulc, Lawrence B. *Active Measures, Quiet War and Two Socialist Revolutions*. Washington DC: Nathan Hale Institute, n.d. https://www.cia.gov/library/readingroom/docs/CIA-RDP90-00806R000200720008-2.pdf.

Sun, Tzu. *The Art of Warfare*. Translated by Roger T. Ames. New York: Ballantine, 1993.

Sun, Yat-sen. *Fundamentals of National Reconstruction*. Taipei: China Cultural Service, 1953.

Suri, Jeremi. "Explaining the End of the Cold War: A New Historical Consensus?" *Journal of Cold War Studies* 4, no. 4 (October 1, 2002): 60–92. https://doi.org/10.1162/15203970260209518.

Sutyagin, Igor. "Zapad-2017: Why Do the Numbers Matter?." *Commentary* (blog), Royal United Services Institute, September 12, 2017. https://rusi .org/commentary/zapad-2017-why-do-numbers-matter.

Suwaidi, Jamal S., ed. *Iran and the Gulf: A Search for Stability.* London: I. B.Tauris, 1996.

Svechin, Aleksandr. *Strategy.* Minneapolis MN: East View Press, 1992.

Swaine, Michael D., and Ashley J. Tellis. *Interpreting China's Grand Strategy: Past, Present, and Future.* Santa Monica CA: RAND, 2000. http://www .rand.org/pubs/monograph_reports/MR1121.html.

Szabo, Ernest. *Operational Issues of Insurgency/Counter Insurgency: The Maccabean Revolt.* Fort Leavenworth KS: Army Command and General Staff College, 1997. http://www.dtic.mil/docs/citations/ADA331346.

T & R Productions LLC and ANO TV-Novosti. "Exhibit A to Registration Statement Pursuant to the Foreign Agents Registration Act of 1938, as Amended." November 11, 2017. https://www.fara.gov/docs/6485-Exhibit -AB-20171110-2.pdf.

Tabnak News. "ABNA Site Was Filtered in Saudi Arabia and Bahrain." March 13, 2011. http://www.tabnak.ir/fa/news/153150.

Tap, Bruce. *Over Lincoln's Shoulder: The Committee on the Conduct of the War.* Lawrence: University Press of Kansas, 1998.

TASS Russian News Agency. "Russian Government Approves 2018 State Arms Procurement Program." December 22, 2017. http://tass.com/defense /982420.

——. "Russian State Armaments Program to Focus on Precision Weaponry—Defense Official." November 23, 2017. http://tass.com/defense/977195.

——. "Russia's Gas Pipelines to Europe by 2018." January 29, 2015. http:// tass.com/infographics/7275.

Taylor, Adam. "'Novorossiya,' the Latest Historical Concept to Worry About in Ukraine." *Washington Post,* April 18, 2014. https://www.washingtonpost .com/news/worldviews/wp/2014/04/18/understanding-novorossiya-the -latest-historical-concept-to-get-worried-about-in-ukraine/.

Telhami, Shibley. "Al Jazeera: The Most-Feared News Network." *Brookings Institution* (blog), June 15, 2013. https://www.brookings.edu/articles/al-jazeera -the-most-feared-news-network/.

Than, Krisztina. "Special Report: Inside Hungary's $10.8 Billion Nuclear Deal with Russia." Reuters, March 30, 2015. http://www.reuters.com/article /us-russia-europe-hungary-specialreport-idUSKBN0MQ0MP20150330.

Thant, Myint-U. "Why Burma Must Reset Its Relationship with China." *Foreign Policy,* January 12, 2016. https://foreignpolicy.com/2016/01/12/why -burma-must-reset-its-relationship-with-china/.

Thomas, Timothy. "Nation-State Cyber Strategies: Examples from China and Russia." In *Cyberpower and National Security,* edited by Franklin Kramer, Stuart H. Starr, and Larry Wentz, 465–90. Lincoln NE: Potomac, 2009.

————. "New Developments in Chinese Psychological Warfare." *Special Warfare* 16, no. 1 (April 2003): 2–11. https://apps.dtic.mil/sti/pdfs/ADA434978.pdf.

————. "Russia's Reflexive Control Theory and the Military." *Journal of Slavic Military Studies* 17 (2004): 237–56. https://www.rit.edu/~w-cmmc/literature /Thomas_2004.pdf.

Thompson, Mark. "Iranian Cyber Attack on New York Dam Shows Future of War." *Time*, March 24, 2016. http://time.com/4270728/iran-cyber-attack -dam-fbi/.

Tiku, Nitasha. "The Line Between Big Tech and Defense Work." *Wired*, May 21, 2018. https://www.wired.com/story/the-line-between-big-tech-and -defense-work/.

Tomkins, Richard. "NATO Interception of Russian Planes in Baltics Rise." United Press International, January 11, 2016. http://www.upi.com/Business_News /Security-Industry/2016/01/11/NATO-interception-of-Russian-planes-in -Baltics-rise/3031452534461/.

Tomlinson, Lucas. "More Russian Spy Planes, Bombers Approach Alaskan Airspace." Fox News, April 21, 2017. https://www.foxnews.com/us/more -russian-spy-planes-bombers-approach-alaskan-airspace.

————. "Russian Spy Ship Spotted Back off U.S. Coast." Fox News, March 15, 2017. http://www.foxnews.com/us/2017/03/15/russian-spy-ship-spotted -back-off-u-s-coast.html.

Tor, Deborah. "The Islamisation of Iranian Kingly Ideals in the Persianate Furstenspiegel." *Journal of the British Institute of Persian Studies* 49 (2011): 15–22. https://www.academia.edu/1280808/The_Islamisation_of_Iranian _Kingly_Ideals_in_the_Persianate_Furstenspiegel.

Towfighi, Parviz S. *From Persian Empire to Islamic Iran: A History of Nationalism in the Middle East*. Lampeter, Wales: Edwin Mellen, 2009.

Toynbee, Arnold J. *A Study of History*. Vol. 1. Third Impression ed. Oxford, UK: Oxford University Press, 1945.

Trask, David F. *The AEF and Coalition Warmaking,1917–1918*. Lawrence: University Press of Kansas, 1993.

Treisman, Daniel. "Why Putin Took Crimea." *Foreign Affairs*, April 18, 2016. https://www.foreignaffairs.com/articles/ukraine/2016-04-18/why-putin -took-crimea.

Trenin, Dmitri. "The Georgian-Russian Crisis: Objectives, Strategies, and Outcomes." *Carnegie Moscow Center* (blog), http://carnegie.ru/2006/10/13 /georgian-russian-crisis-objectives-strategies-and-outcomes-pub-18786, accessed October 4, 2017.

Trofimov, Yaroslav. "After Islamic State, Fears of a 'Shiite Crescent' in Mideast." *Wall Street Journal*, September 29, 2016. http://www.wsj.com/articles/after -islamic-state-fears-of-a-shiite-crescent-in-mideast-1475141403.

Trotsky, Leon. *The Third International after Lenin*. Atlanta GA: Pathfinder Press, 1996.

Troy, Thomas. *Donovan and the* CIA: *A History of the Establishment of the Central Intelligence Agency.* Frederick MD: University Publications of America, 1981.

Trubowitz, Peter, Emily O. Goldman, and Edward Rhodes. *The Politics of Strategic Adjustment: Ideas, Institutions, and Interests.* New York: Columbia University Press, 1999.

Truman, Harry S. "President Harry S. Truman's Address before a Joint Session of Congress." Washington DC, March 12, 1947. http://avalon.law.yale .edu/20th_century/trudoc.asp.

Tsiang, T'ing-fu. "China and European Expansion." *Politica* 2, no. 5 (March 1936): 1–18.

Tsou, Tang. *The Cultural Revolution and Post-Mao Reforms: A Historical Perspective.* Chicago: University of Chicago Press, 1999.

Tsvetkova, Maria. "Exclusive: Russian Private Security Firm Says It Had Armed Men in East Libya." Reuters, March 13, 2017. http://www.reuters.com/article /us-russia-libya-contractors-idUSKBN16H2DM.

Tucker, David, and Christopher J. Lamb. "Restructuring Special Operations Forces for Emerging Threats." *Strategic Forum*, Institute for National Strategic Studies, January 2006. http://permanent.access.gpo.gov/lps496 /Strforum/sf219/SF_219.pdf.

Turse, Nick. "The Special Ops Surge: America's Secret War in 134 Countries." *TomDispatch* (blog), The Nation Institute, January 16, 2014. http://www .tomdispatch.com/blog/175794/.

Twining, David T. "Soviet Strategic Culture—The Missing Dimension." *Intelligence and National Security* 4, no. 1 (January 1, 1989): 169–87. https://doi .org/10.1080/02684528908431992.

United Nations. *United Nations Treaties and Principles on Outer Space.* New York: United Nations, 1999. http://www.unoosa.org/pdf/reports/ac105 /AC105_722E.pdf

U.S. Army Special Operations Command. *"Little Green Men": A Primer on Modern Russian Unconventional Warfare, Ukraine 2013–2014.* Fort Bragg NC: U.S. Army Special Operations Command, n.d. https://info.publicintelligence .net/USASOC-LittleGreenMen.pdf.

U.S. Department of Defense. *Annual Report to Congress: Military and Security Developments Involving the People's Republic of China 2016.* Arlington VA: Office of the Secretary of Defense, April 2016. https://www.defense.gov/Portals /1/Documents/pubs/2016%20china%20military%20power%20report.pdf.

———. *Defense Directive 5111.11.* Washington DC: Government Printing Office, August 2001.

———. *Summary of the 2018 National Defense Strategy of the United States of America: Sharpening America's Competitive Edge.* Arlington VA: Office of the Secretary of Defense, January 2018. https://www.defense.gov/Portals/1 /Documents/pubs/2018-National-Defense-Strategy-Summary.pdf.

U.S. Department of State. "Message of the President of the United States to the Two Houses of Congress, at the Commencement of the Second Session of the Thirty-Seventh Congress." *Foreign Relations of the United States*, 1861. http://digicoll.library.wisc.edu/cgi-bin/FRUS/FRUS-idx?type=header&id=FRUS.FRUS1861v01&isize=XL.

———. New Strategic Arms Reduction Treaty, Appendix on Inspection Activities. Prague, Czech Republic, April 8, 2010. http://www.state.gov/documents /organization/141293.pdf.

———. *Soviet Influence Activities: A Report on Active Measures and Propaganda, 1986–87*. Washington DC: Department of State, October 1987. http://www .iwp.edu/docLib/20140714_SovietInfluenceActivities.pdf.

U.S. Department of Treasury. "Fact Sheet: Treasury Designates Iranian Entities Tied to the IRGC and IRISL," December 21, 2010. https://www.treasury .gov/press-center/press-releases/Pages/tg1010.aspx.

———. "Fact Sheet: U.S. Treasury Department Targets Iran's Support for Terrorism. Treasury Announces New Sanctions Against Iran's Islamic Revolutionary Guard Corps-Qods Force Leadership." Press Center, August 3, 2010. https://www.treasury.gov/press-center/press-releases/Pages/tg810.aspx.

———. "Update on the Continuing Illicit Finance Threat Emanating from Iran." June 22, 2010. https://www.fincen.gov/resources/advisories/fincen -advisory-fin-2010-a008.

U.S. Government Accountability Office. "Iran: U.S. and International Sanctions Have Adversely Affected the Iranian Economy," no. GAO-13-326 (February 25, 2013). https://www.gao.gov/products/GAO-13-326.

Van Alstyne, Richard W. *The Rising American Empire*. 2nd ed. New York: W. W. Norton, 1974.

Verstappen, Stefan H. *The Thirty-Six Strategies of Ancient China*. San Francisco: China Books & Periodicals, 1999.

Vesti. "Белоруссия получила российский кредит на $700 млн" ["Belarus received $700 million in Russian credit"], September 15, 2017. Accessed September 25, 2017. http://www.vestifinance.ru/articles/91025 (site discontinued).

———. "Потребительский сектор стран ЕАБР на пути к росту" ["The consumer sector of EDB countries is on the way to growth"], September 8, 2017. Accessed September 25, 2017. http://www.vestifinance.ru/articles /90712 (site discontinued).

Villamor, Felipe. "Duterte Says Xi Warned Philippines of War Over South China Sea." *New York Times*. May 19, 2017. https://www.nytimes.com /2017/05/19/world/asia/philippines-south-china-sea-duterte-war.html.

Vittori, Jodi. "How Anonymous Shell Companies Finance Insurgents, Criminals, and Dictators." *Council on Foreign Relations* (blog), September 7, 2017. https://www.cfr.org/report/how-anonymous-shell-companies-finance -insurgents-criminals-and-dictators.

Voeten, Erik, and Paul R. Brewer. "Public Opinion, the War in Iraq, and Presidential Accountability." *Journal of Conflict Resolution* 50, no. 6 (December 1, 2006): 809–30. https://doi.org/10.1177/0022002706291054.

Wagstyl, Stefan. "Merkel Sharpens Attack on US Sanctions against Russia." *Financial Times.* June 16, 2017. https://www.ft.com/content/6fbafa0c-528e -11e7-bfb8-997009366969.

Waldron, Arthur. *The Great Wall of China: From History to Myth.* Cambridge, UK: Cambridge University Press, 1992.

Waley-Cohen, Joanna. "Militarization of Culture in Eighteenth-Century China." In *Military Culture in Imperial China,* edited by Nicola Di Cosmo, 278–95. Cambridge MA: Harvard University Press, 2009.

———. *The Culture of War in China: Empire and the Military under the Qing.* London: I. B. Tauris, 2014.

Walt, Stephen M. "Alliance Formation and the Balance of World Power." *International Security* 9, no. 4 (1985): 3–43. https://doi.org/10.2307 /2538540.

Walt, Vivienne. "Why France's Marine Le Pen Is Doubling Down on Russia Support." *Time,* January 8, 2017. http://time.com/4627780/russia-national -front-marine-le-pen-putin/.

Walton, C. Dale. *Grand Strategy and the Presidency: Foreign Policy, War and the American Role in the World.* Milton Park, UK: Routledge, 2012.

Waltz, Kenneth N. "The Stability of a Bipolar World." *Daedalus* 93, no. 3 (1964): 881–909.

———. *Theory of International Politics.* Long Grove IL: Waveland, 2010.

Wang, Robert S. "China's Evolving Strategic Doctrine." *Asian Survey* 24, no. 10 (1984): 1040–55. https://doi.org/10.2307/2644218.

Wang, Yuan-kang. *Harmony and War: Confucian Culture and Chinese Power Politics.* New York: Columbia University Press, 2010.

Ward, Steven R. *Immortal: A Military History of Iran and Its Armed Forces.* Reprint ed. Washington DC: Georgetown University Press, 2014.

Wass de Czege, Huba. "Systemic Operational Design: Learning and Adapting in Complex Missions." *Military Review,* February 2009, 2–12.

Watkins, Eli. "Trump Chastises Intel Chiefs after They Contradict Him on Iran and Claims of Foreign Policy Success." CNN, January 30, 2019. https://www .cnn.com/2019/01/30/politics/trump-intel-chiefs-foreign-policy-iran-isis -north-korea/index.html.

Watts, Barry. "Barriers to Acting Strategically: Why Strategy Is So Difficult." In *Competitive Strategies for the 21st Century: Theory, History, and Practice,* edited by Thomas G. Mahnken, 47–68. Redwood City CA: Stanford Security Studies, 2012.

Wee, Sui-Lee. "China's New Cybersecurity Law Leaves Foreign Firms Guessing." *New York Times,* May 31, 2017. https://www.nytimes.com/2017/05/31 /business/china-cybersecurity-law.html.

Weeks, William Earl. *Building the Continental Empire: American Expansion from the Revolution to the Civil War.* Chicago: Ivan R. Dee, 1997.

Wehrey, Frederic. "Ominous Divide: Shiite Iran v Sunni Gulf." United States Institute of Peace. *Iran Primer* (blog), February 18, 2014. https://iranprimer .usip.org/blog/2014/feb/18/ominous-divide-shiite-iran-v-sunni-gulf.

———. "Saudi Arabia Has a Shiite Problem." *Foreign Policy*, December 3, 2014. https://foreignpolicy.com/2014/12/03/saudi-arabia-has-a-shiite-problem -royal-family-saud/.Error! Hyperlink reference not valid.

Wehrey, Frederic, James Dobbins, Kaye Dalia Dassa, and Alireza Nader. "How to Defuse Iran's Nuclear Threat." *RAND Review* 36, no. 1 (Spring 2012): 18–24. https://www.rand.org/pubs/periodicals/rand-review/issues/2012 /spring/iran.html.

Wehrey, Frederic, Jerrold D. Green, Brian Nichiporuk, Alireza Nader, Lydia Hansell, Rasool Nafisi, and S. R. Bohandy. *The Rise of the Pasdaran: Assessing the Domestic Roles of Iran's Islamic Revolutionary Guards Corps.* Santa Monica CA: RAND, 2009. http://www.rand.org/pubs/monographs/MG821 .html.

Weigley, Russell Frank. *The American Way of War: A History of United States Military Strategy and Policy.* Bloomington IN: Indiana University Press, 1977.

Weinstein, Allen, and Alexander Vassiliev. *The Haunted Wood: Soviet Espionage in America—The Stalin Era.* New York: Random House, 2000.

Weiss, Michael. "Revealed: The Secret KGB Manual for Recruiting Spies." *Daily Beast*, December 27, 2017. https://www.thedailybeast.com/the-kgb-papers -how-putin-learned-his-spycraft-part-1.

Wesslau, Fredrik. "Putin's Friends in Europe." *European Council on Foreign Relations* (blog), October 19, 2016. http://www.ecfr.eu/article/commentary _putins_friends_in_europe7153.

The White House. *International Strategy for Cyberspace.* Washington DC, May 2011. https://obamawhitehouse.archives.gov/sites/default/files/rss_viewer /international_strategy_for_cyberspace.pdf.

———. *National Security Strategy of the United States.* Washington DC, December 2017. https://www.whitehouse.gov/wp-content/uploads/2017/12/NSS -Final-12-18-2017-0905.pdf.

———. "Office of Management and Budget Historical Tables: Outlays for Discretionary Programs: 1962–2023." Washington DC, January 4, 2019. https://www.whitehouse.gov/omb/historical-tables/.

White, Leonard. "The Embargo." In *The Causes of the War of 1812: National Honor or National Interest?*, edited by Bradford Perkins, 32–37. New York: Holt, Rinehart and Winston, 1962.

Whittle, Richard. "Former NSC Cyber Head Clarke Calls for Global Cyber Treaty." Breaking Defense, June 16, 2016. http://breakingdefense.com/2016 /06/former-nsc-cyber-head-clarke-calls-for-global-cyber-treaty/.

William, Katie Bo. "Trump Renews Attacks on U.S. Intelligence Community for Contradicting Him." *Defense One*, January 30, 2019. https://www.defenseone.com/politics/2019/01/trump-renews-attacks-intelligence-community-contradicting-him/154539/.

Williams, William Appleman, Andrew J. Bacevich, and Lloyd C. Gardner. *The Tragedy of American Diplomacy*. 50th anniversary ed. New York: W. W. Norton, 2009.

Willis, David. "Warplane Classic: Boeing B-29 and B-50 Superfortress." *International Air Power Review* 22 (2007): 136–69.

Wilson, Scott. "Lebanese Wary of a Rising Hezbollah." *Washington Post*, December 20, 2004. https://www.washingtonpost.com/archive/politics/2004/12/20/lebanese-wary-of-a-rising-hezbollah/a09fad05-e608-4b58-97da-fcb0971bcda3/.

Wilson, Woodrow. "President Woodrow Wilson's Fourteen Points." Address to Congress, Washington DC, January 8, 1918. http://avalon.law.yale.edu/20th_century/wilson14.asp.

———. *The Papers of Woodrow Wilson*. Vol. 44, edited by Arthur S. Link. Princeton NJ: Princeton University Press, 1984.

Wing, Joel. "A History of Iraq's Islamic Dawa Party, Interview with Lowy Institute for International Policy's Dr. Rodger Shanahan." *Musings on Iraq* (blog), August 13, 2012. http://musingsoniraq.blogspot.com/2012/08/a-history-of-iraqs-islamic-dawa-party.html.

Wittaker, Alan G., Frederick C. Smith, and Elizabeth McKune. *The National Security Policy Process: The National Security Council and Interagency System*. Washington DC: National Defense University, October 8, 2010. https://www.hsdl.org/?view&did=690866.

Wojcieszak, Magdalena, Amy Brouillette, and Briar Smith. *Outside In: The Practices of Iranian Diaspora*. Philadelphia: Iran Media Program, University of Pennsylvania, Winter 2013. http://repository.upenn.edu/iranmediaprogram/11.

Wojcieszak, Magdalena, Briar Smith, and Mahmood Enayat. *Finding a Way—How Iranians Reach for News and Information*. Philadelphia: Iran Media Program, University of Pennsylvania, n.d.

Wolfers, Arnold. "'National Security' as an Ambiguous Symbol." *Political Science Quarterly* 67, no. 4 (December 1952): 481–502.

Wortzel, Larry M. "The Chinese People's Liberation Army and Space Warfare." *Astropolitics* 6, no. 2 (June 24, 2008): 112–37.

X [George F. Kennan]. "The Sources of Soviet Conduct." *Foreign Affairs*, July 1, 1947. https://www.foreignaffairs.com/articles/russian-federation/1947-07-01/sources-soviet-conduct.

Xie, Tao. "How Did China Lose South Korea?." *Diplomat*, March 9, 2017. http://thediplomat.com/2017/03/how-did-china-lose-south-korea/.

Xinhua. "China Welcomes More Japanese Investments: Premier Li." September 12, 2019. http://www.xinhuanet.com/english/2019-09/12/c_138384906.htm.

Xu, Beina, and Eleanor Albert. "Media Censorship in China." Council on Foreign Relations, February 17, 2017. https://www.cfr.org/backgrounder/media-censorship-china.

Yang, Bin. *Between Winds and Clouds: The Making of Yunnan (Second Century BCE to Twentieth Century CE)*. New York: Columbia University Press, 2009.

Yardley, Jim, and Hari Kumar. "Kashmir Erupts over Reports of Koran Desecration." *New York Times*, September 13, 2010. http://www.nytimes.com/2010/09/14/world/asia/14kashmir.html.

Yeo, Mike. "China Upgrades Military Infrastructure on South China Sea Islands, Report Claims." *Defense News*, February 9, 2017. https://www.defensenews.com/naval/2017/02/09/china-upgrades-military-infrastructure-on-south-china-sea-islands-report-claims/.

Yu, Yingshi. *Trade and Expansion in Han China: A Study in the Structure of Sino-Barbarian Economic Relations*. Berkeley: University of California Press, 1967.

Yufan, Hao, and Zhai Zhihai. "China's Decision to Enter the Korean War: History Revisited." *China Quarterly*, no. 121 (March 1990): 94–115.

Yung, Christopher. *China's Expeditionary and Power Projection Capabilities Trajectory: Lessons from Recent Expeditionary Operations*. Before U.S.-China Economic and Security Review Commission, United States House of Representatives (January 21, 2016).

Yutang, Lin. *The Importance of Living*. New York: Harper, 1937.

Zakharova, Maria. "Брифинг Официального Представителя МИД России М.В.Захаровой, Москва, 3 Ноября 2016 Года." Russian Ministry of Foreign Affairs Press Conference, November 3, 2016. http://www.mid.ru/foreign_policy/news/-/asset_publisher/cKNonkJE02Bw/content/id/2513436?p_p_id=101_INSTANCE_cKNonkJE02Bw&_101_INSTANCE_cKNonkJE02Bw_languageId=en_GB.

Zarakhovich, Yuri. "Putin's Reunited Russian Church." *Time*, May 17, 2007. http://content.time.com/time/world/article/0,8599,1622544,00.html.

Zhang, Feng. "Confucian Foreign Policy Traditions in Chinese History." *Chinese Journal of International Politics* 8, no. 2 (June 1, 2015): 197–218. https://doi:10.1093/cjip/pov004.

Zhao, Suisheng. "China's Power from a Chinese Perspective (I): A Developing Country Versus a Great Power." In *Assessing China's Power*, edited by Jae Ho Chung, 251–70. London: Palgrave Macmillan, 2015.

Zhou, Fangyin. "Equilibrium Analysis of the Tributary System." *Chinese Journal of International Politics* 4, no. 2 (July 1, 2011): 147–78. https://doi.org/10.1093/cjip/por005.

INDEX

Ba'ath Party, 98
Bacevich, Andrew, 248
Bäckman, Johan, 68
Bahrain, 104, 105, 109, 110
balance: conscious act of, 10; principle of, 125. *See also* power, balance of
Balticconnector, 63–64
Baltic States, 62; gas for, 63–64; incursions into, 82; NATO and, 85–86
Bank of America, 107
Barbary Wars, 192–93
Basij Resistance Force, 95, 112
battlespace, 139, 195, 284n60
Bay of Pigs, 219–20
BBC, 37, 102–3
behavior, 24, 69, 189, 250; adversarial, viii, 16, 258–59, 261n2, 269n93; Chinese, 135, 144, 154–55, 161, 163; cyberspace, 165; revanchist, x
Belarus, 84–85; reliance on Russia by, 273n175; trade with, 70–71
Belt and Road Initiative, 148
Benton, William, 266n43
Berlin Wall, collapse of, 227
Bill of Rights, 216
bin Laden, Osama, 232
bipolarity, 10, 11, 13, 231
Bletchley Park, 208
Boers, x, 20
Bolsheviks, 31–32, 38, 49
Borogan, Irina, 52
botnets, 54, 108
Breedlove, Philip, 46
Bretton Woods, 211
British Secret Service, 188
Bronze Night demonstrations, 54, 270n110
bureaucracy, 39, 120, 150, 246; federal, 216, 238, 240, 252–53; national security, 213, 217, 234, 240, 256–57
Bush, George W., 231

Cambridge Five, 43
capabilities, ix, 6, 22, 28, 168, 281n24; asymmetric, 14, 27, 55, 116, 119, 118, 120, 140; cyber-defense, 106; military, 95, 115–16; modernization, 164; perception of, 262n14

capitalism, 31, 32, 38, 132; countering, 38; experience with, 44; free-market, 212; trade and, 113
Carter, Jimmy, 224
Casey, William, 41, 225
casualties, aversion to, 138, 139, 140, 141, 178, 204, 228, 229, 259, 259
Cathedral of the Assumption (Moscow), 74
Catherine the Great, 30
CCP. *See* Chinese Communist Party (CCP)
CCTV. *See* China Central Television (CCTV)
censorship, 106, 149, 151, 287n121; economic growth and, 150
Central Committee (CPSU), International Department of (Soviet), 39–40
Central Intelligence Agency (CIA), 213, 218, 222, 225, 227, 230; Bay of Pigs and, 219–20; Department of Defense and, 220–21; intelligence estimate by, 37–38; Iranian Coup and, 93; NSC 10/2 and, 214
Central Military Commission, 169
Central Propaganda Department (CPD), 287n121
Central Security Bureau (Russia). *See* KGB
Century of Humiliation, 177
challenges, xii, xiii, 78, 248, 249, 254; addressing, 230; creating, 209–10; doctrinal, 278n40; governance, 30; national-security, 163, 233, 234, 235, 244; solving, 179; strategic, x, 123, 246, 298n8; warfare, 20, 98
checks and balances, 186, 215
Cheka, establishment of, 41
Chesapeake-Leopold Affair, 193–94
Chiang Kai-shek, 133, 134, 177
China. *See* People's Republic of China (PRC)
China Central Television (CCTV), 150, 152
China National Radio, 150
China-Pakistan Economic Corridor, 175
China Radio International, 150
Chinese Coast Guard, 223
Chinese Communist Party (CCP), 133, 146, 149, 164, 170, 240; censorship/economic growth and, 150; CPD of, 287n121; doctrinal uniformity and, 169; ideology and, 134; nationalism and, 138; regional hegemony and, 26–27; social media and, 151, 152

Chinese embassy (Belgrade), bombing of, 138
Churchill, Winston, 207, 210–11
church-state relations (Russia), 74, 75, 76
CIA. *See* Central Intelligence Agency (CIA)
CIS. *See* Commonwealth of Independent States (CIS)
CIS-EMO. *See* Commonwealth of Independent States–Election Monitoring Organization (CIS-EMO)
civil defense, 67, 173
civilization, 121, 201, 203; Chinese, 128, 129, 178; Iranian, 120; Islamic, 90
civil-military relations, 22, 124, 203, 206, 207, 210; Chinese, 169, 175, 179
civil society, 95, 220, 254, 259; media and, 153; organizations, 219, 295n70
Civil War (U.S.): military development following, 196–210; origins of, 181–96
Clausewitz, Carl von, 2, 4, 5, 134, 153, 199, 202, 203, 252, 265n13
Cleveland, Grover, 200–201
Cold War, ix, 14, 15, 25, 41, 45, 56, 214, 215, 219, 231, 235–36, 241, 242, 244, 245; as balancing cycle, 10; bipolarity and, 11; end of, viii, 1, 7, 49, 88, 97, 227, 237, 238, 239; incursions and, 82; politics of, 43; strategic landscape and, 97
colonialism, 30, 182, 183
Color Revolution, 59, 71
Comintern, 40
command, 23, 86, 163, 171, 186, 213, 225, 226; chain of, 39; establishment of, 21; improving, 153, 169, 227; special operations, 49, 80, 81
command and control, 153, 169, 171, 215, 216
Commonwealth of Independent States (CIS), 69–73, 273n169
Commonwealth of Independent States–Election Monitoring Organization (CIS-EMO), 72, 172, 274n188
communication, 166, 203, 295n70; Chinese, 171, 174; Russian, 57; sea lanes of, 159; space-based, 161; vulnerability for, 53
communism, 132, 212, 219, 220, 228; containing, 33, 217, 223; expansion of, 35, 38,

235; ideological war with, 51; moral code of, 36; promise of, 32; threat of, 266n26; Western iterations of, 134
Communist bloc, 62, 64, 65
Communist movement, 31, 39, 43, 265n13
Communist Party of the Soviet Union (CPSU), 31, 32, 43, 74; active measures by, 44; Communist movement and, 39; information and, 41
Communist Party of the United States of America (CPUSA), 33, 40
competition, 102, 127, 161, 180, 191; aimless, 230–36; comprehensive view of, 225; cross-competition, 249; cross-domain, 249; defining, 242; machinery of, 223; military, 21, 185; nonmilitary modes of, 101, 142; realms of, 23; strategic, 44, 299n21; understanding, 240–41, 249; ways of, 15–24, 234. *See also* international competition
competition short of war: conceptualizing, 29–44, 88–94, 123–32, 181–210; contemporary, 44–47, 94–97, 132–38, 210–27
complacency, xi, 24, 236, 260; competition and, 21; power and, 28; reducing, 259
Confederacy (U.S.), 197, 198, 199, 294n47
conflict, 36, 203, 206; armed, 12, 70, 101, 142, 240, 241, 244, 255; cyber, 163, 165; dynamics, 22; environment, 168; international, 9, 39, 155, 160, 229; low-intensity, 116, 182; overt, 144; zones, 49
Confucianism, 128, 129, 134, 155, 178
Congressional Research Service, 245
Congress of Vienna (1814–15), 9
Constitutional Convention, 186
Constitutional Revolution (Russia), 92
Consultative Assembly (Saudi Arabia), 110
Continental Congress, 186
conventional forces, viii, 116, 118, 119, 161, 165, 185, 215
cooperation, 22, 75, 76, 226, 241; bilateral, 154; international, 10
counterespionage, 30, 205
counterinsurgency, 20, 21, 220, 221, 232
Counterinsurgency Field Manual (U.S.), 232
counterterrorism, 231–32, 234

economics, 61, 181, 235

economy, 95, 243, 259; approaches to, 113, 115, 141; censorship and, 150; Chinese, 178; domain of, 22, 23, 68, 92, 159, 252; domestic, 113; growth of, 32, 121, 141, 168, 196; influence of, 73, 117, 146, 153–54; influence operations of, 51–77, 100–116; Iranian, 112–16; issues with, 23, 77, 86, 142, 145, 199, 214, 226, 233–34; market-style, 44; measures of, 69–70, 73; policies of, 144, 194, 206; reforms of, 115, 137, 169; resistance of, 113; Russian, 70, 85

education, 68, 150, 169; military, 295n65; vulnerability, 53

efficacy, 239, 260; decline in, viii-ix, 1; lack of, 27; maximizing, 28; power and, 10; question of, 2–8, 9; understanding of, 3, 13–14

Eisenhower, Dwight, 218, 219, 227

Eisenstadt, Michael, 96, 277n33

election: interference, 26, 59–60, 73; monitoring groups, 71–73, 273n180

electrical-grid attacks, 53

Elements of Military Art and Science (Halleck), 195

embargoes, 193, 194

energy, 162; policy/Soviet, 45; renewable, 63; revenues from, 61; sector, 61, 66, 88

the Enlightenment, 4, 5, 196

environment: cultural, 131; information, 41, 153, 161, 164; political, 59; security, 100; strategic, 2, 18, 121, 124, 180

espionage, 30, 198, 205; cyber, 164; industrial, 33; operations, 34, 126, 166; Russian, 63; Soviet, 33–35

Estonia, 63, 64; cyberattacks against, 54

European Parliament, 65

European Reassurance Initiative, 46

European Union (EU), 46, 65; NATO and, 66; non-NATO states of, 66–69; Russian trade with, 66, 271n149; surge capacity and, 61

Europe of Nations and Freedom (ENF), 65

EW. *See* warfare, electronic

Executive Office of the President, 246, 248

existential crises, 185–86, 187, 202, 244, 249

expansionism, 191, 194, 196, 235; impe-

rial, 265n7; Iranian, 89; messianic, 31; national, 30; object of, 209; principled/moralistic view of, 190; U.S., 187, 293n21

extremism, Islamic, viii, 230, 231

Fairbank, John, 136

Fancy Bear, 54, 56, 270n117

Federal Bureau of Investigation (FBI), 33, 205

Federalists, 187, 189, 190, 192, 193

Federal Security Service (FSB) (Russia), 80; expansion of, 47

Fennovoima nuclear power plant, 69

Fillon, Francois, 271n150

First Ranger Battalion, 208

first-use principle, 80, 157, 170–171

flexibility, 117, 124, 227, 229–30, 241

force allocation, 126, 128, 157

foreign affairs, 92, 155, 189, 248

Foreign Assistance Act, 223

foreign direct investment, 148, 250

foreign policy, 47, 57, 144, 176, 186, 214, 223, 246, 253; direction of, 221–22; efficacy of, x-xi, 8; focus on, 256–57; imperialistic, 295n58; innovation in, 221; military and, viii; objectives of, ix; Russian, 44, 46, 64; Soviet, 39; strategies and, 257; tools of, 219; U.S., 199, 200, 224, 227

"Foundations of the State Cultural Policy" (Russia), 50

"Fourteen Points" speech, 201

Franklin, Benjamin, 187, 188

Freedman, Lawrence, 263n32, 263n33

freedom-of-navigation exercises, 147

Freedom of Navigation Operations, 250

Friedberg, Aaron, 24

Front National (FN), 65

FSB. *See* Federal Security Service (FSB)

Fuller, J. F. C., 204

Garrard, Carol, 275n206

Garrard, John, 275n206

gas imports, 61, 62–64, 65, 68, 70

Gas Interconnection Poland-Lithuania, 63

Gazprom, 67

GCC. *See* Gulf Cooperation Council (GCC)

General Board (U.S.), 199, 200

General Political Department of the People's Liberation Army (GPD) (China), 143, 157

General Security of Military Information Agreement (GSOMIA), 154

General Staff (China), 163, 174

General Staff (U.S.), 200

General Staff of the Armed Forces of Russia, 48

genius, 121, 249, 252, 257; absence of, 5, 260; emergence of, 260; military, 4, 193

geography, 19, 29, 89, 189, 235

George, Alexander, 12–13, 263n32

Georgia, 50, 69, 70, 71; incursions and, 82; invasion of, 78

Georgia-Russia conflict (2008), 53, 80

Gerasimov, Valery, 48

Gerasimov doctrine, 26

GhostNet, 165–66

Godson, Roy, 38, 267n55

Goldwater-Nichols Act (1986), 226, 227

Gorbachev, Mikhail, 42, 44, 74, 268n79

governance, 23, 30, 127, 134, 188, 191, 235, 254; domestic, 124; global, 158; international economic, 212; internet, 55; patterns of, 24; sclerotic, 131; theoratic system of, 110

Grand Armée, 5

Gray, Colin, 16, 17

gray zone, viii, xi, 299n21

Great Game, 264n51

Great Leap Forward, 137

Green Revolution, 106, 108

GRU. *See* Main Intelligence Directorate (GRU) (Russia)

GSOMIA. *See* General Security of Military Information Agreement (GSOMIA)

guerrillas, 93, 135, 183, 218

Gulf Cooperation Council (GCC), 120, 282n133

Gulf States, 100–101, 104, 121, 278n48

Haas, Ernst B., 9

hackers/hacking, 54, 55, 167, 270n117; independent, 165; Iranian, 107, 108; IRGC-backed, 107

Halleck, Henry, 195

Hamilton, Alexander, 186, 189, 190

Han dynasty, 128, 129

Harkin Amendment, 223

hawala system, 114, 281n121

hegemony, x, 10, 11, 14, 24–25, 264n51; regional, 26–27, 130, 148, 179

Hezbollah, 48, 96, 99, 111, 114, 117

Hitler, Adolf, 205

Hoffman, Frank, 20

Homer, 3

Hoover, J. Edgar, 266n26

Hopkins, Harry, 34, 206, 213, 296n88

Hossein, Sultan, 91

Houthis, 117

Huang Shin-kung, 126

Hudson Institute, 55

human agency, 4, 5–6, 18, 22, 28, 238, 261n5; domestic developments and, 7–8; theory/practice and, 15, 24

human capital, 233–34

humanitarian law, 160

human rights, 72, 223

Hungarian Civic Alliance, 63

Huntington, Samuel, 203, 206

Hussein, Saddam, 98, 110

Hyde, Susan, 274n189

identity: Iranian, 89, 90, 92, 93; Russian national, 76

ideology, 73, 156, 217; Bolshevik, 31; CCP, 134; communist, 36, 38, 265n17; Iranian, 95; non-Communist, 42; noncompatable, 198; Soviet, 74, 224–25; U.S., 235, 237

iFilm, 103, 104

Imam Khomeini Relief Committee, 112

Imperial Court (China), 129–30

imperialism, 132, 136; foreign policy of, 295n58

implementation, 254–58; strategic, 257; tools of, 245

Independence Party, 65, 271n150

indirect approach, 23–24, 66, 221

Industrial Revolution, 29, 199

influence: campaign, 54–55; mechanisms of, 35, 36; operations, 37, 153; propagating, 85, 86; regional, 100; supranational, 155

Marx, Karl, 49
Marxism-Leninism, 144, 178
maskirovka, 36, 52, 84, 215, 266n39
May Fourth Movement, 133
Ma Ying-jeou, 145, 146, 153
media, 40–41, 103, 142, 149–50; campaign, 158; Chinese, 150, 151, 152; civil society and, 153; consumers, 56; control of, 150; entertainment, 151; international, 279n69; Iranian, 104; mass, 102; outlets, 153; public-opinion warfare and, 150–55; skepticism of, 266n27; Soviet, 45; state-run, 101; Western, 104. *See also* social media
Medvedev, Dmitry, 76, 274n198
Merkel, Angela, 66
Merrill, Frank, 208
message-delivery vehicles, 151
microblogging platforms, 151
Middle East, 27, 92, 108, 112, 115, 116, 117, 232; engagement in, 100; Iran and, 120
military, 132, 160, 186, 204, 243; action, 69, 120, 140, 141, 189, 192; action, Chinese, 156, 157, 173, 178; action, Iranian, 94, 113; engagement, 1, 19, 88, 201, 215, 226; engagement, justification for, 191; engagement, limiting, 187; engagement, skepticism for, 193; force, xi, 2, 181; foreign policy and, viii; modernization, 137, 141, 142, 164–77; modernization, Chinese, 164, 168, 171; modernization, Russian, 78–81, 85, 86; modernization, U.S., 233; nuclear force and, 171; permanent, 187; power, viii, 12, 78, 116, 183, 185, 242, 256; strategic gains and, 188; U.S. buildup of, 226, 230. *See also* doctrine, military
Military Information Support Operations, xi
military-shaping operations, 77–84, 116–20; modernization and, 164–77
militias, 184, 185, 194; cyber, 165; maritime, 173; Shi'a, 106, 109, 111, 116, 117
Ming dynasty, 25, 129, 130, 131, 177
Ministry of State Security (China), 143
misinformation, 37, 41, 53, 101
missiles, 45, 79, 80, 84, 171, 226, 228; cyber, 166; surface- to-air, 159; testing, 119

mobilization, 97, 127; mass, 78; understandings of, 269n93; wartime, 207
modernization, 137; initiatives, 81, 167, 168; service-specific, 170–74. *See also* military, modernization
Mogadishu, 229
Mohammed Reza Shah, 93
Molotov-Ribbentrop Pact (1939), 33
Monroe Doctrine, 196, 235
morale, 125, 134, 146, 277n33
Moscow Conference, 210
Moscow Patriarchate, 75, 76
Movement for a Better Hungary (Jobbik Party), 63
Mujahedin-e Khalq, 93
Multi-National Force, 98
multipolarity, 24, 248
Muslims, 6, 61, 91, 103, 104, 111

Najaf, 91, 109, 110
Napoleon Bonaparte, 5, 194, 196, 264n51
narratives: influencing, 152–53; media, 40–41; political, 56, 60; power, 86; preexisting, 56; victimhood, 101
nation, definition, 15
National Defense Act (1916), 202
National Defense Strategy (NDS), xii, 22, 23, 254, 255–56, 257
National Democratic Action Society of Bahrain, 278n48
National Intelligence Estimates, 245
national interests, 54, 112, 142, 167, 192, 199, 206, 240, 243, 260
nationalism: Chinese, 132, 134, 138; Iranian, 94; Russian, 60, 65; U.S., 189, 194
national security, xii, 29, 94, 170, 192, 233, 250–51, 253–54; agencies, 87; challenges, 163; decisions, 258; directives, 258; establishment, 217; funding system, 241; policy, 213, 298n8
National Security Act (1947), 212–13, 214
National Security Action Memoranda 57, 220
National Security and National Defense Strategies (2017–18), 242, 257
National Security Concept (Russia), 75

National Security Council (NSC), 217, 245, 249, 258, 299n23; civil servants and, 246; interagency integration and, 256; NSC-68 and, xii, 38, 214; strategy formulation and, 246, 248

National Security Council (NSC)-68, xii, 38, 214, 215, 216, 222–23; strategic brilliance of, 227

National Security Council Directive (NSC) 10/2, 213, 214

National Security Decision Directive (NSDD)-75, 225

National Security Law, 170

National Security Strategy (NSS), xii, 22, 23, 234, 244, 255

Native Americans, 196, 197; Christianization of, 182; engagements with, 182, 199; fighting style of, 183–84; paternalistic view of, 292n1; population decline for, 184

NATO, 39, 46, 54, 71, 77, 84, 212, 218; confrontation with, 85–86; exercises by, 84; expansion of, 66; formerly communist members of, 62–64; incursions and, 82; military engagements for, 49; Russia and, 48, 64–66; strategic position of, 47; ties with, 69

Naval Infantry (Russia), 81

Naval War College (U.S.), 199

navigation: freedom of, 147, 202, 250; shared use, 170

Navy Act (1916), 202

NDS. See National Defense Strategy (NDS)

near abroad, 31, 59, 70

Net Assessment, 17

Network Centric Warfare, 7

networks: creation of, 178; intelligence-gathering, 165–66; international, 37; patronage, 241; pipeline, 61, 62; state-sponsored, 56; Taiwanese, 166

neutrality, 42, 189, 192, 197

Neutrality Act (1935), 205

New China News Agency, 152

New Deal Democrats, 33

New Look, 78, 81, 218, 219, 227

New York Stock Exchange, 107

Nimr, Nimr al-, 110

"nine-dash line" map, 156–57

Nixon, Richard, 221, 222, 223, 224, 258

"no first-use" policy, 80, 157, 170–71

Nord Stream 2, 67

NotPetya attack (2017), 53, 270n113

Novorossiya, 57, 58

NSC. See National Security Council (NSC)

NSDD. See National Council Decision Directive (NSDD)

NSS. See National Security Strategy (NSS)

nuclear age, 208–9, 242

nuclear power plants, 63, 65, 69

nuclear weapons, 6, 10, 11–12, 26, 38, 44, 97, 107, 211, 216, 242; Chinese, 170–71; power of, 11; Russian, 79, 80

Obama, Barack, 166–67, 232, 290n220

Odoacer, 25

Odysseus, 3

Office for Emergency Management, 206–7

Office of Liberation Movements, 96

Office of Net Assessment, 243, 245, 248

Office of Personnel Management, 167, 251

Office of Policy Coordination, 214

Office of Strategic Services (OSS), 208, 211

Office of War Information, 211, 218–19

officer corps, professionalized, 194

oil imports, 61, 65, 67, 68, 70, 113

Okhrana, 30, 31

Operation Desert Storm, 138, 228

Operation Eagle Claw, 224

Operation Iraqi Freedom, 109, 299n18

Operation Overlord, 34, 207

operations, 35–36, 81, 211, 254, 256

Orange Revolution, 72

Organization for Security and Co-operation in Europe (OSCE), 54, 71–72, 73

Organization for Security and Co-operation in Europe–Office for Democratic Institutions and Human Rights (OSCE-ODIHR), 71–72, 273n188

OSS. See Office of Strategic Services (OSS)

outer space, 10, 161, 165, 177, 179

Pakistan, Chinese relations with, 175

Paks nuclear power plant, 62

Palestinian Liberation Organization, 40, 43

Paracel Islands, 159
paramilitaries, 42, 43, 95
Paris Peace Conference (1946), vii
Passive Defense Organization, 107
Pathé, Pierre-Charles, 43
Paul, T. V., 11
peace, vii; dividend, 230; maintaining, 222; sustainable, 9; war and, 28, 206, 213, 220
People's Daily, 150, 152
People's Liberation Army (PLA), 27, 137, 140, 141, 142, 156, 157, 169, 170, 228; components of, 164; divisions of, 171; EW and, 174; ground forces of, 169; nationalism and, 138; political warfare and, 285n96; three wars concept and, 143; work of, 287n142
People's Liberation Army Air Force (PLAAF), 174
People's Liberation Army Navy (PLAN), 172
People's Liberation Army Rocket Force, 171
People's Party of Our Slovakia, 63
People's Republic of China (PRC), 133, 137, 217; competition with, 180; decline of, 25; disapproval rating for, 147; historical development of, 123–28; infiltration by, 146; internal stability of, 131; strategic thinking and, 284n66
people's war, 135, 137, 177–78, 284n66
percentages agreement, 210–11, 296n81
Persian Empire, 90, 93
Persian Gulf, 117, 228
Persian society, 89–90, 92
Peter the Great, 49
petite guerre, 183, 185
Philippines, relations with, 148, 286n116
phishing, 165, 166
Phoenix program, 220–21
Pillsbury, Michael, 125
Pipes, Richard, 265n13
PLA. *See* People's Liberation Army (PLA)
PLAAF. *See* People's Liberation Army Air Force (PLAAF)
PLAN. *See* People's Liberation Army Navy (PLAN)
Plan Orange, 205
Plato, Forms/Ideas and, 3

pluralism, 51, 59, 85, 225
policy initiatives, 34, 75, 243, 244, 245, 246, 247
Politburo, 39, 267n55
politics, 43, 61, 65, 70, 90, 145, 225; conflict/struggle and, 31; great-power, 202, 223; influence of, 51–77, 100–116; international, 31, 203; issues of, 75, 76, 77, 199, 214; operations of, 60–62, 108–16; war and, 134, 284n53; will and, 7, 12, 28, 139, 215, 236, 238, 259, 281n124
populism, 60, 65, 135
Potemkin, Prince Grigory, 30
power, 25, 47, 86, 178; absolute, 27, 156, 238; air, 228; annihilative, 11; balance of, viii, ix, 8–9, 10, 12, 120, 121, 143–44, 168, 173, 216, 239, 240; coercive, 46; complacency and, 28; consolidation of, 222, 223; cyber-warfare, 107; diminishing, 26, 230; diplomatic, 98; dynamics, 11, 28; economic, 98, 132, 200; evolving application of, 164; expanding, 6, 9, 27, 191, 200; foreign policy, 257; hard, 8, 97, 99, 121, 129, 170; imperialistic, 39; informational, 98; inherent, 246; instruments of, 22; interplay of, 8–14; military, 132, 185; national, viii, xi, 1, 2, 22, 35, 98, 192, 199, 214, 237, 239, 252, 256, 258; naval, 199, 281n132; obligations of, 209; perceptions of, 239, 242; projection of, 117, 226; relative, xii, 8, 10, 13, 14, 24; soft, 109, 115, 121, 130; spectrum of, 242; strategic configuration of, 125; tools of, 19, 44. *See also* military, power
practice, theory and, 2, 3, 4, 7, 28, 261n5
PRC. *See* People's Republic of China (PRC)
Press TV, 103, 105
The Prince (Machiavelli), 3
Progressive Era, 200, 201
propaganda, 51, 63, 68, 135, 153, 188, 198, 204, 207, 223, 225; agitation, 37, 56; anti-American, 36; countering, 56, 222; distributing, 40; domestic, 150; government, 56, 204; recognition of, 149
provocation, 47, 50, 147, 148, 215, 259, 296n94

proxy wars, 10, 11, 27, 96, 217

psychological operations, xi, 126, 139, 144, 149, 153, 204, 217, 220

Psychological Warfare Center (U.S.), 218

public opinion, 42, 57, 149–50, 198, 216, 299n18

Pussy Riot, 50, 275n205

Putin, Vladimir, 86, 88; cultural policy and, 50; defense spending and, 79; Fancy Bear and, 270n117; foreign policy of, 45, 46; influence campaign of, 54–55; KGB and, 47; LePen ties with, 271n150; military campaigns and, 51; military modernization and, 85; near abroad and, 59; nuclear weapons and, 80; rebellion by, 65; revanche and, 264n2; ROC and, 76, 77; Special Operations Command and, 80; Ukraine and, 57; United Russia party and, 60

Qassim, Sheikh Isa, 110

Qing dynasty, 124, 131, 132

Qom, 91, 102, 105, 110

Quds Force, 13, 95, 96

Questions and Replies between T'an Tai-tsung and Li Wei-kung, 126

Quran, 96, 102, 104, 105, 278n52

Rahnema, Ali, 276n12

RAND Corporation, 15, 88

Reagan, Ronald, 224, 225, 226, 227, 258

realpolitik, 23, 191, 222, 224, 227

Red Scare, 37

The Red Web (Soldatov and Borogan), 52

reflexive control, 52–53

reforms, service-specific, 170–74

regimes: authoritarian, 6, 72, 151, 178, 223, 241, 274n189; legal, international/domestic, 155, 157, 233, 249

Regional Comprehensive Economic Partnership, 148

reinvigoration cycle, Iranian, 92, 94, 97, 100, 120, 121

relationships, 24, 75; Chinese, 125–26; civil-military, 169; defense, 175; economic, 115, 175; Sino-U.S., 156

religion, 57, 101, 108–16; hostility for, 73–74; influence of, 92, 109–12

research-and-development system, 88, 175, 176

resources, 85, 214, 256; financial, 241; foreign, 25; Iranian, 109–11; lack of, 191–92; national, 170

Revolutionary War, professional military and, 185–86

revolution in military affairs (RMA), 138, 178

The Rise and Fall of the Great Powers (Kennedy), 115

RMA. *See* revolution in military affairs (RMA)

ROC. *See* Russian Orthodox Church (ROC)

Rocket Kitten, 107, 108

Romanian Orthodox Church, 77

Romans, 24, 25, 264n51; Maccabees and, 20

Roosevelt, Franklin Delano, 32, 34, 204–5, 206, 210, 211, 212, 213, 246, 247, 258, 295n73, 296n88; Neutrality Act and, 205; strategic information and, 208

Russia: historical development of, 29–47; influence of, xiii, 64–65, 71, 84–85, 87–88; strategic position of, 47, 71

Russian Air Force, 79

Russian Empire, 29–30

Russian Federation. *See* Russia

Russian Institute of Strategic Studies, 68

Russian Ministry of Defense, plans by, 79

Russian Orthodox Church (ROC), 26, 46, 60; coup and, 74; influence of, 73–77; Kremlin and, 76–77; resurgence of, 275n206; teachings of, 75–76

Russian Orthodox Church Outside Russia, 75

Russia Today (RT), 56

Russo-Japanese War, 92

Russophobia, 57, 86

sabotage, 41, 205, 213

Saddam Hussein, 98, 99, 231

Sadr, Muqtada-al, 99, 109

Safavids, 90, 91–92, 277n13

Sahar TV, 103, 104

sanctions, 66, 88, 112, 115, 116, 119

Sarafraz, Mohammad, 104

Saudi Aramco, information-technology of, 107

Visegrád Group, 62, 63
Voice of America, 36, 37
von Bulow, Heinrich Dietrich, 193

Wagner Group, 84
Wallace, Henry, 34
Waltz, Kenneth, 10
warfare: asymmetric, 48, 173; attrition, 184; biological, 42; Chinese thinking on, 123, 163; conventional, 185; defining, 19; drone, xi; economic, 207, 213, 222, 225; electronic, 26, 78, 173, 174; expansive view of, 18; guerrilla, 135, 214; hybrid, viii, 20, 26, 48–49; ideological, 230, 231; Iranian approach to, 101, 122; legal, 142, 155–57, 157–64; limited, 185; low-intensity, 20, 183; mechanics of, 35; media, 142, 154; modern, 172; Native Americans conceptions of, 183; net-centric, 141, 239; new forms of, 139–40; nonkinetic, 48; one-size-fits-all, 127; organizational/rhetorical aspects of, 35; perceptions of, 18; pervasive/targeted, 139; political, 35, 36, 40, 143, 145, 225, 266n40, 268n59, 284n53, 285n96; psychological, 106, 142, 144, 145, 146, 147, 157, 165, 214, 217, 218; public-opinion, 149, 150–55; scientific approach to, 2–3, 193, 195, 197; shih and, 126; spiritual/moral dimensions of, 102; unconventional, 207, 214, 218, 220, 221; understanding, 35, 196, 237, 249–54; unrestricted, 39, 178; U.S. conception of, 98, 139, 183, 234–35. *See also* cyber warfare; information, warfare
War of 1812, 194, 197
War Powers Resolution, 223
War Production Board, 33–34

Warring States Period, 155
Washington DC, 200; burning of, 194
Washington, George, 185, 186–87, 191
weaknesses, 11, 14, 243, 247; exploiting, 20; strengths and, 244; weapons, 78, 135; chemical, 233; conventional, 161; export of, 114, 175; precision, 178; transfers, 114. *See also* nuclear weapons
Weigley, Russell, 18, 183, 184, 237, 293n28
West Point, 193, 194, 195, 197
whole of government, 19, 23, 246
whole of society, 19, 246
Wilson, Andrew, 282n7
Wilson, Woodrow, 201–2
World Trade Organization, 138, 156
World War I, 31, 197, 202, 203, 204, 210
World War II, vii, 8, 21, 26, 33, 34–35, 117, 133, 177, 211–12, 214, 254; global order after, xiii; military development up to, 196–210; sustainable peace after, 9

Xi Jinping, 169, 170, 175; Obama and, 166–67
Xinhua news agency, 150, 152

Yangtze River, 128
Yanukovych, Viktor, 72
Yellow Sea, 128
Yeltsin, Boris, 74
Yemen, 40, 117, 119
Yuan dynasty, 283n34
Yuan-kang Wang, 129

Zeman, Milos, 63
Zheng He, 130
Zhou dynasty, 124
Zmiana Party, 63